W9-BNO-953

Interview
Magic

**JOB INTERVIEW
SECRETS FROM
AMERICA'S CAREER
AND LIFE COACH**

Susan Britton Whitcomb

jist
Works
America's Career Publisher

Interview Magic

© 2005 by Susan Britton Whitcomb

Published by JIST Works, an imprint of JIST Publishing, Inc.
8902 Otis Avenue
Indianapolis, IN 46216-1033
Phone: 1-800-648-JIST   Fax: 1-800-JIST-FAX   E-mail: info@jist.com

Visit our Web site at **www.jist.com** for information on JIST, free job search tips, book chapters, and ordering instructions for our many products! For free information on 14,000 job titles, visit **www.careeroink.com**.

Quantity discounts are available for JIST books. Please call our Sales Department at 1-800-648-5478 for a free catalog and more information.

Acquisitions and Development Editor: Lori Cates Hand
Interior Design: designLab, Seattle
Page Layout: Trudy Coler, Deb Kincaid
Cover Designer: Aleata Howard
Proofreader: David Faust
Indexer: Henthorne House

Printed in Canada
08 07 06 05 04   9 8 7 6 5 4 3 2 1

Library of Congress Cataloging-in-Publication Data

Whitcomb, Susan Britton, 1957-
   Interview magic : job interview secrets from America's career and life coach /
   Susan Britton Whitcomb.
        p. cm.
   Includes index.
   ISBN 1-59357-016-3 (alk. paper)
   1. Employment interviewing. I. Title.
   HF5549.5.I6W4594 2005
   650.14'4–dc22   200402358

We have been careful to provide accurate information in this book, but it is possible that errors and omissions have been introduced. Please consider this in making any career plans or other important decisions. Trust your own judgment above all else and in all things.

Trademarks: All brand names and product names used in this book are trade names, service marks, trademarks, or registered trademarks of their respective owners.

ISBN 1-59357-016-3

Dedication

We can do anything we want to do if we stick to it long enough.

—Helen Keller

This book is dedicated to all of the career seekers who faithfully persevere amidst formidable challenges, who choose not to disable themselves with a pessimistic attitude, and who know that life is about progress and not perfection.

Acknowledgments

Sincere appreciation goes to those who contributed insider tips, insights, and industry knowledge for the writing of this book:

Dana Adams, Microsoft Corporation

Lou Adler, Adler Concepts

Reginna K. Burns, AT&T

Michael T. Carpenter, financial services executive

Freddie Cheek, Cheek & Associates Career Connections

Reverend Robbie Cranch

Gerry Crispin, *CareerXroads*

Mary Ann Dietschler, Abundant Life for U

Dean Eller, Central California Blood Center

Meg Ellis, Type Resources

Debra Feldman, JobWhiz.com

Julianne Franke, The Right Connections

Sheila Garofalo, SFC Consulting

Wendy Gelberg, Advantage Resumes

Dr. Charles Handler, Rocket-Hire.com

Bob Heisser, Digital Training Group

Barry Hemly, Corning, Inc.

Mike Johnson, Corning, Inc.

Valerie Kennerson, Corning, Inc.

Martin Kimeldorf

Melvin King, Expert Polygraph

Kate Kingsley, KLKingsley Executive Search

Louise Kursmark, Best Impression Career Services

Murray Mann, Global Career Strategies

Mark Mehler, *CareerXroads*

Don Orlando, The McLean Group

Dr. Dale Paulson, Career Ethic/ Allegiance Research Group

Jean Hampton Pruitt

Richard Reardon, R&R Business Development

Pamela Ryder, Wyeth Pharmaceuticals

Kevin Skarritt, Acorn Creative

Dr. John Sullivan, San Francisco State University

Eileen Swift, Swift Graphic Design

Peter Weddle, Weddles.com

Gwen Weld, Microsoft Corporation

Judy Wile, New England Human Resources Association

Deborah Wile-Dib, Executive Power Coach

Michael A. Wirth, Talent+, Inc.

Unique to *Interview Magic* is its list of industry-specific questions (see chapter 14). A number of people contributed to this compilation, including members of Career Masters Institute and National Résumé Writers' Association (see appendix B). In addition, I extend thanks to the following industry professionals who shared their time and insights:

Susan Bradley, healthcare consultant and attorney

Kevin Bradshaw, Gottschalks, Inc.

Paul Davis, healthcare consultant

Valerie Deveraux, attorney

Michael Giersch, Giersch & Associates Inc. Civil Engineers

Richard Ho, Technology Consultant

Neal Lehman, Sherwood Lehman Massucco

Harry Massucco, Sherwood Lehman Massucco

Steve McDonald, Project Engineer

Larry Narbaitz, Warmerdam Packing

Joanne Riester, Baker Peterson & Franklin CPAs

Hilton Ryder, attorney

Mary Jansen Scroggins, Jansen and Associates

This book came to life because of a terrific team at JIST Publishing. A huge thank you goes to editor Lori Cates Hand, who had the vision to take the *Magic* series further. She truly has the "magic touch" when it comes to development and editing. This, paired with her moral support along the way, has been priceless to me. In addition, a big thank you to Trudy Coler, Aleata Howard, Amy Adams of designLab, David Faust, and Kelly Henthorne of Henthorne House for behind-the-scenes work with expert production, design, desktop publishing, proofreading, and indexing.

Special thanks go to Sandi Tompkins, my friend and "sister," who also happens to be a crack editor. Her editorial guidance helped make the author review process that much smoother. Heartfelt thanks go to my coach Judy Santos, for reading chapters in the middle of the night and believing in me throughout the many projects I take on. And to Jean Gatewood, a huge thank you for reading countless versions of chapters (and enlisting husband Bob's support), bringing me home-cooked meals, taxi-ing my daughter to skating lessons, blessing me with timely prayers, and graciously offering whatever was needed to support me over the long haul—you are a light in this world. And finally, to my husband Charlie, thank you for allowing me to be me.

Access Free Additional Interview Questions and "Magic Words" Strategies

Thank you for selecting *Interview Magic* from a shelf full of interview books. In addition to the questions found in this book, you can also find dozens more industry-specific questions and answer strategies online at www.CareerAndLifeCoach.com (click on Interview Magic).

The author welcomes your comments about this book. E-mail, call, or write to let the author know what you found helpful, what you would like more information on, or what could be done to make this book stronger. Also, feel free to share an interesting or humorous interview story. Please be sure to mention this book's title in your correspondence.

Susan B. Whitcomb, CCMC, CCM, NCRW
Whitcomb Career Strategy
Fresno, CA
Telephone: (559) 222-7474
E-mail: swhitcomb@careerandlifecoach.com
Web site: www.CareerAndLifeCoach.com

About This Book

This resource is for career-minded professionals and managers who need insider secrets that will make them stand out from the competition in the interview process. Although it's titled *Interview Magic,* this book is not about using incantations, spells, or sleight-of-hand to trick an employer into hiring you! It is, however, about tapping into extraordinary power and influence so that employers quickly recognize your value, offer you the job, and pay you top dollar.

Interview Magic is divided into three parts. Part 1 establishes the all-important foundation for interview success. Chapter 1 presents 10 liberating truths that can unlock fears, expose limiting beliefs, and turn around any ineffective strategies regarding the interview process. Chapter 2 sets the foundation by helping you target positions that are the right Career-FIT™. After all, what's the use of acing an interview if it lands you a job that isn't a great fit?

In chapter 3, you'll catalog a series of SMART Stories™; these success stories will help you provide employers with hard evidence of how you can deliver a return-on-investment (ROI) to the company by solving problems or serving needs. Chapter 4 then walks you through the steps to create a memorable career brand—that unique combination of skills or competencies that employers are willing to pay a premium for! Branding is one of the hottest trends in career management.

Hear this! All of the insider tips and strategies shared in this book are nearly useless if you don't (or won't) believe in yourself. Chapter 5 will infuse you with that make-or-break "I CAN" mindset, teaching you how to Inspire yourself daily, Control the controllables, Act now, and Never give up!

In Part 2 of *Interview Magic,* you'll review 10 common types of interviews in chapter 6 and find quick tips for preparing for each type. Chapter 7 will help you be ready to run the gauntlet of online prescreening technology, psychometric interview instruments, and technology-based interviewing simulations. Chapter 8 explains the secrets to a successful telephone interview and how to convert it to a face-to-face appointment.

Behavioral and competency-based interviewing continues to be used heavily by human resource professionals and hiring managers. Chapter 9 explains how to recognize behavioral interview questions, reveals the top 50 competencies most desired by employers, and coaches you on how to deliver a SMART Story™ that packs a powerful punch.

In chapters 10, 11, and 12, you'll learn a proven "4 Cs" model for **C**onnecting with interviewers, **C**larifying the employer's needs in the position, **C**ollaborating on how to deliver results in the position, and **C**losing the interview in a manner that keeps communication lines open and "forwards" your momentum.

In Part 3 of this book, you'll benefit from reviewing more than 100 interview questions, including frequently asked questions (FAQs), industry-specific questions (ISQs), and illegal and awkward questions (covered in chapters 13, 14, and 15, respectively). Answer strategy is provided, along with dozens of "magic words" sample responses. You'll learn how to be positive, precise, and pertinent so that the employer knows beyond a shadow of a doubt that you will contribute to his or her bottom-line productivity and profit.

With a clear picture of your "reality," "comfort," and "dream number" salary ranges, you'll find in chapter 16 the secret to negotiating with power and integrity so that you can receive what you're worth!

One of the nicest features of this book is the tips found at the end of chapters 2 through 16. The "10 Quick Tips" for each chapter will give you a quick overview if you're in a hurry, while the coaching tips will help you take charge and move your career forward with commitment, intention, and momentum. If you're ready to do something awesome for your career, read on!

Contents

Part 3: Preparing for Interview Questions and Negotiating Salary...................................283

Part I

Interview Foundations

10 Critical Truths for Job Interview Success

Men occasionally stumble on the truth, but most of them pick themselves up and hurry off as if nothing had happened.

—Sir Winston Churchill

Success in interviewing requires a two-pronged approach. You must address the *mechanics* and *mindset*—the *visible* and *invisible* elements—of interviewing. Many job seekers focus only on the mechanics of interviewing—what's the "right" answer to this or that question, how do I follow up after the interview, how do I negotiate salary, and so on. Although these "mechanical" elements are important, they are only half of what you need. It's like trying to walk on one leg—a distinct disadvantage. When you incorporate both the mechanics and the mindset into your interview strategy, you set the stage for significant success—you will be able to run, not walk, to your next career move.

Are either of these scenarios of concern to you?

⭑ Sending out resumes but not getting interviews.

⭑ Landing interviews but not getting offers.

In the chapters to come, you'll learn how to weave together mechanics and mindset strategies to get more interviews and offers. (I touch briefly on resumes in chapter 4; for a comprehensive look at the subject, pick up one

of my earlier books, *Résumé Magic*, also published by JIST.) In addition, you'll equip yourself to avoid some of these common interview woes:

- Getting tongue-tied when it comes to proving your worth in the interview.

- Having trouble differentiating yourself within a marketplace that is flooded with competitive candidates.

- Looking like a "clueless candidate"—one who has not done enough research prior to the interview.

- Figuring out how to put a positive spin on skeletons in the closet, such as gaps in your employment, a history of illness, the lack of a critical degree, or perhaps even a clash of ethics with a prior boss.

- Not asking probing questions about the company—if you don't, you might find yourself jumping from the frying pan into the fire with a company that isn't the right fit for you.

- Experiencing a "LACK Attack"—**L**ies **A**bout your **C**apabilities and **K**nowledge. LACK Attacks are often heard by naysayers or, even worse, spoken by that little voice you hear occasionally in your head that accuses you of not knowing enough, not doing enough, not being good enough, and so on.

- Knowing how to follow up after you think you've had a great interview, yet you don't hear back from the company.

- Acing your interviews but hitting a brick wall when it comes to negotiating salary.

If you have picked up this book to remedy any of the preceding situations, or you are proactively preparing yourself so that you don't fall into any of these categories, I applaud you for taking action. Whatever your motives for committing yourself to this book, know that there are some enduring truths that will be critical to your interview success. The following sections discuss each of these truths.

Truth #1: Careers Can Be Made or Broken in the Interview Process

This is a radical statement, perhaps, but it's true. Here's why:

- The interview is not a single event. It is a process that begins the second a recruiter or hiring decision-maker picks up the phone to "chat" with you. Whether you applied for a position or were contacted out of the blue, the evaluation process has begun. The interviewer's first impression of you might make or break your chances.

- You might be interviewing and not know it. The interview often starts well before you speak to the recruiter or hiring decision-maker. In many instances, you unknowingly interview with the secretary who sets up your interview appointment, the employee you spoke with when doing your research, the networking contact who is putting in a good word for you with the hiring manager, the company vendor who gave you the inside scoop on an operational issue, and so on. Each of these people might have a small but cumulative influence in the process, with the power to build you up or break you.

- Hiring managers' standards are higher than ever before. They expect you to know your value and have a clear sense of your vision for both near and mid-term employment. Inability to articulate this vision succinctly and persuasively can knock you out of the running.

- Employers today demand "career accountability" from candidates. You must take personal charge of growing your career. That includes creating a memorable brand (see chapter 4) and crafting a meaningful marketing message for "product you."

- Your interviewing savvy will either open or close doors to the next step in your career. Once those doors are closed, it's difficult to pry them open again.

- Acing an interview—even for a job that isn't perfect for you—will put you on the radar screen of those who can help you in the future. Remember that interviewers have their own network of contacts that will likely be valuable to you.

- Bombing an interview can tarnish your reputation among people who are critical to your success. Interviewers might think, "I heard great things about her, but she sure didn't live up to her reputation during the interview."

- Turning down an interview (because you declined to discuss an opportunity presented by a recruiter) might prevent you from securing a good stepping-stone position or even fine-tuning a position that could lead to a radically different and rewarding career.

How will you set yourself apart from the dozens (or even hundreds) of people competing for your next position? If you aren't sure of the answer to this question, you've picked up the right resource. This book not only helps you win at interviewing, it also shows you how to take control of your career, identify your value, and always be interview-ready.

Truth #2: Your "Career DNA" Is the Secret to Your Value

The secret to radical career success lies in tapping into your "career DNA." You learned in school that DNA is the molecular basis of your heredity. In other words, it's the root of your innate, or natural, talents. For the purposes of this book, I'll refer to DNA in a career-management framework, with the letters standing for your **D**esigned **N**ature and **A**ssets. Let's look at the significance of each of those words.

Designed

You were uniquely designed with a thumbprint, a voice pattern, and an iris that does not match any other human being on this planet (even the eyes of genetically identical twins have iris barcodes as different as unrelated eyes). That individuality makes you distinctively valuable and affords you the ability to create a career like no other. What you choose to do in your work life *does* matter! Without engaging in a deep philosophical discussion, let me capture the essence of your career purpose:

To be radically rewarded and enthusiastically engaged in work that adds value to others.

You were designed with a purpose. That purpose gives you value. Value gives you bargaining power. Bargaining power gives you confidence. Confidence is integral to success. Tap into your designed purpose and you will unlock your passion. Purpose produces passion!

The key to greater workplace productivity and performance is aligning your skills and interests with work you can be enthusiastically and passionately engaged in. Greater productivity and performance doesn't just benefit the employer—it affords you greater career significance and security, as well. Your distinctive value is how you can differentiate yourself from the competition for your next position.

Nature

From birth, you have exhibited certain preferences and personality traits. In fact, if you look back into your childhood for clues that you'd be good at what you do today, you will likely find some interesting evidence. Everyone has those clues. As an example, Grandma Moses, the Vermont artist who gained notoriety after picking up her paintbrushes at the age of 80, actually showed very early signs of her artistic skill. A child of six who loved to draw, she would go out to her family's vineyards and pluck grapes from the vines to experiment with blending colors. Her homemade paints soon had to be put aside for plowshares, as the demands of farm life in the late 19th century left little time for artwork. For more inspiring stories in this vein, see *Why You Can't Be Anything You Want to Be* by Arthur F. Miller, Jr. (Zondervan Publishing, 1999) or *Now, Discover Your Strengths* by Marcus Buckingham and Donald O. Clifton (Free Press, 2001).

Look to your childhood and adolescence for early hints of your nature. For me, I recall an instance that I refer to as my "Puff-is-in-pain story." When in kindergarten, my teacher played the Peter, Paul & Mary tune "Puff the Magic Dragon" for the class. By the time the record finished, I was crying noticeably—presumably, I was the only child in the room who got the deeper meaning of the song. When asked why there were tears, I told the teacher "I'm sad for Puff. He is lonely because Jackie Paper went away." (In case you're wondering, no, the urban legend that the song is about marijuana is not true. According to www.snopes.com/music/songs/puff.htm, it is what its writers have always claimed it to be—a song about the innocence of childhood lost.) That early ability to see Puff's pain was a harbinger of my innate ability to connect with others, which serves me well in my role as a coach.

Your distinctive nature makes it easier for you to do certain things better than others. So, what do you do naturally? Encourage others? Remember facts and figures? Find strategy for a project? Bring logic to a discussion? Envision the future? Create new ideas? In chapter 2, we will look more closely at your Career-FIT™ to help you really hone in on the right interview opportunities.

Assets

Assets include the knowledge, skills, and values you bring to an employer. Knowledge—information, facts, data, experiences—is gained over the course of your education, career, and life. Skills—proficiencies and expertise—are learned and honed through thousands of hours of practice. (If your career spans 10 or more years, you've logged more than 20,000 work hours, assuming a minimal 40-hour work week.) Values—things that are important to you in your career—might be tangible or intangible; for instance, independence, social interaction, intellectual challenge, personal development, creativity, or economic rewards. A clear sense of your values will help you in evaluating different interview opportunities and making wise career choices.

Look to your Designed Nature and Assets—your career DNA—to give you purpose, identify your value, and help you find the ideal place to practice your passion.

Truth #3: There Is a Place for You

While coaching people in career transition, I occasionally hear the question that I sense many are afraid to voice: Is there really an employer out there who will want me and appreciate me? Your answer to that question will be fundamental to your interviewing success. If you doubt there's a positive answer to the question, look to the Biblical wisdom of King Solomon, who offered the timeless quote: "there is a time for every season."

What season are you in now? It might be a season to teach or to learn, to grow or to rest, to move on or to wait. Perhaps one of these career situations sounds right for you at this time in your life:

- **Stepping stone:** A stepping-stone position is not a dream job, but it might lead to one. Perhaps your industry has encountered steep declines and opportunities aren't plentiful. Maybe you just need to remove yourself from a toxic employment situation. Either way, a stepping-stone position might be just the ticket.

- **High yield:** Looking for big rewards based on a significant investment of time and energy in your career? If you are a fast-tracker, you might be ready for a pressure-cooker position where you can stretch and challenge yourself to the extreme.

- **Incubator:** You might have recently endured a significant loss, illness, or setback. If so, an incubator position might be the place where you can heal and regain your strength. Incubator positions do require that you perform work of value, but the work might not be particularly challenging. Incubator positions are temporary and can serve a purpose for certain seasons of your life.

- **Life balance:** Life-balance positions appeal to those who previously sacrificed quality of life by pouring themselves into jobs that required 60, 80, or even 100-hour work weeks. Typically a lesser-paying position than what you've come from, a life-balance position can offer less tangible but more meaningful payoffs. It might even include a flex-time or job-sharing arrangement.

- **Lobster:** Ever wonder how a lobster can grow to be so big? It has to shed its shell periodically. You might feel cramped or stifled in your current position. If so, it might be time to find a place where you can grow.

- **Circuit rider:** In the 1800s, a circuit rider was a clergyman who would spread himself among multiple towns. The concept of dividing time among two or three companies might be appropriate for you, especially if you're working in an industry that is cash-strapped and cannot afford a full-time arrangement.

- **Free agent:** Similar to a circuit rider, a free-agent position allows you to move quickly between or within companies where your skills are in highest demand. Reminiscent of workers in the film industry, where work is project based, free agents typically accept work by the project, as opposed to a traditional, open-ended employment situation.

- **Site seeing:** Do you like what you're doing but perhaps just need a change of scenery? A site-seeing position is one that allows you to do similar work but with different surroundings or people. Sometimes a simple change of scenery can do wonders.

- **Portfolio:** A portfolio position allows you to use and further develop a variety of special skills. This type of position is especially appealing to those who thrive on variety and a spontaneous, flexible approach to life and work.

- **Destination:** A destination position is one that you've been aiming at for a number of years. This type of position is typically at the top of the career ladder for your functional area.

It's obvious that up and ahead are not the only options when it comes to a new position. Instead, your goal should be progress, not perfection. Progress includes anything that is right for you at this juncture in your life. With all these different options in mind, there *is* an employer out there who will benefit from your career DNA.

Truth #4: Employment Relationships Are Symbiotic

The balance between employer power and employee power shifts depending on various economic and industry factors. During the dot-com days of the late 1990s, it was an employee's ballgame, with many techies passively sitting back as they were courted by startup companies willing to give them huge signing bonuses and lucrative stock options. The downturn associated with the triple blow of the dot-com bust, the 9-11 tragedy, and the normal business slowdown following a long period of sustained economic growth caused it to become an employer's ballgame. Tens of thousands found themselves "RIF-ed" (losing their jobs through reduction-in-force layoffs), scrambling to find jobs that were as rare as hen's teeth.

The reality is this:

There is nothing more important to a company than hiring top talent.

Without talent, companies cannot produce products or serve customers. Without companies, talent has a limited framework in which to work (aside from the one-man/woman entrepreneurial show—and even these operations have a tendency to grow and then need—you guessed it—more talent!). When employers let employee relationships languish, employees leave. When employees do not perform up to par, they are let go. Yet, top talent will always be in demand.

It's your job to make sure that you are, indeed, top talent—an "A" or "B" player. "A" players are considered the cream-of-the-crop star performers, the ones with the biggest salaries and recognition. Often, these "A" players are motivated by extrinsic (external) rewards, such as salary, fringe benefits, recognition, or impressive titles. According to a recent *Harvard Business Review* article, "B" players can be just as productive and valuable as "A" players, yet don't demand the top salaries or recognition. Instead, they require intrinsic (internal) rewards from their jobs, finding motivation through the work itself, a job well done, personal growth, or involvement in a meaningful cause. You do *not* want to be a "C" player—those with a reputation for not meeting goals, not showing initiative, or not being a good match for the job. The fact that you are reading this book proves that you don't want to be a "C" player. Throughout the book, you will find tips on how to further avoid "C" player status.

Truth #5: You DON'T Have to Memorize Answers to 101+ Interview Questions

Competency-based interviewing is the latest innovation in interviewing techniques. It involves carefully matching job descriptions with an individual's innate competencies (also known as *strengths* or *themes*), as well as required skills for the job. For instance, when hiring an executive, an employer might look for someone with themes that represent futuristic and strategic thinking. When hiring a customer service representative, an employer might identify problem-solving and relational skills as core competencies for the position.

Industry-leading companies such as The Home Depot, The Ritz-Carlton, General Electric, Corning, and many others have found competency-based interviewing key to a rise in worker productivity, with the added corporate benefits of competitive market advantage and higher profits.

What does competency-based interviewing mean for you, the job seeker? There are two items of particular importance:

⭐ To be considered for an interview, you *must* target positions that are a good fit (see chapter 2 for more on the Career-FIT™ system). Indiscriminately applying to job postings is akin to career graffiti, and technology is now helping shield employers from the deluge of unqualified applicants.

⭐ You don't have to memorize answers to a hundred different interview questions. You do, however, need to be ready with tip-of-the-tongue stories that substantiate your competencies, motivation, and ability to deliver results (see chapter 3).

The latter is good news because throughout the interview process you get to be yourself (on your best behavior, of course). Focusing on your competencies and relevant knowledge removes the stress of trying to figure out the "right" answer to every interview question. When you know yourself and are confident about your career DNA, you will respond with composure to whatever you are asked and won't be thrown off by questions you can't anticipate.

Conversations with countless hiring managers confirm that they wish candidates would simply be themselves in the interview. One district sales manager for an international pharmaceutical company explained it well: "I don't need every candidate to be a top-ranked performer. I need people with a range of strengths and knowledge. If candidates would be honest about their strengths—what they are passionate about—it would make my job easier and, in the long run, make the employee more satisfied because they would be doing work they enjoy. Satisfied employees make more productive teams."

What happens if you encounter an employer that doesn't espouse competency-based interviewing and fires off a series of dated or irrelevant interview questions? In chapter 11, you will learn tips for converting the interview from a confrontational interrogation to a collaborative business meeting so that you can deliver the one thing every employer wants.

Truth #6: You Can Control Your Success

How? Control the controllables (those things you can be in charge of). In real estate, the maxim is "location, location, location." In interviewing, it involves three P's:

- Preparation
- Preparation
- Preparation

Preparation is non-negotiable. It's your job to be more prepared for the interview than the interviewer. That means knowing your strengths and value proposition. It also means taking the time to learn the key concerns and trends within the industry, the company's strengths and weaknesses, any problems the prior incumbent experienced, how the position fits in with the company's entire strategic plan, and how the company will tangibly measure your success in the next 60, 180, 360 days and beyond. (See appendix A for resources for researching your target companies.)

Truth #7: You Can Control Your Performance

Truth #6 requires preparation, preparation, preparation. Truth #7, controlling your performance, requires another three P's:

- Practice
- Practice
- And more practice!

Lou Adler, author of *Hire with Your Head,* trains recruiters and hiring managers how to interview and select candidates. Adler also is an executive recruiter. In this role, he advises his candidates to spend 10 or more hours preparing for every interview. Although some of that time will be devoted to research, a good portion should be spent verbally practicing your responses. Having information in your head and articulating that information with your mouth are two very different activities. In even more grueling advice, some speech coaches claim that an hour of preparation is required for every minute you are on stage. Sound like hard work? Consider the return on investment you will reap. Divide your annual income by the number of hours you spend preparing for the interview. At an annual income of $50,000 a year, 10 hours of preparation equates to $5,000 an hour. At $100,000, it's $10,000 an hour. And, once you've become comfortable with describing your success stories and strengths, 10 hours won't be necessary for each and every interview.

Truth #8: You Will Be Judged on Three Dimensions

Employers use a number of frameworks to gauge candidates. These boil down to three C's:

- ✨ Competency
- ✨ Chemistry
- ✨ Compensation

In measuring competency, you will focus on proving you can do the job based on your experience, skills, knowledge, innate strengths, and motivational drive to exceed employer expectations. Chemistry involves *you* connecting with the company's mission, its people, and its customers, as well as the employer connecting with you. Compensation—the often-dreaded salary-negotiation phase—entails making sure the company is paying within the industry range (preferably the upper end of that range) and demonstrating how you will deliver a strong ROI (return on investment) for your salary.

Truth #9: Bottom Line—Every Employer Wants One Thing from You

In a word: value. It's the one thing *every* employer wants from its employees. Value refers to a fair return in services (your job performance) for something exchanged (most notably, salary).

We see and hear the term *value* so frequently that there is a tendency to take the word for granted, and yet it is worth a closer look. We *value* an item to determine its worth. When something is *of value* it is worthwhile. To be *invaluable* is to be beyond price. Companies provide *added-value* in an effort to provide customers with a bigger bang for their buck. Wall Street is interested in *shareholder value*. Salespeople extend a *value proposition* to infer that a transaction is of worth. Employees are *evaluated* to measure their performance. Interviewers will make a *value judgment* about your candidacy.

In the employment marketplace, *value* means working in a manner that will make your employer a better, stronger, more productive, and profitable company. Gwen Weld, former General Manager of Staffing for Microsoft, related the story of a candidate who impressed the Microsoft interview team because of his competencies of courage, conviction, and passion for technology. These competencies, coupled with his substantive skill and absence of ego, led Weld to extend an employment offer. Says Weld about the candidate, "he would make Microsoft a better Microsoft."

How will you make your new employer a better company? Therein lies your value. Communicating your value in the interview is critical.

Truth #10: You Can Give 'em What They Want

This book is devoted to identifying and communicating your value—helping you find the *magic words* to "give 'em what they want." It's based on a reliable coaching model that enables you to do the following:

- **Connect** with the employer and establish a relationship. Remember that one of the three C's mentioned in Truth #8 is Chemistry. People hire people, not automatons. If it comes down to two candidates who have equal competencies, the decision factor will usually be in favor of the candidate who had the better chemistry. You *must* connect!

- **Clarify** the employer's needs with respect to the position and the company. What is the real position and the key deliverables that will measure success? How will this position impact the overall goals of the company in the near term and over the long haul?

- **Collaborate** on strategies to perform in the position. In this phase, you'll display how you've done similar work in the past (or used transferable skills) and how you would tackle the position in question. Like test-driving a new car, you want the employer to actually see how you can hit the road running. Collaboration turns interviews from an interrogative session into a cooperative business meeting.

- **"Close"** throughout the interview process. Good sales representatives *test close* throughout the sales cycle to gauge the interest of the prospective buyer and overcome any objections. You'll learn how to close by asking questions that will help you gauge the interest of prospective employers. In doing so, you can shore up any weak areas, understand what the employer is thinking, follow up intelligently after the interview, and negotiate the best possible compensation package.

The remainder of this book digs into the mechanics and mindset for successful interviewing. If you're cramming for an interview that's right around the corner, review the 10 Quick Tips at the conclusion of each chapter (you'll also gain momentum by answering the "magic" coaching questions at the end of each chapter), and focus on the material in the latter half of the book. Otherwise, let's start with first things first: going after what you really want. Turn to chapter 2 to learn how.

Chapter
2

First Things First: Focus on the Right F.I.T.

The best vision is insight.

—Malcolm Forbes

A re you suffering from fish fever? Fish fever is an ailment peculiar to Alaskan bear cubs who manage to go hungry despite standing in the middle of rivers thick with salmon. While studying the starving cubs, wildlife biologists observed them lunging indiscriminately after any airborne fish that appeared in their paths. Their fishing strategy yielded minimal success. The biologists came to the conclusion that the cubs were too immature to focus on just one target. In comparison, the nearby mother bear would choose a fishing spot that offered promise, hone in on one fish, and then strike. Her fishing strategy yielded frequent success. Mama bear's target fish was usually underwater, less noticeable than those jumping about, but more promising in the end.

Too often, I see job seekers with symptoms of fish fever. One opportunity pops up that looks appealing (for example, "I want to be a pharmaceutical sales rep") and the job seeker pursues that direction. Then another opportunity comes into sight ("I want to broker loans") and the job seeker pursues this new direction. And then another opportunity, and another. Like the hungry bear cubs, these job seekers end up losing their catch despite the many opportunities at their feet.

Although it's wise to be on the lookout for interesting opportunities, the key to successful job search and interviewing is to be *discriminating* about which opportunities are right for you. To be discriminating, you must know what you want. Hiring managers and recruiters *expect* you to have self-knowledge about your functional strengths, interests, passions, and motivators. AT&T's Director of Talent Acquisition, Reginna K. Burns, offers supporting advice: "Step 1 in the job search process is really about understanding yourself—your skills, your values, your priorities—and what kind of work you want to do."

Why Job Seekers Jump at the Wrong Opportunities

Why do some job seekers jump at *any* opportunity that flies by? Table 2.1 outlines several reasons. Check any of these reasons that might apply to you.

Table 2.1: 7 Reasons Job Seekers Might Jump for the Wrong Opportunity

✓ If Cause Applies to You	Antidote
☐ **Lack of financial reserves— the reality of making ends meet leads to career compromises.** If you are unemployed and have limited financial reserves to sustain a job search, don't despair.	Strategically target one of the options noted in chapter 1 (see Truth #3), such as a stepping-stone or incubator position. Do your best to choose a position that offers "rècycling" potential, where you can learn new skills or make new contacts that will be useful down the road.
☐ **Salary—the compensation for a new job is alluring.** It might, however, come at a heavy price once the realities of overtime and other stressors surface. Income is important but loses its luster if it robs us of energy that could be spent on other aspects of our lives.	In Beverly Kaye and Sharon Jordan-Evans' bestselling book on employee retention, *Love 'Em or Lose 'Em*, the authors surveyed why employees stay with a company. The top three reasons were exciting work and challenge; career growth, learning, and development; and working with great people. Fair pay, or salary, appeared fourth on the list. The exercises in this chapter will help you identify what constitutes exciting and fulfilling work.

✓ If Cause Applies to You	Antidote
☐ **Convenience—the new position is an easy commute.** With the aggravation of congested freeways and long commutes, many job seekers jump at an opportunity that is close to home, only to find that there are other bigger frustrations associated with the job.	Some of the questions in chapter 11 will help you with your "due diligence" to get a realistic picture of your target company and its culture.
☐ **Prestige—the company or position title is impressive.** One job seeker went to work for one of the world's hottest technology companies, headquartered in California's Silicon Valley. A few years down the road, she was happy to leave her impressive title, which had led to stress-related illnesses and difficulty conceiving (several years later, she is now the mother of two beautiful little girls).	Evaluate the opportunity in light of your priorities, looking carefully at the "Things That Matter" category in the Career-FIT™ exercise later in this chapter.
☐ **Pressure—the job seeker conforms to someone else's goals or desires.** Is there a spouse, parent, family member, friend, or admired colleague who thinks, "you should be a _____ [fill in the blank]," when you know in your heart that this isn't the right direction? Or, perhaps there is someone who has put you in a box and says, "you'll only be a _____ , and how silly of you to think you could be more?" Or this one, "you'll never make any money doing that!" (Caveat: *Do* make sure that your dream goal is well-researched in terms of market demand.)	Often well meant, these pressure-packed messages don't always have *your* best interest at heart. Sometimes there's a payoff for the other person to see you stay where you are—that other person might be scared to watch you grow, develop, and find joy or enthusiasm, especially if that person isn't him/herself growing, developing, and finding joy and enthusiasm. Breaking free of other people's expectations requires courage, but the rewards are huge. Ultimately, when you are healthy, happy, and whole, your energy and creative thinking can be unleashed and liberated to work in a way that you never dreamed.
☐ **Lack of confidence—the job seeker sets sights too low and settles for a lesser position.** Two job seekers with equal qualifications might land very different jobs, depending on their confidence in themselves and belief that the "right" position is out there for them.	If you sense that lack of confidence is undermining your interview performance, you'll have a chance in chapter 3 to identify your success stories, which can boost your self-confidence by a notch or two. Chapter 5 will also help with mindset.

(continued)

(continued)

✓ If Cause Applies to You	Antidote
☐ **Lack of focus—the job seeker hasn't explored options or committed to a focus.** Lack of focus is often at the root of other points described in this list. Some job seekers have "fallen" into careers because they've followed in a parent's footsteps or an opportunity serendipitously appeared. Sometimes these careers work out, and sometimes they don't.	Take the time to confirm that the career direction you're heading in is, indeed, what you want. That's the whole point of this chapter!

In this chapter, you can avoid "fish fever"—jumping indiscriminately at unpromising opportunities—by getting a clearer picture of what you want. You'll use the Career-FIT™ model, with the acronym FIT standing for ingredients that are critical to career success:

- ★ F—**F**unction and **F**ulfillment
- ★ I—**I**ndustry/**I**nterests and **I**dentity
- ★ T—**T**hings That Matter and **T**ype

Invest the time now to zero in on these essentials. Skipping this process is like planning your dream vacation without having a destination in mind. When you have completed this chapter, you'll find that the information and insights gained will allow you to

- ★ Make strategic choices to act offensively rather than defensively in your job search.
- ★ Leverage your time by pursuing the "right" opportunities.
- ★ Impress interviewers by knowing what you want.
- ★ Gain confidence targeting positions you can be enthusiastic about.
- ★ Increase your career satisfaction.

The Solution to Job Stress

The National Institute for Occupational Safety and Health reported that 25 percent of employees see their jobs as the primary stressor in their lives, and 75 percent feel that workers today have more job stress than a generation ago. You can alleviate much of that stress by proactively choosing employment situations that are a good Career-FIT™!

Identify Your Career-FIT™

Merriam-Webster defines the verb *fit* this way:

To be suitable for or to harmonize with

When your work is not a good fit with who you are, it yields stress and frustration. The analogy of relationships illustrates the importance of finding a good fit. You've likely experienced a relationship where the other person needed something from you that you didn't have the capacity or desire to give; for example, an introspective friend who loves to engage in hourslong, one-on-one philosophical conversations when your idea of a good time is to participate in an action-packed motocross race with some of your closest friends.

You can see the parallel: If your job isn't a good fit, it can give you fits! Imagine working in a position that required you to write computer programs all day (a somewhat solitary and monotonous task that calls for precision and logic) when what really energizes you is to work with teams in a creative setting, conceptualizing and developing marketing ideas. Even a more subtle mismatch can lead to career dissatisfaction. Diane, one of my coaching clients, loved working in healthcare management; however, her last position was at the corporate headquarter level, which prevented her from having close contact with patients—part of the reason that she chose a career in healthcare in the first place. Using the Career-FIT™ system, she realized what interested her and mattered most. She then targeted healthcare management positions that allowed her face-to-face contact with patients. She quickly found a new opportunity that fit her to a "T."

It's clear that when your work is in alignment with things that are important to you, there is harmony and satisfaction. Instead of being a "square peg in a round hole," you can perform work that "fits like a glove."

Success is getting what you want. Happiness is wanting what you get.

—Anonymous

Figure 2.1 gives you a closer look at the elements within the Career-FIT™ model. You'll note that there are two layers for each of the letters in FIT. The first layer—Function, Industry/Interests, and Things That Matter—focuses on external elements that are easily observable. The second layer—Fulfillment, Identity, and Type—hones in on internal elements that are less easily identifiable, but just as important.

Later in this chapter, you'll have a chance to flesh out each Career-FIT™ item as it relates to you. In the meantime, table 2.2 briefly describes each element.

Figure 2.1: The Career-FIT™ model.

Table 2.2: Elements of the Career-FIT™

	F	**I**	**T**
External Variables	**F**unction Function represents job titles and tasks; for example, titles such as accountant, copywriter, or customer service representative or tasks such as analyzing, planning, or writing. Although you're capable of doing a number of different functional jobs or tasks, you'll want to concentrate on your innate talents and skills, and favorite experiences.	**I**ndustry/Interests Industry refers to *where* you will apply your functional skills. Frequently, your functional interests can be used within a number of industries. For example, a customer service representative (Function) with a passion for organic products might target call centers (Industry) or retailers (Industry) that specialize in natural products (Interests).	**T**hings That Matter Wouldn't it be wonderful if you could open the medicine cabinet each morning and pop a pill that would motivate you to go to work? That pill *does* exist! It takes the shape of having your values and needs met. In the "Things That Matter" category, you'll identify what's most important to you in your next position. Understanding and aligning your work with these values and needs can take your job from humdrum to fun, and your career from good to great!

	F	**I**	**T**
Internal Variables	**F**ulfillment Fulfillment is synonymous with purpose. Remember in chapter 1 that I described your career purpose as being "radically rewarded and enthusiastically engaged in work that adds value to others." Your definition should capture the essence of how you will bring value to your employer, as well as how you will fulfill yourself. It's something you can intentionally look forward to on a Monday morning and say, "this is what I am committed to," as well as look back on Friday afternoon and say, "I have accomplished my purpose."	**I**dentity Identity refers to how you see yourself—your internal self-image. It is the way in which you define yourself. What distinguishing characteristics do you want others to note in you? What do you *believe* you are capable of accomplishing? How do you want others to perceive you? Those who experience the greatest meaning and fulfillment in life and work periodically redefine themselves and move beyond their previously accepted limitations.	**T**ype Type refers to your personality. You came wired-at-birth with four main personality preferences: where you focus your energy (your outer world or inner world); how you take in information (concretely or intuitively); how you make decisions (based on logic or feelings); and how you approach the world (in a planned or spontaneous manner).

If you're thinking that it will be a challenge to find a position that ideally suits all six elements—your functional skills, ideal industry/interests, things that matter, fulfilling purpose, evolving identity, and personality type—don't be discouraged. It *is* possible (I am living proof, along with many others I know!). However, recognize that it is a process of fine-tuning your career over time. Start by making sure you're clear about the first-level elements—Function, Industry/Interests, and Things That Matter—as you target new positions. Then, weave in your second-level elements—Fulfillment, Identity, and Type—to take your career to the next level.

As you walk through this process, it's important that you commit to taking action toward your future. Oscar Hammerstein once said, "If you don't have a dream, how are you going to make a dream come true?" I'd like to make a request that will take you closer to seeing your career dreams come true. My request is that you do whatever it takes to discover and pursue career choices that best *fit* your individual needs. To solidify your intention, develop a commitment statement, similar to one of the examples shown here:

- I am committed to being enthusiastically engaged in and radically rewarded by work that adds value to others.

- I am committed to pursuing my Career-FIT™ so that my work will be uniquely fulfilling.

I am committed to regularly reassessing my identity in a way that breaks through previously accepted limitations and allows me to engage in radically rewarding work.

Choose one of the preceding statements or use your own words to capture the essence of your commitment, and then write it here:

I am committed to:

_____

_____

_____

Speak the commitment out loud. Make sure it rings true for you. Know that this little step can lead to big rewards as you live out that commitment on a daily basis.

Loving Your Career Leads to Career Contentment

In *The Millionaire Mind,* Thomas J. Stanley, Ph.D. (Andrews McMeel Universal, 2001), catalogs the top 30 success factors of millionaires. Near the top of the list at number 6 is "Loving my career/business." Topping the list at number 1 is "Being honest with all people," followed by "Being well disciplined," "Getting along with people," "Having a supportive spouse," and "Working harder than most people." Whether or not your sights are set on millionaire status, it's clear that loving your career will lead to career contentment.

My hope for each of you is that you get a glimpse of a larger, grander, and more fulfilling career—one that causes you to look forward to jumping out of bed each morning. The Career-FIT™ model is the vehicle to get to that goal. In the remainder of this chapter, you'll complete six steps using some simple checklists and easy exercises that will help you identify specifcs for each of the Career-FIT™ elements.

Step 1: Find the Right Function

Step 1 in the Career-FIT™ process begins with brainstorming functional areas (titles and tasks) that fit with your skills and talents. In the following Function Checklist, place a checkmark next to the functions that seem to make sense or feel right to you at this time. You'll have a chance to prioritize these functional areas later.

Function Checklist

- ☐ Accounting
- ☐ Actuarial work
- ☐ Administration
- ☐ Advertising
- ☐ Affirmative action
- ☐ Architecture
- ☐ Assembly labor
- ☐ Auditing
- ☐ Automation
- ☐ Board leadership
- ☐ Budgeting
- ☐ Call center operations
- ☐ Cash management
- ☐ Category management
- ☐ Clerical
- ☐ Coaching
- ☐ Consulting
- ☐ Copyright law
- ☐ Corporate relations
- ☐ Counseling
- ☐ Credit and collections
- ☐ Customer service
- ☐ Design
- ☐ Development/fund raising
- ☐ Diversity
- ☐ Economics
- ☐ Education
- ☐ Engineering
- ☐ Environmental

- ☐ Financial
- ☐ General management
- ☐ Graphic arts/design
- ☐ Help desk
- ☐ Healthcare
- ☐ Human resources
- ☐ Industrial labor
- ☐ Information technology (IT)
- ☐ Intellectual property
- ☐ International relations
- ☐ Investor relations
- ☐ Laboratory work
- ☐ Law
- ☐ Light industrial
- ☐ Logistics
- ☐ Management consulting
- ☐ Manufacturing
- ☐ Market research
- ☐ Marketing
- ☐ Materials management
- ☐ Materials planning
- ☐ Medical
- ☐ Merchandising
- ☐ Mergers and acquisitions
- ☐ Minorities
- ☐ Networks/LAN/WAN
- ☐ Nonprofit
- ☐ Nursing
- ☐ Operations

(continued)

(continued)

☐ Packaging	☐ Senior executive management
☐ Paralegal	☐ Senior financial management
☐ Personnel	
☐ Planning	☐ Senior IT management
☐ Plant management	☐ Senior operations management
☐ Process control	
☐ Product development	☐ Systems analysis
☐ Product research	☐ Systems development
☐ Production	☐ Systems implementation
☐ Project management	☐ Tax planning/management
☐ Public relations	☐ Technical
☐ Purchasing	☐ Technical support
☐ Quality assurance	☐ Telecommunications
☐ Regulatory affairs	☐ Therapy
☐ Research and development	☐ Trademark law
☐ Risk management	☐ Trading
☐ Safety professional	☐ Training
☐ Sales	☐ Venture capital
☐ Scientific	☐ Writing
☐ Secretarial	☐ Other
☐ Security	

Need more options? The most exhaustive list of position titles and functional areas is housed in the *Occupational Outlook Handbook* at the U.S. government's Bureau of Labor Statistics page online (the book is also available in print at libraries and booksellers). Go to www.bls.gov/search/ooh.asp?ct=OOH and click on one of the letters under the A–Z index.

In addition to choosing functional areas from a list, you can take career assessments that will aid in inventorying your functional skill set. Many of these assessments are reasonably priced and take less than an hour to complete. If you have never taken this type of an inventory, I recommend doing so and working with a career coach to explore the results. Several career assessments are available at my Web site: www.careerandlifecoach.com (click on Assessments).

After identifying your preferred functional areas, you will need to prioritize the items you checked. Choose the top two that have the most appeal to you and make the most sense at this point in your career. If you find that your top options are very similar to one another, you can target these options in your job search. Examples of similar options would be health-care professional and nursing or budgeting and financial. If your top options are dissimilar, such as accounting and writing or law and marketing, it would be wise to spend time on "career reconnaissance," where you can explore and learn more about each area so that you can later target the one best functional area for you. Targeting two areas in your job search will likely slow your progress and send a mixed message to your networking contacts.

Too Many Options?

If you are having trouble narrowing down your list, try the "butler" method. Envision a butler approaching you with two small silver trays, one in each hand. The tray in his left hand holds a richly embossed invitation with the name of one of your options printed on it. The tray in his right hand holds a similarly beautiful invitation with the name of another option printed on it. Choose the invitation that makes the most sense or feels right for you at this time in your life. When using this method, first pair a strong option in one hand with a weak option in the other. Continue this process until you have identified the one best option.

In the space below, write your top functional areas for your Career-FIT™:

Functional Preferences

_____

_____

_____

_____

Step 2: Identify Your Ideal Industry and Interests

Step 2 helps you pinpoint industries where you can apply your functional talents. The following list of industries will serve as a starting point. The basis for the Industry Checklist in this section was contributed by Resume Machine.com, a reputable Web-based resume-distribution service. Place a checkmark next to the industries that appeal to you.

Industry Checklist

- ☐ Accounting
- ☐ Advertising
- ☐ Aerospace
- ☐ Aggregates
- ☐ Agriculture/agribusiness
- ☐ Apparel
- ☐ Automotive
- ☐ Banking
- ☐ Biotechnology/equipment
- ☐ Boats/marine
- ☐ Broadcasting
- ☐ Brokerage
- ☐ Building products/systems
- ☐ Chemicals
- ☐ Communications
- ☐ Computer services
- ☐ Computers
- ☐ Construction
- ☐ Consulting
- ☐ Consumer packaged goods
- ☐ Cosmetics
- ☐ Credit/credit cards

- ☐ Data processing
- ☐ Defense
- ☐ Direct marketing
- ☐ E-commerce
- ☐ Education
- ☐ Electronics
- ☐ Energy
- ☐ Engineering
- ☐ Entertainment
- ☐ Environmental
- ☐ Equipment
- ☐ Executive search
- ☐ Fashion
- ☐ Film
- ☐ Financial services
- ☐ Food and beverages
- ☐ Forest products/pulp/paper
- ☐ Franchising
- ☐ Furniture and fixtures
- ☐ Government
- ☐ Hazardous waste
- ☐ Healthcare/hospitals

- ☐ High-tech
- ☐ Higher education
- ☐ Hospitality
- ☐ Hotels/restaurants
- ☐ Human resource services
- ☐ Import/export
- ☐ Industrial
- ☐ Information technology (IT)
- ☐ Instruments
- ☐ Insurance
- ☐ International
- ☐ Internet
- ☐ Investment banks
- ☐ Laboratories
- ☐ Law firms
- ☐ Leasing
- ☐ Leisure/recreation
- ☐ Lighting
- ☐ Lumber
- ☐ Machinery
- ☐ Managed care
- ☐ Management consulting
- ☐ Manufacturing
- ☐ Marketing
- ☐ Measuring equipment
- ☐ Media
- ☐ Medical
- ☐ Medical devices
- ☐ Metals
- ☐ Mining

- ☐ Motor vehicles
- ☐ Natural resources
- ☐ New media
- ☐ Non-profits
- ☐ Oil and gas
- ☐ Paper
- ☐ Perfume
- ☐ Pharmaceuticals
- ☐ Plastics
- ☐ Printing
- ☐ Public administration
- ☐ Public relations
- ☐ Publishing
- ☐ Real estate
- ☐ Recruiting
- ☐ Research and development
- ☐ Retail trade
- ☐ Rubber
- ☐ Security services/products
- ☐ Semiconductors
- ☐ Services
- ☐ Soap
- ☐ Software
- ☐ Specialty materials
- ☐ Sports
- ☐ Stone/gravel/silica
- ☐ Telecommunications
- ☐ Television
- ☐ Test equipment
- ☐ Textiles

(continued)

(continued)

☐ Transportation	☐ Waste
☐ Travel	☐ Wholesale trade
☐ Trucks	☐ Wireless communications
☐ TV/radio/cable	☐ World Wide Web
☐ Utilities	☐ Other
☐ Venture capital	

You can find more industry options at the Bureau of Labor Statistics' Web site: www.bls.gov/oco/cg/home.htm. Once there, click the links on the right side of the page to explore exhaustive information on various industries. You can also search the North American Industry Classification System (NAICS) at the National Institutes of Health Small Business Office: http://epic.od.nih.gov/naics/ (click **New to the NAICS?**).

Can't Decide on an Industry?

Healthcare/Pharmaceutical, Finance, and Professional Services look to be popular hiring industries in the near future. The aging baby boomer population and a rapid research and development rate in healthcare and pharmaceutics will fuel opportunities in these sectors. (Source: DBM.)

Rank your industry choices in order of preference. If your top choice is an industry where hiring is at a standstill due to transition conditions or economic factors, consider pursuing your second industry choice. In the following space, write the industry you've decided to target. (You can include more than one industry preference if they are closely related.)

Industry Preference(s):

_____

_____

Now let's hone in further by looking at interests within your industry preference. Interests tap into subjects that naturally appeal to you or things about which you are enthusiastic and passionate. When you're engaged in an innate interest, time seems to pass more quickly. To unearth your interests, consider one of these exercises:

⋆ **Do a documentary.** Interview friends and colleagues and ask them what they see as your primary interests. Sometimes an objective third party can identify something you've missed that was right under your nose. Chris found himself in job search mode after his pharmaceutical company announced a post-merger reduction in headcount. A conversation with his sales manager helped him recognize that he was the team's go-to person for Internet research and timesaving technology shortcuts. These technology skills (Interests) areas gave him added value when pursuing sales positions (Function) in the pharmaceutical industry (Industry).

⋆ **Niche yourself with a specialty.** Many physicians specialize in a niche—cardiology, neurology, oncology, pediatric ophthalmology— giving them a clear target market for patients and, many times, greater financial rewards. Examine your industry for specialty categories and identify where your interests lie. For instance, in the field of human resources, there are specialty areas of compensation and benefits, recruiting, employee relations, and organizational development, to name a few. What industry niche might be your specialty area?

⋆ **Inside-the-box thinking.** Walk around your home or office and carefully notice items that are important to you. Put those items into a large box. Analyze the items in the box. Is there a common thread or pattern that emerges? As an example, someone who loves making quilts with special Chinese silks might take an Industry focus of import/export to a more meaningful level by targeting companies that import hard-to-find silk fabrics.

⋆ **The time trap.** Keep a log for an extended period of time and note what you love to spend hours doing, both on and off the job. Even if it's watching soap operas, you might be able to incorporate this interest into your industry focus. For instance, one smart entrepreneur took her Industry focus on entertainment a step further by creating the *Soap Opera Digest* based on her love of daytime drama.

⋆ **Find a hole.** Look carefully at your industry for unmet needs and untapped opportunities. Perhaps there is a hole that needs to be filled. Every gadget and innovative service we enjoy today was born out of somebody's need and subsequent frustration. Cordless phones came about because people wanted mobility while they chatted. Personal chefs are in demand today because busy professionals don't have time to cook. Have you created a solution for something that frustrates you on the job? If so, perhaps you can transform it into a niche that will increase both your job satisfaction and your marketability.

Based on the results of the above exercises, note the special interests you would like to incorporate within your industry target:

Interests

Step 3: Think About the Things That Matter

Step 3 identifies your "career needs"—those things that really matter to you. Everyone has unique needs. Some of those needs are extremely basic and common to us all, such as feeding and watering ourselves on a daily basis. Our bodies have a clear system to signal hunger or thirst—our stomachs growl and our mouths get dry. We also have higher-level needs that are less readily apparent, such as the need to be imaginative on the job or the need to have appreciation expressed for our work. Unfortunately, the signaling mechanism for these career-related needs is not always so clear. Instead of a growling tummy to signal hunger, we might have a growling temper, a lack of energy, or a sick feeling in our stomachs on Monday mornings to signal that our career-related needs are not being met.

Needs are key to understanding motivation. Psychologist Abraham Maslow developed a Hierarchy of Needs model in the 1940s that is acknowledged today by both psychologists and business leaders as fundamental to understanding human motivation. The hierarchy presents five basic levels of need:

1. Physiological: Food, water, shelter, sleep

2. Safety: Security, freedom from fear

3. Belonging and Love: Friends, family, spouse, affection, relationships

4. Self-Esteem: Achievement, mastery, recognition, respect

5. Self-Actualization: Pursuit of inner talents, creativity, fulfillment

The theory states that people are motivated by unsatisfied needs. The lower-level needs (physiological and safety) must be met before a person is motivated to satisfy a higher need (self-esteem and self-actualization). For example, someone who has not eaten for three days (level-1 needs) will not be motivated to pursue achievement and mastery (level-4 needs).

I have identified some career counterparts to Maslow's model, as table 2.3 illustrates.

Table 2.3: Hierarchy of Career Needs

Maslow's Hierarchy of Needs	Career Counterparts
Level 1: Physiological (food, water, shelter, sleep)	Basic paycheck, manageable work hours
Level 2: Safety (security, stability, freedom from fear)	Work environment free of violence, abuse, pollutants, danger, or continual threat of job loss
Level 3: Belonging and Love (friends, family, spouse, affection, relationships)	Organizational culture and camaraderie; relationships with supervisor, peers, coworkers, customers
Level 4: Self-Esteem (achievement, mastery, recognition, respect)	Impressive title; awards; a sense of appreciation received through praise/thanks, promotions, level of responsibility or authority, upper-range salary, perks; a belief that company policy is fair and respectful of the employee; career activity synergizes personal/life goals
Level 5: Self-Actualization (pursuit of inner talents, creativity, fulfillment)	Personal growth; full utilization of talents on the job; enthusiastic engagement in work; experiencing the "tingle factor"

When the "Things That Matter" are present in your work, your attitude can soar and your satisfaction can skyrocket. A chain reaction then occurs that benefits employers, customers, and shareholders. The Gallup organization, in a survey on the impact of employee attitudes on business outcomes, noted that organizations where employees have above-average attitudes toward their work had 38% higher customer satisfaction scores, 22% higher productivity, and 27% higher profits.

In the following list, place a check next to the needs and values that are important to you. Check as many items as you like.

The Things That Matter to Me

☐ Autonomy—you want freedom to act independently

☐ Achievement—you enjoy completing goals or projects

☐ Advancement—you want your career to allow upward mobility

☐ Adventure—you want excitement associated with your work

☐ Ambition—you enjoy pushing yourself to continually move forward

☐ Authority—you want to hold power and clout within your organization

☐ Beauty—you want surroundings that are aesthetically pleasing

☐ Casualness—you want a company environment that is low-key and easygoing

☐ Communication—you want to keep others informed and involved; you want to be kept in the loop

☐ Courage—you want to stand up for your beliefs

☐ Creativity—your work will require imagination and innovation

☐ Cultural diversity—your work will embrace and further matters of diversity

☐ Entrepreneurialism—you want to be able to create something new; you want to own your work

☐ Ethics—your want a work environment that supports a high level of ethics

☐ Excellence—you want to have mastery of existing and new skills in your work

☐ Honesty—you want to work where honesty is valued by leadership and others

☐ Independence—you want the ability to manage your time and work at your own pace

☐ Influence—your input will influence strategy and direction

☐ Intellectual stimulation—you want ongoing intellectual challenges

☐ Job security—you want a position that offers long-term career stability

☐ Leadership—you want to manage organizations or influence others

☐ Learning—you want the opportunity to continually add new layers of skills or knowledge

☐ Location—you want the geographic location of your work to be a good fit

☐ Logic—you want your work to require you to apply reasoning and judgment

☐ Loving—you want your work to allow you to show warmth, respect, and consideration to others

☐ Meaningful work—you want to find deep satisfaction in your work

☐ Monetary reward—you want your salary to be at the top end of the range for your industry

☐ Movement—you want physical activity to be an important part of your work

☐ Order—you want your work environment to be organized and efficient

☐ Personal development—work will afford you ongoing growth and understanding

☐ Recognition—you want to receive credit and appreciation for your work

☐ Relationships—you want strong working relationships on the job

☐ Respect—you want to earn respect from others

☐ Responsibility—you want decision-making responsibilities

☐ Risk—you enjoy work that involves a measure of risk

☐ Service—you want to help others in your work

☐ Size of company—whether boutique-ish, midsize, or corporate giant, company size is important to you

☐ Spirituality—you want spirituality to be expressed and honored in your workplace

☐ Teamwork—you want the ability to work regularly with others

☐ Time—your work will allow time for home-life and external interests

☐ Traditional—you want the company environment to be well-established or conservative

☐ Travel—you want your work to require travel

☐ Uniqueness—you want to be known for an exclusive or unique skill

☐ Variety—you want your work to involve a range of activity

In the following spaces, prioritize up to 10 of your choices. These "Things That Matter" will be important to uncover as you interview for a new position.

The Things That Matter to Me

1. _____
2. _____
3. _____
4. _____
5. _____
6. _____
7. _____
8. _____
9. _____
10. _____

Step 4: Define Fulfillment

Step 4 will transform your job from "paycheck" to "purpose" as you write a fulfillment statement for your career. Fulfillment, or purpose, is the reason *why* you work. If the primary reason behind your work is simply to earn a paycheck, I propose with confidence that there can be much, much more. If you're wondering whether I'm advocating that you trade in your paycheck for purpose, the answer is a resounding *no!* Purpose and poverty don't need to go hand in hand. I am very much in favor of you earning an attractive income, if that is important to you. The secret is to pair your purpose with market demand—there must be employers or customers who will need and pay for your services or products. When this is the case, you can find profound fulfillment because you have identified your passion, which drives perseverance, enthusiasm, creativity, productivity, and income to peak levels.

Passion Can Pay!

Srully Blotnick, a columnist for *Forbes*, helped confirm that passion can pay with his study of 1,500 business school graduates' financial success. Blotnick separated the graduates into two groups. Group A was made up of 1,245 people who were focused on making money first, with plans to indulge in what they really wanted to do only after their financial goals were met. Group B was made up of the remaining 255 graduates, who bypassed lucrative offers upon graduation to follow their passions and real interests, trusting that financial returns would eventually come.

Twenty years later, there were 101 millionaires from the sample. Of these, only one came from Group A—those initially focused on making money. The remaining 100 millionaires came from Group B—those who had followed their passions first. The earnings curve for Group B increased slowly, if at all, for many years and then suddenly spiked. He concluded that Group B's passion had fueled the drive to excel for the extended time they needed to be successful, noting "the overwhelming majority of people who have become wealthy have become so thanks to work they found profoundly absorbing."

To find what profoundly fulfills you, look for the "tingle factor." The tingle factor is that goose-bumpy feeling that comes from doing something you absolutely love. The tingle factor causes you to think, "I can't believe they pay me to do this!" Recognize that it is unrealistic to experience the tingle factor on a continuous basis. We're not in search of nirvana! Instead, your ideal work should allow you to experience the tingle factor randomly but regularly. For me, it comes a few times each week. For instance, as a coach, I experience the tingle factor when a client sinks her teeth into a liberating new truth and comes away encouraged, inspired, and confident. As a writer, I experience it after I've wrestled with and won the words that perfectly capture the concept I want to express.

The positive impact you make on others, as well as your own life, is often a clue to uncovering fulfillment. The answers to these questions can provide insight into what is uniquely fulfilling to you:

- What is your personal purpose? What is your professional purpose? How do these complement each other?
- What difference do you want to make in the workplace?
- What do you want to be known for?
- What gifts, or core strengths, do you bring to your supervisor, colleagues, customers, or clients?

Based on the answers to these questions, you can begin drafting a fulfillment statement. It should be short, just one or two sentences, and resonate with you. Here are some examples that various professionals have penned:

- To encourage professionals to value their inborn talents and worth, and use their strengths to enrich the world (founder of Career Coach Academy).

- To cause students to think, examine their belief systems, and grow in their knowledge and understanding (teacher).

- To connect consumers with products and services that enhance their lives (salesperson).

- To provide technology solutions that serve, rather than restrict, business owners (IT sales liaison).

- To direct the design of robotics systems that take technology to new levels and add value to my company, its customers, and consumers (technology executive).

- To write and orchestrate music for films that entertains and moves people to be inspired and touched on an emotional/spiritual level (musician).

This recipe might help you in writing your own fulfillment statement:

Action Verb + Who and What + Benefit to Others

Using this format, table 2.4 illustrates how some of the above examples can be broken down.

Table 2.4: Example Fulfillment Statement Recipes

Action Verb	Who and What	Benefit to Others
To encourage	professionals to value their inborn talents and worth and use their strengths to	enrich the world
To cause	students to think, examine their belief systems, and	grow in their knowledge and understanding
To provide	technology solutions to business owners	that serve, rather than restrict, business owners

Use the blank rows in the following box to write a few drafts of your own fulfillment statement. When you're comfortable with the wording, finalize your statement in the final row.

Draft Your Fulfillment Statement

Action Verb	Who and What	Benefit to Others
Draft 1:		
Draft 2:		
Draft 3:		
Fulfillment Statement:		

Step 5: Enhance Your Identity

Step 5 involves an assessment of how you want to see yourself and what you believe you are capable of accomplishing. You should do this identity assessment periodically because life and work experiences cause us to change and grow. It's obvious when children grow: They need a larger size of clothing. It's not so obvious when adults grow: It takes a very conscious examination of our thought patterns, level of self-reliance, and degree of confidence to recognize when it's time for us to try on a larger size of life—an enhanced identity.

In enhancing your identity, it's helpful to start with a simple list of adjectives that capture the essence of you. For instance, here's a 10-point list of how I view myself: encouraging, inspirational, knowledgeable, leading, conscientious, thorough, capable, intuitive, gracious, successful. Having these priorities in focus helps me to act in concert with them.

What characteristics describe your career identity? Check any of the words in the following checklist that are part of your career identity and will be important to prospective employers.

Ingredients of My Career Identity
That Are Important to Employers

- [ ] Accountable
- [ ] Accurate
- [ ] Adaptable
- [ ] Aggressive
- [ ] Ambitious
- [ ] Amenable
- [ ] Articulate
- [ ] Assertive
- [ ] Authentic
- [ ] Awesome
- [ ] Bright
- [ ] Bottom-line–oriented
- [ ] Broad-minded
- [ ] Capable
- [ ] Calm
- [ ] Caring
- [ ] Cheerful
- [ ] Chic
- [ ] Clean
- [ ] Clever
- [ ] Collaborative
- [ ] Committed
- [ ] Compassionate
- [ ] Competitive
- [ ] Compliant
- [ ] Composed
- [ ] Communicative
- [ ] Confident
- [ ] Connected
- [ ] Conscientious
- [ ] Consistent
- [ ] Cosmopolitan
- [ ] Courageous
- [ ] Creative
- [ ] Credible
- [ ] Daring
- [ ] Deadline-oriented
- [ ] Delightful
- [ ] Detail-oriented
- [ ] Direct
- [ ] Driven
- [ ] Dutiful
- [ ] Dynamic
- [ ] Eager
- [ ] Efficient
- [ ] Elegant
- [ ] Encouraging
- [ ] Energetic
- [ ] Enthusiastic
- [ ] Entrepreneurial
- [ ] Ethical
- [ ] Exclusive
- [ ] Even-tempered
- [ ] Experienced
- [ ] Extroverted
- [ ] Fashionable

☐ Fast	☐ Meticulous
☐ Flexible	☐ No-nonsense
☐ Forgiving	☐ Open-minded
☐ Free-spirited	☐ Optimistic
☐ Friendly	☐ Organized
☐ Fun-loving	☐ Passionate
☐ Funny	☐ People-oriented
☐ Future-oriented	☐ Perseverant
☐ Generous	☐ Persuasive
☐ Gracious	☐ Polite
☐ Helpful	☐ Positive
☐ Honest	☐ Precise
☐ Imaginative	☐ Productive
☐ Independent	☐ Professional
☐ Influential	☐ Problem-solving
☐ Innovative	☐ Quality-oriented
☐ Inspirational	☐ Quick
☐ Intellectual	☐ Quiet
☐ Intelligent	☐ Relational
☐ Introverted	☐ Reliable
☐ Intuitive	☐ Research-driven
☐ Just	☐ Resilient
☐ Knowledgeable	☐ Resourceful
☐ Leading-edge	☐ Respected
☐ Level-headed	☐ Respectful
☐ Logical	☐ Savvy
☐ Loving	☐ Self-starting
☐ Loyal	☐ Sincere
☐ Mature	☐ Smart
☐ Methodical	☐ Sophisticated

(continued)

(continued)

☐ Spontaneous	☐ Top-ranked
☐ Strategic	☐ Tough
☐ Street-smart	☐ Trendy
☐ Stylish	☐ Trustworthy
☐ Successful	☐ Upbeat
☐ Supportive	☐ Visionary
☐ Tasteful	☐ Well-trained
☐ Team-oriented	☐ Wise
☐ Thorough	☐ Witty
☐ Thoughtful	☐ Other

From the words you checked off, write the top 10 terms that capture the essence of your work identity here.

The Essence of My Work Identity

1. _____
2. _____
3. _____
4. _____
5. _____
6. _____
7. _____
8. _____
9. _____
10. _____

What do you believe you are capable of accomplishing? At 20 years of age, you will have a different answer to this question than you will at 30, 40, 50, and so on. The next job you target is directly linked to what you believe you are capable of accomplishing. The good news is that you are usually capable of much more than you believe. Let's raise the bar on your beliefs! When reflecting on any self-imposed limitations you've held in the past, you set the stage to adopt beliefs that serve you better and allow you to move forward in your career.

In the following space, write a few sentences that raise the bar on what you believe you are capable of accomplishing in your next position:

What I Can Accomplish in My Next Position

_____

_____

_____

_____

_____

Step 6: Know Your Personality Type

Step 6 allows you to better understand personality type and how it relates to your behavior, both on and off the job. Type theory stems from the work of influential psychiatrist Carl Jung who, more than 80 years ago, proposed that differences in peoples' behavior were the result of preferences related to basic functions of personality. These basic functions include how we take in information and how we make decisions.

Taking Jung's work to another level, the mother-daughter team of Katharine Briggs and Isabelle Myers developed an assessment to classify people's observable behavior. With this effort, the assessment known as the Myers-Briggs Type Indicator® (MBTI®) was born and is now administered to more than 2.5 million people each year. Briggs' and Myers' two-fold purpose for developing the MBTI® was noble: 1) to better match people and jobs; and 2) to contribute to world peace through a better understanding of people's type.

When you understand type, you can pursue positions that will complement, not clash with, your personality preferences.

Using Personality Type to Have a Better Interview

A basic understanding of personality type can give you insights into your interviewers' personality and how to best communicate with him or her. For instance, an interviewer who asks for lots of details or says "wait a minute, I missed hearing a step in your response" might prefer information delivered in a sequential, concrete, and ordered fashion. Conversely, an interviewer who seems impatient with step-by-step details and wants the big-picture view might appreciate responses that use metaphors and weave together multiple concepts. For more on connecting with interviewers, see chapter 10.

The basic tenets of personality type measure four scales:

1. **Energy:** The direction in which your energies typically flow—outward, toward objects and people in the environment (*Extroversion,* or its abbreviation *E*) or inward, drawing attention from the outward environment toward inner experience and reflection (*Introversion,* or its abbreviation *I*).

2. **Perception:** Whether you prefer to take in information through your five senses in a concrete fashion, focusing on "what is" (*Sensing,* or *S*) or with a "sixth sense" in an abstract or conceptual manner, focusing on "what could be" (*iNtuiting,* or *N*).

3. **Judgment:** Whether you make decisions based on facts and logic (*Thinking,* or *T*) or based on personal or social values (*Feeling,* or *F*).

4. **Orientation:** Whether you orient your outer world in a methodical, deliberate manner, seeking closure (*Judging,* or *J*), or in a spontaneous, play-it-by-ear approach, remaining open to more information (*Perceiving,* or *P*).

The assessment yields a four-letter code, such as *INFJ* or *ESTP,* to indicate your personality preferences. These four preferences, according to Jung, become the core of our attractions and aversions to people, tasks, and events. The following examples shed light on Jung's and Myers-Briggs' theory as it relates to career choice:

People with a clear preference for "Extroversion" (E) will likely be attracted to work where they can interact with people extensively or with large groups of people. People with a clear preference for "Introversion" (I) will be attracted to occupations where they can interact one-on-one or with small groups, or concentrate quietly on ideas, impressions, or information.

⭐ Those with a combined preference for "iNtuiting" and "Feeling" (NF) will likely be attracted to work such as advocacy, facilitation, or counseling; conversely, these same people would likely have an aversion to work that requires repetitive tasks, such as a production line job.

⭐ Those with a combined preference for "Sensing" and "Feeling" (SF) often choose occupations that require work with details in a way that allows them to help others. Accordingly, professions such as healthcare (physician, nurse, medical records technician, therapist), management or administration (often in social services or education programs), data management (bookkeeping, librarian, secretary), or law enforcement (police detective, guard, site administrator) might be appealing.

⭐ Those with preferences for "Sensing" (S), "Thinking" (T), and "Judging" (J) will likely be drawn to task-oriented work that might involve measurement, logistics, monitoring, or management.

⭐ People with a combined preference for "iNtuiting" and "Thinking" (NT) will likely be attracted to work that involves problem-solving, brainstorming, strategy, or leadership.

Personality type clearly impacts career choice. For instance, the *MBTI Manual* (Third Edition, Consulting Psychologist Press) indicates that, on a national basis, only a small percentage of the population have the NT preference (10.3%). Yet when comparing this percentage of the population with a sample of MBA students, the percentage of students reporting an NT preference was almost double that of any other type. Often, MBA graduate programs lead to an executive career track, something that's likely to be attractive for the NT group (although not a guarantee of excellence on the job).

Use table 2.5 as a starting point to identify your preferences for the four scales of energy, perception, judgment, and orientation. This is not a test—there are no right or wrong answers! This is about identifying your natural preferences, just as you have a natural preference for right-handedness or left-handedness. When responding, don't think about what is most socially acceptable or how you've trained yourself to be on the job. Instead, think about how you would naturally respond, with no one looking over your shoulder or judging you. Read the paired items from left to right, and then check the box that best describes your preference. Mark only one box for each of the pairs.

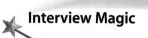

Table 2.5: Identify Your Energy, Perception, Judgment, and Orientation Preferences

Extroversion	Introversion
Energy: How You Recharge and Focus Your Attention	
☐ Devote more energy toward outer world, focusing energy and attention to objects and people in the environment	☐ Devote more energy toward the the inner world, focusing attention on clarity of thoughts, ideas, impressions
☐ Prefer group settings	☐ Prefer individual or small-group settings
☐ Like expanding your social circle and sphere of friends	☐ Carefully consider adding new friends due to the time and energy commitment of maintaining deep relationships
☐ Energized by starting and engaging in conversation; mingle easily with strangers	☐ Find it draining to keep the conversation going; small talk with strangers is taxing
☐ Process thoughts by thinking out loud; often have a quick response or witty comeback	☐ Process thoughts internally before speaking; often think of the perfect response hours later
☐ Active, enthusiastic, energetic, animated	☐ Reflective, calm demeanor, understated
☐ Enjoy entertainment that involves action	☐ Enjoy entertainment that sparks mental stimulation
☐ Prefer variety in workday; dislike working on one thing for a long time, especially if on their own	☐ Enjoy working on one thing for a long time
☐ Enjoy the spotlight	☐ Happy to work behind the scenes
☐ Prefer to have a breadth of interests	☐ Prefer to have a depth of understanding about a few interests
_____ Total checkmarks for Extroversion column	_____ Total checkmarks for Introversion column

Circle the preference that received the most checkmarks (if there is a tie, select Introversion):

Extroversion (E) or Introversion (I)

Sensing	iNtuiting

Perception: How You Take In Information

☐ Trust information you can take in through your five senses	☐ Trust information you can take in through inspiration, inference, impressions
☐ Enjoy details and concrete, physical data	☐ Enjoy abstract ideas and meanings
☐ Use precise, literal language; give detailed explanations	☐ Use general, figurative language; speak in metaphors and analogies
☐ Present or take in information in a step-by-step, sequential fashion	☐ Present or take in information tangentially
☐ Are pragmatic and results-oriented	☐ Are conceptual and idea-oriented
☐ Hands-on; trust experience	☐ Theoretical; trust ideas
☐ Realist, "what-is" perspective	☐ Visionary, "what-if" perspective
☐ Past or present, "here-and-now" orientation	☐ Future orientation
☐ See facts and details before seeing underlying patterns or whole concepts	☐ See behind-the-scenes before seeing individual facts and details
_____ Total checkmarks for Sensing column	_____ Total checkmarks for iNtuiting column

Circle the preference that received the most checkmarks (if there is a tie, select iNtuiting):

Sensing (S) or iNtuiting (N)

Thinking	Feeling

Judging: How You Make Decisions

☐ Base decisions on logic and reasoning	☐ Base decisions on personal or social values
☐ Focus on analysis and objectivity	☐ Focus on people and harmony
☐ Deem it more important to be truthful than tactful	☐ Deem it important to be tactful as well as truthful

(continued)

(continued)

Thinking	Feeling
☐ Prefer objective, analytical presentation of facts	☐ May sense that your or others' feelings are not being valued when discussion centers on an objective, analytical presentation of facts
☐ Value fair treatment for everyone, with a one-standard-for-all philosophy	☐ Evaluate situations based on the individual, with an exception-to-the-rule viewpoint
☐ Tend to be critical; point out flaws	☐ Easily show appreciation to others; overlook others' flaws
☐ Detached, aloof; process-oriented	☐ Connected to people; people are integral to the process
☐ Often oblivious to others' feelings	☐ May be viewed as overly accommodating or overemotional
☐ Facts drive decisions	☐ Impact on others factors heavily into decisions
☐ Make tough decisions despite any negative personal reactions	☐ Tender; effect of a decision on others can be more important than logic
_____ Total checkmarks for Thinking column	_____ Total checkmarks for Feeling column

Circle the preference that received the most checkmarks (if there is a tie, select Feeling):

Thinking (T) or Feeling (F)

Judging	Perceiving
Orientation: How You Orient Your Outer World	
☐ Prefer a planned, organized, systematic approach to life	☐ Prefer a spontaneous, flexible approach to life
☐ Prefer to have things settled	☐ Prefer to leave things open
☐ Formal and orderly; efficient	☐ Informal and easygoing; casual
☐ Like expectations to be clearly defined	☐ Are comfortable with ambiguity

Judging	Perceiving
☐ Make lists, enjoy completing a task on time or early	☐ Starting the task is fun; finishing a task on time is optional
☐ Prefer to take in only the amount of information necessary to make a decision	☐ Remain open to new information as long as possible in order to miss nothing that might be important
☐ Start early to reduce stress of deadline pressure	☐ Do most creative work when under deadline pressure
☐ Let's get this done	☐ Let's wait and see
☐ Enjoy organization; apply procedures to help structure task	☐ Enjoy variety and diversity; procedures can impede creativity
☐ Decide quickly on goals and stay the course in achieving them	☐ Change goals when made aware of new information
_____ Total checkmarks for Judging column	_____ Total checkmarks for Perceiving column

Circle the preference that received the most checkmarks (if there is a tie, select Perceiving):

Judging (J) or Perceiving (P)

Write your preferences for each of the four scales in the blanks that follow:

My Preferences

Energy (Extroversion or Introversion):

_____

Perception (Sensing or iNtuiting):

_____

Judgment (Thinking or Feeling):

_____

Orientation (Judging or Perceiving):

_____

Identifying your individual preferences for energy, perception, judgment, and orientation is only the first step in understanding type. Together these four preferences mesh to create a richly complex personality type, which can best be understood by completing the MBTI® (or, for career purposes, the MBTI® Career Report). If you have not had the opportunity to take this assessment, I encourage you to do so. The results will enable you to target tasks that you find interesting and express your preferences on the job, which is like cycling with the wind at your back rather than in your face. You will need to work with an individual who is specially qualified to administer the MBTI® assessment (many career coaches and counselors possess this qualification). Alternatively, you can use an assessment similar to the MBTI called the Keirsey Temperament Sorter, which is available online at www.advisorteam.com. Two other great resources are the books *Do What You Are* (Little, Brown) by Paul D. Tieger and Barbara Barron-Tieger and *What's Your Type of Career?* (Davies Black) by Donna Dunning, which provides detailed information about how type relates to career choice.

Introverts in Sales Careers

Should an introvert avoid positions in sales? Absolutely not. One of my clients, a sales professional, identified his preference for introversion, and yet he was the #1 sales representative in the nation for a Fortune 500 company and the #1 sales manager in the country for a national consumer packaged goods company. When we explored this preference for introversion further, he noted that, although he loved being with people, the solitary driving time between clients was just what he needed to be able to reflect, process, and reenergize before he called on the next client.

Step 7: Set Your Salary Range

In addition to steps 1–6, you'll need to add one more item to your Career-FIT™ so that it truly FITS! That final item is *salary*. Identify the range that you're targeting for your next position. Of course, you won't be mentioning your salary requirements to many people at this early stage. However, it's important that you put pencil to paper to calculate what you would accept on the low end, what the industry average is, as well as what your ideal or dream salary would be. If you need help getting a handle on what these numbers should be, ask colleagues what they consider to be the range for your target position (the phrasing "what is the range?" will be better received than "what do you make?"). Also, visit www.salary.com for salary information adjusted for hundreds of metro areas throughout the U.S. The basic salary report from this site is free; a personalized salary report is available for approximately $30.

List your three salary figures in the following box.

Salary Figures

Low-end salary I would be willing to accept:

$ _____

Industry average:

$ _____

Dream-job salary:

$ _____

Finalize Your Career-FIT™

After completing the six steps in the Career-FIT™ system, use table 2.6 to pull it all together. For easy future reference, transfer each of your responses from Steps 1 through 7 to the following table.

Table 2.6: My Career-FIT™ Elements

	F	I	T
External	Step 1: *Function*	Step 2: *Industry/ Interests*	Step 3: *Things That Matter*
Internal	Step 4: *Fulfillment*	Step 5: *Identity*	Step 6: *Type*
Step 7: Salary	Low-End Salary $ _____	Industry Average $ _____	Dream-Job Salary $ _____

Create Your Focus Statement

Based on the work you've completed in finding your Career-FIT™, you're ready to write your focus statement for your next position. The benefits of doing so are threefold:

- **Motivation:** Your focus combines the unique ingredients that will energize and motivate you throughout your job search.

- **Meaning:** Your focus hones in on what *you* want, as opposed to striving after the dreams of someone else (be it parents, spouse, friends, or coworkers).

- **Map:** Your focus will keep you on course as you make decisions about what interview opportunities to pursue.

I've provided an example focus statement to help get you started.

> *I am committed to targeting opportunities that will use my branch management skills in the field of financial services, specializing in mutual funds, where I can develop management and marketing strategies that will grow shareholder value and investors' net worth. This type of position is in sync with my personality preferences for "intuiting" and "thinking" (seeing the big picture, brainstorming, making decisions based on logical facts) and meets my core values and needs of intellectual stimulation, leadership, logic, and monetary reward (with salary in the range of $75,000–$90,000).*

Here's how the target statement relates to the Career-FIT™:

I am committed to targeting opportunities that will use my

[step 1, Functional abilities] __branch management skills__

[step 2, Industry] in the field of __financial services__, specializing

in [step 2, Interests] __mutual funds,__ where I can

[step 4, Fulfillment] __develop management and marketing strategies that will grow shareholder value and investors' net worth__.

This type of position is in sync with my personality preferences for

[step 6, personality Type] __"intuiting" and "thinking" (seeing the big picture, brainstorming, making decisions based on logical facts)__

and is consistent with my self-image [step 5, Identity] and values [step 3, Things That Matter], such as

__intellectual stimulation, leadership, logic__, and __monetary reward__ (with salary in the range of $_____ to $_____).

In the following template, write your own target statement using the information you filled in earlier in table 2.6.

I am committed to targeting opportunities that will use my
[Functional abilities]

_____

[Industry] in the field of

_____, specializing

in [Interests] _____ where

I can [Fulfillment]_____

_____

_____

_____

This type of position is in synch with my personality preferences for
[personality Type]_____

_____

_____

_____

and is consistent with my self-image [Identity] and values [Things That
Matter], such as

_____,

_____,

_____,

_____, and

_____, as well as my salary needs of

$_____ to $ _____.

When networking, you might want to use just the first sentence in your focus statement to help others know what you are looking for. Omit the second sentence and reserve salary for discussions with hiring managers. In chapter 4, we'll look more closely at developing sound bites for networking and interviewing. In the meantime, this focus statement will help keep you on course as you evaluate new job opportunities.

Chapter Wrap-Up

Remember that achieving career contentment is a process. It doesn't happen overnight. It requires honing in on and weaving together all six of the

Career-FIT™ elements. Gaining a new awareness of each item puts you on the right path. And, if you've fleshed out answers to each of the six steps, you'll be far ahead of the competition for your target job.

An intentional focus on these FIT elements will allow you to be "radically rewarded and enthusiastically engaged in work that adds value to others." The final four words in that definition of career purpose—adds value to others—contain an important truth. Your work must bring value to others, specifically your company, colleagues, or customers, so that your career is in sync with marketplace demands. Chapter 3 outlines how to add value so that interviewers will view you as a competitive candidate.

10 Quick Tips for Focusing on the Right Career-FIT™

1. **Step 1—Find the right *F*unction.** Functions represent job titles and tasks, such as engineer and graphic artist or market research and product development.

2. **Step 2—Identify your ideal *I*ndustry and *I*nterests.** Industry refers to *where* you will apply your functional skills, whereas Interests tap a specialty area that you connect with or are especially enthusiastic about. For instance, a nurse might target oncology as an Industry and then focus on pediatric oncology as a special Interest within oncology.

3. **Step 3—Think about the *T*hings That Matter.** When what you do from 8 to 5 aligns with your values and needs, you will find greater energy, motivation, and career satisfaction. Employers value employees with energy and motivation. What motivates you? Autonomy? Authority? Influence? Monetary reward? Recognition? Teamwork? Variety? Know the top 10 things that matter most to you in your career.

4. **Step 4—Define *F*ulfillment.** Fulfillment transforms your job from paycheck to purpose. Fulfillment, or purpose, is the reason *why* you work. To define fulfillment, pay attention to the "tingle factor"—that goose-bumpy, addictive feeling that comes when you do something you absolutely love. Be sure to pair your purpose with market demands to ensure that you don't compromise your paycheck for purpose!

5. **Step 5—Enhance your *I*dentity.** Your identity, what you believe about yourself, is directly linked to the type of position you'll target. You are usually capable of accomplishing much more than you believe you can. Raise the bar on beliefs! Blast through self-imposed limitations. Adopt beliefs that serve you better and allow you to move forward in your career.

6. **Step 6—Know your personality *Type*.** Understanding your type allows you to pursue positions that complement, rather than clash with, your personality preferences. The basic tenets of personality type measure four scales: Energy—the focus of your energy and attention flows to the outer world or is directed toward inner experiences and reflection (Extroversion or Introversion); Perception—your preference for taking in information via "what is" or "what could be" (Sensing or iNtuiting); Judgment—your preference for making decisions based on facts and logic or personal/social values (Thinking or Feeling); and Orientation—your preference for coming to closure or remaining open to more information (Judging or Perceiving).

7. **Step 7—Set your salary range.** In addition to the six FIT steps, your last step adds a final "S," for *salary,* so that your target truly FITS! Identify a range for your target position, listing the industry average for your position, a low-end salary figure that you would be comfortable with (one that won't make you feel as though you're being taken advantage of), and a top-end, dream-job number.

8. **Avoid "fish fever"**—jumping indiscriminately at any opportunity that pops onto the radar screen.

9. **Commit to the long haul.** Finding the perfect Career-FIT™ will take time. Keep an aerial perspective on your progress, proceed with small steps, and be patient with yourself. First, be clear about your functional strengths (step 1 in the process), and then systematically work through the remaining steps.

10. **Remember the benefits of the right fit.** An intentional focus on the FIT elements will allow you to leverage your time by pursuing the right opportunities, to impress interviewers by knowing what you want, to gain confidence targeting positions you can be enthusiastic about, and, ultimately, to land a position that is radically rewarding.

★ **Magical Coaching Questions**

Which of the Career-FIT™ elements had you already incorporated into your prior positions?

_____

_____

_____

(continued)

(continued)

Which Career-FIT™ elements will you focus on incorporating into future positions?

_____

_____

What system or reminder can you put in place to ensure that you weigh those new elements when considering new opportunities?

_____

_____

Chapter
3

Capture Your Value with "Smart" Success Stories

The basic building block of good communications is the feeling that every human being is unique and of value.

—Author Unknown

E = MC² captures Einstein's brilliant theory of relativity. I've translated that memorable formula into job search terminology so that *you* can be brilliant in your quest for new employment! In the realm of job search, E = MC² reads like this:

Employment = Mechanics × Commitment-Squared

Let's explore what each of those terms means to you:

- **Employment:** Receiving, and accepting, a job offer that is in sync with your career goals
- **Mechanics:** Applying savvy strategies, systems, and tactics—the ins and outs—of job search and interviewing
- **Commitment-Squared:** Holding optimum mindset, emotional energy, and intelligent attitude throughout the job search process.

If you've purchased this book, I'll assume that employment—a new job— is your goal. To get to that new job, you'll need to put into practice the nuts and bolts of job search and interviewing, which I've referred to as "mechanics." Add to that a double portion of commitment. Together, these ingredients translate not just to employment, but to career success—radical rewards and enthusiastic engagement in work that adds value to others.

Some of the next steps that you're now ready to walk through include the following:

- Developing success stories and sound bites for your job search campaign
- Targeting companies and networking to identify opportunities and openings
- Communicating your value and return-on-investment to hiring managers as you network and interview

The work you do now will enable you to avoid the most common downfall of many candidates: going to interviews unprepared.

Conveying Value to Interviewers

Truth #9 from chapter 1—Every Employer Wants *One* Thing from You— holds the key to landing an offer. That one thing, *value,* should be at the heart of your interviewing message. Use it to describe how you'll work in a manner that will make your employer a better, stronger, more profitable company. Value can be woven into your interview responses at every turn. Three methods for conveying value include

- Linking your past successes and future solutions to employer buying motivators
- Demonstrating a return on investment (ROI)
- Emphasizing benefits instead of features of your qualifications

Let's look at each of these three methods more closely.

The Employer's Motivation to "Buy"

"Walk a mile in my moccasins." This old Indian adage can help you adopt an employer-focused mindset. Consider the hiring manager's perspective in what will motivate him or her to engage your services as an employee. Yes, the hiring manager will be thinking about how you can benefit the company and the team. But she is also thinking about how you will help her individually, whether it is to lighten the load in her inbox or solve a pressing issue. Whatever the situation, recognize that she will want you to make her look good. You can approach the interview with confidence, knowing that you (unlike many candidates) understand her concerns about getting the job done and keeping costs down while keeping morale up.

Numerous "Employer Buying Motivators" drive business. These 10 buying motivators are key to why hiring decisions are made:

- Buying Motivator #1: Make Money
- Buying Motivator #2: Save Money
- Buying Motivator #3: Save Time
- Buying Motivator #4: Make Work Easier
- Buying Motivator #5: Solve a Specific Problem
- Buying Motivator #6: Be More Competitive
- Buying Motivator #7: Build Relationships, Brand, and Image with Internal/External Customers, Vendors, and the Public
- Buying Motivator #8: Expand Business
- Buying Motivator #9: Attract New Customers
- Buying Motivator #10: Retain Customers

In chapter 4, you'll have a chance to explore how you can link your strengths to each of these 10 buying motivators.

What's Your ROI?

ROI, short for *return on investment,* is a business term widely used by companies to determine how quickly their decision to invest in new equipment, advertising, or an expansion will pay for itself. In the case of a hiring decision, the employer is investing in salary, benefits, training, work space, and equipment.

In the corporate world, savvy career professionals concentrate on generating a return on investment for their employers. For instance, a top sales performer can show that a $125,000 salary will be justified by her ability to bring in $500,000 in new sales contracts. A materials manager might find methods to reduce waste or recycle scrap, which may add up to a six-figure savings. A production line worker might make a suggestion that, when implemented, leads to a spike in productivity, which can be tied to the bottom line. Whatever your role, challenge yourself to look for ways to boost your employer's success, and then document that success.

Benefits vs. Features

As with most people, hiring managers are tuned to radio station WIFM, or "what's in it for me?" Benefits explain what's in it for them! High-paid advertising copywriters know that benefits sell, whereas features can put you to sleep. Let's compare features and benefits for a minute by using career coaching services as an example.

A few features that a career coach might have:

- Certified Career Management Coach
- Nationally Certified Resume Writer
- Graduate of Career Coach Academy
- Member of Career Masters Institute

You'll note that the features are title-oriented. Yawn. Features might carry some weight, but they don't really describe the benefit of what a career coach can do.

On the other hand, these statements describe benefits:

- Helping people who feel stuck in their careers uncover options that can move them from drudgery to dream job.

- Equipping job seekers with insider strategies that shorten the time it takes to find a new job.

- Helping people eliminate the guesswork and frustration from career transition and job search.

- Helping job seekers who wish networking would just go away to find self-marketing methods that are both comfortable and compelling.

- Enabling mid-career professionals to bloom where they're planted, using a 10-step formula that transforms their current job from surviving to thriving.

- Lighting a fire under the dream you've relegated to the back burner, helping you break through roadblocks and find meaningful life-work…purpose produces passion!

The preceding benefits use carefully chosen language to address needs that a prospective client might have. Part of your goal in writing success stories is to address the needs, or pain points, of a prospective employer. To do so, concentrate on knitting in benefit-oriented words such as these verbs and nouns:

Accelerate	Eliminate	Free
Build	Enhance	Gain
Create	Equip	Grow
Decrease	Find	Guarantee
Discover	Formula	Help

Honor	Proven	Strategies
How To	Reduce	Strengthen
Improve	Relief	Techniques
Increase	Relieve	Tips
Less	Save	Uncover
More	Secret	
Numbers	Steps	

S.O.S.

The familiar Morse code of S.O.S. stands for **S**ave **O**ur **S**hip. Although most companies with which you'll interview aren't necessarily sinking, they will likely need some help bailing out from an overflow of work or plugging a hole caused by someone's absence.

When writing your success stories and sound bites, offer your own S.O.S. Response, in the form of **S**olutions **O**r **S**ervices. Positioning yourself as a provider of solutions or services will give your candidacy favored status.

Inventorying Your Success Stories

In this section, you'll take stock of your success stories. When I give the upcoming exercise to my clients, I sometimes hear, "I don't have any success stories." They assume that if they didn't single-handedly initiate and execute a project of monumental proportions, they have no success stories. However, *any* information that helps support your candidacy qualifies as a success story. Although you'll want the majority of your success stories to have a positive outcome, it's also acceptable to include a few anecdotes that describe an unsuccessful attempt or lesson learned. Interviewers will be suspicious if you can't admit to having met with some failure or disappointment over the course of your career. Later, you'll identify and think through your response to potential negatives so that you're ready with a positive response in the interview. The key is to *leverage the lessons learned*. In doing so, the situation can be categorized as a success!

Everyone can uncover success stories, especially when this definition is adopted:

Success Story: An anecdote or account providing evidence that you have the knowledge, hard and soft skills, and motivation to excel in the target job.

Let's expand on the elements in this definition. *Anecdotes*—short descriptions of a relevant incident—can be interesting, amusing, or biographical in nature. *Knowledge* can be gained through employment, education (class activities, group projects, case studies), and unpaid experience (internships, work study, job shadowing). Even community service, team or sports involvement, and parenting can contribute to your knowledge bank. *Hard skills* refer to your technical skills and talents, whereas *soft skills* are those less-tangible but often-important interpersonal and communication skills. Beyond knowledge and skills, employers today are also interested in whether you have the inner drive and ambition to do the job. *Motivation* stems from being rewarded and engaged by work that aligns with your Career-FIT™ (see chapter 2). The verb *excel*—the final part of the definition of a success story—implies that you are bottom-line oriented, with a commitment to delivering results that help add revenue, reduce costs, or boost productivity.

Each of these examples illustrates a success story that conveys value:

- **Materials Management Success Story (materials coordinator describing a reduction in order-cycle time):** In my last position as a materials coordinator at Lanco Foods, I participated on a team that cut our order cycle time by about 75 percent. We analyzed turnkey processes and identified two key areas for improvement: order placement and payment closure. I then took the lead on writing new procedures for order placement and taught our customer service team how to implement the procedures. Within six months, our order cycle was shortened from 45 days to 11 days.

- **Marketing Success Story (retail marketing specialist describing an increased return on trade spending):** I inherited a retail marketing specialist position where the return-on-investment on trade spending was below the target of 10:1—it was actually at 8:1, and we ended up delivering a 50 percent increase. After analyzing syndicated data and interviewing marketing specialists at other stores to learn what they were doing to get higher returns, I initiated a campaign to increase the displays in some of our top customers. I prepared proposals and accompanied sales reps as they made presentations to store managers. Within three months, my action plan allowed us to exceed the benchmark in trade spending with a return ratio of 12:1 versus the target of 10:1.

- **Secretarial Success Story (executive secretary to litigation attorney describing an initiative that increased her boss' billable hours):** I noticed that the attorney whom I supported was frustrated about keeping up her billable client hours. After observing her typical days and thinking about where I could help, I approached her about letting me handle some of her e-mail, which seemed to be stealing a lot

of time from her day. She agreed, so I designed a series of boilerplate auto-responses that allowed me to respond to approximately 30 percent of her e-mail. This action allowed her to reclaim an hour or more a day in billable time. At $250 an hour, this translated to almost $6,000 per month in additional revenue. The attorney mentioned our system to the managing partner, and we're now in the process of data-basing those auto-responses so that all of the legal secretaries can use them to lighten the administrative load of the rest of the attorneys.

Event Planning Success Story (stay-at-home mom transitioning back into the work force describing her lifelong skills in event planning): I'd like to tell you about how I recently generated a 200 percent increase in revenue through my event planning—I'm certain I was born with these skills, so I'll first share a quick story about my earliest recollection of planning an event. When I was only five years old, I invited four of my neighbor friends for a dog party. I unknowingly covered all the event-planning bases: program, theme, publicity, food and beverage, etc. Everyone was to bring their dog, with the plan that we would train them to do a trick, have them wear party hats, and feed them doggie treats. I had a 101 Dalmatians theme, advertised the event with posters on my front-yard tree, and talked my mother into baking cookies and making punch. Several decades later, I'm the one that the principal of Johnson Middle School calls on to help with the Fall Festival, our chief fund-raising event of the year. I've expanded the event significantly to include in-kind and cash donations from local businesses, entertainment by television soap stars, and additional revenue centers, such as the silent auction. Before I became involved, our highest earnings were only $4,500; this past year, we raised $14,000.

Teacher Success Story (kindergarten teacher describing her success with language arts): I was challenged by teaching a kindergarten class at Washington Elementary, where 80 percent of the students were from non-English–speaking homes. I addressed the needs of emergent readers through phonemic awareness, phonics, concepts of print, decoding, guided reading, and shared reading. Writing skills were cultivated through modeled, shared, interactive, and journal writing, and I introduced spelling at the appropriate developmental level. By the end of the year, all of the students were at or above grade level in their reading scores, excited about "graduating," and confident about entering the first grade. My success with these students led to my principal asking me to share my strategies with the other kindergarten teachers.

Executive Success Story (responding to the question, "tell me about your biggest failure"): As Chief Executive Officer of XYZ Company in the late '90s, the Board asked me to lead the company through a critical transition period after the founder, who had held the reins for 20 years, died unexpectedly in a plane accident. I addressed a number of pressing marketing, operations, and morale issues and was proud to be at the helm as the company reached 50 percent gross margins—a record in its 20-year history. At the same time, the dot-com world was exploding, which led me to launch the company's e-commerce venture. The concept was strong but the business model wasn't sustainable, so after nine months I made the decision to cut our losses. The good that came out of it is that I gained some firsthand knowledge of what does and does not work in the dot-com world. Since that time, I've launched another e-commerce site that is profitable, in large part due to the lessons learned at XYZ Company. I can give you some details on that project if you'd like.

Questions to Elicit Success Stories

Answers come when you are asked the right questions. Here are 25 questions to ask yourself that will help percolate great ideas for your success stories:

1. What are you most proud of in your career?

2. What are you most proud of in each of your past positions?

3. What challenge or crisis did you face on the job and what was your approach for solving each situation?

4. In what way did you help your employer generate more revenue?

5. In what way did you help your employer save money?

6. In what way did you help your employer increase productivity?

7. What was the most interesting suggestion or project you initiated?

8. When were you complimented by a supervisor, coworker, or customer?

9. What positive comments (or ratings) were documented in your performance evaluations?

10. When do people say to you, "You are amazing…you make it look so easy!" or "How do you do that!?"

11. What skills or talents are you especially known for?

12. What kinds of work activities cause you to lose track of time?

13. What special projects or teams have you worked on?

14. How were goals and productivity measured on the job?

15. When did you go above and beyond the call of duty?

16. What do you do that your coworkers don't do? What would happen if you weren't on the job?

17. What would others point to as evidence of your success?

18. When did your actions motivate or influence others to do something that they initially did not want to do?

19. When did you have to make a tough decision under pressure?

20. Under what circumstances did you display character and integrity?

21. How did you overcome a challenging situation with a coworker or team member?

22. When did you have to quickly learn new information or skills? How did you go about this?

23. When did you use your verbal communication skills to influence or improve a situation with a coworker, team member, or customer?

24. When did you diplomatically address a politically delicate situation?

25. How did you go about making a presentation to internal or external stakeholders? What was the outcome?

Questions for Recent Graduates

If you are a recent graduate, your college work counts! Consider these questions:

1. In thinking back over your time in college, what are you most proud of?

2. What classes did you enjoy the most? Describe several assignments from each of those classes.

3. What was the most difficult assignment you received? How did you handle it?

4. What assignments did you have that involved business simulations, case studies, or a hands-on practicum? What problems did you have to solve?

5. If you had a difference of opinion with a professor, how did you handle it?

6. If you also held a job while attending college, how did you manage your time?

7. What co-curricular activities were you involved in? Describe a situation where your group had a challenging task to complete.

8. In what situations did you display leadership skills?

9. Was there a time when you stood up for your convictions about an issue where others disagreed with you?

10. How did you persuade or influence others?

11. How did you manage your time when it came to juggling class, studies, and personal needs?

12. What extra effort did it take to get a good grade in a challenging class?

13. If you were chosen to lead a study group or project group, what goals, actions, and results were achieved?

14. If you were involved in sports, what team accomplishment were you proud of?

15. What positive comments did your professors make about your presentations or papers?

16. Apart from college, what personal accomplishments are you most proud of?

Questions for People Returning to Work

Perhaps you're returning to work after a hiatus. If this is the case, first use the initial 25 questions as a starting point for your success stories. In addition, these questions might help build stories for your recent time away from work.

1. While you were away from the business world, what did you do to stay abreast of new trends or issues in your field?

2. You might have been away from work to raise children or care for a terminally ill loved one; or, perhaps you were recuperating from a challenging illness or accident. If so, what were some of the biggest challenges associated with this time? Write individual stories to describe how you managed each of these challenges.

3. If your hiatus involved travel or exploration, what planning was required? What insights did you gain from this time away? How did the experiences help you grow personally? What will you bring to the work world because of these experiences?

4. If you were involved in volunteer work, in what roles did you serve? If you were in a leadership role, what projects or tasks did you plan, execute, and achieve results around? If you were in a support role, what did your collective efforts help achieve? What were some of the challenges associated with team communications or motivating volunteers?

5. What parallels can you draw between the focus of your non-work time and your professional career?

Using the SMART Format to Answer Behavioral Interview Questions

Many interviewers prefer that you deliver your responses to behavioral interview questions using a format that first outlines what was happening, then what you did about it, followed by what resulted from the actions. Common variations on this format include the following:

- **STAR: S**ituation/**T**ask, **A**ction, **R**esult
- **CAR: C**hallenge, **A**ction, **R**esult
- **PAR: P**roblem, **A**ction, **R**esolution

In coaching candidates for interviews, I've found that a variation on this format called the SMART Story™ works well. SMART stands for

- **S**ituation and **M**ore
- **A**ction
- **R**esults
- **T**ie-in or **T**heme

A SMART Story™ will allow you to craft your responses with a definitive beginning, a middle, and a dynamite ending and provide the many details that interviewers are hungry to hear about. It also is unique in that the final step positions you to neatly link the response back to the employer's competency question, inquire further into the employer's needs, and focus the conversation on how you can *do* the job instead of simply *auditioning* for the job. Here's how it breaks out:

- **Situation and More:** Frame the story with contextual details, offering specific numbers about the situation. What was the specific situation you were faced with? Use numbers to describe who and what was involved? Where and when did it occur? What was the impact of the situation? What was the timeframe for the story?

- **Action:** What specific action did you take to tackle the task, overcome the challenge, or resolve the issue? If others were closely involved, how did you interact with them? What were your thoughts or decision-making process? What was your specific role in relation to the team?

Results: Essential to your success story are numbers-oriented, bottom-line results. They will help you convey your return-on-investment (ROI) value and give you leverage in salary negotiations.

- What measurable outcome did you achieve? Think beyond your own work role to how others were impacted, including your boss, your team, your department, your company, your customers, your community, or your industry.

- If it was a group effort, what measurable outcome did the group achieve or contribute to? Did you contribute to a 5 percent increase in productivity; support a team that met or exceeded goal by 9 percent in a difficult economy; participate in an effort that improved customer satisfaction scores; collaborate with team members to accomplish work with 25 percent less staff; or provide ideas that halted a conflict or impasse that had held up progress?

- If the outcome wasn't rosy, what conclusions did you reach or what positives did you learn from the experience?

- Compare your performance. You can make comparisons to a variety of numbers, including your prior work performance, the company's past record, the industry standard, or your competitor's average.

Tie-in and Theme: Use a question or statement to link this story back to important issues or link it to a theme of key competencies sought by the employer. Statements might convey enthusiasm or knowledge gained:

- "I found that I thrived in these sorts of situations, as they give me a chance to use my problem-solving skills," or

- "I learned that it's important to regularly communicate progress status to every member of the team," or

- "My supervisors have commented that my problem-solving, customer relations, and innovation were key to being a good fit for the position," or

- "From the conversation I had with one of your vendors, it sounds like my strengths in vendor relations would be of help."

An occasional question can also be effective in tying the story back to the employer's needs. For instance,

- "Would you like additional detail or another example?" or

- "How will this experience relate to your current needs?" or
- "Is the department encountering similar opportunities [or challenges] to the one I just described?"

The SMART Story™ format will help you structure your writing. It will take an investment of time to develop these stories, so keep in mind the payoff:

- Interviewers will be impressed because you offered tangible evidence of your success stories.

- Interviewers will remember you over other candidates who provided vague, unspecific responses.

- You will feel more comfortable and confident during interviews because you have tip-of-your-tongue evidence that documents your ability to do the job.

- You will be fully prepared to answer behavioral interview questions, which require tangible, step-by-step details about your behavior in past situations.

Note the numerous facts and figures included in the following SMART Stories™:

SMART Story™

Situation and More: **My role:** *Production Worker*

> **Where:** *Wamco Manufacturing, my current employer*
>
> **When/Timeframe:** *January through March of this year*
>
> **Who else was involved or impacted:** *Production shift team of 10 and maintenance mechanic*
>
> **What was the task or challenge:** *I managed to work with outdated equipment that continually broke down and caused long down times. The company had been hit hard financially due to industry issues and didn't have the funds to invest in new equipment or even special maintenance.*

Action: **What was your thought process? What steps did you take? What decisions were made? Describe the sequence.**
At first, we waited for the maintenance mechanic to come to fix things— sometimes that took awhile because this guy had to cover our facility and another facility across town, since they had laid off the mechanic for the plant across town. If he was working on a problem at the second facility, it would take him hours to get to us. Sometimes, the boss would let us go home for the day. I hate waiting around, so after about the third or fourth breakdown, I talked to the maintenance mechanic and

(continued)

(continued)

> *asked him if I could help. At first he said no. Then I asked him if I could just watch what he did. He said yes. It wasn't too complicated. So the next breakdown, the mechanic let me work with him on the repairs. Later on, when things broke down on the vacuum-seal line, I was able to work on it.*

Results: **Use numbers to relate your results.**

> *There were at least three times this past month that I had the problem fixed, and we were back up and running in less than an hour. In the past, it might have taken two or three hours to fix it. Our manager wants a goal of 300 units per day, so in a few cases, we kept our production numbers up even with the breakdown. This past month, we made our production goals, which is the first time in several months. Some other factors came into play as well, but part of it was the repair work I did.*

Tie-in/ Theme: *I know that productivity is key to a profitable operation. Are your productivity numbers where you'd like them to be?*

(Competency Theme: *Initiative, problem-solving, teamwork, mechanical ability*)

SMART Story™

Situation and More: **My role:** *Office Manager*

Where: *Inco Insurance, my current employer*

When/Timeframe: *March through September of this year*

Who else was involved or impacted: *Employees (25 claims processors and 5 support staff)*

What was the task or challenge: *My challenge was to stop losses of more than $1,000 per month. I didn't realize that the systems I put in place would not only stop those losses but increase our productivity. Here's what happened...*

Action: **What was your thought process? What steps did you take? What decisions were made? Describe the sequence.**

> *I was new to the position and familiarizing myself with expenses. I compared and analyzed office expense figures with several prior years and realized that, even though our headcount was down by 25 percent, our expenses were up by almost 30 percent. None of our vendors had implemented any price increases, so I began to look for other reasons. I noticed that CDs and boxes of file folders seemed to be "walking off by themselves." In one of our weekly group meetings—something new I implemented to improve teamwork—I explained that one of our goals included cost controls. To help meet that goal, a new check-out system would be*

implemented for items valued in excess of $20, but that incidentals would be on an "honor system." I posted a bar graph in the supply room reflecting volume in use of supplies over the past six months, along with reduction goals for each ensuing month. I asked staff members for suggestions on incentives and decided what would be feasible. When we reached our monthly goals, I rewarded staff with their choice of an early-dismissal day or a catered box-lunch party.

Results: **Use numbers to relate your results.**
Supply costs were not only reduced more than 35 percent, there was greater camaraderie among the team. It led to the claims processors openly sharing helpful resources and making suggestions, some of which were implemented and helped improve our productivity numbers by about 15 percent.

Tie-in/ *It confirmed to me that communicating clear objectives to staff, along*
Theme: *with soliciting their input, is a wise management policy.*

(Competency Theme: *Communications, problem-solving, analytical, motivator*)

SMART Story™

Situation and More: **My role:** *Vice President, Business Development Manager*

Where: *State Bank & Trust*

When: *The current calendar year, June 200x–May 200x*

Who else was involved or impacted: *A 30-branch Northern State Community Banking District*

What was the task or challenge: *I enjoy telling my "how-I-went-bald" story! It started with being given the charge by my Senior VP to turn around a two-year history of double-digit declining revenues for the district. At the time, the district was ranked last among 17 for revenue performance and had been through four business development managers over the course of three years.*

Action: **What was your thought process? What steps did you take? What decisions were made? Describe the sequence.**
Here's the storyboard. I piloted a new business-development program for the district, which included creating sales strategies for a full complement of products and services (commercial loans, trust and investment services, cash management services, retirement and depository accounts, government guarantee programs, computerized banking, and alliance banking). I scheduled a two-day meeting for the 30 branch managers in the district, and I used a very motivational "All-Star" theme. At the meeting, I created a vision for what could be accomplished, laid out the program, and then used interactive

(continued)

(continued)

> train-the-trainer systems so that they could teach the strategies to 150+ sales reps in the district. I laid down the challenge, telling them that if we reached our goal early, I would shave my head! I had already cleared this with the Senior VP.

Results:	**Use numbers to relate your results.**
	Bottom line, we secured 44 new customers with $16+ million in loan commitments approved, added nearly $4 million in deposits, and secured first-time fee revenue of $162,000 from establishing new international business. We broke all records for loan and deposit growth in the district's 30-year history and boosted the district's ranking from #17 among 17 to #2 in less than two years. And, yes, I was proud to be bald for a time!

Tie-in/ Theme:	*In visiting some of your branches, I had a few ideas about how fee-based revenue could be introduced.*

(Competency Theme: *Leadership, motivator, innovation, strategic, analytical, communication*)

SMART Story™

Situation and More: **My role:** *Mother*

> **Where:** *Home*

> **When:** *The past six years*

> **Who else was involved or impacted:** *Children, husband.*

> **What was the task or challenge:** *Adapting to my new role as mother after having had a record-setting career in sales.*

Action:	**What was your thought process? What steps did you take? What decisions were made? Describe the sequence.**
	I remember the mind shift I had to go through when I first had my daughter. It felt odd to be out of the business world, where I had been regularly recognized for my sales abilities. Being so goal-driven, I knew that I had to have goals in place for myself. The goals I started with may not sound too exciting, but they were appropriate goals for that time of my life—things like not losing my patience when the baby had a fussy night—no small feat when you're seriously sleep deprived. A few years later, I graduated to bigger, more lofty goals, like "selling" broccoli to my 4-year-old!

Results:	**Use numbers to relate your results.**
	Bottom line, I recognized that an innate value for me is performance—setting and achieving goals, for every aspect of my life, whether personal or professional. It's what allowed me to rank among the top 10 percent in a region of 46 while in my last position at Cosamar, Inc.

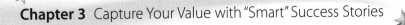

Tie-in/ Theme:	*I know that my initiative and problem-solving skills will serve me well in the position you need to fill. Could you tell me a little more about your clients?*

(Competency Theme: *Initiative, problem-solving, goal-oriented*)

Writing Your Success Stories

Use the blank forms that follow to capture your stories. Be generous with the contextual details. In the form, you'll see a Competency & Keyword area. Leave it blank for now. You'll come back later to complete this section. Don't be concerned about finding the perfect wording or magic words at this stage. And, remember that you'll be delivering these stories in verbal rather than written format. That means you don't have to be concerned about perfect punctuation or syntax as you write. Spoken language is far more flexible and forgiving than written language.

Before you get started on your stories, I want to make a somewhat unusual request. I'd like the first SMART Story™ that you write to be about your current job search situation. Write about the Situation and More in past tense, such as: "I conducted a job search while still employed, working a 60-hour work week," or "I conducted a job search during a time when my industry had experienced a severe downturn." The Action, again in past tense, might include "I read *Interview Magic* (and its predecessor *Résumé Magic*), developed a solid set of success stories, networked beyond my comfort zone, enlisted the support of a job search group, and said 'no' to certain activities so that I could devote as many as 20 hours a week to my job search while I was also working full time." The Result will be written in present tense. Make it a vision statement, such as "I am employed with one of the leading widget companies in the area, performing radically rewarding work that is in sync with my personality, talents, interests, and values." And, finally, tie it to a Theme: "The experience underscored my self-initiative and perseverance, gave me the ability to learn new research strategies, and sharpened my communication skills. In addition, I have an acute understanding that career success is all about providing value to employers."

After you've written about your current situation, you can then dive into your other SMART Stories™.

Some Points to Guide You

These points will guide you in the writing process.

- **Use the "it's about them, not me" perspective when describing your stories.** This means that, ultimately, your SMART Stories™ must be related to "them"—the employer—and *their needs.* Think in terms of what will motivate the employer to buy, the return-on-investment you offer, and your benefits vs. features.

✴ **Use the same standards of quality that a judge or jury would accept.** Choose vivid examples, weave in expert testimony (for instance, from customers, coworkers, vendors, or supervisors), and incorporate appropriate statistics.

✴ **Write SMART Stories™ about your work for each of your past employers.** The heaviest concentration of stories should be about your current or most recent experiences. Pen a SMART Story™ for each recent accomplishment on your resume.

✴ **Assign themes to your SMART Stories™ that underscore competencies needed for the target position.** For instance, competencies for a customer service rep might include customer-focused orientation, interpersonal judgment, communication skills, teamwork, problem solving, listening skills/empathy, and initiative.

✴ **Write SMART Stories™ for non-work experiences if you are just entering the work force.** It is fair game to draw on volunteer work, school experiences, and general life incidents. (If you sense you need additional experience, identify and quickly act on how you can best prepare yourself through reading, attending a course, job-shadowing, volunteering, or taking a relevant part-time job.) Regardless of what point your career life is at, *everyone* should recollect influential or life-altering events throughout youth and adulthood. Write SMART Stories™ about these times.

✴ **Numbers speak louder than words!** Load the stories with numbers, dollar amounts, productivity measurements, comparisons, and the like. (Be cautious about conveying proprietary or confidential company information. In these cases, use year-to-date or quarterly comparisons and translate the numbers into percentages.) Be specific and offer proof. Instead of saying, "I learned the program quickly," make it crystal clear with language like, "I studied the manual at night and, in three days, I knew all the basic functions; in two weeks I had mastered several of the advanced features; and by the end of the month, I had experienced operators coming to me to ask how to embed tables into another program."

✴ **Include emotions and feelings.** Yes, feelings. When describing the situation, don't be afraid to include details such as these: "the tension among the team was so serious that people were resigning"; "the morale was at an all-time low"; or "the customer was irate about receiving a mis-shipment that occurred because of our transportation vendor." When writing about emotions or feelings, be mindful *not* to whine or disparage anyone, even through a veiled reference.

* **Avoid personal opinions.** You can, however, include the opinion of a supervisor or another objective party. Instead of saying, "I believe my positive outlook really helped keep the customer happy," rely on someone else's opinion: "My supervisor commented in a memo how my outlook helped us save a key account that was in jeopardy of being lost. I have a copy of that memo if you'd like to see it."

* **Choose your words carefully.** There might be a tendency to say, "I was chosen to lead this project" when it would be more powerfully worded as, "The VP sought me out, from among 12 eligible specialists, to spearhead this critical project."

* **Pace the stories so that each is approximately two to three minutes in length.** Set up the story briefly with facts, place the greatest weight on the action portion of the story, wrap it up with numbers-driven results, and tie it back to the interviewer's needs. Occasionally, vary the delivery by dropping in a result at the front end of the story.

* **Make the stories relevant.** You have myriad experiences in your background. Sift through them and select the stories that best substantiate your competencies, knowledge, skills, and motivation to excel in the target job.

Remember to review the 25 questions listed earlier in case you encounter writer's block. Enjoy the process...and may you gain a clearer picture of your value and grow in confidence as the stories emerge!

Two Heads Are Better Than One!

If you prefer to collaborate on your SMART Stories™, enlist the support of a colleague, mentor, or trusted friend. If you'd like to benefit from working with a professional coach, visit Career Coach Academy (www.careercoachacademy.com) for a list of Certified Career Management Coaches around the country.

Catalog Your SMART Stories™

I'd like you to develop a *minimum* of 10 stories. Sound like a lot? I want you to feel fully confident and completely prepared! DBM, a leading global workplace consulting firm, revealed that job seekers participated in five to seven interviews per job opportunity. This is common in a tight economy where jobs are few, applicants are plentiful, and employers are willing to take their time and sort through top candidates to find just the perfect fit. Ten stories will get you started; however, if you anticipate an extended series of interviews, consider writing 20 or more stories so that you have enough "ammunition" to shine throughout the process. (For additional blank forms, go to www.careerandlifecoach.com and click on Interview Magic to download an MS Word version of the form; or just photocopy the form on page 75.)

Complete the Situation and More, indicating your role, where (what company), when (what time period and for how long), who was involved or impacted, and what was the specific situation. Describe the Action taken, as well as the Results. Leave the Keywords and Competencies and Potential Interview Questions sections blank for now. You'll fill them in later as you work through chapter 9 and link job postings or job descriptions to your various success stories.

SMART Story™ Worksheet

Situation and More:

Your role: _____

Where: _____

When: _____

Who else was involved or impacted: _____

_____

What was the task or challenge: _____

_____

_____

Action:

What was your thought process? What steps you take? What decisions were made? Describe the sequence.

_____

_____

_____

_____

Results:

Use numbers to relate your results.

_____

_____

_____

Tie-in / Theme:

Keywords & Competencies: _____

_____

Potential Interview Questions: _____

_____

Rate Your Stories

After you've completed writing your SMART Stories™, you can rate each one. For each story, give yourself a point for every item you can say "yes" to on this 10-point quiz.

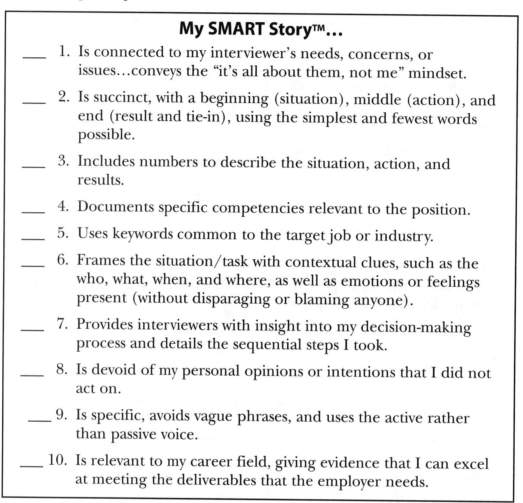

My SMART Story™...

___ 1. Is connected to my interviewer's needs, concerns, or issues...conveys the "it's all about them, not me" mindset.

___ 2. Is succinct, with a beginning (situation), middle (action), and end (result and tie-in), using the simplest and fewest words possible.

___ 3. Includes numbers to describe the situation, action, and results.

___ 4. Documents specific competencies relevant to the position.

___ 5. Uses keywords common to the target job or industry.

___ 6. Frames the situation/task with contextual clues, such as the who, what, when, and where, as well as emotions or feelings present (without disparaging or blaming anyone).

___ 7. Provides interviewers with insight into my decision-making process and details the sequential steps I took.

___ 8. Is devoid of my personal opinions or intentions that I did not act on.

___ 9. Is specific, avoids vague phrases, and uses the active rather than passive voice.

___ 10. Is relevant to my career field, giving evidence that I can excel at meeting the deliverables that the employer needs.

How did you score? If most of your SMART Stories™ earned a 9 or perfect 10, reward yourself. If your stories scored in the 7–8 range, this is a great start. They will probably require the addition of a few details or numbers to become 9s or 10s. If most of your stories scored 6 or less, take a break and rest your brain a bit. (Chapter 5 offers some ideas for jump-starting yourself.) When you come back, look at the pattern of the stories to determine where they can be shored up, and edit wherever appropriate.

Chapter Wrap-Up

Remember Truth #6 from Chapter 1? "You *Can* Control Your Success." That truth is contingent on being prepared. You should be feeling like the proverbial Eagle Scout now! Know that the work you've completed in this chapter is key to "controlling the controllables"—the systems and steps that you can control in the process. Evidence-based success stories are at the heart of your interview message. When you're ready to move on, chapter 4 will help you convert your success stories into a cohesive career brand… one that can position you as a trusted expert, attract your ideal employer, and communicate the value of hiring you.

10 Quick Tips for Capturing Your Value

1. $E=MC^2$ in a job search context refers to Employment = Mechanics × Commitment-Squared, meaning that a job offer is gained through mechanics (strategies, systems, tactics) multiplied by a double dose of commitment (mindset, emotional energy, attitude). Focusing on providing value to the employer is an essential employment strategy.

2. Avoid the most common mistake of candidates—going unprepared to interviews. A critical step in preparation is to craft relevant success stories.

3. Use the SMART Story™ method to structure relevant success stories, remembering to include contextual situational clues, sequential actions, numbers-driven results, and a tie-in to the employer's needs.

4. Translate your value into ROI (return on investment).

5. Tap into the 10 reasons employers are motivated to *buy* (hire you).

6. Focus on benefits rather than features to inject value into your stories.

7. Load your stories with numbers, such as year-to-year comparisons, records, past highs, past lows, target goals, size of project, number of persons involved, and budget or project figures (when not confidential).

8. Add flavor to your stories using emotion, humor, and metaphors.

9. Write *S.O.S.* responses that provide **S**olutions **O**r **S**ervices.

10. Remember the mindset mantra, "them, not me," when writing your stories. Employers will filter everything they hear through the screen of "will the candidate's skills help me?"

Magical Coaching Questions

What's the greatest insight you've gained from your work in this chapter?

_____

_____

_____

How will you use what you've learned to move your search forward?

_____

_____

_____

_____

Communicate Your Value Via a Career Brand

There are four ways, and only four ways, in which we have contact with the world. We are evaluated and classified by these four contacts: what we do, how we look, what we say, and how we say it.

—Dale Carnegie

Ask yourself these two questions:

- ✦ What do you want to be known for?
- ✦ What kind of employer do you want to connect with?

These two questions capture the essence of what branding is all about: image and connection. Think of your brand as a uniquely individual image with a magnet attached to it. What unique combination of skills or competencies do people recognize in you? Why do people in the work world trust you? What do you want to contribute to your world of work? What kind of employer will be drawn to, connect with, and pay a premium for that?

How Can a Career Brand Help You in Interviews?

Perhaps you're thinking, "I don't need a brand...I just need to know how to ace the interview." You might be surprised to learn that a brand *will* help you ace the interview because many of the same dynamics behind why a consumer chooses Crest over Colgate also apply in hiring.

The benefits of a brand are numerous. A compelling career brand can

- Make you more attractive to employers, even when there are no formal job openings
- Control what interviewers remember most about you
- Lower the barriers to hiring by creating trust and conveying value
- Elevate you from the status of commonplace commodity to one-of-a-kind service
- Differentiate you from the competition
- Guide you in your decisions about which interviews to pursue
- Create employer desire to buy (hire)

What happens if you don't create a brand? Obviously, the opposite of everything in the preceding list. Worse yet, potential employers will determine your brand for you, and it might not be the brand you intended to project! It's a bit like looking at Rorschach ink blots. Two people, with no suggestions to sway them, often see two very different things in the ink blots. But, if one points out that there is a butterfly in one of the ink blots, the other will likely look hard to find and focus on that butterfly. The same is true with branding. Without prompting from you, the employer will see what he wants to see in you. With a few sound bites that bring your brand into focus, the employer is more likely to concentrate on the strengths or value you want him to see.

The Elements of Your Brand

No longer reserved for corporate giants, brands are now applicable to career-minded individuals like you and me. For your brand to accomplish its purpose, it must knit together these three A's:

- Authentic Image
- Advantages
- Awareness

The good news is that you have already put in place the first two of the three A's. Your Authentic Image is the genuine you—not costumed to play the part of someone else, but cast in the right role...a role that allows you to be radically rewarded and enthusiastically engaged in work that adds value to others. Your Career-FIT™ work in chapter 2 pointed you toward your Authentic Image. The second A, Advantages, is synonymous with benefits and value. You concentrated on identifying benefits and value in chapter 3, especially in writing numbers-oriented results for your SMART Stories™. The final A, Awareness, refers to communicating your brand in a manner that makes people attentive and responsive to it.

Authentic Image, Advantages, and Awareness add up to one word: *Marketing*. In a job search, you are the product and your employer-to-be is the consumer.

Job Search = Marketing

In chapters 2 and 3, the focus was on what you want and what you can offer to an employer—your product, so to speak. Now it's time to look at your product through the eyes of consumers (employers) and their awareness and perception of your product. In this and future chapters, the focal point will be what the employer needs and whether the employer perceives that you can meet those needs better than your competitors.

Verbal Branding—Creating Your Sound Bites

Sound bites, like success stories, will help you feel prepared to meet any networking or interview situation. Sound bites should be short, from 20 seconds to two minutes in length, and can be used for these types of situations:

- To convey your unique key strengths in an interview
- To articulate your goals and help networking contacts understand what you are looking for
- To offer a brief, value-packed introduction of yourself

To be prepared for these and other job search conversations, you'll equip yourself with three key sound bites:

- **Three-Point Marketing Message** (a succinct sound bite, less than 30 seconds, used to convey your unique key strengths and integrated throughout your resumes and cover letters, networking, informational interviews, and job interviews)
- **Verbal Business Card** (a succinct sound bite, less than 30 seconds, used in networking, informational interviewing, and job interviewing to articulate your goals and the benefits you offer)

⟡ **Mini-Bio** (a short message, between one and two minutes, the elements of which can be mixed and matched to offer a relevant career capsule in networking, informational interviewing, or job interviewing)

You saw earlier that companies often communicate their brand in as few as three or four words with a pithy tagline. Luckily, in job search, you'll be able to use more than a few words—written or spoken—to capture the essence of who you are. The theme and language used in your resume and cover letter can support your brand from a written perspective. Moreover, the success stories and sound bites you choose when communicating with interviewers can support your brand from a verbal standpoint. (Note that for our purposes, I'll include written words as part of verbal branding because taglines and other written messages take on a verbal connotation when we say them—albeit sometimes silently in our minds—to make sense.)

Your Three-Point Marketing Message

A Three-Point Marketing Message is the most recyclable sound bite you'll use when networking and interviewing. You can use it again and again. The three-point message should be part of your response to the age-old interview question, "tell me about yourself." It's also a great way to wrap up the interview and leave the interviewer with a clear message about your qualifications. You can weave the three points throughout your job search communications, including resumes, inquiry/approach letters, and follow-up letters. The following example is especially memorable because of its catchy alliteration:

Sound Bite of Three-Point Marketing Message:	As a sales representative for the hotel industry, my strengths lie in the areas of Research, Relationships, and Revenue Enhancement.

Customize Your Message for Each Employer

Ideally, your Three-Point Marketing Message should be customized for each employer. Remember, it's not about you; it's about them. Always connect your strengths to what the employer needs most.

Combining Your Three-Point Marketing Message with Other Job Search Tools

Figure 4.2 shows an example of how to integrate the three points into your resume. The strengths are listed under the Strengths subheading near the top of the resume.

You can also vary the wording on your Three-Point Marketing Message and combine it with a SMART Story™:

Variation on Three-Point Marketing Message:	The reason I've exceeded quota in all my positions—and the reason I'm confident I could do the same for you—is that I've mastered the 3 R's of sales: Research, Relationships, and Revenue Enhancement.
SMART Story™:	In my last position, where we were faced with stagnant revenues, my research skills helped me unearth a prospect list that included Fortune 1000 companies, including ABC Company, DEF Company, and GHI Company. I turned that cold data into warm leads, and gained access to decision makers at 9 of the 10 target companies. Bottom line, our revenue increased 45 percent during my tenure and our average sale increased 17 percent. Based on what you've told me about your operation, it sounds like research might be an area that you'd like to concentrate on first.

What Your Three-Point Marketing Message Should Include

Your Three-Point Marketing Message should convey your three most marketable selling points. They are likely common themes in your SMART Stories™ or the focus of your resume. These three points might be functional strengths, unique experiences, or even soft skills. This social work

CHRIS CABALLERO

555 East Serena
Los Angeles, CA 90000   Relocating to Chicago   (555) 555-5555
      c_caballero@hotmail.com

SALES / BUSINESS DEVELOPMENT

Hospitality ◆ Convention ◆ Meeting ◆ Visitors Bureau

Strengths:

Research—Developed qualified business leads using traditional and online research methods.
Relationships—Quickly established loyal and trusting relationships with key accounts and networking contacts.
Revenue Enhancement—Set new records for group and convention business at major-brand and boutique hotels.

PROFESSIONAL EXPERIENCE

Assistant Director of Sales—MAJOR HOTEL, Los Angeles, California   1/00–Present
(396-room property, with 42,000 sq. ft. of function space)

Manage more than $2 million in group business. Prospect and book national and state association accounts. Attend national and regional trade shows to increase market share. Travel 4–6 times per year for sales trips and trade shows. Coordinate familiarization trips with Bureau and hotel for lead generation. Exclusively sell and coordinate Rose Bowl group business. *Contributions:*

◆ Increased revenue 45% during tenure, with average sale up 17%.

◆ Delivered record group bookings first year in position, with 25,000 group room nights in 2000.

◆ Increased total bookings each subsequent year (despite challenge of post-9/11 market)…on track to close 32–34,000 group room nights this year.

◆ Maximized Rose Bowl business by working closely with Tournament of Roses Association and targeting Fortune 500 companies that sponsor floats and host VIPs. This year, sold out before July (in past years, sell-out occurred as late as December for this New Year's Day event), while also increasing minimum stay and rates.

◆ Expanded communications and working relationships with Convention & Visitors Bureau, gaining more business from special events such as the People's Choice Awards, Emmy Awards, and major Broadway shows.

National Sales Manager—GRAND HOTEL, Los Angeles, California   9/98–12/99
(800-room property, with 40,000 sq. ft. of function space)

Recruited to manage convention and group business within the Southeast Region. Prospected new business and expanded existing accounts. Traveled 6–8 times per year for sales trips and national trade shows. *Contributions:*

◆ Met and exceeded quota, earning maximum bonus for revenue increases.

National Sales Manager—EXCLUSIVE HOTEL, Los Angeles, California   11/96–9/98
(84-room boutique hotel located inside historic private club)

Developed and executed marketing plan to capture untapped group business. Established relationship with Bureau, offering niche-market services for convention-goers desiring full workout facilities in an upscale setting. *Contributions:*

◆ Grew group business from virtually nil to more than 2,500 room nights per year (record still unsurpassed).

Prior Experience with major brands—management trainee, convention service manager, sales manager.

EDUCATION, PROFESSIONAL DEVELOPMENT & AFFILIATIONS

BA, Sociology—Northwestern University (1995)
Seminars—Dale Carnegie, Professional Selling Skills (PSS), Professional Sales Negotiation (PSN), Hilton Sales College
CSAE (California Society of Association Executives)

Figure 4.2: A resume with a Three-Point Marketing Message integrated into it.

case manager identified two functional strengths (counseling and teaching) and one soft skill (client advocacy) as part of her Three-Point Marketing Message:

Sound bite of Three-Point Marketing Message:

As a case manager with more than 15 years of experience, my greatest assets for this position are counseling, teaching, and client advocacy.

It's likely that you have more than three key skills or strengths for your target position. However, it's unlikely that your networking contacts or interviewers will be able to remember much more than three things about you. One interviewer, who understandably requested anonymity as he related this story, admitted that after interviewing a string of candidates and taking indecipherable notes in the process, he and his fellow interviewers couldn't even remember the name of their star candidate. I'll give you some tricks for using physical "plops" and other memory-enhancing artifacts for your listeners in the chapters to come. Recognize, however, that when it comes to verbal delivery of your strengths, simple is better.

Creating Your Message

What will your Three-Point Marketing Message be? Here's an easy two-step process to create your marketing message. First, select an introductory phrase. You can choose one of these or write your own:

☐ My background is unique because…

☐ Throughout my career as a _____ [functional title], I've always been drawn to…

☐ As a _____ [functional title], I'm known for…

☐ The reason I've exceeded quota in all my positions—and the reason I'm confident I could do the same for you—is that I'm an expert in…

☐ My strengths as a _____ [functional title] lie in the area of…

☐ At the heart of my experience are these three strengths…

☐ I am passionate about…

☐ My former supervisors and coworkers concur that the key to my success is…

☐ Clients frequently compliment me for…

☐ I've developed a reputation for…

☐ I'm very good at…

Second, add your three key points to the introductory phrase. Use grammatically parallel language in describing the three terms or phrases so that the wording flows better. For instance, these three phrases are parallel, "researching prospects, building relationships, and driving revenue." These terms are also parallel: "research, relationships, revenue." You can see, then, that this wording is not parallel—"researching, relationships, and drove revenue"—making it sound awkward and stilted.

Identify and write your three key points here:

1. _____

2. _____

3. _____

Now, combine the introductory phrase you selected previously with your three key points and write it here:

_____

_____

_____

Speak the Three-Point Marketing Message aloud. Make any adjustments needed until it feels comfortable and sounds strong.

Your Benefit-Driven Verbal Business Card, or "What's in It for Me (the Employer)?"

Similar to the focus statement you developed in chapter 2, a benefit-driven Verbal Business Card helps networking contacts or employers recognize both the type of opportunity you want and the benefits you bring to the table. As you saw in chapter 3, hiring managers are tuned to radio station

WIFM, or "what's in it for me?" Now's your chance to tell them. In the preceding chapter, I listed 10 employer buying motivators (also known as benefits), each of which addresses the employer's profit need or pain point—a situation where the employer is hurting and needs help solving a problem. When you focus on benefits, you

- Appear business-savvy
- Connect with the employer
- Indicate your understanding of the need for profitability and productivity
- Demonstrate a track record for contributing to the bottom line

What benefits do you bring to a prospective employer? What are you better at than others who have similar credentials? What "invisible" factors might be behind your success? The answers to these questions will strategically reposition you from run-of-the-mill to out-of-the-ordinary.

I'd like you to brainstorm ideas on how you can benefit an employer in each of the 10 buying motivations. To illustrate that this exercise isn't just for people in executive or sales positions, table 4.1 shows examples for an administrative assistant who worked in a small real estate office.

Table 4.1: Examples Tied to Employer Buying Motivators

Employer Buying Motivator	Example Brainstorming on Solutions or Services That Benefit My Target Employers
Buying Motivator #1: Make Money	Worked overtime to help boss close a multimillion-dollar real estate transaction that generated $240,000 in commission.
	Developed administrative systems that supported a new fee-based consulting line of business for the company. Revenues on this grew from startup to $60,000 in one year.
Buying Motivator #2: Save Money	Shopped for better pricing on office supplies. Cut costs on key expenses by approximately 10 percent.

(continued)

(continued)

Employer Buying Motivator	Example Brainstorming on Solutions or Services That Benefit My Target Employers
Buying Motivator #3: Save Time	Wrote and cataloged standardized word-processing clauses to speed document processing and project completion. System saved an average of 20 percent time.

I wouldn't ask you to do anything that I wouldn't be willing to do myself! To make certain that any business-related professional can link their activity to employer buying motivators, I put myself to the test. Table 4.2 outlines benefits related to my services as a career coach:

Table 4.2: Examples Tied to Employer (Client) Buying Motivators

Employer (Client) Buying Motivator	Example Brainstorming on Solutions or Services That Benefit My Target Employers (Clients)
Buying Motivator #1: Make Money	Help career-minded professionals with strategy to campaign for a raise or promotion. Help job seekers with salary negotiations.
Buying Motivator #2: Save Money	Help job seekers sort through the career marketing scams on the Internet. Help job seekers identify strategies to stretch their job search dollars.
Buying Motivator #3: Save Time	Offer insider job search strategies that short-cut the length of time to reemployment. Offer professionals time-management strategies so that they can concentrate on projects that will give their careers the greatest traction and leverage.

Now it's your turn. In table 4.3, list as many benefits as come to mind for each of the Employer Buying Motivators. Remember to make it an S.O.S. (solutions or services) response whenever possible (see chapter 3).

Table 4.3: My Benefits That Relate
to Employer Buying Motivators

Employer Buying Motivator	Brainstorming on Solutions or Services That Benefit My Target Employers
Buying Motivator #1: Make Money	
Buying Motivator #2: Save Money	
Buying Motivator #3: Save Time	
Buying Motivator #4: Make Work Easier	
Buying Motivator #5: Solve a Specific Problem	
Buying Motivator #6: Make the Company More Competitive	
Buying Motivator #7: Build Teams or Individuals; Enhance Relationships or Image with Customers	

(continued)

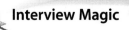

(continued)

Employer Buying Motivator	Brainstorming on Solutions or Services That Benefit My Target Employers
Buying Motivator #8: Expand Business	
Buying Motivator #9: Attract New Customers	
Buying Motivator #10: Retain Customers	

To finalize your Verbal Business Card, combine your Career-FIT™ Function and Industry targets from chapter 2 with the benefit ideas you listed in table 4.3. This example for a communications professional pairs function and industry (pinpointed in chapter 2) with benefits:

> I'm a communications professional targeting director-level opportunities with industrial manufacturers where I can leverage my track record for developing award-winning creative teams and delivering record returns on marketing communications.

Table 4.4 shows how the preceding Verbal Business Card relates to each of the elements from chapter 2:

Table 4.4: Elements and Wording of a Verbal Business Card

Element	Sample Wording
Function	I'm a communications professional targeting director-level opportunities with…
Industry	industrial manufacturers…
Benefit (linked to Buying Motivators #1 and #7)	where I can leverage my track record for developing award-winning creative teams and delivering record returns on marketing communications.

Use the following worksheet to create your Verbal Business Card.

My Verbal Business Card	
Element	**Draft Wording**
Function	I'm a _____
	targeting _____ opportunities
Industry	in the _____ industry
Benefits	that will allow me to _____
	_____
	_____
	_____ .

Your Mini-Bio

The final sound bite to be crafted for your verbal branding is a short biography, which we'll call a Mini-Bio. Also known as an "elevator pitch," this is another sound bite you'll need to have down pat. Some (but not all) of these elements will appear in your bio:

- Three-Point Marketing Message
- Number of years of experience
- Prestigious employer(s)
- Title or functional area
- Scope of responsibility (budget, staff, special projects)
- Verbal business card
- Key selling points or strengths
- Key accomplishments
- Impressive educational degree or credentials
- Fulfillment/purpose/mission statement
- SMART Stories™
- Tagline
- Inquiry/call to action

Building on the communication professional's example cited previously, let's look at how these elements can come to life. In table 4.5, the left column notes the element, whereas the right column breaks down the Bio.

Table 4.5: Elements and Wording for Mini-Bio

Element	Sample Wording
Verbal Business Card	I'm a communication professional targeting director-level opportunities with industrial manufacturers where I can leverage my track record for developing award-winning creative teams and delivering record returns on marketing communications.
Number of years of experience	Over the past 10 years,
Prestigious employer(s)	I've worked with the region's leading lighting manufacturer
Title or functional area	in senior-level positions as an Advertising Manager and Director of Communications
Scope of responsibility	with charge of a staff of 25 and six-figure project budgets.
Sound bite of Three-Point Marketing Message	Throughout my career as a creative director, I've been recognized for my expertise in advertising strategy, project management, and creative development.
Key accomplishments (tied to Three-Point Marketing Message)	I can offer some examples if you'd like. As an advertising strategist, my skills delivered an ROI of 15:1 on marketing funds, which, as you know, is well above average.
	As a project manager, I have numerous contacts with artists, copywriters, and printers and have a track record for bringing projects in on time and on a shoestring budget. It wasn't unusual for me to save $5,000 on printing costs when our total budget was $25,000.
	And, because of my strong creative background, many of the campaigns I directed earned national advertising awards.

Element	Sample Wording
Tagline	I'm known for turning ideas into dollars.
Inquiry/call to action (use when speaking to a networking contact)	What companies come to mind that might benefit from someone with my background? OR What companies are you aware of that are doing interesting work with their marketing communications?

You're allowed some wiggle room with the length of your Mini-Bio. It can be about a minute or two. Keep in mind that if it's too short, you won't be able to give people a good sense of who you are, what you're looking for, and what you can do for others. If it's too long, you'll confuse people and risk sounding long-winded.

What's Your Tagline?

Some job seekers borrow (with appropriate credit) company taglines or corporate references to describe themselves. For instance, one insurance sales rep described his tenacity and perseverance with this sentence, "When it comes to cold calling, I'm like the Energizer Bunny: I just keep going and going and going." A project manager conveyed his track record in this way, "My boss likes to call me Mr. FedEx because I have a reputation for delivering projects on time."

Create your Mini-Bio using the outline in the following worksheet. At this point, fill in each box; however, you do *not* have to use every element when you introduce yourself. In fact, it will probably sound too wordy if you do. Instead, you can mix and match the different elements so that you have some variety when speaking to people. I've placed an asterisk (*) next to the ingredients that are most important and should be mentioned in most every introduction. This should be a fairly simple exercise because you have already developed much of the information needed. The example in table 4.5 will give you ideas for phrasing and connecting the different elements of your introduction.

Table 4.5: Elements of My Mini-Bio

Element	Wording
Sound Bite of Three-Point Marketing Message (you completed this earlier in the chapter)	
Number of years of experience	
Prestigious employer(s)	
*Title or functional area (you identified this in chapter 2)	
Scope of responsibility	
*Verbal Business Card	
*Key selling points or strengths	
*Key accomplishments (tied to Three-Point Marketing Message)	
Impressive educational degree or credentials	

Element	Wording
Fulfillment/purpose/ mission statement	
SMART Story™ (choose an impressive one from your work in chapter 3)	
*Tagline	
*Inquiry/call to action (use when speaking to a networking contact)	

It's important that you practice speaking your Bio. Start by practicing alone in front of a mirror. Then ask someone to critique you. Know the material inside and out, backwards and forwards. Make adjustments until you can comfortably deliver it without feeling like you're a telemarketer following a script!

Like Tinker Toys, you can combine your elements in ways that will bring your career brand to life. This section has given you the gist of verbal branding. There are certainly other tactics you can use to convey your brand, so be creative. For instance:

- Add your tagline to your e-mail signature.
- Include the themes from your Three-Point Marketing Message on your personal business card.

- Create a portfolio that is divided into sections for the three themes of your Three-Point Marketing Message.
- Use a relevant success story in an interview thank-you/follow-up letter.
- Have pens or stickies made with your name and tagline.

What else can you think of?

Visual Branding—Look and Act the Part!

In chapter 1, Truth #8, I forewarned that you would be judged on three dimensions: chemistry, competency, and compensation. The first dimension, chemistry, requires a reciprocal connection between you and the company. Yes, *your* opinion of the company does count in this matter! You must connect with the company, its people (especially the hiring manager), and its customers. The converse is also true. The company's people (again, especially the hiring manager) must connect with you. In visual branding, we'll concentrate on how your visuals—image and dress—can create some good chemistry.

Your Image

Entering a room to meet a new employer can be like walking into a whole new chapter of your life. At that moment, you can influence the employer's perception of you based on your actions, attitudes, and attire. To illustrate this point, recall the movie *Catch Me If You Can*, an extraordinary true tale of a brilliant young master of deception. Eluding a dogged FBI agent (played by Tom Hanks), the story follows Frank W. Abagnale, Jr. (played by Leonardo DiCaprio) as he successfully passes himself off as a pilot, a lawyer, and a doctor, all before his 21st birthday.

Abagnale was able to hoodwink so many people because he *confidently acted* the part in every respect. The result? An image that people perceived as real. Of course, I am not in the least suggesting that you lie about yourself. I do suggest, however, that as part of your visual branding you *confidently act the part in every respect.*

Role Models

To confidently act the part, you'll need a clear description of the image you want to project. One of the best ways to do this is to look for role models. Who in your industry do you admire? Who is successfully doing the type of work you want to do? Even better, who is a notch above the role you'd like to be in?

Why Are Role Models Important?

I'll let you in on a secret. When employers are ready to interview, the first place they go to is the desk of their top performers. Hiring managers painstakingly analyze top performers to determine the behaviors and competencies that make them so successful. In turn, those behaviors and competencies will be the high-water mark you're measured against. Find and emulate a successful role model and you'll improve your chances for interview success.

Once you've identified a role model or two, study their image by asking yourself these 10 questions:

1. How would you describe this person?
2. What actions does he or she take that cause success?
3. What do you like about the way he or she treats others?
4. What is his or her mindset and attitude?
5. Who does he or she associate with?
6. How does he or she dress?
7. What is his or her posture like? How does he or she stand, walk, sit?
8. How does he or she communicate with others? What, and how much, does he or she say? Not say?
9. Is there something about the way he or she spends lunch or free time that feeds success?
10. What does your role model *not* do (for example, avoid making excuses, blaming others, stretching the truth, and so on)?

It's sometimes difficult to see yourself as others perceive you. To give you a fresh perspective, compare yourself with a role model using the questions in table 4.6. In approaching this exercise, make sure that your self-talk is inspirational and encouraging, not critical and disapproving. Think to yourself, "This enhanced image that I want to project is something worthwhile and attainable."

Table 4.6: Positive Traits of Role Models

Questions	What I Admire About the Role Model	Success Traits I Already Possess	Choices I Can Make to Improve My Image
How would you describe this person?			
What action does he or she take that causes success?			
What do you like about the way your role model treats others?			
What is this person's mindset and attitude?			
Who does he or she associate with?			
How does your role model dress? (style, colors, and so on)			
What is this person's posture like? How does he or she stand, walk, sit?			

How does your role model
communicate with others?
What, and how much, does he
or she say? Not say?

Is there something about the
way this person spends his or
her lunch or free time that
feeds success?

What does your role model not
do (for example, avoid making excuses,
blaming others, stretching the
truth, and so on)?

If needed, enlist the support of a trusted colleague on this role model exercise. If you do solicit a support partner, make sure you choose someone who will be respectful and kind, yet direct and honest—someone with a heart for helping people become all that they can be. First, ask the person to tell you what you're doing right. Then, give the person permission to tell you things you might not want to hear. Further, give permission to point out where this person senses you're resisting change. We cannot change until we are aware of what we need to change!

Finally, let me make perfectly clear that I'm *not* asking you to become a clone. Instead, I'm suggesting that you adopt elements of what you like best from others to enhance your own individuality and marketability.

Bugged by Being Compared to Others?

It is frustrating to think that people are judging you based on your image. However, the reality is that image does factor into the hiring process—even if it isn't supposed to. In the hiring game, when two candidates have equal skills and one has an image that fits better with the company, the candidate with the right chemistry will get the job. Candidates who don't examine this topic with fresh eyes put themselves at a disadvantage.

How People Perceive You

How would you like others to describe you? When it comes time to hire, it's not unusual to hear an employer say something like this to employees: "We need to replace Lori in the bookkeeping department while she's on maternity leave—do you know anyone with a bookkeeping background who is very detail-oriented and trustworthy?" The employer is looking not only for competencies, but chemistry.

Image is part of chemistry. Image is about behaving in a manner consistent with how you want people to perceive you. Review the list of 10 adjectives you identified in chapter 2 ("Step 5, Enhance Your Identity") and answer the following questions.

Image Worksheet

1. Are these terms you identified in chapter 2 in sync with top performers in your target field? If so, great. If not, what adjustments should you make to your list?

   _____

   _____

   _____

   _____

2. Write a few sentences about how you want networking contacts and potential employers to perceive you.

   _____

   _____

   _____

   _____

3. What behaviors or attitudes do you already exhibit that are consistent with this description? What do you need to do to ensure that these behaviors or attitudes are evident to an interviewer?

   _____

   _____

   _____

> 4. What image elements will you improve on or enhance? How will you do so?
>
> _____
>
> _____
>
> _____

Your Wardrobe

Remember that corporate America uses colors and visual images as part of its branding. In career branding, your colors and visual images are communicated through your wardrobe. As we discuss wardrobe, consider that your attire for the interview shouldn't be an anomaly, like a one-night tuxedo rental for a special occasion. One candidate dressed beautifully for an interview and, once hired, didn't don a suit coat again, much to the chagrin of the executive team. Your interview attire should be part of who you are, as well as who you are committed to becoming.

Always Look the Part

Attire for networking meetings should be similar to that for interviews. If you aren't dressed professionally or groomed meticulously when meeting with an influential networking contact, that contact might be hesitant to recommend you to an employer. Pay attention to every detail, including the type of pen you carry, the quality of your business card holder, and the style of notepad you use to take notes.

A picture is worth a thousand words. When it comes to meeting influential contacts and potential employers, _you_ speak a thousand words—even before you open your mouth. Approach your business wardrobe as if you were mute and the wardrobe were going to do all the talking. That's how important dress is to your interview success.

With business attire across the board these days, a one-size-fits-all recommendation on this subject won't fit. Use good judgment. Assess the type of companies you'll be targeting and dress to their standards. Image experts offer varying advice regarding dressing for interviews. Some counsel you to dress a little nicer than the norm for the business; others advise you to dress the same as your interviewer, just cleaner! Either can work. I defer to the advice of my dear mother when it comes to dress: If you err, err on the side of formality…dress a little nicer than the norm.

Dress for Women

The wardrobe recommendations that follow apply to traditional business environments. From head to toe, here are some guidelines:

- **Suits and shirts:** Two-piece matching suits (with the same fabric for the jacket and skirt or pants) give the best impression. For the most conservative companies, opt for solid colors or subtly patterned fabrics in deep blues, greys, or black; complement the suit with a solid or light-colored blouse or sweater. Pants with a matching or complementary jacket are acceptable. For less conservative atmospheres, follow and have fun with fashion trends! As this book goes to press, print blouses are in, along with a skirt and jacket that blend but don't necessarily match.

- **Dresses:** In formal environments, consider a smart-looking dress with a jacket that matches or complements the dress. For less formal environments, business dress *sans* jacket is fine, especially if you're applying for a nonmanagerial role.

- **Fabrics:** Pick tried-and-true fabrics that are tasteful, hang well, and don't wrinkle excessively. Linens are lovely, but you'll likely be wildly wrinkled before you get to your meeting. Reserve fabrics with a high sheen (such as satin) for the evening.

- **Hosiery:** Hose should be natural color, with no patterns.

- **Shoes:** Close-toed shoes, pumps, or flats should complement the suit or dress. Avoid extremes in heel height or style, such as stiletto heels that could double as a weapon. Avoid sandals or strappy shoes. Polish any scuffs and repair worn heels.

- **Jewelry:** Avoid anything that jingles, clanks, or makes noise. Limit jewelry to one ring per hand, one bracelet per wrist, and one earring per ear. Necklaces may be worn as long as they are not the focal point—you want interviewers concentrating on your face, not your necklace. Avoid any body piercing beyond earrings.

- **Hair:** Clean and neatly cut. Style long hair in a conservative manner, making sure it doesn't fall in your face or cause you to touch your face to push it away. Avoid an overly styled hairdo that involves excessive mousse or hairspray. If you color your hair, make sure that roots are hidden.

- **Makeup:** Conservative and natural-looking is safest; avoid bright colors. Stay away from excessive face powder that gives a pancake-makeup, aged appearance.

- **Nails:** Use neutral or clear polish; French manicures are acceptable. If you have to resort to a pencil or other device to dial the phone, shorten your nails.

- **Scents:** For those with a tendency toward perspiration or body odor, carry a fresh blouse or change into your interview suit in an inconspicuous area just prior to the interview. Perfumes, lotions, or creams should be very subtle—remember that many people have chemical allergies and are bothered by what you might consider pleasant. If you want a very light scent, spray cologne into the air and walk through it. This trick will leave a nice close-up scent without being overwhelming.

- **Special touches:** For some, visual branding includes a signature item that is a staple of the wardrobe, such as a tasteful lapel pin or silk scarf.

- **Modesty:** Modesty is becoming a lost art. The interview is not a date. Avoid clingy, see-through fabrics and low-cut blouses. When sitting, skirt lengths should not go more than an inch or two above the knee. Even if it's in fashion to show some tummy, don't do it in the workplace. Wear the right size! Squeezing into snug clothing will make you look heavier than you really are. Cover any visible tattoos with makeup and light powder.

Not So Extreme Makeovers

If you're in the market for an image update, enlist the support of an expert. One of my trusted authorities on the subject is Mary Ann Dietschler (www.CoachMaryAnn.com).

Dress for Men

Men, if you have an inkling that you need guidance in putting together an impressive interview wardrobe, don't hesitate to enlist the support of someone who is known for his or her taste in clothing. Better to be embarrassed before just one friend (your wardrobe advisor) than in front of several strangers (your interviewers).

- **Suits and shirts:** A navy blue or gray suit is your surest bet. Choose a white, long-sleeved dress shirt to accompany it, even in summer. Make sure it is crisp, clean, and not fraying or balling from wear. Opt for conservative fabrics. If you need guidance in purchasing (or borrowing) a suit, ask a friend who has a sense of style to come along as your haberdashery consultant. Many companies promote business-casual dress. Even so, men should wear a suit and tie; or if the atmosphere is very casual, opt for a sharp navy blazer and dress slacks when interviewing.

⚡ **Belts:** The belt should fit your suit pants—typically one inch wide—with no unusual or distracting buckle. The belt should be appropriate for the suit color (black belts for black, gray, or navy suits; brown belts for brown suits).

⚡ **Socks:** Dark dress socks are required with suit pants or dress slacks. Avoid socks that do not match your shoe color.

⚡ **Shoes:** Leave the athletic shoes at home. Leather lace-up shoes, freshly polished, are best. Pay attention to the health of the heels and the shine of the shoes; if needed, get your interview shoes to the shoe repair shop for new soles or a general rejuvenation.

⚡ **Jewelry:** A watch and one ring are fine, along with conservative cufflinks. Avoid gold chains and earrings, even a small diamond in one ear.

⚡ **Hair:** Make sure your hair is clean and freshly cut, with your neck neatly shaved. Facial hair might be a part of your normal look, but if it isn't a part of the company's normal look, it could cost you some points in the chemistry and connection department.

⚡ **Nails and facial care:** Gentlemen, spa services are no longer just for metrosexuals (urban males who spend a great deal of time and money on appearance and lifestyle)! For most men who frequent spas, it's not about pampering or looking good; it's about not looking bad. This might be the time to go the extra grooming mile to tidy the fingernails and cuticles (no polish), exfoliate the face, and remove excessive hair from the nose, ears, or upper back.

⚡ **Scents:** You might be tempted to add an extra splash of aftershave or cologne for good measure. Don't do it! Interviewers don't want to smell you before they see you. Again, be considerate of the thousands of individuals who endure life with allergies to fragrances.

The Psychology of Color

What color will you wear to your interview? What will it communicate? When selecting an interview suit, consider these color implications:

⚡ **Blue:** Researchers tell us that wearing blue to an interview indicates dedication and loyalty. Blue also relaxes the viewer's nervous system. Men, stick to dark navy. Women, you have a broader range of choice—one of the best power shades of blue is a deep blue, which falls between the blue of a hyperlinked e-mail address and midnight blue.

* **Black:** Always a classic, black is formal and sophisticated, conveying authority and power in the business world. It is associated with reliability, discretion, and wisdom. And, if you're looking to camouflage a few pounds, black clothing can be slimming to the figure. Women can soften black with a complementary blouse color.

* **Gray:** Gray cycles in and out of fashion favor. Psychologically, gray suggests caution, focus, dedication, and commitment. When wearing a gray suit, consider a lively accent color, such as a red tie.

* **Brown:** Reminiscent of earth, brown communicates credibility, strength, and maturity. Be careful in choosing brown for interviewing; some shades of brown can appear dull or drab. And, it isn't perceived to be as powerful as blue or black.

* **Red:** Attention women! Although red is considered powerful, uplifting, and energizing, be cautious about wearing it to an interview. Some suggest that red means confrontation—not your goal in an interview. Consider red as an accent color in a tie or scarf. When you choose red for accent colors, consider the deep-hued reds and avoid the orangey reds.

* **Purple:** The color of royalty, purple symbolizes luxury, wealth, and sophistication. Women, if choosing purple for your interview attire, lean toward the deeper amethyst colors and steer clear of the pastel hues.

* **Green:** Associated with nature and wealth, certain shades of green are acceptable for interview attire, including dark green, olive green, and (only for women) emerald green or a deep teal green. Avoid yellow greens.

When selecting wardrobe colors, also consider what is most flattering for you. Women, if black causes you to look pale, consider an alternate power color, such as navy blue.

As you prepare for your next networking meeting or formal interview, remember that visual branding—image and wardrobe—will either contribute to or take away from the chemistry you want to create with others.

Chapter Wrap-Up

You covered a lot of important ground in this chapter. Applause, applause! With the work accomplished thus far, I can guarantee you've gained an edge over your competition. Why can I confidently say this? Because most job seekers have tunnel vision when it comes to interviewing—they see an interview as an isolated event, the focus of which is submitting to a series of interrogative questions that should be answered in a polished, perfect manner. It isn't.

In reality, interviewing is a holistic, big-picture process marked by a series of business meetings between you and networking contacts, and ultimately you and the hiring decision maker. The focus of these meetings is achieving an outcome where both parties get their needs met. The employer wants value or return on investment, and you want a good *fit* where you can be radically rewarded and enthusiastically engaged in your work. Recalling Truth #4 from chapter 1, this win-win perspective gives you equal footing with employers and adds to your confidence and bargaining power.

So, congratulate yourself on having an edge. Over the past few chapters, you have

- Intelligently targeted a position that takes into account your Career-FIT™ (functional strengths and fulfillment, industry and interests, things that matter, and personality type)

- Developed success stories and sound bites that focus on benefits (solutions or services) and value (return on investment and employer buying motivators)

- Taken steps to look and act the part with a cohesive image and compelling career brand

Now it's time to go find some great opportunities!

10 Quick Tips for Communicating Your Career Brand

1. Job search is marketing. You are the product and the employer is the consumer. A clear and compelling career brand helps employers perceive the benefits of your product, giving you an advantage in the job market.

2. Successful career brands weave together three A's: Authentic image, Advantages, and Awareness. Project an image of your authentic self, focus on the advantages the employer receives from you getting the job done, and make employers aware of those advantages.

3. Branding can be accomplished through verbal and visual means. Verbal branding includes your sound bites and success stories, whereas visual branding is accomplished through your actions, attitude, and attire.

4. Hone your product benefits into a Three-Point Marketing Message that conveys your unique strengths. This is a critical sound bite.

5. Create a Verbal Business Card to keep you focused, help networking contacts know how to help you, and explain your value to interviewers. Align your statement with employer buying motivators.

6. Mix and match your success stories and sound bites to create a comfortable yet compelling Mini-Bio. Consider using a tagline that helps people remember you in a unique and favorable light.

7. Practice. You must be able to deliver your sound bites naturally, without appearing as though you've memorized a script.

8. Visual branding means you must look the part. Ask for wardrobe advice from someone who is successful and has a good sense of style. If uncertain about how to dress for interviews or networking, err on the side of formality.

9. Visual branding also means you must act the part. Candidly evaluate your mindset, beliefs, behaviors, and attitudes. Are these consistent with others in your field who have attained notable success?

10. Find a person or two who will respectfully and selflessly support you in your commitment to shaping and enhancing your ideal image.

 Magical Coaching Questions

Envision life a year or two down the road. As you grow personally and develop your ideal image, what will the rewards be? Be specific with respect to the positive impacts on your career, work relationships, personal relationships, self-esteem, finances, and so on.

_____

_____

_____

Thinking back to the image description you wrote earlier in this chapter, who can support you in achieving this goal?

_____

_____

_____

(continued)

(continued)

In the next seven days, what small step can you take to get started toward your ideal image?

_____

_____

_____

What system or structure will you put in place to build momentum and periodically track your progress?

_____

_____

_____

_____

_____

Manage the "Buoy Factor"—How Mindset Can Sink or Support You in Interviews

It is your attitude and not your aptitude that determines your altitude.

—Zig Zigler

Buoys—those brightly colored objects that aid in nautical navigation—remain afloat, day in and day out, whether calm seas or rough waters. Beaconage buoys, seen by seagoing vessels, are equipped with radio-beacon technology to mark channels and guide mariners to safe passage. Closer to shore, buoys denote boundaries or caution you of submerged danger, such as a reef or shoal. Certain shapes of buoys, horseshoe and crown, also serve as life preservers.

Regardless of their shape or function, buoys have two things in common. They float, and they are anchored in some fashion.

What allows you to stay afloat?

What are you anchored to?

As a verb, *buoy* refers to raising one's spirits. In the process of accessing and acing interviews, you will likely encounter days that feel like smooth sailing, whereas others might be reminiscent of stormy seas. To be successful, you must address both the mechanics and mindset of job search and interviewing. Previous and future chapters cover the mechanics in detail. This chapter is devoted to the mindset piece of the equation, specifically the mental, physical, and emotional factors that will keep your attitude afloat. We'll call it the Buoy Factor.

The Buoy Factor

The Buoy Factor is a measurement of how quickly you regain your self-confidence and recover from discouragement. The operative word here is *recover*—not that you won't encounter days of discouragement (you will), but how fast you'll make a comeback (you can).

People with a high degree of buoyancy display several common characteristics. They are

- Purposeful
- Confident of their value
- Persevering
- Proactive
- Optimistic
- Empowered, with inner strength
- Anxiety-free
- Balanced
- Diligent about self-care
- An inspiration to others

The Buoy Factor doesn't require perfect and unwavering self-confidence, just the skills to regain it in an appropriate amount of time. Henry Ford said, "Whether you believe you can do a thing or not, you're right."

The "I CAN" Mindset

When operating in full force, your Buoy Factor will enable you to say, "I *CAN* do this." You *can* do it, when you apply this meaning to the I CAN acronym:

 I–Inspire Daily

 C—Control the Controllables

 A–Act Now

 N–Never Give Up!

This chapter is an *a la carte* chapter—choose the sections that best relate to your circumstances. Not everyone will be coming from the same place. As you read this, you might be in a "good" place—with minimal pressure to find a new position, you're certain about your course and have the energy and optimism to proceed with confidence. Others of you might be in a "not-so-good" place—perhaps there is pain from an unexpected layoff, discouragement about an extended period of unemployment, fear regarding low financial reserves, or frustration stemming from other pressing issues.

If you're in need of inspiration, focus on the "Inspire Daily" segment of the chapter; if you feel like things are out of control, concentrate on the "Control the Controllables" segment; and so on.

Gauge Your Buoyancy

To help gauge your buoyancy, use the quick quiz in table 5.1. Circle the score that best represents your response to each item, with 1 meaning true, 2 mostly true, 3 occasionally true, 4 mostly false, and 5 false. I suggest using a pencil and dating the exercise, as you might want to reassess yourself down the road to measure your progress.

The point of the exercise in table 5.1 is to become aware of your mindset. The good news is that once awareness is present, you are in a position to do something about it. If your scores are lower than you would like, do not be discouraged and *do not* disparage yourself. Instead, view them as a signal that it's time to act.

Very low scores might indicate that there has been a significant loss, health issue, or other difficult episode in your life. If this is the case, treat yourself with the same devotion, concern, and tenderness you might use in caring for a loved one with a serious illness. In some cases, speaking to a counselor or therapist might be beneficial—if so, give yourself permission to take the time necessary to regroup and make a comeback.

Review where your scores are low. Then, as you read through the following chapter sections, concentrate on the strategies that will allow you to bump up your Buoy Factor. Remember, this is an a la carte chapter, so munch on the material that your mind, body, or spirit is most hungry for.

Table 5.1: Gauge Your Buoyancy

Lately, I find that I am...	1 = True	2 = Mostly True
1. Feeling overwhelmed about what needs to be done	1	2
2. Lacking energy to do the important things or procrastinating about the important things	1	2
3. Dealing with stress in ways that aren't healthy for me	1	2
4. Forgetting what really matters in life; losing the ability to laugh at myself	1	2
5. Impatient with people; yelling at my kids or the dog	1	2
6. Over-reacting to things that aren't that important	1	2
7. Doubting my abilities or value	1	2
8. Fearful or anxious about the future; discouraged or lacking hope	1	2
9. Focusing more on the negatives than I do the positives in my life	1	2
10. Unable to give myself fully to roles as spouse, partner, parent, or close friend	1	2
11. So focused on one compartment of life that other areas have suffered	1	2

3 = Occasionally True	4 = Mostly False	5 = False
3	4	5
3	4	5
3	4	5
3	4	5
3	4	5
3	4	5
3	4	5
3	4	5
3	4	5
3	4	5
3	4	5

(continued)

(continued)

Lately, I find that I am...	1 = True	2 = Mostly True
12. Not making the time or finding the energy to care for my physical needs (exercise, nutrition, regular medical checkups, and so on)	1	2
13. Lacking enthusiasm or inspiration; not involved in anything that excites, stimulates, or challenges me	1	2
14. Feeling isolated or lonely; withdrawing from people and situations	1	2
15. Lacking the support I need to accomplish my goals	1	2
16. Lacking calmness and peace of mind	1	2
17. Distracted by issues that I have no control over	1	2
18. Complaining about circumstances but not taking action	1	2
19. Blaming others for my circumstances	1	2
20. Having trouble being grateful for much	1	2
Subtotal your scores for each column	=	=
Add each column subtotal for a grand total My total score:		

Steps to Scoring:

1. After circling a number for each item, add up each column.
2. Then, add the column totals across and enter your total score on the last line.
3. Identify your score in the scoring key below.

Scoring Key

91–100	Your focus, energy, peace, and optimism are at a peak and you bounce back instantaneously; you're a beacon of hope and optimism for others.
80–90	You have the mental, physical, and emotional strength to bounce back quickly from most discouraging circumstances.

3 = Occasionally True	4 = Mostly False	5 = False
3	4	5
3	4	5
3	4	5
3	4	5
3	4	5
3	4	5
3	4	5
3	4	5
3	4	5
=	=	=

70–79	Your self-confidence is intact, but there are periods when you don't bounce back as quickly as possible.
60–69	There is some leakage in your mental, physical, or emotional reservoir, causing you to lose time, focus, energy, or peace of mind; your buoyancy could be bumped up a notch or two.
46–59	Your mental, physical, or emotional reserves are low.
31–45	Your mental, physical, or emotional reserves are nearly bankrupt.
20–30	Your situation might benefit from the intervention of a therapist or medical professional.

Inspire Daily

Recall a time when you felt utterly inspired, ready to take on the world, confident that everything would work out for the best. What would your career be like if you could have that feeling on a daily basis? Tasks would get tackled immediately, people would want to have you on their team, ideas would flow, and energy would be focused on what really matters. Successful people have mastered the art of recharging themselves with daily inspiration. You can, too! Here's how.

Master the Law of Inner Action

In the physical life, the action of sowing a sunflower seed will yield a sunflower plant, given the right growing conditions. In the inner life, the seeds you sow will spread as swiftly as narcissus plants. Sowing seeds of pessimism only yields more gloom-and-doom thoughts. Conversely, sowing seeds of optimism yields hope, giving your mind the right growing conditions to plan and be open to how things can work out. Formally stated, the Law of Inner Action is simply a variation on the biblical adage, "you reap what you sow."

Gottfried de Purucker's esoterical writings yielded a number of insights, including this memorable quote: "Sow an act, and you will reap a habit. Sow a habit, and you will reap a destiny, because habits build character. This is the sequence: an act, a habit, a character, and a destiny." I would add two items to lead off de Purucker's sequence: *a thought, and a choice.*

Thoughts and choices, or inner action, precede outer action. To get to action that will bolster your Buoy Factor, bolster your thought life. Thoughts and choices either *empower* or *impale* us.

From your work in table 5.1, identify items where you scored a 1, 2, or 3. For your convenience, the 20 items from table 5.1 are presented again in table 5.2, along with a column to identify any self-defeating thoughts associated with the item and a column to rewrite those thoughts into self-supporting thoughts. If you scored a 2 for the first item, "Feeling overwhelmed about what needs to be done," list the self-defeating thoughts that are associated with that statement, followed by new self-supporting thoughts. I've provided an example near the beginning of the table.

Table 5.2: Rewriting Thoughts

Lately, I find that I am...	Self-Defeating Thoughts	Self-Supporting Thoughts
EXAMPLE: Feeling overwhelmed about what needs to be done	My to-do list is overwhelming. I'll never get this all done. I'm feelings crushed. I should have said "no" to serving on that committee.	I am committed to tackling these tasks in priority order. I am learning to give myself permission to let go of the low-priority items. I will ask Joe for help on a couple of these tasks.
1. Feeling overwhelmed about what needs to be done		
2. Lacking energy to do the important things or procrastinating about the important things		
3. Dealing with stress in ways that aren't healthy for me		
4. Forgetting what really matters in life; losing the ability to laugh at myself		
5. Impatient with people; yelling at my kids or the dog		
6. Over-reacting to things that aren't that important		
7. Doubting my abilities or value		
8. Fearful or anxious about the future; discouraged or lacking hope		
9. Focusing more on the negatives than I do the positives in my life		

(continued)

(continued)

Lately, I find that I am…	Self-Defeating Thoughts	Self-Supporting Thoughts
10. Unable to give myself fully to roles as spouse, partner, parent, or close friend		
11. So focused on one compartment of life that other areas have suffered		
12. Not making the time or finding the energy to care for my physical needs (exercise, nutrition, regular medical checkups, and so on)		
13. Lacking enthusiasm or inspiration; not involved in anything that excites, stimulates, or challenges me		
14. Feeling isolated or lonely; withdrawing from people and situations		
15. Lacking the support I need to accomplish my goals		
16. Lacking calmness and peace of mind		
17. Distracted by an issue that I have no control over		
18. Complaining about circumstances but not taking action		
19. Blaming others for my circumstances		
20. Having trouble being grateful for much		

Be in Charge of Your Own Inspiration

Inspiration starts with the letter *i*, reminding us that *I* alone am in charge of inspiring myself. No one else can do this for you. Take the first two letters of the word—*in*—and realize that you must also *in*ternalize the inspirational message for it to shift from head to heart. Do any of these activities inspire you?

- Attending workshops (industry conferences, meetings with motivational speakers)
- Talking with others who have persevered and succeeded
- Recalling your past successes
- Journaling about what you'd like to accomplish in the future
- Setting specific goals
- Meeting small or big goals
- Learning something new
- Exercising
- Taking action
- Reading inspirational material
- Attending religious services
- Praying or meditating
- Getting away to refresh and reinvigorate

Need a Dose of Daily Inspiration?

Browse the archives at www.dailymotivator.com or pay a small fee and receive daily e-mails with inspirational quotes and stories.

Inspirational Triggers Worksheet

As a career professional in the 21st century, it is a prerequisite of success to know what inspires you. Don't wait for someone else to do this for you! Use the following lines to catalog your inspirational triggers:

_____

_____

(continued)

(continued)

_____

_____

_____

How will you weave these inspirational activities into your daily or
weekly habits?

_____

_____

_____

Keep a Future Focus

Victor Frankl, a psychiatrist and survivor of a Nazi concentration camp,
chronicles his Auschwitz experience in *Man's Search for Meaning*. Beyond the
despicable deeds done, the dehumanization, and the loss of touch with
loved ones, Frankl describes the psychological severity of not knowing
when, or if, the imprisonment would end. In order to bear the terrible *how*
of his existence, Frankl looked for a *why*—an aim—that brought meaning.
He personally applied this philosophy to endure the torture of the concentration camp. Later in his life, he applied this philosophy in working with
patients, asking them to focus on the future and create assignments that
were to be fulfilled. As part of Frankl's future focus while imprisoned, he
pictured how he would someday stand in front of audiences and lecture on
his experiences—a vision that became reality.

Job seekers who are between jobs can hold a twofold focus that incorporates rewards in both their career and personal lives. The career focus
might be tied to your Fulfillment statement, which you wrote in chapter 2.
For instance,

> **When I am in my new position, I will enjoy developing history lessons that
> cause students to think critically, examine their belief systems, and grow in
> their knowledge and understanding...I will start outlining a unit now and
> explore what new resources might be available.**

Note how the resultant action step keeps this job seeker involved in and
current about his profession.

The personal focus might be something like, "this time next year, my credit cards will be paid off." Or, "this time next year, I will have put away enough money to take that trip I've been thinking about."

Use the lines that follow to write out your future focus. You might want to preface your statement(s) with one of these phrases:

* Next year this time I will…

* I look forward to the day when I will…

* What I'll do when I've landed this next job is…

Future Focus Worksheet

My Career Future Focus

_____

_____

_____

My Personal Future Focus

_____

_____

_____

Symbols Help Create a Future Focus

Consider one of these symbols to help keep your future focus:

* A collage of pictures and words representing you in your new, successful role

* A job description written by you that includes the ideal responsibilities and challenges you'd like in your next position

* A diagram that shows the people you'll network with to generate leads, the names of interviewers you'll speak with, the company you'll be working at, the money you'll be making, and the new opportunities that will be open to you

(continued)

(continued)

- A photo of yourself at a time in your life that you felt very successful or were demonstrating who you are in a positive way

- The wrong side of a tapestry or stitchery project that, from the underside view, looks scrambled and gives no clue to the beauty on the upside

- A picture of a road that reminds you that life is a journey

- A rosebud that will open shortly

- A desk plate that contains your name and professional title (these can be custom-made for a reasonable price at many sign shops or copy shops)

Remind Yourself of Your Value

Value is at the heart of your self-esteem. At least once a day, recall your value. The benefit-oriented ideas generated in table 4.3 and the Verbal Business Card Worksheet in chapter 4 can serve as the basis for your affirmations—positive statements that something is *already* so. These affirmations describe a marketing professional's value:

I am of value to employers because of my ability to connect with customers and establish strong relationships. Employers love to have me on their team because of my ability to quickly unravel complicated problems and come up with creative solutions that a lot of my colleagues are amazed by. Certain companies are clamoring for someone with my background because my marketing skills contributed to gaining #1 market share for two of the last three products I worked on.

Affirmations Worksheet

If you find the process of writing out affirmations helpful, do so below. I've provided a few suggested phrases to get you started:

- I bring value to employers because I am good at…

- I bring value to employers because I help impact the bottom line by…

- I bring value to employers because I help solve problems associated with…

- I bring value to employers because I help save time and money through my ability to…

Use present tense when writing and make sure the statements ring true for you; if you overstate or stretch the truth, your mind won't believe them and you'll undermine the purpose of the affirmations—reminding you that something is *already* so.

_____

_____

_____

_____

_____

_____

Make your affirmation sentences a part of your self-talk—that conversation with yourself that goes on inside your head throughout the day. In addition, post them on index cards and say them aloud at least daily.

Reframe the Situation with a New Perspective

Reframing is a technique described in *Co-Active Coaching* (Davies-Black Publishing), a coaching how-to textbook authored by veteran coaches Laura Whitworth, Henry Kimsey-House, and Phil Sandahl. Reframing involves looking at a seemingly negative situation with a fresh perspective and a sense of renewed possibility.

The ancient Daoist parable about a ruler and his son helps illustrate the concept of reframing. One day, the son's horse runs away. The ruler responds, "Surely, this is a bad thing." The next day, the horse returns with three more wild stallions by his side. The ruler responds, "Surely, this is a good thing." The following day, the son sets about taming one of the new horses, only to fall off and break his arm. The ruler responds, "Surely, this is a bad thing." The next day, the military comes to recruit all able-bodied young men for war and passes over the son because of his infirmity. The ruler responds, "Surely, this is a good thing."

When you are faced with a problem, deficiency, or obstacle, ask yourself these questions:

- How might this be a good thing?
- What's the silver lining here?

⭐ What's the flip side to this?

⭐ What opportunities are present in this challenge?

⭐ What can I learn from this situation?

⭐ If I had to convince someone that this seemingly negative situation is a good thing, what would I point to?

⭐ If you feel like you're saying goodbye or losing something in your particular career transition, what might you be gaining or saying hello to?

In addition, consider adding a theme to your situation, such as "this will be a time of allowing more awareness into my way of being."

Deal with the Do-Be's

Are you a do-be? Do-be's are people who find their value in doing, rather than being. (I myself lean toward do-beism but have made great strides toward recovery!) There is a tendency to think that doing (working) is the sole avenue for fulfillment and self-worth. When that avenue is taken away (unemployment), there can be an identity crisis. Unemployment can be hard on do-be's. The secret lies in recognizing that your value is intrinsically in you and being who you were meant to be, both on the job and off the job.

Try one of these strategies for curbing the do-be's:

⭐ Remind yourself that compensation is not the only measure of your value. Whether you're employed or between opportunities, remind yourself that you are still the same talent-filled being.

⭐ Do not rely on someone else to define your value—not your boss, coworker, friend, spouse, parent, or anyone else. On your own, or through the eyes of the God who loves you, you must find the *immeasurable* worth that you have as a human being. Recognize that worth in others, as well.

⭐ Acknowledge that life work, which encompasses everything outside of your work life (relationships, recreation, self-care, home environment, spiritual growth, personal growth, and so on) is as significant as career work. And, without tending to these elements, you will not be able to function optimally at work.

⭐ Identify job search-related outlets for your skills. For instance, if you're a project manager, project manage your interview preparation. If you're a customer service rep, provide excellent customer service to your potential employers in all your interviews and follow-up communications. If you're a teacher, educate your interviewers about how you can improve learning.

 Live in the moment, be aware of your surroundings, and focus on the small miracles.

 Make a list of things that you like about yourself apart from work. *(I like the way my intuition serves me in figuring out problems. I like that I'm a good friend to others. And so on.)*

Control the Controllables

One of the secrets of buoyant people is that they concentrate on what they can control. You *can't* control how interviewers will respond to you, nor the competition you face for a particular job. You *can* control how you respond to interviewers, and the manner in which you convey your advantages as a candidate. You *can't* control whether networking contacts will pass along leads or ideas to you. You *can* control how frequently you will network, to some degree *who* you will network with, and how easy you will make it for people to help you.

This concept—controlling the controllables—is foundational to all the other strategies in this chapter. Let's look at what you can control.

Control the Basics

A few of the job search and interviewing items that are in your range of control include

 Number of networking calls you will make each week

 Number of hours per day you will spend on your search

 Types of activities you will focus on in your search

 Amount of time you will devote to your job search (if you're unemployed, put in a full work week of 32 to 40 hours; if employed, put in 10 to 15 hours each week to generate momentum)

 Amount of time you will devote to developing SMART Stories™ and preparing for interviews (5 to 10 hours per interview; this can be part of your allotted job search time)

 Developing a "plan B" should "plan A" not come to fruition

 Developing a dynamite resume and support marketing materials

 Sending a follow-up note to interviewers or networking contacts

 Showing up prepared, on time, well-groomed, and with an upbeat attitude to every networking meeting or interview

- Participating in professional associations that will increase your visibility and reputation among hiring managers

- Studying press releases about your target company

- Reading professional journals and checking news/media sources to stay current on your industry

- Taking a course to keep your skills and knowledge fresh and ahead of the curve

- Making a name for yourself by writing articles or through public speaking

Personal things that are in your range of control include the following:

- Amount of exercise, rest, sleep, and nutrition you give yourself

- Attitude and self-talk—what you believe and tell yourself quietly in your head

- Acting "as if" you are already successful (see "Act Successful" later in this chapter)

- Accountability vs. entitlement mentality—echoing John F. Kennedy's sentiments in "ask not what your country can do for you, but what you can do for your country," ask not what the company can give you, but what you can give the company

- News and media you'll allow yourself to consume (is it inspirational or depressing?)

- Time each day for activity that will boost your spirits (stopping to smell the roses, reading to your child, exercising, reading an inspirational autobiography, and so on)

Are You Feeding on Garbage?

GIGO, an acronym for *Garbage In, Garbage Out,* is a famous computer axiom meaning that if invalid data (garbage) is entered into a system, the resulting output will be trash. Although originally applied to computing, the axiom holds true for other systems, such as production, manufacturing, or decision making. As it relates to the Buoy Factor and your mental well-being, "garbage in" might be overdosing on depressing news coverage, consuming television programs that have no redeeming quality, eating up time at Internet sites that offer no value, or even spending too much time with people who are not supportive and uplifting. Is there something you're mentally digesting that might qualify as "garbage?"

Controlling the Controllables Worksheet

To make progress in controlling the controllables, first make a list of those things you'd like to let go of. For instance, worries about money, discouragement about a setback, or concerns about how to gain access to an important networking contact or employer.

Things I will let go of:

_____

_____

_____

_____

_____

Now, itemize the things you can control (draw from the earlier list of bulleted items for ideas or create your own).

My controllables are

_____

_____

_____

_____

_____

What actions can you take to help shift your list of controllables from a conceptual phase to a firm commitment?

_____

_____

_____

Find Bone-Marrow People

Every one of us gets through the tough times because somebody is there, standing in the gap to close it for us.

—Oprah Winfrey

At some point, we all need someone who can stand in the gap for us—someone who selflessly comes by our side in good times and bad. I call them bone-marrow people.

Bone marrow is where new blood cells are formed. Dean Eller, CEO of the Central California Blood Center, describes marrow this way: "It's where life is produced." He knows first-hand the importance of bone marrow and blood. Dean stood by his daughter Jennifer as she battled acute myelogenous leukemia—one-third of those diagnosed die within 30 days. Jenny was blessed with an additional four years of life, in large part because of blood donations and a marrow transfusion. During her illness, virtually every ounce of blood in her body was there because people had donated hundreds and hundreds of pints of blood. A marrow transfusion requires a perfect match—about one in 20,000 are compatible. Diseased marrow is a death sentence. With a successful marrow transfusion, the body has a chance to regenerate with new, healthy blood cells. Some transplant recipients even celebrate a "re-birthday" because new marrow means renewed life, hope, and possibilities.

Just as bone marrow creates life for your body, Bone-Marrow People create life for your mind and spirit. When you've been in the presence of Bone-Marrow People, you become more, not less—closer to, not farther from, your ideal self. My business coach and life coach—Judy Santos and Heather Scheferman—fit this description. My best friend Jean Gatewood also fills the bill, as do several other friends and career-coaching colleagues. I am rich in the support department, which helps me find the "I CAN" energy to be **I**nspired daily, **C**ontrol what I can control, **A**ct now, and **N**ever give up.

Bone-Marrow Worksheet

Who are the bone-marrow people in your life?

_____

_____

How frequently do you need a transfusion of their wisdom and support?

_____

What specifically do you need them to be or do?

_____

_____

> If you don't have those special people in your life, how can you tell those closest to you what you need from them?
>
> _____
>
> _____
>
> To whom are you a bone-marrow person? In what way?
>
> _____
>
> _____
>
> How can you be a bone-marrow person to yourself?
>
> _____
>
> _____
>
> _____

If you have bone-marrow people in your life, consider yourself blessed. If not, hire a coach. That's what we do best!

Do's and Don'ts for Friends and Family Supporting You in a Job Search

Consider suggesting a few of these do's and don'ts to people supporting you in your job search. Authored by Robbie Cranch, who recently endured the slings and arrows of an extended job search, the advice is especially helpful when you're faced with a prolonged search:

DO'S for Support Partners

- Ask your friend to describe the ideal position and industry she or he is targeting.

- Ask for a copy of your friend's resume, and read it.

- Offer sincere acknowledgment of your friend's strengths.

- Ask how you can specifically support him or her.

- Be careful that your kindness or generosity does not translate to charity.

- Keep your eyes peeled and pass along *any* potential opportunity.

- Offer leads, not advice.

- Be sensitive to your friend's changed financial picture.

- Unless your friend needs to talk things through, keep the conversation light and upbeat. At the same time, let your perspective be transparent—while you understand this is a serious bump in the road, you believe in him or her.

DON'TS for Support Partners:

- Never ask "how are you," if you're not willing to hear a truthful answer.

- Avoid saying, "I know how you feel" unless you, too, have been on an extended job search.

- Don't assume your friend is just dabbling in a search if she or he has a two-income household.

- Never ask, "What do you do all day?" or wonder aloud why it is taking so long to find a job (the number of ads seen in the classifieds usually has *no* relation to your friend's real job picture).

- Be careful about saying, "I know you'll find something terrific." It might sound like encouragement, but to a person dealing with prolonged unemployment, it might come across as patronizing and superficial. Instead, try something like, "I know this is a really hard time, and I'm wishing you all the best."

Choose Positive Thoughts

The greatest discovery of our generation is that human beings can alter their lives by altering their attitudes of mind. As you think, so shall you be.

—William James

Think positive! It sounds hackneyed, but it's true. Master your thought life, and you'll master your world. We are capable of thinking only one thought at a time—we alone choose whether we'll put a positive or negative spin on it. Ever notice how people who choose the positive spin typically have

positive outcomes? Likewise, those who hold a doom-and-gloom perspective often attract a negative outcome. If you have a tendency to assume the worst before knowing all the facts, pick up an interesting book by Martin Seligman, *Learned Optimism: How to Change Your Mind and Your Life* (Free Press). In it, Seligman details how to shift from negative to positive thinking—a skill that will boost anyone's Buoy Factor.

Consider these exercises to increase hope-filled thinking:

- **Flipping:** When you hear yourself thinking negatively, ask yourself, what's the opposite of that thought?

- **Affirmations:** Review the section on "Remind Yourself of Your Value" for how to write affirmations. If you're not comfortable making an absolute statement ("I am successful"), alter the affirmation slightly to indicate you're growing toward the goal ("I am equipping myself with the knowledge and action plans to make this project a success").

- **Joy Journal:** I'm an advocate of journaling. Here's a new twist on the idea. Keep a Joy Journal—a diary devoted exclusively to things you're grateful for. Reread the pages when negative thoughts creep up.

- **A Great Day:** Set aside a day or evening where every syllable you utter reflects only optimism, gratitude, and hope.

- **The Pedometer:** Similar to wearing a pedometer that clocks the number of steps you take on a walk or run, consider clocking the accomplishments you've made this hour, day, week, or month. Review those accomplishments frequently to help remind yourself of the miles covered and progress made.

An Attitude of Gratitude

"My father's heart condition is precarious, my friend's husband just died of cancer leaving her with two little boys to raise on her own, my daughter just informed me that her school concert is tomorrow night (something I hadn't planned for in an already-too-busy week), my car needs to go in the shop (for the umpteenth time), my book deadline is looming, I'm coming down with a flu bug, and I'm dragging my chin on the floor." That was an abbreviated list of complaints I shared with my friend recently. Frankly, I was irritated when she responded by asking me to make a list of the things I was grateful for and pointing me to a Bible verse that says "Rejoice always...in everything give thanks." I knew she was right. And, it was timely advice, given my concurrent writing of this chapter. A bit unenthusiastically, I scribbled my list of "thankful for's" (I found tiny positives in every aforementioned complaint), I rejoiced (halfheartedly), and I gave thanks (aloud, not *for* the challenges but *in the midst of* the challenges).

After doing so, although none of the circumstances on my list had changed, I truly *felt* better. Gratitude is a recipe for feeling better and more buoyant.

Instead of focusing on the things that have gone wrong (the roadblocks with research, the hot lead that ended in a dead-end, the interviewer who offered the job to someone else), be grateful for what has gone right (the chance to master an important new skill, the knowledge you gained in the midst of following the lead, the chance to practice interviewing so that you're all the more prepared for the next one, and so on). Attitude is a controllable. What are *you* thankful for?

Be Agile

Expect the unexpected. How can you control the unexpected? By being alert, nimble, and responsive to the need to change. There will always be something that pops up to either derail our plans or, in some cases, shift our plans so that we get on an even better track. It is a powerful thing to be able to adjust—to our surroundings, our circumstances, the people we encounter, and the curves that come our way in life. If we expect all these things to adjust to us, our rigidity invites disappointment and frustration. There is power and freedom in expecting the unexpected.

Bolster Reserves of Time, Energy, and Finances

Reserves are extras of important things—extra time, extra energy, extra finances, extra space, and so on. Reserves give you a cushion and a safety net from which to operate. Having extras of good things lowers stress and gives you the freedom to take calculated risks. For instance, an abundance of energy makes you feel invincible, as though you can tackle a big project; an abundance of finances gives you the freedom to wait for the right career opportunity; an abundance of interview opportunities allows you to operate from a position of power and choice. Even if you're currently operating from a position of low reserves, there are some steps you can take to rev up your resources.

Time Management for Job Search and Interviewing

How much time should you spend on your search? These guidelines will help:

- **Part-time search:** If you're conducting a part-time search (you're still employed), time will be your most precious commodity. A campaign with momentum requires 10 to 15 hours a week.

- **Full-time search:** If you're conducting a full-time search (between opportunities), time is on your side, but it needs to be managed well.

For a strong search, clock 30 to 40 hours a week, just as if it were a full-time job. Interview preparation will range between 5 to 10 hours per interview. This is what it takes to thoroughly research a company, talk to insiders, understand critical needs, and practice your SMART Stories™ and sound bites.

These questions will help you to create reserves of time in your schedule:

- What are the priority projects or people you will say "yes" to?

- What projects or people should you say "no" to in order to free up more time?

- If you have trouble saying no to people, what system can you put in place to make it easier to say no? For instance, start by memorizing the line, "I'd love to help with that, but my prior commitments won't allow it."

- What typically interrupts or distracts you and causes you to lose time?

Chunk Your Time

Try this tip from Tim Wright of www.wrightresults.com for creating time. "Chunk" your time by evaluating your energy level and allotting, say, the next 30 minutes to one particular task. Do absolutely nothing other than the designated task for the next 30 minutes. When 30 minutes is up, reevaluate whether you'll spend the next chunk of time on the same task or a different task, and what amount of time you will devote to the task. If you're at home practicing your SMART Stories™ for an interview, for example, assess how much energy you have to focus on the task—is it 20 minutes, 30 minutes, an hour? Set a timer if need be. Then, do nothing other than rehearse your SMART Stories™ during that chunk of time. Do not distract yourself by getting a cup of coffee, checking e-mail, or even using the restroom (you can allot the next five-minute chunk of time for that!). This is a great method for staying focused and getting the most out of your time.

Energy

How can you build reserves of energy? The answer rests in self-care—making decisions and taking action that will support and sustain you. Those decisions and actions might include any of the following

- **Structure:** Orchestrate your day so that priorities are taken care of *first*.

- **Habits/rituals:** Practice daily or weekly routines that make you feel strong and empowered.

- **Exercise:** This is your secret weapon in fighting stress and fighting feelings of being overwhelmed.

- **Rest:** Pushing yourself will only further deplete your energy.

- **Nutrition:** *You* know what foods nourish you and what foods drag you down.

- **Water:** Eight glasses a day keep the ailments away; also limit alcohol intake during your job search.

- **People:** Stay away from "toxic" people and stick to bone-marrow people.

- **Projects:** Say "no" to projects that are draining or pull you from your focus.

If you don't take care of your body, mind, and spirit, who will?

Finances

If finances are tight during your search, look into an emergency loan, consider what material items you might sell, explore temporarily downsizing your living accommodations if possible, and simplify wherever possible. Look into part-time, temp, contract, or consulting positions that might ease cash flow. Be frank with immediate family about the situation and make cost-cutting a group effort. There are some great free money-stretching resources on the Web—type *"frugal," "cheapskate," and "bargain"* at www.google.com and you'll have dozens of ideas. Shop at consignment boutiques for interview attire—these shops are often loaded with gently worn, but low-cost, designer garments. With respect to job search, never pay money to an employment agency to place you in a position, and be wary of career marketing firms that guarantee they will help you find a job for a high-priced investment.

If it's been a while since you've had a paycheck and debt is a concern, there are free or low-cost sources that can help. The National Foundation for Credit Counseling provides credit counseling, debt-reduction services, and education for financial wellness. Member locations can be found by calling 800-388-2227 for 24-hour automated office listings, or visit their Web site at www.nfcc.org or their affiliate Web site www.debtadvice.org. Many churches also offer financial counsel through Crown Financial Ministries (www.crown.org), or call 800-722-1976 to obtain the name of one of their local financial counselors.

Manage Any Negative Emotions

If you are a casualty of a corporate layoff or left your job for reasons other than your own volition, you might be experiencing some negative emotions. If so, it's important that you deal with them before they derail you. Interviewers can sense it when interviewees are worried, scared, sad, angry, and so on. They can also spot candidates who harbor resentment against past employers. Those candidates have a slim chance of being hired, as employers are suspicious that they'll speak negatively about others down the road. Jettison a negative emotion by

- Acknowledging it—objectively note that the emotion is there
- Expressing it—in a socially acceptable manner
- Releasing it—let go and move forward

Act Now

If we were as relentless in our commitment and action as life is in its daily demands, success would be certain. Act. Persist. Success will be certain!

The 80/20 Principle

Choose your actions wisely. Devote the greatest part of your energy to that which yields the greatest results. The 80/20 principle recognizes that it is the minority (20 percent) of the effort that yields the majority (80 percent) of results. For instance, 80 percent of a company's profits come from 20 percent of its customers. It might be a slightly different proportion, but it is virtually always heavily unbalanced.

These activities might be "20-percenters," yielding the greatest results for your investment of time:

- Meeting with your career coach
- Attending a networking meeting that will put you in front of hiring decision makers
- Rehearsing your two-minute profile and SMART Stories™
- Getting insider information on one of your target companies
- Meeting with people in your target companies
- Attending an event that pumps up your spirits (job clubs, motivational speaker, and so on)

These activities might be "80-percenters," not yielding the momentum and leverage you need:

- Looking for job postings on career sites

- Attending job fairs

- Networking with people who don't have access to decision makers

---

80/20 Worksheet

What is the 20 percent activity that will yield the 80 percent result for you?

_____

_____

_____

What do you need to do more or? Less of?

_____

_____

_____

Join a Job Search Support Network

"I wish I had found my job club sooner," notes a neighbor of mine who admirably weathered an 18-month job search. The job search resources and synergy that come from these networks is undeniably powerful. Frequently, they include access to insider leads and guest speakers who are experts in resume writing, interviewing, and networking. National organizations such as the Five O'Clock Club (www.fiveoclockclub.com) have an excellent reputation. Many areas have locally operated groups that are free to members, with the requirement that they give back in volunteer time. To find these local organizations, inquire with local temporary agencies, the unemployment office, employment development department, or Chamber of Commerce. If there are no job search groups in your area, start your own. Make up a flyer with telephone tear-off slips and post it in a public place. Churches, upscale grocery stores such as Whole Foods Market, and neighborhood shopping malls often have a bulletin area to help people connect.

Multiple Benefits to Job Search Networks

A Boston-based client noted, "even though I've only received a few leads from the network, I've benefited from sitting down and talking with others in similar circumstances...and, in brainstorming job search strategies, it gives me an opportunity to feel like I'm helping someone else."

Another benefit of a job search club is the camaraderie and comfort of being with people who have walked a mile in your moccasins. The format and dynamics of a support group are proven, as demonstrated in formal organizations such as Alcoholics Anonymous and Weight Watchers, as well as in informal grief-support groups. Fortunately, job search groups are more upbeat than the latter. When newcomers to the group see someone land a job, it rekindles hope. It also provides an outlet for helping others. Tossing around strategies that might help another job seeker will make you feel good, and might give rise to ideas that will also apply to your own search.

Get on the Radar Screen

If it seems as though things have stalled (the interviewer hasn't called back, you can't get in to see networking contacts, and so on), consider a radar screen activity—action that gets you in front of decision makers. It might be sending a follow-up letter, making a call, or e-mailing an informative article to a networking contact or interviewer. Another smart radar screen activity involves attending a seminar or meeting. During the event, be sure to ask an intelligent question or make a comment that makes your presence known!

Put a "Plan B" in Place

Options are a good thing. They give us choice, flexibility, and hope. Even if that interview you're headed off to seems like a sure thing—avoid going in without some other opportunities that you've considered. If the interview doesn't work out, you won't have to go back to square one and rebuild your momentum. What do you need to do to get some more balls in the air?

It's important that Plan B has several options within it. If you really want your next position to be in a particular field, list another four choices that you can live with.

You can also apply a "Plan B" to a particular interview. If the interviewer doesn't call back, what is your alternative plan to stay in the running? What is your plan to out-position your competition?

Finally, I recommend having a personal post-interview plan. Immediately after the interview, follow up with a handwritten note to the interviewer (you can even add a telephone call). Then, have a plan in place for some positive activity, whether it be a trip to the gym, a meeting with a friend, a session with your coach, and so on.

Act Successful

We are what we pretend to be, so we must be careful what we pretend to be.

—Kurt Vonnegut, Jr.

Act "as if." Act as if you already have that dream job you're after. Attitudes, actions, vocabulary, dress, posture, knowledge, habits, self-talk, and mindset all play a part. How do you need to act to be successful in your job search and interviewing? Even if you're conducting a full-time search and don't have an office to go to, put on nice clothes *every* day. Attend to your grooming each morning as if you were headed to work, even if you plan to spend the day at home sending out follow-up letters and making phone calls. Plan to have lunch with a friend occasionally before going back to "work."

Consider Volunteering

If you're conducting a full-time search, consider allotting some time to volunteering. Donating your talents has a twofold reward. It gives you an avenue to use your skills and feel of value. When performed in an organization where potential hiring decision makers can see your work product, it can produce job leads and potential offers.

Be discriminating about your investment of time. And, approach your volunteerism with a service-oriented attitude. If on day one of your volunteer project, you start asking for job leads or introductions to potential networking contacts, you might appear too self-serving.

Pump Up Another Part of Your Life

Feel like all you do is live and breathe job search? If so, it might be helpful to take a short break and pump up some other part of your life. Now might be the perfect time to

- Refresh relationships with friends or family members.

- Read a little something other than industry trends and interviewing books.

- Catch up on some much-needed fun and recreation.

- Spend time doing something you really enjoy.

- Choose to be with people who have a knack for making you laugh and feel good.

- Reconnect with the spiritual side of yourself.

- Do things that are good for your physical health.

- Pick up an old or new hobby.

- Tackle a home improvement project that can be done in a short period of time.

The latter can be as simple as tidying the pantry or cleaning out closets. For me, there's something therapeutic about clearing clutter from closets. I love the feeling of spaciousness and order that comes, and it gives the sense that there is room for something new to move into my life.

Never Give Up!

When things go wrong as they sometimes will;
When the road you're trudging seems all uphill;
When the funds are low, and the debts are high
And you want to smile, but have to sigh;
When care is pressing you down a bit—
Rest if you must, but do not quit.
Success is failure turned inside out;
The silver tint of the clouds of doubt;
And you can never tell how close you are
It may be near when it seems so far;
So stick to the fight when you're hardest hit—
It's when things go wrong that you must not quit.

—Author Unknown

Perseverance is one of the characteristics of someone with a strong Buoy Factor. Job search and interviewing requires perseverance extraordinaire. You learned some good techniques in the three preceding "I CAN" sections. Here are some final strategies that will ensure that you never give up.

Persevere

Thomas Edison noted that "genius is 1% inspiration and 99% perspiration," while Woody Allen quipped that "80% of success is showing up." There aren't too many short cuts when it comes to job search and interviews, and nothing substitutes for hard (and smart) work. Enough said!

"Nadia" Doesn't Know the Word "No"

Age and health challenges didn't stop Nadia from persevering. She endured a life-threatening back injury that confined her to bed for nearly two years. After what seemed an eternity of doctors' visits, surgery, and therapy, she was able to walk again. With a new lease on life and her children now grown, she decided to enter the work force at age 44, initially as a teacher. Shortly thereafter, she landed a position with the Department of Energy where, for the next seven years, she launched and managed some of the most successful consumer educational programs in the history of the department. She then set her sights on a position with the United Nations. It took two years of planning, writing, and calling on people before the UN opportunity opened up. After her time at the UN came to a close, she found herself in job search mode during the worst job market in decades. With the additional challenge of being a "mature" worker, Nadia, at age 66, spent one year of constant networking and interviewing. Her hard work and buoyant spirit paid off, eventually landing her a position with a leading telecom manufacturer at a six-figure salary. Nadia never gave up!

Don't Take Things Personally

"We found a candidate who was a better fit." If you hear this response in your interview travels, do not take it personally. If you do, it can send you into a downward spiral of discouraging self-doubt. Eleanor Roosevelt once said that "No one can make you feel inferior without your consent." You must not give your consent! And, if your mix of experiences and personality aren't right for the company, the *we-found-a-candidate-who-was-a-better-fit* response might have saved you from a frustrating career situation. Remember that every "no" brings you one step closer to a "yes!"

I encourage my clients to adopt the "happy puppy syndrome" when job searching and interviewing. Puppies are notorious for *expecting* that you're happy to see them and want their company. Their Buoy Factor is usually quite high! When it seems that an interviewer might be avoiding follow-up with you, examine your belief system. Is that a certainty? Or is it that the interviewer might have gotten busy and had to put the hiring process on the back burner? If you've ever been in a position to interview others, you know that this can easily happen.

One client of mine, Paula, seemed to be getting the brush-off from a recruiter who, at one point, had told her she was a top candidate in the running for a management position. Paula could have immediately assumed she was at fault with thoughts of, *he must have found a better candidate* or *he doesn't want me,* but she didn't. Instead, she continued to leave polite voice-mail messages and send proactive follow-up notes every Friday for at least six consecutive weeks. It turned out that Paula *was* still in the running, but a confidential internal problem that involved shifting Paula's would-be boss into a different position had to take place before the search could be resumed. Paula never gave up, didn't take things personally, and ended up impressing the recruiter even more because of her perseverance.

When following up, avoid communicating your frustration or anger. This is a great opportunity to demonstrate your professionalism.

Interviewing Is Like Dating

Interviewing is a little like looking for a good dating partner—you can't expect every date to be Mr. or Ms. Right. At the same time, you should do all you can to ensure that your qualifications are highly competitive. When an interview doesn't result in an offer, follow up with something like this, "I'd like to bring value to your organization and be considered for future opportunities. What would you suggest I do to enhance my qualifications when a similar position opens up?"

Listen for the Leading

Coincidence—God Winks—are little messages to you on your journey through life, nudging you along the grand path that has been designed especially for you.

—SQuire Rushnell, *When God Winks*

Coincidence, intuition, synchronicity, serendipity, the hand of God? SQuire Rushnell, in his short book *When God Winks: How the Power of Coincidence Guides Your Life* (Atria Books), chronicles dozens of stories that defy an explanation of random chance—stories that encouraged people to persevere and move ahead.

Rushnell writes of Beth, whose sobbing in the airport over her father's unexpected death caught the attention of fellow traveler Kevin Costner. Costner expressed sincere condolences, also mentioning "good things always come from sad times." He then extended an open invitation to Beth to stop by and watch the filming of a movie he was shooting in her home town. Two months later, Beth had opportunity to do so. The film's public relations executive was called over to sit with her—it was love at first sight. That night she called her mother to say, "Today, I met the man I'm going to marry." Within eight months, they were husband and wife.

Rushnell also tells of his own God Wink that helped confirm the direction his career would take. At the youthful age of 15, his dream was to be a radio announcer. A job interview 10 miles away with the general manager of a local television station required that he hitchhike, a relatively safe undertaking in those days. The traffic on his rural road was sparse. Every car passed him by. Fearful he hadn't left enough time to get to his appointment, he began to lose faith. Eventually, the car that did stop to scoop him up was driven by none other than his favorite disc jockey, his pop hero at the time. The DJ knew the GM and told Rushnell to pass along a hello. Rushnell made it on time, *and* he got the job. That first position eventually led the wannabe radio announcer to an award-winning 20-year career as an executive with the ABC Television Network.

Winks Worksheet

What *winks* have you seen that hint of good things to come?

_____

_____

_____

What events, places, or persons have been encouraging signs along your way?

_____

_____

_____

Enjoy the Adventure of Not Knowing

Job search can seem fraught with not knowing. How long will it take? Will I find work before my unemployment checks or savings runs out? Will it be work that I enjoy? Will they call me back for a second interview?

Dealing with uncertainty is one of *my* least favorite tasks! My tendency is to want to know what the future holds, to have details pinned down. Many of us do. Recall from chapter 2 where we discussed Type and the four preference scales of Introversion-Extraversion, Sensing-Intuiting, Thinking-Feeling, and Judging-Perceiving. That fourth dimension, Judging-Perceiving, can lend insight into how you manage the *not knowing*. Those with a preference for Perceiving (P) enjoy leaving their options open and often take a wait-and-see attitude. If this describes you, the *not knowing* might actually be fun and adventurous. Those with a preference for Judging (J) enjoy closure and are less comfortable with ambiguity, making the *not knowing* doubly frustrating. If you are a J (like me), adopt some of the mindset of a P: let your search be more of an adventure!

An Attorney Manages the Not Knowing

Valerie was leaving her law firm and exploring whether she would continue working as an attorney or pursue a different career direction. To help manage the current uncertainty, she was able to look back to a time several years ago when she had another period of unemployment. During that time, she was able to help care for her terminally ill grandmother. The day her grandmother passed away, she received a call about a new position. In retrospect, she describes the time with her grandmother as "a precious gift" that she would not have otherwise had. The entire experience helped her trust that things would again unfold in her current circumstances.

Not Knowing Worksheet

What can you point to that will help you enjoy the adventure of not knowing? The answers to these questions might help:

Be an historian. Look back into your history for an event where you had to wait to learn the outcome. What were the positive things associated with this time?

_____

_____

_____

(continued)

(continued)

> Where did you receive emotional or material provision for your needs?
>
> _____
>
> _____
>
> In cases where the outcome wasn't positive, what did you learn from that situation that will make this one easier?
>
> _____
>
> _____
>
> What's the worst that might happen in your current situation?
>
> _____
>
> _____
>
> What actions will you take to minimize that risk?
>
> _____
>
> _____

Finally, give yourself permission to *not* have all the details figured out. Like going on a first date with someone, you rarely know whether this will be "the one." Instead, trust that as you walk it out—with steadfast commitment, focused energy, and intelligent action—your story will unfold and answers will come.

Leverage What Works

Similar to the 80/20 principle, leverage means to focus on the self-care activities that work best for you. If you know that getting to church or temple is crucial to your mental well-being, get yourself there (find an accountability partner if necessary). If you know that exercise is the linchpin in your emotional well-being, get out and move (write it into your calendar if necessary). If you know that being around bone-marrow people is the difference between delight and depression, see those people (schedule several appointments each week if necessary). If you know that time alone is the best way for you to recharge, steal away during a lunch hour or schedule an entire weekend of solitude.

As Nike advises, *just do it!*

Chapter Wrap-Up

Employers prefer to hire people with energy and enthusiasm—people who conduct themselves with purpose, confidence, and perseverance—people with buoyancy! Buoyant workers have an optimistic outlook when problems arise on the job. They bounce back quickly from setbacks. They are an inspiration to others, affecting morale and productivity. They get hired and promoted faster. *You* can be that person. Just say *I CAN!*

10 Quick Tips for Managing Mindset

1. **Mindset can either sink or support you in your job search and interviewing.** To keep your attitude afloat and boost your Buoy Factor—that measurement of how quickly you regain your self-confidence and recover from discouragement—adopt the I CAN mentality: **I**nspire Daily; **C**ontrol the Controllables; **A**ct Now; and **N**ever Give Up.

2. **Inspire yourself by mastering the Law of Inner Action.** Success starts on the inside, with the inner action of thought and choice. Sow positive inner actions, and you'll reap positive outer actions—behaviors that lead to more leads, interviews, and offers. Consciously be aware of your thought life and convert any self-defeating thoughts into self-supporting thoughts. Always hold a positive picture of the future, remind yourself of the value you offer employers, and frame situations from a possibility perspective.

3. **Inspire begins with the letter *i*, reminding us that *I* alone am in charge of inspiring myself.** Identify your inspirational triggers (being with other people, reading inspirational stories, exercising, and so on) and weave them into your daily or weekly habits.

4. **Control the controllables.** Controllables include "soft" items like your attitude, self-talk, and self-image, as well as "hard" items, such as devoting a certain number of hours each week to networking and preparing for interviews, putting contingency plans in place, managing your time, and taking care of yourself.

5. **Surround yourself with bone-marrow people**—individuals who selflessly stand beside you with encouragement, ideas, and inspiration.

6. **Act now!** Apply the 80/20 principle, focusing on the minority (20 percent) of effort that yields the majority (80 percent) of results. Twenty-percent activities might include meeting with your coach, attending meetings that put you in front of hiring decision makers, rehearsing for interviews, getting insider information on a target company, meeting with people in target companies, or attending an event that pumps up your spirits.

7. **Act successful.** Act like you've already got the job. Act like you have value (you *do*). Adopt the attitudes, actions, vocabulary, dress, posture, knowledge, habits, self-talk, and mindset that personify people who are successful in your target position.

8. **Never give up.** Be as relentless in your action as life is in its daily demands. Success will be certain.

9. **Leverage what works.** When the stress piles on, focus on the self-care activities that give you the most momentum, whether it be exercising, going to church/temple, meeting with friends, or finding time for introspection.

10. **Success in interviewing goes well beyond the mechanics of what to say to an interviewer.** It requires a buoyant spirit that embodies purpose, confidence, and perseverance. Tending to your mental, physical, and emotional health is a sure way to boost your Buoy Factor.

Magical Coaching Questions

A buoyant mindset stems from a combination of mental, physical, and emotional health. What individual daily habits need to be in place for each of these elements to thrive?

_____

_____

_____

When a significant setback comes, what do you need to do that hour, or that day, to care for your mental, physical, and emotional needs?

_____

_____

_____

What do you need to do to empower yourself today?

_____

_____

_____

Part 2

The Interview

Chapter 6

The 10 Types of Interviews

Knowledge itself is power.

—Francis Bacon

Flexibility, agility, resiliency…these are a few of the key traits that "A" candidates possess. You will need each of these skills to be alert and responsive to the many types of interviews you might encounter on your job search journey. Ten of the most popular types include the following:

- Telephone screening interviews
- One-on-one interviews (structured or unstructured)
- Behavioral and competency-based interviews
- Situational interviews
- Stress interviews
- Panel or committee interviews
- Group interviews
- Simulation interviews (situational judgment tests, case studies, demonstrations)
- Videoconference interviews
- Lunch or dinner interviews

Although there are several more varieties of interviews, we'll focus our discussion on these 10, which you will be most likely to encounter. Use this chapter as a quick reference with tips to guide you through each of the more common interview genres. At the end of the chapter, you'll note these helpful lists of Top 10's:

- ✦ 10 Quick Tips for Managing Different Types of Interviews
- ✦ 10 Quick Tips for Any Interview
- ✦ 10 Common Interview Mistakes Made by Candidates

Shortly ahead in this part of the book, you'll note separate chapters devoted to the more prevalent types of interviews: telephone interviews (chapter 8) and behavioral and competency-based interviews (chapter 9). Then we cover the ins-and-outs of managing traditional interviews in detail in chapters 10, 11, and 12.

Telephone Screening Interviews

In telephone interviewing, the name of the game is staying in the game. Interviewers use telephone screening interviews to pare down their list of applicants. They are probing for reasons to scratch candidates from the list.

Telephone interviews are usually a sort of Dragnet, just-the-facts-ma'am, interview. Be wary of volunteering information beyond what is asked; it could work against you.

Here are some tips for telephone interviews:

- ✦ Treat every telephone call from any key networking or employment contact as a telephone interview. Whether you realize it or not, you are continually being judged.
- ✦ Set up your Phone Zone (see chapter 8).
- ✦ Buy time if a phone interview makes you feel caught off guard. It's critical that you be focused and centered.
- ✦ Follow the lead of the interviewer. If he or she is business-like and wants only facts, match his or her pace and tone of voice and give just the facts. If the interviewer is more conversational in manner, interact and build rapport.
- ✦ Refer to chapter 8 for a thorough look at telephone interviews.

One-on-One Interviews

Once you've run the telephone screening gauntlet, you'll normally be invited to a one-on-one interview. This type of interview may take any number of forms, such as a behavioral interview, a situational interview, or a stress interview. We'll cover one-on-one interviews thoroughly in the chapters to come.

Here are some tips for one-on-one interviews:

* Don't forego thorough research on the company and position.

* Practice responding to questions. Thinking about what you will say and actually verbalizing it are two very different animals.

* Treat every interview as a *first* interview, regardless of whether it is the fifth time you've met with the same person.

* Beware the interviewer who does all the talking. You are either at the mercy of an ill-trained interviewer or in the presence of a manager desperate to fill a position and doing his best to sell you on the job!

* Refer to the 10 Quick Tips at the end of chapters 11, 12, and 13 for guidelines on connecting with interviewers, clarifying what needs to be done, collaborating on how to do it, and closing an interview.

Behavioral and Competency-Based Interviews

Behavioral interviews are a common favorite of interviewers. The underlying principle is that past performance is the best indicator of future performance. Behavioral questions will be closely linked to competencies and essential functions of the position. We cover behavioral interviews to a greater degree in chapter 9.

Here are some tips for behavioral interviews:

* Watch for questions that start with "Tell me about a time when…, Describe a situation where you had to…," or "What have you done that…." These are the prefaces to behavioral interview questions.

* Be specific and detailed in your responses.

* Use the SMART Story™ format from chapter 3 to describe the **S**ituation and **M**ore, **A**ction taken, **R**esults achieved, and **T**ie-in to the interviewer's question or competency **T**heme.

* Be ready for follow-up probes, such as "How did you decide which task to do first?," "What could you have done differently?," or "How has that experience affected the way you do business today?"

Situational Interviews

Situational interviews are similar to behavioral interviews, with the distinction that situational interviews probe or ask the candidate to demonstrate what he or she *would do* in certain circumstances versus what he or she *has done* in certain circumstances. For instance, in a situational interview, you might be directed to do the following:

- Persuade your work team that your new idea to redesign product packaging is better than the current packaging.

- Now inform your team leader that you do not agree with a decision regarding the project.

- Inform the head of another department that you will not be able to meet his deadline for an important report.

Here are some tips for situational interviews:

- Let your SMART Stories™ from chapter 3 guide your responses and actions. For instance, if you are asked, "How would you tell a customer that their important order will not be delivered on time?," you might think back to a time when you had to do just that.

- If you're unsure of what to say, admit that you don't have the whole picture. For instance, tell the interviewer, "Now, I recognize that I don't have all the history and information I might need to make the best decision. When actually in the job, I would take the time to involve other key parties."

Stress Interviews

Stress interviews are a deliberate test of your coping skills. The interviewer might be intentionally sarcastic, argumentative, or rude, or you may be kept waiting for an extended period. The interviewer will assume that your reaction to stress in the interview will be similar to your reaction to stress on the job. You want to assure them that you can handle it.

Here are some tips for stress interviews:

- Don't take things personally. This is absolutely key!

- Remain calm.

- Endure the silent treatment, a technique often seen in stress interviews. If the interviewer remains silent for more than a minute, ask whether he or she needs clarification or elaboration on your last comment.

✦ Use good judgment. If the interviewer steps beyond the line of putting you through a stress interview to treating you in a downright offensive or degrading manner, stand up for yourself. Consider a comment like this: "I base my business relationships on mutual respect. I'd like our relationship to be the same. May we continue in a manner that would allow us to build bridges and explore our mutual needs?" If they say no, be ready to stay and be humiliated or walk away.

✦ Or, call them on it. "I recognize that you may intentionally be putting me through the paces of a stress interview. Please understand that my current position requires me to manage stressful situations and clients on a daily basis, which I do quite well. If you were a client that I was servicing, I would set expectations that would raise the bar for professional conduct. I'd like to continue in that vein from this point forward."

Panel or Committee Interviews

The panel interview—with its roots in academia and health care—has made solid inroads into the corporate sector. Here, two or more individuals, frequently representing different departments of the organization, will play tag-team interviewing as they ask a series of questions. A panel interview measures how you interact with other people, many of whom will be your supervisors and colleagues.

Here are some tips for panel or committee interviews:

✦ Relax, focus, and breathe! Take it one question at a time, one person at a time. Address your response primarily to the individual asking the question, while also making eye contact with the rest of the panel.

✦ Look for the key decision-maker on the panel—he or she is often the person who is last to the meeting because of a busy schedule, or the person to whom all the other heads turn when there is a question.

✦ Prepare as thoroughly as you would for a one-on-one interview, and then some. Memorize your resume—you want answers on the tip of your tongue. Study the job description to understand what the interviewers are looking for. If possible, get basic bio information on each of the panel members (sometimes a Google or Google News search will yield information on distinguished panel members).

✦ Send a separate thank you/follow-up note to each panel member.

Group Interviews

In a group interview, a pool of candidates is assembled under one roof. Interestingly, this is often the only time you can get a glimpse of your competition. In some cases, employers will bring all the candidates in at the same time. The same question may be put to multiple candidates or a different question may be given to each candidate. Your goal is to answer in a manner that makes you stand out and proves that you can keep your cool under pressure as your competition looks on. Fortunately, this type of interview isn't all that common.

Group interviews are also used to uncover the leadership potential of prospective managers and employees. Candidates are directed to gather for an informal sort of town hall meeting. The interviewer may introduce a subject and start off the discussion. Or, you may be given a group exercise, where the group will be watched to see who takes charge, how well he or she delegates, and how the others react to his or her leadership. During group interviews, you will be observed for attire, manners, and body language, as well as key competencies, such as interpersonal, persuasion, communication, teamwork, leadership, organizational, and stress-management skills. Frontrunner candidates are then invited to one-on-one interviews.

Here are some tips for group interviews:

- Stand out (in a professional way) and be noticed.
- Be a leader rather than a follower, or at least an active participant rather than a casual observer.
- Involve other team members and delegate tasks efficiently.
- Give and receive (graciously) constructive criticism.
- Focus on resolving the issues at hand.
- Review case studies later in this chapter to improve your ability to improvise.

Simulation Interviews

At larger, leading-edge companies, you may encounter a relatively new breed of cognitive ability test: job simulations. These simulations may come in the form of situational judgment tests, case studies, or demonstrations.

Situational Judgment Tests

Situational judgment tests, sometimes called role-plays or inbox exercises, are an excellent method for interviewers to determine whether you can walk your talk! Some companies create a formal simulation on-site, while others send candidates for testing to resources such as DDI, a global human resource consulting firm specializing in leadership and selection. The more sophisticated setups videotape you for playback and analysis by company decision makers.

A common simulation for management candidates involves an inbox exercise to assess prioritization, time management, decision-making, leadership, and interpersonal skills. The candidate is equipped with a computer and telephone and tasked with responding to typical business challenges ranging from routine to crisis level, such as the following:

- E-mails both urgent and low-priority
- Telephone interruptions
- Employees who are having a squabble
- A staffing or technology problem, such as your secretary calling in sick or notice that the server will be down for three hours from noon to 3 p.m.
- A public relations crisis
- A request from your immediate supervisor to prepare materials by the end of the day for an important meeting

Responses from the exercise are later analyzed and graded according to important competency areas, such as those seen in figure 6.1.

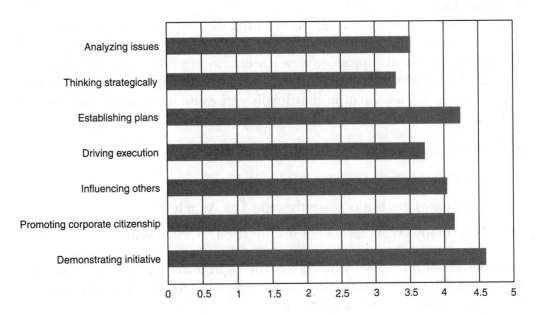

Figure 6.1. Results of an inbox simulation graded by competencies.

Take a Peek at an Inbox Exercise

Wilson Learning, a leader in assessment and selection systems, has a demo of an inbox simulation at its Web site. Visit http:// asp.wilsonlearning.com/amc_demo.asp to get an idea of how an inbox exercise for middle-level managers might be structured.

When tasked with a complex role-play or inbox exercise, keep these tips in mind:

★ Carefully read any introductory information and make note of key players, such as the name of your direct supervisor, as well as important issues.

★ Focus on completing the top three priorities—usually items that affect your direct supervisor and the company's key initiatives.

★ Flag lower-priority items for follow-up.

★ Be mindful of core competencies the interviewers might be looking for and focus on demonstrating those competencies.

★ If you sense you didn't do well on an inbox exercise, express this to the interviewer and offer how you might have handled items differently if you had it to do over again.

Case Studies

Case studies are common when you're interviewing at consulting firms, such as Accenture, McKinsey & Company, and Boston Consulting Group. Smaller firms may also propose a case scenario to evaluate a candidate's analytical skills while introducing him or her to the type of issues the company confronts. The situation may involve an estimation (also called numerical cases) or actual or theoretical client questions.

Numerical estimations may ask questions such as these:

★ How many cows are there in Canada?

★ How many gas stations are there in Los Angeles?

★ How many DVD players are sold in the U.S. each year?

Interviewers don't expect you to have the right answer to any of these questions. Instead, they are interested in hearing what logical structure you would use to arrive at the answer.

Actual or theoretical client questions might sound like these:

- ABC Automaker is losing money. What would you suggest they do?

- FedEx is going to offer a new service where customers can drop a package directly into a driver's vehicle. What issues need to be thought about?

- A popular vocalist wants to start a recording company. How would you advise her?

These tips will guide you in managing a case-study interview:

- Listen intently and take notes.

- Clarify the case. After hearing the information regarding a client issue, restate your understanding of the case to the interviewer.

- Outline what additional information is needed, as well as what the critical issues are. Tell the interviewer, "The key issues I am focusing on are…."

- Ask the interviewer questions. Remember that this is a dialogue, not a monologue!

- Create a structure for your approach. Converse with the interviewer to analyze the problem, such as "That issue could be approached in a few ways. The one I would use is…."

- Think out loud so that the interviewer understands your thought processes.

- Identify potential findings from your analysis, offer solutions, and present a hypothesis for future analysis and discussion. Draw a visual if it will help in presenting the solution.

- Summarize the case.

- Have fun. Interviewers want to see a passion for analyzing issues and strategizing solutions.

For a thorough analysis of case interviews, see the books *Case in Point: Complete Case Interview Preprartion*, Third Edition, by Marc Cosentino (Burgee Press, 2004) or *Ace Your Case! The WetFeet Insider Guide to Consulting Interviews* (WetFeet Press, 2003).

Test Your Skill in an Interactive Online Case Study

McKinsey & Company, one of the world's top management consulting firms, offers a simulated case study at its Web site. Visit www.mckinsey.com/aboutus/careers/ and click on On-Line Case Study to test your analytical prowess.

Demonstrations

Demonstrations should be a requisite part of *every* interview. Were this true, the candidate who is most qualified would win the offer instead of the candidate who interviewed best! A demonstration allows the interviewer to take a "test drive" and see how you will perform and contribute. In addition, he or she can begin to visualize you as a natural part of the team. At the same time, demonstrations give you an opportunity to focus on what's most important—doing the job—instead of talking about how you can do the job.

Demonstrations can apply to a wide range of candidates—from a dental hygienist cleaning teeth or a medical transcriber transcribing chart notes to a programmer writing code or a sales manager creating a strategy to boost sales. One vice president of talent strategies for a Fortune 500 company mentioned that demonstrations are often a part of hiring candidates in marketing or sales-facing positions. For example, the company will fly the marketing candidate along with other company management to a location that needs to increase its market share. There, the candidate has an opportunity to view the retail situation, analyze the competition, and then come up with marketing strategies to support a sales increase.

Some companies ask candidates to deliver a presentation around an issue relevant to the position. For an example, see the PowerPoint presentation in chapter 11 (see the section titled "Phase 3: Collaborate on How to Do the Job").

When presenting a case study or demonstration, remember to add in an occasional comment, such as, "As your marketing manager, I would, of course, have access to in-house information that might change some of the strategy involved here." Or, "I'd, of course, make a point of communicating with the Director of Sales and Director of Manufacturing on these issues." Interviewers are more interested in your approach to a situation, your thought processes as they relate to problem solving, and the general quality of your work. We cover demonstrations more fully in chapter 11.

The type of demonstration will drive the details of how to manage a demonstration exercise. Here are some general tips:

- Exhibit key competencies for the position in your demonstration. For instance, if expert analytical skills are the most important competency for the position, mention "In analyzing the consumer landscape, I found...." Or, "The analytical process I used to create this strategy included...."

- Care about the interviewers' needs—it's a sure-fire strategy to suppress self-consciousness. Interact with them. Ask questions to open further dialogue about their needs.

✴ This is more about *doing* the job than delivering a perfect stage performance.

✴ If asked to create a demonstration or presentation that would normally take a week to prepare for, negotiate by suggesting something like this: "I'd love to accommodate you with that request. Normally, I'd devote 15 to 20 hours [or whatever is normal] to a project of that significance. Given my current client commitments and that you need this tomorrow, may I focus on just one important portion of the presentation, say, the industry analysis or competitive analysis?"

✴ In some cases you can create a template presentation that can be tweaked for interviews at other companies.

✴ If the employer has not asked for a demonstration, ask permission to share your demonstration. You will stand out as an "A" candidate for having this material *and* give them a chance to see you in action.

Depending on the company and its nomenclature, there may be overlap in situational judgment tests, inbox exercises, case studies, and demonstrations. The greatest commonality is that each of these is an opportunity to display your talents, enthusiasm, and passion for the job.

In fact, every job seeker should create some sort of "test-drive demo" so that interviewers can understand your on-the-job thought processes, see you performing key competencies for the job, and begin to visualize you as a natural, contributing part of the team. Demonstrations give you an opportunity to focus on what's most important—doing the job—instead of talking about how you can do the job.

Videoconference Interviews

Videoconferencing is gaining in popularity as employers recognize the benefit of not having to fly candidates or corporate managers in for interviews. The company will set up the details and direct you to go to a certain location (for instance, a local Kinko's) for the actual videoconference. Treat this interview like any other—be thoroughly researched, rehearsed, and ready to solve and serve!

Here are some tips for videoconference interviews:

✴ Ask the person who is handling the camera to get a head and shoulders/desk shot of you rather than full-body.

✴ Minimize any background movement (avoid sitting in front of a window where people or cars would be seen in the background).

- Be aware of the microphone. If it's on your lapel and you reach for papers or hold a report near the mic, the sound will be annoyingly amplified.

- Never touch, tap, or scratch your face, head, neck, ear, and so on. Hands should never go above shoulder height.

- Write down the names of the interviewers, and use those names when appropriate so that it's clear to whom you are directing a question or comment.

- Face powder isn't just for ladies! Men should consider a very light dusting of translucent matte powder (choose something close to your skin color) to eliminate any shine, especially on the nose or a receding hairline. Another secret is rice paper, an oil-absorbing tissue with rice powder that can be used to blot excess oil.

- Ladies should consider using a hydrating mask before applying makeup for a videoconference. Your skin will look more moist. You may want to have your makeup done by a professional for the videoconference. If so, do a test-run first to make sure the makeup artist will give you the look you want. Many department stores have makeup artists at their cosmetics counters.

- Avoid salty foods several days prior to the videoconference to eliminate any puffiness around your eyes or face.

- Look directly into the video camera, as if you were looking into someone's eyes. If you sense that you are stiff, imagine someone you really like inside that camera (your child, a loved one, and so on). Avoid looking around the room or shifting your eyes when answering.

- Avoid profile shots—full-face is best.

- Keep hand gestures subtle. Avoid excessive "talking with your hands" or large arm movements because they will appear exaggerated on camera.

- Dress conservatively in solid colors. Whites can cause glare while tans may make you look washed out. Blues are often great videoconference colors.

- Notify the interviewer immediately if you are experiencing any technical problems, such as difficulty hearing the question or an excessive delay in the sound or picture. Recognize that there will be a slight delay as data is compressed and transmitted. This can be to your advantage because you'll have a few more seconds to think of your responses.

Lunch or Dinner Interviews

An interview that involves food is designed to test both your competencies and your social skills. Don't let the casual setting cause you to lower your guard. The same rules apply for professionalism and decorum as in any other type of interview.

These helpful "ABCs of Good Restaurant Manners" are courtesy of Executive Communications Group:

- **A**nswer an invitation within twenty-four hours.

- **B**riefcases and handbags should be placed out of the way and out of sight. Don't put them on the table or block the waiter's path.

- **C**hew with your mouth closed and be careful not to make any distracting noises.

- **D**on't pass the salt without the pepper.

- **E**xcuse yourself if you must leave. Fold your napkin neatly and place it on your chair. Push your chair back into the table before you walk away.

- **F**ood should be tasted first. Then, if you need to, use salt and pepper.

- **G**rasp any stemmed glass with your thumb and first two fingers cupping the bowl and your last two fingers lightly touching the stem.

- **H**andle any cancellations yourself. Don't have a secretary or assistant call for you. Make arrangement for another meeting promptly.

- **I**nquiries will get you information. Ask your host what's good at the restaurant and use his or her suggestions to determine a safe price range. For example, "The prime rib here is wonderful," means you don't have to worry about ordering an expensive item off the menu.

- **J**ust in case, call the morning of your engagement to confirm all details. Check the time, directions, dress code, etc.

- **K**eep pace with your companions. Skip a course if you are lagging behind. Slow down if you are bolting ahead.

- **L**ipstick should be blotted unobtrusively with a tissue before the meal. Don't leave marks on glasses or cups.

- **M**ention any problems (if you drop your fork, for example) to your host. It's your host's job to call the waiter to the table, not yours.

- **N**apkins belong on your lap, not tucked under your chin. When you're through with your meal, place your napkin to the left of your plate; never on a dirty dish.

⭐ **O**rder last if you are the host. Help your guests feel comfortable, however. Tell them about a good appetizer so they know it's okay to order a first course.

⭐ **P**lace settings demystified: bread plates to the left, liquids to the right; use the utensils farthest from the plate first and work inwards with each course.

⭐ **Q**uench any desire to comb, smooth, or even touch your hair.

⭐ **R**efrain from eating until the guest of honor (seated to the host's right) begins [author's note: in an interview, treat the senior-most person as the guest of honor]. If you are the guest of honor, do not begin eating until everyone has been served. However, if the food is hot and the gathering is large or the service is slow, use your judgment.

⭐ **S**it when the host gestures you toward a seat. Don't just walk up and grab a place at the table. Likewise, if you're the host, plan where you'll seat your guest beforehand.

⭐ **T**oothpicks are not to be used in front of your companions.

⭐ **U**tensils should not be placed on the table between bites. Instead, balance them on the edge of your plate.

⭐ **V**ent about poor service, poor quality food, etc., in a letter to the manager of the restaurant the next day. During dinner, however, don't make a scene that could make your guests feel uncomfortable. Simply say, "This restaurant isn't up to its usual high quality tonight," and leave it at that.

⭐ **W**ait for your hosts or guests if they are late. Don't order a drink, unfold your napkin, or start eating the bread. The table should be clean when your companions arrive.

⭐ **eX**pect the host to pay the check. Don't argue when the check comes.

⭐ **Y**our mouth shouldn't be full of food when you take a sip of water. Chew, swallow, and then take a drink.

⭐ **Z**ipper your mouth. Never, never, never complain when you are the guest. If the food is terrible, grin and bear it. If you spot a bug on the wall, look the other way.

Reprinted with permission from Executive Communications Group, Division of E.C.G., Inc. (www.ecglink.com).

Chapter Wrap-Up

Whether you're having a telephone interview or a simulation interview, your goal as a candidate is to communicate your ability to help make the organization more efficient, productive, and profitable. It's all about conveying value!

10 Quick Tips for Managing Different Types of Interviews

1. **Telephone screening interviews:** Your goal in a telephone interview is to get a face-to-face interview. Treat every telephone call from an important networking or employment contact as a telephone interview.

2. **One-on-one interviews:** The follow-up to a successful telephone interview is a face-to-face interview, usually with one individual. You may go through a series of one, two, three, four, or more one-on-one interviews with various people from the organization. Don't let your guard down. Treat every interview as a *first* interview!

3. **Behavioral interviews:** This popular style of interviewing is based on the premise that past performance is the best indicator of future performance. With their questions, interviewers are looking for evidence of competencies and essential functions for the position. Respond to behavioral interview questions with SMART Stories™ (see chapter 3).

4. **Situational interviews:** Situational interviews probe for what you *would do* in certain circumstances versus what you *have done* in certain circumstances. Interviewers may ask you to demonstrate or describe how you would handle any number of situations relevant to the position.

5. **Stress interviews:** Designed to test your coping skills, stress interviews assume that your reaction to stress in the interview will be similar to your reactions on the job. Stay cool and don't take things personally.

6. **Panel or committee interviews:** Two or more individuals will interview you at the same time. Prepare thoroughly. Don't be afraid to glance at your notepad to review key points you want to make. Take notes. These actions will help you feel less like you're on the witness stand and more like you're in a business meeting.

7. **Group interviews:** A pool of candidates will assemble and be given a variety of tasks, from individual questions to answer to collaborative group assignments. The key is to look like a leader, or at least a standout professional.

8. **Simulation interviews:** Whether a situational judgment test, case study, or demonstration, simulation interviews can be your best friend. Interviewers have a tendency to give the job to the person who interviews best, not the person who does the job best. Simulations allow you to show how well you can do the job.

9. **Videoconference interviews:** Wear solid colors and avoid noisy jewelry. Use a light dusting of face powder to eliminate any oily shine. Look directly into the camera and allow for lag time from data compression and transmission. Relax, look comfortable, and enjoy the process. If the company is comfortable using videoconferencing technology, they also want someone who is comfortable with technology!

10. **Lunch or dinner interview:** This isn't about nourishment. Interviewers offering to take you out for a meal are interested in observing your social skills. This is a good time to remember all those rules of etiquette your mother drilled into you when you were young!

11. **Bonus tip:** Regardless of the type of interview, go in fully researched, rehearsed, and ready to solve or serve. Focus on demonstrating your ability to do the job smarter, faster, or better than your competitors.

10 Quick Tips for Any Interview

1. **Value:** Know your value. Remember your value. Convey your value. Value, above all else, is the key to being confident, calm, and centered.

2. **End in mind:** Take a lesson from Stephen Covey—"begin with the end in mind." What are your goals for the interview? What key message about your background do you want the interviewer to be absolutely clear about? What do you want to know about the interviewer/company? What ultimately do you want from the interviewer? In most cases, it will be a good relationship, a subsequent interview and, eventually, a job offer.

3. **Clued-in:** Be a clued-in candidate (being the opposite, a clueless candidate, won't win you any points). Clued-in candidates are thoroughly prepared and practiced. They know the company's TOP issues (**T**rends, **O**pportunities, **P**rojects/**P**roblems) and who the key players are inside the company and in the industry. And, they have rehearsed many times over their SMART Stories™ in anticipation of various interview questions.

4. **Props and "plops":** Bring your file on the company, a notepad with questions you'll want to ask, extra copies of your resume, and a portfolio/brag book. The latter can contain work samples, a writing example, spreadsheet analysis, photographs of you in action, an

especially impressive letter of recommendation, an "attaboy" letter from a satisfied boss or client, and other material that will help make your case. Master the use of the "plop," a term coined by Dr. John Sullivan, a respected recruiting consultant to Fortune 500 companies. Plops are documents or artifacts that you can plop down on the interviewer's desk to help illustrate your point. These might be one of the traditional items that are part of your portfolio. They can also be unusual items, such as a small bag of M&Ms to explain to interviewers that you have both the **M**echanics (skills) and the **M**indset (attitude) to excel in the job.

5. **Image:** Look the part (review "Your Wardrobe" in chapter 4). Dress on par or a notch above the interviewer. Be squeaky clean. Visit the dry cleaners so that interview suits are crisp and spotless; shoes should be polished with no tatty heels. See that you have a fresh haircut/shave, very subtle scents (if any), tasteful makeup and jewelry, and so on. And, it should go without saying: Show up early, thank the interviewer for seeing you, be mindful of manners, send a thank-you/follow-up note within 24 hours, and so on.

6. **Connection:** It's easy for interviewers to determine whether you have the hard skills (competencies) to do the job. Hard skills are technical proficiency, knowledge, and so on. What's more elusive to determine is whether you have the soft skills (chemistry) to excel in the job and be a good fit with the organization. Do everything in your power to enhance the chemistry (see chapter 10). Pay attention to both your and the interviewer's body language and eye contact. Stand and sit tall. Let your voice be warm, energetic, and similar to the interviewer's pace.

7. **Deliverables:** Focus on learning what is most important to the employer (see chapter 11). What is in their inbox that isn't getting done? What is getting done but not done well? What are the priorities they'd like to see accomplished in the next 6 to 12 months?

8. **Demonstration:** Once you are clear on the deliverables, don't just describe your ability to do them, demonstrate it. Collaborate with the employer on how they want the job done, how you've approached it in the past, and what you would do in the future. Let them see you in action!

9. **The 3 *P*'s:** Filter every word that passes from your lips through the 3 *P*'s—positive, pertinent, and precise. Positive—put a positive spin on everything. Pertinent—choose the most relevant story or information and resist any urge to elaborate on nonessentials, tell tales, or bare your soul. Precise—be brief, succinct, and specific, always backing up SMART Stories™ with numbers, numbers, numbers!

10. **SOS attitude:** Enter the interview with a Solve Or Serve (SOS) attitude. Focus on making the employer's life easier, your boss-to-be look good, and the organization's bottom line more profitable. It's about them, not you.

10 Common Interview Mistakes Made by Candidates

Avoid the interview mistakes noted in the following list compiled by the New England Human Resources Association HR Network (reprinted with permission of Northeast Human Resources Association. This article can be found on www.nehra.com):

1. Unprepared
- No knowledge of what company does, company history, values, mission, industry
- Unsure of what job and responsibilities are

2. Lack of Interest/Enthusiasm
- No questions asked
- Unable to communicate why they are interested in job/company

3. Inappropriate Attire
- Too casual, too much perfume/cologne/makeup
- Rule of thumb: Wear conservative business attire—always!

4. Poor Body Language
- No eye contact/facial expressions
- Leaning on chair/desk/table
- Fidgeting
- Weak handshake

5. Lack of Resume Knowledge
- Cannot articulate accomplishments/provide specific examples
- Overstated/incorrect work history

6. Lack of Punctuality
- Being late without reason
- Arriving too early
- Rule of thumb: Arrive 10 to 15 minutes before scheduled time

7. Unprofessional

* Talking negatively about past company/manager/employees

* Chewing gum

* Using inappropriate language

8. Rambling Answers

* Talking so much that question is not answered

* Bragging/displaying arrogance rather than confidence

* Rule of thumb: Keep answers concise, 2 to 3 minutes

9. Cell Phones

* TURN THEM OFF!!!

Although the New England Human Resources Association HR Network list does not include this last item, I'll add "Poor Listening" to round out the list to an even 10:

10. Poor Listening

* Missing the point of the question

* Responding before the interviewer finishes the question

* Not taking notes

⭐ Magical Coaching Questions

If you encounter a stress interview, how can you remind yourself that the interviewer is doing this intentionally and to not take things personally?

_____

_____

_____

Review the A–Z items in the "Lunch or Dinner Interviews" section of this chapter. What new facts did you learn? If it won't create a hardship financially, consider going out to eat at your favorite restaurant as a reward for all your hard work in this book to date. At your meal out, practice the items in the A–Z list. How many items did you get right? Any violations?

(continued)

(continued)

_____

_____

_____

What sort of demonstration exercise can you prepare to help employers see you *do* the job rather than only *talk* about how you'd do the job?

_____

_____

_____

_____

Note the Top 10 Mistakes near the end of this chapter. Which of them, if any, might you be prone to making? What action can you take to correct these potential interview busters?

_____

_____

_____

Chapter

7

Pass Online Prescreens and Assessments with Flying Colors

Patience and perseverance have a magical effect before which difficulties disappear and obstacles vanish.

—John Quincy Adams

Online screening and assessments are becoming more and more popular with employers. Dr. Charles Handler, recognized thought leader in the development of online screening and assessment technology, shares that companies use these tools to make sure they're hiring the best person for the job. Handler's *Buyer's Guide to Web-Based Screening & Staffing Assessment Systems* offers examples that underscore the financial rewards to employers:

✦ RadioShack found that the use of staffing-assessment tools for hourly workers was associated with an increase in revenue of about $10 per hour per employee. This translates to an annual revenue increase of more than $12,000 per part-time hourly employee. Given that RadioShack has well over 1,000 part- and full-time hourly employees, the total return on investment (ROI) from this assessment system easily exceeds $12 million a year.

* Neiman Marcus integrated Web-based assessment tools into its hiring process for sales associates and saw a substantial drop in average turnover of new hires and a major increase in average new-hire sales per hour. These changes translate into several million dollars in annual revenue gains.

* Sherwin-Williams estimates that its use of automated assessment tools reduced the number of employment interviews conducted each year by more than 5,000.

Look for prescreening and assessments to increase as more surveys like these continue to tout a solid ROI to employers. You'll encounter them during two phases of your application and interviewing process:

* **During the application process:** These tools are used early in the staffing process, oftentimes from your home computer when you submit your resume to the company's Web site. Prescreening assessments ask you to respond to questions about your experience, skills, and qualifications in order to identify whether you meet minimum job requirements.

* **During the interview process:** Typically used with professional, technical, and management candidates once face-to-face interviews are under way, these tools are used when companies want a more in-depth evaluation of candidates. Formal assessments are scientifically based tools that look at measurements of personality and intelligence. Other exercises and activities that are loosely grouped under the heading of assessments include culture and work environment inventories, talent and skill measures, knowledge tests, integrity and reliability tests, situational tests, and job simulations. These tests are usually taken at the employer's place of business or at a third-party site (such as a consulting firm specializing in hiring or performance management) designated by the employer.

In this chapter, we look at online prescreening tools and assessments in more depth.

Online Prescreening Tools

Prescreening tools are typically short, taking from 15 to 30 minutes to complete, and presented at the time you apply for a position posted on a company's Web site. Salary requirements and relocation are often key screening devices, and information about your personality, work experiences, or work values may be collected. Results of the assessments are typically evaluated in conjunction with your resume. If you appear to be a good match, you'll likely be considered for a telephone screening interview.

The technology used to collect screening information is referred to as an *applicant tracking system,* or ATS. Applicant tracking systems enable companies to screen and hire dozens if not hundreds of people quickly. For instance, using an ATS, Citigroup is able to keep up with processing the 25,000-plus resumes it receives weekly, which leads to the hiring of approximately 500 people every week.

An ATS will screen for one or more of the following areas:

- Resume data
- Automated qualifications screening
- Index of "job fit"
- Biodata and personality questions

When will you encounter these electronic gatekeepers? A survey by Rocket-Hire, a consulting firm that advises companies on employee selections systems, indicates that 54 percent of companies that make less than 150 hiring decisions per year have or are installing an ATS, whereas 95 percent of companies that make between 151 and 500 hiring decisions per year have or are installing an ATS. Clearly, the larger the company, the greater the possibility you'll have to jump through online screening hoops.

What to Expect from Prescreening Tools

When applying at companies that use an ATS, be prepared to answer questions about these topics:

- Salary requirements
- Geographic preference
- Ability to relocate
- Ability to work days, evenings, weekends, holidays (you'll see this question frequently when applying with retailers)
- Willingness to travel and what percentage of the time
- Education, including details about your major and GPA
- Number of years of experience in certain occupational areas or with certain products
- Countries in which you are legally authorized to work
- Willingness to work on a performance-based pay structure that includes bonuses and various award incentives
- Willingness to attend ongoing training sessions

- Willingness to complete a background investigation check or credit check as a condition of employment

- Your current status—employed, on a leave of absence, or on a layoff from any company

- Whether you have been discharged (fired) from any employer

- How many work days you have missed in the last 12 months

- Ever been convicted of a crime

- Service in the military, along with dates and what branch served in

- Eligibility to work in the United States

Job Fit and Personality Questions

Questions about job fit and personality might look like these examples, which have been adapted from the careers page of a Fortune 100 company:

Compared to others in your current (or most recent) full-time job, which statement best describes your situation

- I receive more promotions than my coworkers.

- I have more responsibility than my coworkers.

- I have more freedom than my coworkers.

- I receive more awards/recognition than my coworkers.

- I have never held a full-time job.

Which statement best describes how you feel about supervision at work:

- I prefer to know exactly what's expected of me.

- I prefer to know the limits of my job.

- I prefer to help my supervisor set my assignments and goals.

- I prefer very little guidance from my supervisor.

- I don't know.

Personality-Based Questions

According to Rocket-Hire, employers consider biodata, or personality-based questions, to be the most effective form of screening. Here, you'll likely be asked to agree or disagree with statements such as these:

- Working well under pressure is one of my strengths.

- I can do several things at once and still maintain the quality of my work.

- I adapt well to frequent changes on the job.

- When I finish a task, I am usually proud of the result.

How to Prepare for Prescreening Tools

Follow these tips when you encounter prescreening questions online:

* Know your basic requirements with respect to salary range and availability for relocation ahead of time.

* Have a printed version of your resume nearby to help jog your memory about details, such as the number of years of experience you have in certain skill areas. This way, you'll be sure that your information is consistent.

* In general, offer as broad an answer as possible without lying. For example, The Home Depot's extensive online screening tool asks about knowledge of different home improvement areas, from paint to plumbing. If the extent of your knowledge in these areas extends to painting a room in your house or running a snake through a drain, you may be able to make a case for truthfully having *knowledge* of these areas. If you don't have knowledge of an area that appears to be important to employers, do whatever you can as quickly as possible to gain the knowledge needed. Enroll in a class, research information online, job-shadow an individual in your target field—control the controllables!

* Use discretion. Some screening tools require you to indicate a level of knowledge, such as minimal, general, or advanced. Employers understand that it will be tempting to exaggerate your knowledge level. However, don't overinflate your skills. You'll likely be asked for more details in the interview and won't want to compromise your candidacy by coming up short in the live interview.

* Buy time. If you encounter online screening questions that you'd like to give more thought to:

  * Print the page, or copy and paste the questions from the Web site into your word-processing program.

  * Go through the full series of online screening pages (you might need to insert *x*'s into the blank textboxes in order to proceed to subsequent pages).

  * Do *not* click the final "submit" button.

    Sit down and take some time to determine intelligent answers to the questions asked.

  * Go back to the Web site and complete the online screening process.

* Don't think about falsifying information on screening questions. Most end with legalese to this effect:

- Applicant hereby certifies that the answers to the foregoing questions are true and correct. I agree if the information is found to be false in any respect, including omission of information, I will be subject to dismissal without notice. I authorize you to investigate all information in this application. I hereby authorize my former employers to release information pertaining to my work record, habits, and performance. I understand that additional background investigation may be necessary for certain positions.

Want to do a second take? If you complete the screening questions and realize you didn't provide the best answers, there may be hope. One of my persevering clients figured out a way around the system by revisiting the site and using her maiden name. Her revised, but still truthful, responses landed a face-to-face interview (under her maiden name). If you've already given them your Social Security number, there's not much you can do because systems allow for only one entry per Social Security number. Some systems allow you to reapply after a certain time period.

When you encounter requests for your Social Security number online, be discriminating. It might be safe to provide it at larger, well-established companies that have thorough security for your data. Look closely at the employer's Web site name: If there is an *s* after the *http*, standing for *secure*, your data has a greater measure of security. Secure sites will read https://www.websitename.com instead of http://www.websitename.com. If given the option, do not provide your Social Security number for an initial screening. Many larger companies request your Social Security number and date of birth, stipulating that it is used only for background checks and not provided to people in the hiring process until an offer of employment has been extended.

Once you've made it past the online screening gauntlet, you'll move to the next phase of screening: the telephone interview. See chapter 8 for information about this phase of the interview process.

Assessments

Formal assessments—instruments that offer test-retest reliability and validity—are becoming increasingly popular with employers as a screening device. The Association of Test Publishers notes that business for employment testing companies has increased 10 to 15 percent per year for the last three years. The two most common genres of assessments you might encounter during the face-to-face interview phase are those that measure psychometrics (personality traits) and those that measure cognitive ability (mental ability and aptitude).

Psychometric Assessments

Psychometric tests, or the evaluation of psychological attributes, allow employers to gauge your flexibility, sociability, employee relations skills, management style, leadership qualities, fit with a particular organization's culture, and other traits. We'll look briefly at behavioral assessments and ethics and integrity assessments, both of which fall under the umbrella of psychometric assessments.

Behavioral Assessments

Although there are a number of assessments that measure behavior, most instruments are built around what psychologists call the "Big Five" personality factors:

- Extroversion (social leadership)

- Emotional stability (the opposite of anxiety)

- Receptivity (openness to new experiences)

- Accommodation (agreeableness)

- Self-control (conscientiousness)

Assessments commonly used for behavioral personality factors include 16PF, DiSC®, PIAV (Personal Interests, Attitudes & Values), Predictive Index, Hogan Personality Assessment, The Profile, and the Enneagram.

> *Note* Although ethical guidelines for administering the MBTI® warn that it is not to be used in hiring decisions, some companies do use it in the interview process. As discussed in chapter 2, the MBTI® is a highly reliable instrument for understanding type and therefore identifying career choices that will be in synch with your natural preferences.

16PF

Raymond Cattel's Sixteen Personality Factor (16PF) Questionnaire is a popular psychological assessment. Built on the premise that behavior can be predicted in various situations based on 16 underlying traits, the candidate is measured on these traits, which include warmth, reasoning, emotional stability, dominance, liveliness, rule-consciousness, social boldness, sensitivity, vigilance, abstractedness, privateness, apprehension, openness to change, self-reliance, perfectionism, and tension.

PIAV

The PIAV (Personal Interests, Attitudes & Values) is based around one's attitude toward six value clusters:

- Theoretical attitude (a passion to know, seek out, and systematize the truth)
- Utilitarian attitude (a passion to gain a return on investment for time, money, or resources)
- Aesthetic attitude (a passion to enjoy and experience the world through creating, writing, or exploring)
- Social attitude (a passion to help others achieve their potential)
- Individualistic attitude (a passion to lead or control your own destiny)
- Traditional attitude (a passion to pursue a systematic pattern of living that works for you)

These attitudes are not considered good or bad; instead, they support beliefs that drive behavior. For instance, someone with a strong theoretical attitude might enjoy careers in education or research, while someone with an aesthetic attitude might enjoy sculpting or interior design as a career. Employers looking to hire people hard-wired for research would likely question a candidate whose dominant attitude was aesthetic.

DiSC

The DiSC® assessment is also gaining in popularity as an interview screening device. This instrument created by Dr. William Marston is based on his theory that behavior is influenced by two factors: one's perception of the environment (favorable or unfavorable) and one's perception of self (more powerful or less powerful). Marston identified four key dimensions to describe these perceptions:

- D, or Dominance: How people respond to problems or challenges
- i, or Influence: How people influence others to their point of view
- S, or Steadiness: How people respond to the pace of the environment
- C, or Compliant: How people respond to rules and procedures set by others

Marston's theory states that those with a high Dominance score have high ego strength and are direct and decisive, self-confident, problem solvers, risk takers, and self-starters. People with a high i score, for Influence, are enthusiastic, people-oriented, persuasive, talkative, trusting, optimistic, creative problem-solvers, and motivators. The Steadiness dimension reflects

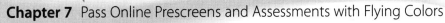

someone who is loyal, a team player, a good listener, friendly, patient, and predictable. Compliant refers to someone who is accurate, analytical, conscientious, careful, systematic, and precise. Should you wish to take the DiSC®, you can find it at my Web site: www.careerandlifecoach.com (click on Assessments).

Favored Responses to Behavioral Questions

Regardless of which psychometric assessment you encounter, employers will typically favor responses that reflect socially desirable traits associated with the Big Five mentioned earlier:

- Accountable
- Achievement-oriented
- Agreeable
- Calm
- Confident
- Conscientious
- Emotionally stable
- Flexible
- Imaginative
- Intellectually curious
- Optimistic
- Outgoing
- Sociable
- Reciprocal (understands needs of others)
- Respectful
- Responsible
- Responsive
- Self-assured
- Self-disciplined
- Self-sufficient
- Talkative
- Venturesome

With Extroversion Among the Big Five, What Do I Do if I'm an Introvert?

Although extroversion is considered one of the Big Five traits, this doesn't mean that those with an inclination toward introversion aren't desired by employers. Some psychologists use the term *extroversion* synonymously with Social Leadership, Social Activity, Ambition and Sociability, or Dominant-Initiative. If you are introverted, simply answer questions in light of what is socially desirable.

As was covered in "Know Your Personality Type" in chapter 2, recall that the extroversion-introversion preference refers to the direction in which your energies typically flow—outward, toward objects and people in the environment (extroversion) or inward, drawing attention from the outward environment toward inner experience and reflection (introversion).

(continued)

(continued)

Introversion is by no means synonymous with antisocial. In fact, introverts can often be seen as more loyal, sincere, and persevering when contrasted with their extrovert colleagues. For a deeper look at the advantages of introverts, pick up *The Introvert Advantage: How to Thrive in an Extrovert World* by Marti Olsen Laney, Psy.D. Her Web site (www.theintrovertadvantage.com) lists the top 10 advantages introverts possess, from creative, out-of-the-box thinking and analytical skills that integrate complexity to maintaining long-term relationships and working well with others, especially in one-to-one relationships. Dr. Laney also provides introvert coping strategies for recharging, work, relationships, and socializing, which are relevant to optimal mindset and effectiveness during a job search.

If you are an introvert, embrace it instead of trying to be someone you are not.

Ethics and Integrity Assessments

Also falling under the broad category of personality assessments are tests for ethics and integrity. These assessments help predict whether candidates' attitudes will create good or poor customer relations and a disruptive or harmonious workplace environment. Employers may assess candidates' inclinations on several scales. Dale Paulson, Ph.D., developer of the CareerEthic™ assessment (available at www.CareerEthic.com), highlights nine scales in measuring ethics and integrity:

Ethics and Integrity Traits

- Justice Arbitration versus Flexibility: Those who lean toward justice arbitration have a propensity to defend one's rights, a strong sense of right and wrong, or the compulsion to intervene in a controversy.

- Relationship Accounting versus Accommodation: Relationship accounting describes a tendency to keep track of obligations as well as perceived slights and insults, and may have the propensity to persist in attempts to "correct" the situation.

- Deservedness versus Reward-Sharing: Those with a high deservedness score may assume that they are not being rewarded sufficiently, tend to see work as an obligation rather than an opportunity, and may have a sense of entitlement.

- Insubordinate versus Deferential: Insubordinates tend to doubt people in authority and the chain of command; may question that "rank has its privileges"; and, are oftentimes unwilling to seek help from a superior.

- Risk-Inclined versus Risk-Averse: The risk-inclined individual generally is unwilling to delay decisions in order to get more information; disinclined to check with others; and has limited regard for record keeping.

- Non-Traditional versus Traditional: Non-traditionals oftentimes have little desire to understand past events, rules and regulations, or work-related ceremonies.

- Egocentric versus Other-Oriented: Egocentrics may be disinclined to assist fellow workers, have limited obligation to customers, and a general unwillingness to make sacrifices for the good of the organization.

- Accountability-Oriented versus Self-Disciplined: Accountability-oriented individuals have a limited commitment to finish projects without supervision.

- Non-Reciprocal versus Reciprocal: Those with a non-reciprocal tendency have limited understanding of the needs and desires of other people and generally accepted social obligations.

Source: www.CareerEthic.com; reprinted with permission.

In the CareerEthic™ assessment, the latter of the paired items is the preferred trait. For instance, flexibility is preferred over justice arbitration, and accommodation is preferred over relationship accounting. You've probably encountered someone along your life journey who is into relationship accounting—someone who keeps score, holding a you-owe-me attitude over your head for any good deed done for you or your loved ones. This self-focused attitude is certainly not conducive to teamwork and camaraderie!

How to Prepare for Psychometric Assessments

Although psychometric assessments aren't the kind of test you can study for, these tips will help you prepare:

- **Think "work mode" when completing personality assessments.** Many personality assessments are configured in a forced-choice model, meaning you must choose between a pair of opposite statements that best describe you. Put yourself in a work frame of reference when answering because your behavior at home may be different than your behavior at work. (Ideally, your persona for home and work should be similar.)

- **Don't try to ace a personality test.** Many tests have scales built in to detect socially desirable responding, or what assessment experts call "faking good." Answer honestly, using a work environment as your frame of reference for responses. For instance, the following sample question from the DiSC® assessment asks you to circle which of the items is most like you and which of the items is least like you. Your answer may differ for a social or family setting as opposed to a work setting.

Item	Most Like Me	Least Like Me
Results are what matter	M	L
Do it right, accuracy counts	M	L
Make it enjoyable	M	L
Let's do it together	M	L

Give yourself the benefit of the doubt. If a question states, *I am an upbeat person,* answer True if this is true most of the time (even if you're not feeling particularly upbeat at the moment).

Watch for terms like "never" and "always." For instance, answering True to a statement such as, *I never have disagreements with coworkers* would, at best, paint you as trying to "fake good" or, at worst, characterize you as timid, unassertive, or oblivious to social situations.

Go into the test fully aware of and focused on your value and your positive traits. We all have areas in our life that can be worked on, but this is *not* the time to focus on them! Don't allow personal stress, work stress, or other factors to cloud your true traits.

If time permits, read through an integrity test first. Then answer consistently because most integrity tests are designed to catch inconsistent responses.

When answering questions that are testing for integrity or ethics, use common sense and answer with the employer's best interest in mind. (After all, that's the attitude you'll have on the job, right?) The following sample questions will give you an idea of what to expect. The parenthetical note following each question explains what the employer is measuring:

- *If you were sure you wouldn't get caught, would you keep an extra $2 that a cashier mistakenly gave you when providing change for a purchase?* (The employer wants to know whether you'll think nothing of ripping off a ream of paper, notepads, and so on. Answer *No.*)

- *Do you believe that children or spouses are more important than anything?* (This question is designed to determine whether your family will interfere with your job. The preferred answer is *No.*)

- *A coworker spins the facts when making a sales pitch to an important new customer. Is this person honest?* (This is an ethics question designed to learn whether you'll lie to get what you want. The best answer is *No.*)

- *There is only one true religion.* (This can be a tricky one for those who believe there is only one true way to heaven. An answer of *True* can brand you as rigid and closed-minded when, in reality, you may be more respectful and accepting of others because of your religious beliefs. The underlying question here is whether you are open to new ideas. If so, the preferred answer is *False.*)

- *How often do you blush?* (You may be prone to blushing at hearing an off-color joke or being praised for good work. That's not what the test-writers are looking for. Presumably, blushing occurs because one is guilty of some illegal act. Choose an answer that indicates you seldom blush.)

- *It would be better if almost all laws were thrown away.* (Do you have little appreciation for rules, regulations, and work-related ceremonies? Answer *False.*)

- *I have nightmares every few nights.* (Have you done something that your subconscious is making you feel guilty about? The preferred answer is *False.*)

- *How often do you make your bed?* (The question purportedly determines whether you have a propensity for sloth and can be counted on to clean up after yourself. If you don't make your bed every day but do pick up after yourself, then the best answer would be *Every Day.*)

- *My soul sometimes leaves my body.* (Unless you're applying for a position with a paranormal researcher, the answer to this should be *False.*)

Cognitive Ability and Aptitude Assessments

Instruments that measure cognitive ability (your general intelligence or aptitude) are certainly the least entertaining for candidates. They are purposefully difficult and frequently designed so that you cannot finish them in the allotted time. Cognitive assessments can determine what you know, how you think, and how quickly you learn. Typically, batteries of these tests are created by teams of industrial psychologists and other professionals.

Cognitive Ability Assessments

Common cognitive ability tests include the Wonderlic Personnel Test™, Thurston Test of Mental Agility, Watson Glaser Critical Thinking Index Test, and Profiles International's Style Test.

See how you do on the following 15 sample questions from The Wonderlic Personnel Test™. Set a timer for five minutes, don't peek at the answers, and give it a go!

1. Look at the row of numbers below. What number should come next?

   8   4   2   1   ¹/₂   ¹/₄   ?

2. Assume the first two statements are true. Is the final one:

   a. True   b. False   c. Not certain

   The boy plays baseball. All baseball players wear hats. The boy wears a hat.

3. Paper sells for 21 cents per pad. What will four pads cost?

4. How many of the five pairs of items listed below are exact duplicates?

   Nieman, K.M.   Neiman, K.M.
   Thomas, G.K.   Thomas, C.K.
   Hoff, J.P.   Hoff, J.P.
   Pino, L.R.   Pina, L.R.
   Warner, T.S.   Wanner, T.S.

5. RESENT RESERVE • Do these words

   a. have similar meanings,   b. have contradictory   c. mean neither the
                                    meanings,   same nor opposite?

6. One of the numbered figures in the following drawing is most different from the others. What is the number in that figure?

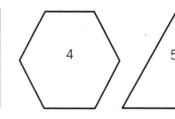

7. A train travels 20 feet in ¹/₅ second. At this same speed, how many feet will it travel in three seconds?

8. When rope is selling at $.10 a foot, how many feet can you buy for sixty cents?

9. The ninth month of the year is

   a. October   b. January   c. June
   d. September   e. May

10. Which number in the following group of numbers represents the smallest amount?

    7   .8   31   .33   2

11. In printing an article of 48,000 words, a printer decides to use two sizes of type. Using the larger type, a printed page contains 1,800 words. Using smaller type, a page contains 2,400 words. The article is allotted 21 full pages in a magazine. How many pages must be in smaller type?

12. The hours of daylight and darkness in SEPTEMBER are nearest equal to the hours of daylight and darkness in:

    a. June　　　　b. March　　　　c. May　　　　d. November

13. Three individuals form a partnership and agree to divide the profits equally. X invests $9,000, Y invests $7,000, Z invests $4,000. If the profits are $4,800, how much less does X receive than if the profits were divided in proportion to the amount invested?

14. Assume the first two statements are true. Is the final one:

    a. true　　　　b. false　　　　c. not certain?

    Tom greeted Beth. Beth greeted Dawn. Tom did not greet Dawn.

15. A boy is 17 years old and his sister is twice as old. When the boy is 23 years old, what will be the age of his sister?

    These are sample test questions and are intended for demonstration purposes only. The Wonderlic Personnel Test is published by Wonderlic, Inc.

Answers

1. $\frac{1}{8}$
2. (a) true
3. 84 cents
4. 1
5. (c) mean neither the same nor opposite
6. 4
7. 300 feet
8. 6 feet
9. (d) September
10. .33
11. 17
12. (b) March
13. $560
14. (c) not certain
15. 40 years old

Wonderlic Personnel Test™. Reprinted with permission.

Aptitude Assessments

There are also special cognitive ability tests designed to measure aptitude for a variety of fields, such as accounting, banking, computer programming, engineering, finance, insurance, law, mechanical trades, reporting, sales, securities trading, and more. Sales aptitude tests are very common because employers want to make sure they're not hiring a clerk when they need a closer.

Following are some of the traits and skills sought in sales associates:

Achievement or goal-oriented	Patient
Analytical	Perseverant
Articulate	Proficient in closing
Assertive	Proficient in cold calling
Competitive	Proficient in presenting
Cooperative	Proficient in qualifying
Diplomatic	Resilient
Driven	Self-confident
Emotionally mature	Self-motivated
Ethical	Sociable
Extroverted	Team-oriented

How to Prepare for Cognitive Ability and Aptitude Assessments

Other than having paid attention throughout elementary and secondary school, there's not a lot of prep work you can do at this point. These tips will make the assessments go as smoothly as possible:

- **Get plenty of rest the night before.** A clear head is the best thing you can bring to these types of tests.

- **Breathe deeply to get oxygen flowing to your grey cells, and relax.** Read the directions carefully. Read each question thoroughly. (I missed a question on the sample Wonderlic Personnel Test™ simply because I rushed through the question!)

- **If you do not know the answer to a question on a cognitive ability test, skip it and come back to it later.** If you are uncertain about an answer, mark it to come back and review it later. If you have time, double-check all your answers.

- **If English is not your native language, let the test administrator know this.** Not knowing idiomatic expressions of language can flaw the results. The test administrator can take this into account when preparing his or her report for the employer. One candidate who spoke flawless English scored poorly on a cognitive ability test. The interviewer, surprised by the results, probed to help reconcile the results in his mind. It was then that the interviewer learned that

English was the candidate's third language, which had contributed to her lower score.

*   **Remember your reading glasses and any other items that will make you feel comfortable and prepared, such as a handkerchief, tissues, or bottled water.** Ask the test administrator whether a calculator is allowed.

*   **Unless directed otherwise, dress as you would for an interview.** The individuals administering the tests often provide a written report about you and have been known to include comments about your appearance and professionalism.

*   **Turn off your cell phone or pager** so that you or other test-takers are not distracted mid-test.

*   **Understand your rights and responsibilities as a test taker.** The sidebar titled "The Rights and Responsibilities of Test Takers" outlines 10 rights and 10 responsibilities. Although Right #8 indicates that you should receive an explanation of your test results, as a general rule most employers do not share results.

The Rights and Responsibilities of Test Takers: Guidelines and Expectations

**Test Taker Rights and Responsibilities
Working Group of the Joint Committee on Testing Practices
August, 1998**

As a test taker, you have the right to:

1. Be informed of your rights and responsibilities as a test taker.

2. Be treated with courtesy, respect, and impartiality, regardless of your age, disability, ethnicity, gender, national origin, religion, sexual orientation, or other personal characteristics.

3. Be tested with measures that meet professional standards and that are appropriate, given the manner in which the test results will be used.

(continued)

(continued)

4. Receive a brief oral or written explanation prior to testing about the purpose(s) for testing, the kind(s) of tests to be used, if the results will be reported to you or to others, and the planned use(s) of the results. If you have a disability, you have the right to inquire and receive information about testing accommodations. If you have difficulty in comprehending the language of the test, you have a right to know in advance of testing whether any accommodations may be available to you.

5. Know in advance of testing when the test will be administered, if and when test results will be available to you, and if there is a fee for testing services that you are expected to pay.

6. Have your test administered and your test results interpreted by appropriately trained individuals who follow professional codes of ethics.

7. Know if a test is optional and learn of the consequences of taking or not taking the test, fully completing the test, or canceling the scores. You may need to ask questions to learn these consequences.

8. Receive a written or oral explanation of your test results within a reasonable amount of time after testing and in commonly understood terms.

9. Have your test results kept confidential to the extent allowed by law.

10. Present concerns about the testing process or your results and receive information about procedures that will be used to address such concerns.

As a test taker, you have the responsibility to:

1. Read and/or listen to your rights and responsibilities as a test taker.

2. Treat others with courtesy and respect during the testing process.

3. Ask questions prior to testing if you are uncertain about why the test is being given, how it will be given, what you will be asked to do, and what will be done with the results.

4. Read or listen to descriptive information in advance of testing and listen carefully to all test instructions. You should inform an examiner in advance of testing if you wish to receive a testing accommodation or if you have a physical condition or illness that may interfere with your performance on the test. If you have difficulty comprehending the language of the test, it is your responsibility to inform an examiner.

5. Know when and where the test will be given, pay for the test if required, appear on time with any required materials, and be ready to be tested.

6. Follow the test instructions you are given and represent yourself honestly during the testing.

7. Be familiar with and accept the consequences of not taking the test, should you choose not to take the test.

8. Inform appropriate person(s), as specified to you by the organization responsible for testing, if you believe that testing conditions affected your results.

9. Ask about the confidentiality of your test results, if this aspect concerns you.

10. Present concerns about the testing process or results in a timely, respectful way, if you have any.

Copyright 2000, Joint Committee on Testing Practices (http://aace.ncat.edu/). Reprinted with permission.

Chapter Wrap-Up

Whether you're facing a battery of online prescreening questions or formal assessments, relax and recognize that the employer is only trying to make the best possible match. A good match is good for everyone. The employer gets a happier, more productive employee. You get to do work that you're wired to do and enjoy.

10 Quick Tips for Managing Online Prescreening and Assessments

1. When applying for a position at a company's Web site (especially larger companies), be prepared to answer questions about salary requirements, geographic preference, relocation, schedule, education, experience, skill level, legal authorization to work in the U.S., criminal record, work history, military service, and more.

2. Keep a printed version of your resume nearby to help jog your memory about details so that your responses are consistent.

3. For online screening questions, offer as broad an answer as possible without lying. Employers assume that there will be a tendency to inflate your skill level. Just make sure that your online screening responses don't compromise your integrity when it comes time for the live interview.

4. If you're stumped by online screening questions, print the page or copy and paste questions from the Web site into your word-processing program. Repeat this process for pages with questions you want to consider more carefully. Close your browser (do not click the Submit Application button) and then take some time to determine intelligent answers. Return to the site and restart the application process.

5. Don't be surprised if you're given assessments as part of the screening process. The two most common types are psychometric assessments (those that evaluate psychological attributes) and cognitive ability assessments (those that measure intelligence).

6. Employers typically prefer candidates with psychological attributes that correlate to the "Big Five" personality factors: extroversion (social leadership), emotional stability, receptivity (openness to new experiences), accommodation (agreeableness), and self-control (conscientiousness). Employers generally favor answers that reflect these factors.

7. Don't try to ace a personality test or "fake good" any psychometric assessment. Most of these tests are constructed to detect socially desirable responding.

8. When taking personality tests, focus fully on your value and your positive traits. We all have areas in our lives that can be worked on, but this is *not* the time to be concentrating on them! Don't allow personal stress, work stress, or other factors to cloud your true traits.

9. Although it is difficult to study for assessments, you can prepare by being rested, breathing deeply to stay relaxed, and answering questions from the perspective of how the employer would like to see you operate within a work environment.

10. When it comes to assessments, understand your rights and responsibilities by reviewing the sidebar in this chapter titled "The Rights and Responsibilities of Test Takers."

 **Magical Coaching Questions**

If you are applying online, what steps you can take to better prepare yourself for prescreening questions?

_____

_____

_____

Regarding the "Big Five" personality factors preferred by employers (extroversion/social leadership, emotional stability, receptivity/openness to new experiences, accommodation/agreeableness, and self-control/conscientiousness), list the area you are strongest in first, followed by your next strongest area second, and so on.

1. _____

2. _____

3. _____

4. _____

5. _____

How can you leverage one of your strongest areas (#1, #2, or #3 on your list) to improve your least strong area (#5 on your list)? For instance, if you listed self-control as your strongest factor and extroversion as your least strong area, you might boost your extroversion skills by disciplining yourself to initiate more conversations in social/work circumstances.

_____

_____

_____

Make a Great First Impression in Telephone Interviews

You never get a second chance to make a first impression.

—Author Unknown

Quick quiz! Your primary goal in a telephone interview is to

    A. Persuade the interviewer you are the right person for the job.

    B. Convert it to a face-to-face meeting.

    C. Determine whether the position is of interest to you.

If you answered *B*, you're on the right track. *A* is part of the answer—you must convince the person you can do the job, but at this point you don't have to convince them that you're the number-one candidate for the job. *C* is a component of your agenda, but it's not your primary goal in a telephone interview.

The employer has a different goal than you when conducting a telephone interview. It is either to

   A. Establish continued interest in you as a candidate (read: keep you on the list), or

   B. Determine that you don't sufficiently meet the job's specifications (read: cross you off the list).

Let's look at what you can do to keep yourself on the list.

Telephone Interviews: The Qualifying Phase

Similar to a sales professional who "qualifies" a prospect to determine whether he or she is a good fit for the product being sold (and therefore worth spending more time on), the employer will qualify you for a preliminary determination of whether you are a good fit for the position being offered (and therefore worth spending more time on in a face-to-face interview). During this phase, offer concise evidence that shows you meet the job's specifications.

Set Up Your Phone Zone

Beware the casual call from a recruiter. It is an interview in disguise. "Many candidates don't recognize that interviewing starts before they even agree to be a candidate," reveals Kate Kingsley, president of KLKingsley executive search and former partner of Korn/Ferry International. This is a reminder that *any* conversation with a key employment or networking contact may be a form of an interview.

To avoid getting caught off guard, set up your "phone zone." This should be a quiet space without the potential for interruptions, where you have easy access to the following:

- Resume
- Three-Point Marketing Message, verbal business card, and mini-bio (from chapter 4)
- SMART Stories™ (from chapter 3)
- Company research
- Questions you'd like to ask the company
- Answers to questions you anticipate being asked
- Computer, notepad, pen, calculator, stickies (write your interviewer's name on a stickie so that you can readily use his or her name in your conversation)
- Appointment book or PDA
- Clock
- Water (should you experience a dry mouth or frog in your throat)

Employers may call at the least expected hour. If necessary, use one of the following phrases to buy time and get centered:

- When you need a few seconds to take some deep breaths, say: "Thank you for calling. May I put you on hold for a moment while I close the door?"

- When you need a few minutes to eliminate background noise (at all costs, avoid dogs barking, television noise, kid noise, and so on), consider this response: "I'm so pleased to hear from you. May I call you back in five minutes? I was just finishing up something and I want to give you my complete attention."

- When you need a few hours, try this: "Thank you for calling. I'm anxious to speak with you but I'm just walking into (or out for) an appointment. When would be a convenient time for me to call you back?"

- When you need better reception quality if you're on a cell phone: "You've caught me on my mobile number in an area where there isn't good reception. May I call you back on a land line? When would be a good time? Actually, now that I think of it, I can be in your area this afternoon or tomorrow morning. Which of those would be better for your schedule?"

- When you need some confidentiality if the interviewer has called you at work: "You've caught me at work. May I call you back around the noon hour (or at my next break)?" Or, "It's difficult for me to speak freely here. May we schedule a time to meet at your office?"

What to Expect During a Telephone Interview

During the telephone screening, which may last between 15 and 45 minutes, interviewers will determine whether

- You meet basic qualifications for the job (if they haven't already done so online).

- Your answers are consistent with information on your resume/application.

- You understand the position.

- You have expressed interest in, and *enthusiasm* for, the position.

- You have asked relevant questions.

Depending on the company, you may be screened by a human resource professional, a third-party recruiter, or even the hiring manager. Human resource professionals will typically ask questions that verify you have the "hard skills" to do the job, such as the right degree and certification, number of years of experience in certain areas, and so on. Third-party recruiters or hiring managers will likely ask more in-depth questions. When the telephone interview gets underway, anticipate some of these frequently asked questions:

1. "What are the top duties you perform in your current/most recent position?"

2. "What types of decisions do you frequently make in your current/most recent position? How do you go about making them?"

3. "What is the most significant project or suggestion you've initiated in your career?"

4. "How many years of experience do you have with _____ [the type of product or service you'll be providing at the company]?"

5. "How would you describe your ideal work environment?"

6. "Why are you leaving your current employer?" (or "Why did you leave your last employer?")

7. "What do you know about (or expect from) the position?"

8. "What do you know about our company?"

9. "What contribution do you anticipate being able to make in this position?"

10. "How does this position fit into your long-term career plans?" (or "Where do you see yourself in 5 to 10 years?")

11. "Why are you the best candidate for this position?"

12. "When would you be available?"

13. "Is the salary range for the position within your acceptable range?"

14. "What questions do you have?"

You might encounter several variations on these questions. Refer to chapter 13 for the Magic Words strategy for frequently asked questions. Because employers often consider your reasoning ability and thought process as important as the answer itself, verbalize more than you might normally in a conversation. This will help the interviewer judge your decision-making process and get to know you better.

Questions to Ask in a Telephone Interview

What questions will you ask to determine whether this position is worth pursuing? Unfortunately, you won't often have a lot of time to ask questions in a telephone interview. The interviewer is more interested in confirming facts than establishing a relationship at this point. There are, however, a few key questions that will help you understand the position:

⭑ "How would you describe the ideal candidate for this position?"

⭑ "What are the top-priority projects or tasks for this position in the next 3 to 6 months?"

⭑ "How does this position fit into the company's long-term plans?"

Notice that there are no questions about salary or benefits among these questions. It's more important at this stage that you learn how you can contribute value to the company or department. From the information you uncover, you can begin thinking about how you might approach the position and contribute value to the team or organization.

If the interviewer is open to answering more questions, you can proceed to uncovering whether the position is a good fit for you. To do so, listen carefully to the interviewer's description of the company and the position. Evaluate the information in light of the "Things That Matter" priorities you identified in chapter 2. Create questions that will help you better determine whether the position is aligned with your priorities. When doing so, make sure the questions are phrased in a manner that underlines *it's all about them, not me.* For instance, if personal development is near the top of your list of Things That Matter, avoid a question like this:

Before
"How will your organization provide opportunities for my personal development?"

Instead, this phrasing sounds more employer-oriented:

After
"I am committed to adding value to my employer by continually growing my skills. I do that by attending conferences, working with mentors, and tackling challenging projects…what kind of ongoing skill development do you like to see in your employees and how do you support that?"

A Dozen Must-Do's in Telephone Interviews

There are some unique disadvantages to telephone interviews to be aware of. For instance, you don't have the benefit of making eye contact or reading body language, nor is it as easy to hold someone's attention on the phone as it is in person. These 12 tips will help make your telephone time a success:

⭑ **Gather dashboard data:** You'll need the caller's name and title, company, address, telephone, and e-mail address for your thank-you letter and follow up. Asking for this information shows interviewers that you are alert and attentive to details.

* **Listen like a blind person:** You won't have the benefit of visual clues on the telephone. To truly hone in on what is being asked, consider closing your eyes to block out distractions. Another trick is to *silently* repeat a few sentences that the interviewer says (don't do this for more than a minute or two). This silent-echo technique will help you focus on what's being said.

* **Avoid background noises:** Children, animals, music, lawnmowers, and so on must all be silenced. One recruiter told me of a telephone call with a candidate who had a squawking parrot in the background. Not surprisingly, the candidate didn't win a face-to-face interview.

* **Use SMART Stories™:** Have your SMART Stories™ memorized or at hand. Interviewers will appreciate concise and specific responses to questions. Never omit the "R" in SMART—providing results will definitely set you apart from your competition.

* **Use verbal nods and avoid long pauses:** When face to face, you can smile, use eye contact, and nod your head to show a listener you are interested. Because you can't do these things on the telephone, use an occasional "I see" or "go on" or "I understand" to indicate that you're listening carefully. If you must pause to think of an answer, avoid "dead air" by saying something like, *"That's an interesting question."*

* **Be aware of your voice:** Is it too high? Too soft? Too loud? Tape record yourself to get an idea of what others hear. Listen for pitch, tone, volume, and attitude. Wear a smile and add warmth and enthusiasm to your voice (see "Tips for Adding Warmth and Energy to Your Voice" later in this chapter).

* **Monitor your talking:** Consider shortening the length of your responses a tad for telephone interviews. It's easy to lose a phone listener's attention because he or she may have visual distractions that you're not aware of. If you have a tendency to be a talker, pull back so that you don't dominate the conversation. A stopwatch or a small hourglass that measures one or two minutes of time may be just the thing to help you remember to keep responses crisp and brief.

* **Expect the unexpected:** You may be asked to participate in a role-play or answer questions that surprise you. If you need a few seconds to think on your feet, fill in the gap by repeating some of the interviewer's instructions. For instance, "Very good, let me review the scenario so that I'm clear on what you're describing." And then repeat a few of the steps.

* **Take notes:** Note-taking helps you remember the specifics of your conversation and makes you look like a great listener when you bring up important points from the telephone interview at the subsequent live interview.

* **Ask for a face-to-face meeting:** When the interviewer asks a particularly important question, respond with a request for a face-to-face meeting. "That's an important question, and one that I could answer more completely in person." And, if appropriate: "I have some interesting material that would shed more light on that subject. Is it possible to set up a meeting on Thursday or Friday?"

* **Close with a thank you:** Interviewers are typically busy people, with a full plate of responsibilities. Graciously thank them for taking the time out of their busy schedules to speak with you. For instance, "I'm sure that finding the right candidate is an important but time-consuming process. I just want to thank you for taking time from your schedule to speak with me and for setting up our next meeting. I'll look forward to the next steps."

* **Send a performance-based thank you:** Double up with an e-mail thank you (for speed) and a handwritten note (see chapter 12 for a sample of a performance-based follow-up letter).

Is English Your Second Language?

If you are a non-native English speaker interviewing with a native English speaker, you might be at a disadvantage. To help interviewers understand you, consider slowing down the pace of your speech, but not to the point that it puts people to sleep. Enunciate carefully and keep plenty of energy and enthusiasm in your voice. If your English is difficult to understand (ask a native English speaker to give you an honest appraisal of this), you might even say, "I am, of course, authorized to work in the U.S.…you can probably tell that English is relatively new to me—I'm taking evening classes [or working with a tutor] and making excellent progress. Please don't hesitate to ask me to repeat a response if needed." If excellent communication skills are critical to the job you're interviewing for, consider working with a speech coach.

How to Wrap Up the Telephone Interview

At the conclusion of the telephone interview, one of three things will happen:

✦ **Scenario A—Accepted:** You will be invited for a face-to-face interview. There is no doubt in the interviewer's mind that you met the criteria for the position.

✦ **Scenario B—Postponed:** You will be told that the results of your conversation will be reviewed before taking further action. This may not be good news for you. Don't lose heart, though. It may just be that you were the first person interviewed and the interviewers want to hear everyone before making a decision.

✦ **Scenario C—Declined:** You will be told that your qualifications are not suitable or that there is a lack of specific expertise or knowledge in your background.

What to Do When You Are Accepted

If it's Scenario A, congratulations! If the interviewer doesn't provide you with an outline of what to expect next, including whether you'll be required to take assessments, follow with this sort of response:

> "Thank you. I'm certainly looking forward to it. I wonder if you'd help me with a few things so that I can prepare properly."

In a light, conversational tone, ask some of these questions. Of course, wait for a response before asking each subsequent question.

- "Who will I meet with?" (Write down this information.)

- "And their titles?"

- "Will those be individual or group meetings?"

- "When would you be able to send me a job description?" (Instead of asking "if" you can see the job description, this question presumes that one already exists and that you are entitled to see it.)

- "How long should I schedule for the meeting?"

- "What dates and times do you have blocked out?" (This may give you an idea of how many candidates the interviewer will be seeing.)

- "Is it possible that we could make that appointment for as late in the day as possible?" (Sometimes candidates start to blur in the interviewers' minds. Making your interview the first thing or last thing in the day might help prevent this phenomenon!)

- "So that I can be prepared and make best use of everyone's time, what will the focus of our conversations be?"

If it's Scenario B, try these magic words:

> "Thank you for the opportunity to speak with you. This sounds like a position I could really contribute to based on my background in _____ and knowledge of _____ ."

What would you need from me to ensure I'm included on your short-list of candidates to interview? I'd like the opportunity to meet to discuss how I can contribute to some of the issues we discussed."

What to Do if You Are Declined

If it's Scenario C, try this last-ditch effort. Muster all the appreciation and enthusiasm you can, with absolutely no trace of pleading, whining, or resentment in your voice:

"Thank you for the opportunity to speak with you. This sounds like an ideal position based on the research I've done in _____ and my knowledge of _____ . Because I'm committed to contributing to your company in some way, whether immediately or down the road, I'd value a chance to meet with you and learn more about where I might fit in best—perhaps there are opportunities at a different level or in a different department. I'd value your guidance on what actions I can take to increase my ability to be a contributor. Or, perhaps there's someone in another department you'd like to direct me to."

Tips for Adding Warmth and Energy to Your Voice

One recruiter noted that "if a person is boring on the phone, he or she is boring in person…it never fails." To counter any semblance of boringness:

- Genuinely care about the interviewer at the other end of the line—this can add warmth to your voice more than anything. Think of this person as someone you'll be getting to know and building a relationship with in the future.

- Concentrate on the person you are talking to rather than your voice.

- Ar-ti-cu-late…that means remembering to clearly add the *-ing* to words like *going* (not *gonna*) and the *t* to the end of words like *went*, as well as pronouncing words like *Saturday* with a hard *t* (not *Sadurday*) and three clearly enunciated syllables.

- Smile (with your mouth and your eyes) when you speak to a telephone interviewer. A smile does come across in your voice.

- Stand up and use gestures during the call—it will increase your vocal energy.

- Breathe from your diaphragm, drop your voice several tones, and strive for chest resonance rather than nasal resonance.

- Focus on something positive. This might be one of your strengths or it might be something external, such as an inspirational role model, a loved one, or your favorite vacation getaway spot. If you're thinking negative thoughts, it will come across in your voice.

- Interject a favorite quote that will make you or your listener smile, such as "I'm a believer in Thomas Edison's philosophy, who said 'Everything comes to him who hustles while he waits.'"

Which of these tips will you need to practice or concentrate on? Consider posting reminders at your phone zone. Your adrenalin is guaranteed to pump during the phone interview—some proactive practice now will go a long way when it really counts.

Following a successful online screening and/or telephone interview, you'll be invited to a live interview where your competitors may number as many as a dozen. The components of the 4-C strategy to **C**onnect with your interviewers, **C**larify what the actual job is about, **C**ollaborate on strategies for results, and **C**lose the interview are found in chapters 10, 11, and 12. During this phase of the interview process, you may also be asked to complete formal assessments, which you read about in chapter 7.

Chapter Wrap-Up

Virtually any telephone conversation with a key networking contact, recruiter, or employer should be treated as an interview. Memorize one of the sentences in this chapter to buy time so that you don't get caught off guard and say something you'll later wish you hadn't. Remember to communicate with the mantra, "It's about them, not me." This simply means that you'll think from the employer's perspective and filter every situation with the question, "What does the employer need from me as a candidate and how can I meet their needs?"

Good employment situations should be a win-win for both the company and the employee. Focus first on what the employer needs—it's the secret to being less self-conscious and more relaxed throughout the screening process. And, once employers know you can meet their needs, they'll be more likely to accommodate yours!

10 Quick Tips for Telephone Interviews

1. Any telephone call from a recruiter, important networking contact, or employer is a form of an interview. Treat it accordingly.

2. Your goal for the telephone screen is to provide sufficient information and value to the employer so that you are offered a face-to-face interview. If you are not offered one, ask for one.

3. Listen like a blind person.

4. Avoid background noises, including pets, children, radio, music, vacuum cleaners, lawnmowers, and so on.

5. For telephone interviews, operate from a phone zone, a place where you can work in quiet and with concentration. Outfit your phone zone with your resume, Three-Point Marketing Message, verbal business card, SMART Stories™, company research, questions you'd like to ask the company, answers to questions you anticipate being asked, as well as business office paraphernalia (computer, PDA, notepad, pen, pencil, calculator, stickies, clock, water bottle, and so on).

6. For telephone interviews, add warmth to your voice by genuinely caring about the interviewer at the other end of the line. Use verbal nods and avoid long pauses.

7. Monitor your talking. The length of your responses should be a bit shorter than they would be for a face-to-face interview.

8. Add energy to your voice by articulating clearly (for example, "going" and not "gonna") or by standing up and gesturing.

9. Breathe from your diaphragm and strive for chest resonance rather than nasal resonance.

10. Close the phone interview with a warm thank you. Then, send a performance-based follow-up. Be sure to get the person's name and contact information for this purpose.

 Magical Coaching Questions

With respect to telephone interviews, who can help give you an honest, but humane, appraisal of your telephone voice and manner?

_____

Ask this person to rate you in each of these areas:

(continued)

(continued)

	Never True		Sometimes True		Always True
Telephone voice conveys warmth.	1	2	3	4	5
Telephone voice conveys energy (enough breath taken in to use the diaphragm to project the voice).	1	2	3	4	5
Pronounces words clearly and crisply (e.g., speakin' of makin' a presentation, we wen' tah… vs. speaking of making a presentation, we went to…).	1	2	3	4	5
Voice has chest (not nasal) resonance.	1	2	3	4	5
Voice is right volume (not too loud or soft).	1	2	3	4	5
Voice is right pitch (not too high).	1	2	3	4	5
Voice is interesting to listen to (not monotonous).	1	2	3	4	5
Speaks at a good pace (not too fast or slow).	1	2	3	4	5
Avoids verbal "pollution" (does not litter speech with phrases such as "you know" or terms such as "like" or "okay") or other distractions, such as frequent clearing of the throat.	1	2	3	4	5
Offers "verbal nods" to help telephone listeners know they are being heard.	1	2	3	4	5
Avoids long pauses or awkward silences.	1	2	3	4	5
Uses correct speech (avoids slang terms, double negatives, incorrect grammar, and so on).	1	2	3	4	5
Has a good "rate of exchange," allowing for two-way conversation with listener; not overtalking and dominating or, the opposite, under-talking and appearing taciturn.	1	2	3	4	5
Speaks with authority and confidence.	1	2	3	4	5
Communicates thoughts logically and persuasively.	1	2	3	4	5

Chapter 9

Score Points in Behavioral Interviews

No one is any better than you, but you are no better than anyone else until you do something to prove it.

—Donald Laird, American psychologist

Picture this scenario: You're a busy professional who needs help to accomplish your goals. Your success rests *solely* on finding someone who can competently do the things that need to be done. You've screened hundreds of candidates and now have eight willing souls vying for the position. How do you choose the right one?

Recruiting professionals, in their quest to source the very best candidate, have developed and finely tuned selection systems over the past several decades. The latest advancement in these selection systems is *behavioral interviewing*. It is based on the premise that relevant past behavior is the best predictor of future performance in a similar environment.

Behavioral interviewing helps prevent hiring managers from wrongly trusting their intuition or asking questions that don't help them objectively assess job-related skills, abilities, and motivation.

How to Spot a Behavioral Interview Question

As opposed to a series of disjointed, interrogative questions like you might find in a traditional interview, you will find that behavioral interview questions allow for a structured, logical conversational style. Behavioral questions frequently start with these phrases:

✴ Tell me/us about a time when you....

✴ Describe a situation where you....

✴ Give me/us an example of a time when you....

✴ How have you handled _____ in the past...?

✴ When have you had a situation where you had to...?

Behavioral questions can be very specific, such as the following:

✴ As a human resources professional, tell me about a time when you had to present a benefit program to a group of employees to win their buy-in. What was the outcome?

✴ As a nurse, tell me about a time you had to read a physician's illegible handwriting. What did you do?

✴ As a customer care representative, tell me about a process or system that you improved so customers would be better served.

✴ As an accountant, describe a time when you came across questionable accounting practices. How did you handle the situation?

Once you've answered the interviewer's anchor question, a series of probing questions might follow:

✴ What was your specific role?

✴ Who else was involved?

✴ How did you decide which task to do first?

✴ How did the outcome affect the company?

✴ What might you have done differently?

✴ How has that experience affected the way you would approach the situation today?

What Employers Look for in Behavioral Interviews

What are interviewers looking for with these anchor and probing questions? As the term "behavioral interview" implies, they're looking for *behaviors* that are equated with success. They're also after something even more important, the thing that's considered the driver of those behaviors: *competencies*. Competencies are capabilities, skills, and talents that make the behavior easy, enjoyable, and almost addicting. I call the feeling you get from doing work you are good at and love "the Tingle Factor!"

Michael A. Wirth, Director of Business and Application Development for Talent+, Inc., an international human resource consulting firm, offers a helpful illustration to shed some light on the difference between a behavior and a competency. Wirth noted that his grandmother keeps a spotlessly clean floor. She has a competency for cleanliness. When he enters his grandmother's house, he wipes his feet thoroughly, not because he values a spotlessly clean floor but because he wants to respect and please his grandmother. He can *behave* in a way that values cleanliness, but it's not his primary motivation.

The analogy is clear. If you want someone to manage a sterile operating room or a clean manufacturing environment, hire the grandmother. Other people might *behave* in a manner that keeps the place clean, but they may not have much *passion* about it. Competencies are the key to passion.

Sorting Out the Language

Although there are certainly distinctions between the many terms associated with behavioral interviewing, you can make it easy on yourself by considering these terms nearly synonymous: competencies, capabilities, abilities, skills, traits, and talents.

Some employers use the terms *competency-based interviewing* and *behavioral interviewing* interchangeably. Others consider competency-based interviewing a little different from behavioral interviewing because competency questions are future-focused ("What would you do if…") whereas behavioral questions are past-focused ("Tell me about a time when you…"). For the purposes of this book, we'll group both competency-based and behavioral interviewing into the same category.

How Employers Link Competencies to Interview Questions

How do interviewers determine what questions to ask? They must first conduct a thorough job analysis to identify relevant knowledge and skills. They will also look at top performers in a similar position and note what capabilities, or competencies, they possess. These competencies might be technical skills (such as proficiency in certain software programs) and performance skills (such as creativity or intuition).

50 Common Competencies in Demand by Employers

Because employers are looking for competencies in behavioral interviewing, you'll need to know which competencies are in demand. Following are 50 competencies that employers commonly seek.

1. Analyzing issues
2. Attitude/optimism/passion
3. Building relationships/ alliances
4. Building talent resources
5. Change innovation
6. Change management
7. Coaching/inspiring others
8. Collaboration
9. Communication
10. Confidence
11. Conflict management
12. Courage
13. Customer service
14. Decisiveness
15. Delegation
16. Detail-orientation
17. Diversity acumen
18. Ethics/integrity
19. Execution
20. Financial acumen
21. Flexibility/adaptability
22. Follow-up skills
23. Global perspective
24. Independence
25. Influencing others
26. Initiative/motivation*
27. Innovation/creativity
28. Interpersonal skills
29. Judgment
30. Leadership
31. Listening skills
32. Multitasking
33. Negotiation
34. Organization
35. Planning
36. Problem solving
37. Process improvement
38. Project management
39. Quality awareness
40. Quantitative analysis
41. Reliability/responsibility
42. Research skills
43. Self-management/self-learning
44. Sensitivity/intuition
45. Strategic thinking
46. Teamwork
47. Technical/technology skills
48. Tenacity
49. Time management
50. Writing

Initiative (also described as energy or drive) is listed by some recruiting experts as the universal trait of success.

Although this list covers many critical competencies identified by employers today, it is by no means exhaustive. If you were to pare the list to just the 10 most commonly sought competencies, you might find these:

1. Analytical skills

2. Communication skills (verbal/written/interpersonal)

3. Flexibility/adaptability

4. Initiative/drive/energy

5. Leadership skills

6. Planning skills

7. Problem-solving skills

8. Teamwork skills

9. Technical/technology skills

10. Time-management skills

NY Times Survey of Desired Skills

Beta Research Corporation, on behalf of The *New York Times Job Market*, interviewed 250 hiring managers in the New York metropolitan area to learn which skills were most in demand. They said:

- Ability to work in a team environment (89%)

- Ability to learn quickly (84%)

- Presentation/verbal communications (76%)

- Multi-tasking (73%)

- Time management (69%)

Skills most in demand for management candidates:

- Leadership (67%)

- Strategic Thinking (56%)

Skills most in demand for administration candidates:

- Technical (25%)

- Analytical (24%)

Skills most in demand for entry-level positions:

- Ability to learn quickly (32%)

(continued)

(continued)

Further, employers said they were willing to pay more money to candidates who have proficiency in the following:

- Multitasking (65%)

- Can quickly learn on the job (64%)

- Possess strategic thinking abilities (61%)

How Employers Use Competencies to Develop Interview Questions

Once employers pinpoint job-specific competencies, they can craft questions to elicit responses that will help them evaluate the candidate's past behavior.

There are three steps employers follow to get from competency to question:

1. They identify approximately 5 to 10 key competencies for the position. For example, a management candidate may need the capability to:

   - Analyze issues

   - Think strategically

   - Establish plans

   - Drive execution

   - Manage change

   - Build relationships

   - Engage and inspire people

   - Influence others

   - Promote corporate citizenship

   - Demonstrate initiative

2. Behaviors are then defined that describe each of these competencies. For instance, "establish plans" may be defined as *setting clear goals and direction during a project.*

3. From this definition of behavior, questions are teased out to determine whether the person regularly used those behaviors. For instance, they might ask, "Tell me about a time when you established goals and direction for a project."

Mining Job Descriptions for Competencies

It's wise to prepare for interviews by analyzing and making an educated guess as to which competencies the employer desires. Job postings and job descriptions can be an excellent source for identifying job-specific competencies. The following example highlights competencies seen in the Skills and Abilities section of an online job posting.

Position Summary:

Performs all general functions related to the receipt and management of work and service requests using a variety of custom-designed software tools. This includes answering phones, placing outbound service requests, maintaining work management queues, facilitating communication through e-mail, and directing calls to appropriate departments.

Skills and Abilities:

The successful candidate places primary importance on delivering superior customer service; demonstrates consummate people skills [interpersonal] and talent at interacting effectively with people; pursues work with insatiable energy and drive [initiative]; is self-motivated, and thrives on doing a job in a meticulous [detail oriented] and thorough manner and completes quality work on time; works independently, takes initiative, and demonstrates a desire to achieve; seeks out opportunities to help rather than waiting to be asked; minimizes non-productive time [initiative] and fills slow periods with activities that will enable preparation to meet the future needs of the company; has excellent attendance [work ethic], is punctual, and has a consistent professional appearance; has superior organizational skills, is flexible and can adjust to shifting priorities; proficient knowledge of computer programs [technical proficiency] such as Word, Excel, PowerPoint, and various custom-designed software.

In the preceding sample, I highlighted the key competencies in grey and, to help clarify, also inserted common competency terms in brackets. Based on the prior job posting, the employer is looking for these competencies in its next new hire:

- Customer service
- Interpersonal
- Initiative/self-motivation
- Detail oriented
- Work ethic
- Organizational
- Flexible
- Technical proficiency

When a candidate's key competencies are evaluated in an actual interview, the employer might use a form similar to the one in table 9.1.

Table 9.1: Interviewer's Candidate Assessment Form
Candidate's Competency/Skill Level

	1 (low)	2	3 (average)	4	5 (high)	Score
COMPETENCIES						
Customer service			✓			3
Interpersonal				✓		4
Initiative		✓				2
Detail-oriented					✓	5
Work ethic					✓	5
Organizational					✓	5
Flexible		✓				2
Technical			✓			3
OTHER FACTORS						
Experience & industry background				✓		4
Performance trend over time		✓				2
Education & credentials					✓	5
Personality & cultural fit		✓				2
TOTAL						42 out of possible 50

Note how the competencies, along with other factors, are listed in the far-left column. A rating scale of 1–5, with 1 being low and 5 being high, is used for each factor. The far-right column produces scores that can then be totaled. This particular candidate scored 42 out of a possible 50.

Linking Competencies to Your SMART Stories™

Recall from chapter 3 that you developed numerous SMART Stories™. Near the end of that chapter, we discussed leaving blank the "Tie-in/Theme" section on the SMART Story™ worksheet. Now is the time to link your competencies to your SMART Stories™. To do so, follow these steps:

1. Pull out job postings you've applied to (or a job description for an upcoming interview) and highlight the competencies. To aid in this process, review competency terms from the list of 50 common competencies earlier in this chapter. Are there terms in the list that apply to the job postings/description(s)?

2. Compile a master list of competencies from your job postings/descriptions.

3. Next, read through the SMART Stories™ you've written. What competencies are apparent in each story? Review your newly compiled master list or the 50 common competencies earlier in this chapter if you need help identifying competencies. For each SMART Story™, write out a few competencies in the Keywords & Competencies section (found near the bottom of the worksheet).

4. Finally, check to be sure that each of the competencies noted in your master list is illustrated in at least one of your SMART Stories™. This way, when an interviewer asks you to "Describe a situation when you demonstrated initiative" (or any other competency), you'll know which SMART Story™ to offer.

Wouldn't it be lovely if the interviewer would tell you what specific competencies he or she was looking for in the ideal candidate? It's not likely to be that easy. Employers are often hesitant to reveal the competencies they are seeking in a candidate. In *Recruiting, Interviewing, Selecting & Orienting New Employees* (American Management Association), author Diane Arthur advises interviewers "not to identify the qualities being sought in the desired candidate." The interviewer's concern, of course, is that candidates will tell them only what they want to hear.

To counter this, consider these magic words:

> I appreciate your need to make a sound hiring decision. I'll of course be as honest and helpful as I can because I want to make sure that this is the best fit for both of us. If you'd identify some of the key traits that are important for success in the position, I can better offer examples that will help you judge what type of an asset I can be.

Why SMART Stories™ Are Critical in Behavioral Interviews

During a behavioral interview, candidates are asked a series of standardized questions to elicit three key pieces of data:

* **Situation/circumstances:** What was the context in which the behavior or action took place?

* **Behavior:** What actions were actually taken in the situation?

* **Result/outcome:** What was the bottom line of the action taken?

These three segments correlate beautifully with the SMART Stories™ you developed in chapter 3. Recall that the SMART acronym stands for

Situation and **M**ore, **A**ction, **R**esult, and **T**ie-in/Theme. Here's how the SMART Story™ matches up with the three segments interviewers want to know:

- ⭐ **Situation/circumstances** equates to the SMART Story's™ **Situation and More.**
- ⭐ **Behavior** equates to the SMART Story's™ **Action taken.**
- ⭐ **Results/outcome** equates, of course, to the SMART Story's™ **Results.** After explaining results, follow with the **Tie-in/Theme**, where you can engage the interviewer with a relevant "tie-in" comment or question or underscore the theme (competency) of the story (for example, analytical skills).

Make Sure Your SMART Stories™ Are Complete

Be mindful of delivering solid SMART Stories™. Development Dimensions International, a respected leader in behavioral interview training, teaches interviewers to watch for three common *faux pas* made by candidates:

- ⭐ **Vague statements:** These are general statements that might sound good, but provide no specifics of what the person actually did.
- ⭐ **Opinions:** These are personal beliefs, judgments, or feelings about something that, like vague statements, provide no information about what the person actually did.
- ⭐ **Theoretical or future-oriented statements:** These tell what a candidate would do, would like to do, or would likely do in the future, but not what was actually done in the past.

Table 9.2 provides a comparison of SMART Story™ elements that illustrate some of the common mistakes.

Table 9.2: SMART Story™ Analysis

	Before	**After**
Situation and More:	*I was responsible for business development for my district.* [Here, the candidate makes the error of giving a vague statement that doesn't provide the context for the story.]	*I enjoy telling my "how-I-went-bald" story! It started with being given the charge by my senior VP to turn around a two-year history of double-digit declining revenues for the district. At the time, the district was ranked last among 17 for revenue performance and had been through four business development managers over the course of three years.*

	Before	**After**
Action:	*I think it's really important to involve team members in the process.* [The candidate provides an opinion, which is not necessarily wrong—just incomplete.] *I always take the time to find out what's happening in the district, and I've turned around a lot of districts that way.* [This is a vague statement.]	*Here's the storyboard. I piloted a new business development program for the district, which included creating sales strategies for a full complement of products and services (commercial loans, trust and investment services, cash management services, retirement and depository accounts, government guarantee programs, computerized banking, alliance banking). I scheduled a two-day meeting for the 30 branch managers in the district, and I used a very motivational "All-Star" theme. At the meeting, I created a vision for what could be accomplished, laid out the program, and then used interactive train-the-trainer systems so that they could teach the strategies to 150+ sales reps in the district. I laid down the challenge, telling them that if we reached our goal early, I would shave my head! I had already cleared this with the senior VP.*
Results:	*We met our goal, and actually exceeded it, with $16+ million in loan commitments approved.* [This sentence is accurate but lacks impact because no context or comparison is offered.]	*Bottom line, we secured 44 new customers with $16+ million in loan commitments approved, added nearly $4 million in deposits, and secured first-time fee revenue of $162,000 from establishing new international business. We broke all records for loan and deposit growth in the district's 30-year history and boosted the district's ranking from #17 among 17 to #2 in less than two years. And, yes, I was proud to be bald for a time!*
Tie-in/ Theme:	[Many candidates completely miss the opportunity to reemphasize the theme of the story or to tie in their response to the interviewer's desired competency.]	*My communication and motivational skills were foundational to this success. By the way, in visiting some of your branches, I had a few ideas about how fee-based revenue could be introduced.*

Note that the competency themes underscored in this story are leadership, motivation, innovation, strategy, analytical, and communications.

Action

Situation and More

Result and
Tie-in/Theme

Figure 9.1: Shape your SMART™ Story like a bell.

Be Mindful of the Shape of Your SMART Story™

Make your SMART Story™ bell-shaped. Note the picture of the Liberty Bell above.

The bulk of the mass is in the center of the bell. That's where the bulk of your information should be as you tell a story—spend more time on the Action. The lip on either side of the bell is analogous to the beginning (Situation and More) and ending (Result and Tie-in/Theme) of your SMART Story™. Spend less time on the Situation and Results. From the interviewer's perspective, the quality of a behavioral interview response rests in the details (Action) of what you did.

Vary the Length of Your Responses

Vary the length of your responses. For instance, if you've just answered a question that required a lengthy answer with lots of details, you may not want to provide as many details in your next response. You can gauge whether you're giving the interviewer enough information by tagging one of these questions onto your response:

- Would you like more details on that?

- Is that the kind of information you are looking for?

- Would you like another example?

- Two or three other examples come to mind that address that issue. They speak to times when I did _____ and _____ [fill in these blanks with relevant subject matter]. Would those be of interest to you now, or do you have enough information?

Chapter Wrap-Up

Given employers' successes with behavioral/competency-based interviewing, it's likely you'll encounter at least a few behavioral questions if not a full-blown behavioral interview in your job search. Welcome this type of interview because it allows you to be judged on your experience more than your interview stage presence. Behavioral interviews are more about substance than style!

10 Quick Tips for Behavioral Interviews

1. Behavioral interviewing is very common because it works! Its premise is that past behavior is the best indicator of future performance.

2. Recognize behavioral interview questions by introductory phrases such as "Tell me/us about a time when you…," "Describe a situation where you…," "Give me/us an example of…," or "In the past, how have you handled…."

3. Be prepared for very specific anchor questions, such as, "As an accountant, describe a time when you encountered unethical accounting practices. How did you handle it?"

4. After the anchor question, be prepared for probing questions, such as "What was your specific role?" "Who else was involved?" "How did you decide which task to do first?" "How did the outcome affect the company?" "What might you have done differently?" and "How has that affected the way you would approach the situation today?"

5. Competencies drive behavior. Competencies are capabilities, skills, and talents that make the behavior easy or enjoyable to perform.

6. Employers look at the behaviors of top performers in similar positions to identify competencies. If you want to move forward, model yourself after top performers.

7. There are more than 50 common competencies in demand by employers. Among the most important are initiative/drive/energy and communication skills.

8. Mine job postings and job descriptions to create a master list of key competencies for your target position.

9. Review your SMART Stories™ and note several competencies that are illustrated in the story.

10. Avoid making vague statements, giving opinions, or offering theoretical or future-oriented statements when delivering your SMART Story™.

Magical Coaching Questions

Practice delivering your SMART Stories™ to a colleague or friend. Use the following form to score yourself.

Practice Your SMART Stories™

	1 (low)	2	3 (average)	4	5 (high)	Score
Avoids vague statements						
Avoids opinions						
Avoids theoretical or future-oriented statements						
Situation and more described						
Action described						
Action comprises the bulk of the story						
Results are specific with numbers						
Competency theme or tie-in is present						

What are you doing right/well when delivering your SMART Stories™?

_____

_____

What part of your SMART Stories™ do you want to enhance?

_____

_____

What is one step you could take in the next 24 hours to make that happen? What will be the benefit of doing so?

_____

_____

Connect with the Interviewer—How to Create the Right Chemistry

Most conversations are simply monologues delivered in the presence of a witness.

—Margaret Miller

Interviewing is about helping others (the employer) become more successful while also moving your career forward into an ideal state (for example, gaining meaningful employment, adequate remuneration, responsibility, recognition, and so on). To better understand how that happens, we can turn to a coaching framework. The model we'll use involves four C's:

- Phase 1: Connect
- Phase 2: Clarify
- Phase 3: Collaborate
- Phase 4: Close

You'll note that interviewers structure interviews roughly in this manner, although perhaps not consciously. At the beginning of the face-to-face interview, they *Connect* with you so that you'll be able to relax and be yourself;

they'll also be evaluating the subjective chemistry between you and the interview team. They then *Clarify* whether you can do the job. In some instances, they ask you to *Collaborate* on how to get the job done. And, if they sense that you can get the job done, they *Close* the deal.

As a candidate, you can also follow this format, but with a slightly different perspective. Your job will be to

✦ *Connect* with the interviewer to enhance chemistry.

✦ *Clarify* the primary deliverables of the job (what needs to be done).

✦ *Collaborate* on how you would do the job.

✦ *Close* in a respectful manner that indicates your desire for the position and commitment to the company.

In this chapter, we'll focus on the all-important first phase of Connecting. We'll save *Clarify* and *Collaborate* for chapter 11, and *Close* for chapter 12.

Phase 1: Connect with the Interviewer

Recall from chapter 1, Truth #8, that you will be judged by your interviewers on three dimensions: Chemistry, Competency, and Compensation. This first dimension—Chemistry—is critical. You'll want to connect with the company's mission, its people, and its customers. You'll also want the interviewer to connect with you!

You've heard the phrases before: "We really connected"…"Talk about chemistry—we just clicked!"…"There's something about her—I just feel a good connection." On the other end of the scale are comments like these: "Boy, I don't know, there seemed to be a big disconnect…I just couldn't seem to relate to him"…"Like oil and water don't mix—we just didn't connect."

What does it mean to connect with someone? To get clear on this, think about someone in your work world with whom you connect well. When you speak to this person, what is present in the conversation? When you interact, how does this person behave? Chances are good that, in addition to having some things in common, the person you're thinking of respects you, supports you, and is a good listener and communicator. You can do the same in your interview.

Follow the 6 Keys to Connecting

To connect with interviewers, do the following:

A Simple Connecting Device: Live Life on Lombardi Time

The famed football coach Vince Lombardi invented a strategy that he recommended to his coaches and players. It came to be known as Lombardi Time and embodied a valuable habit that will serve you well as a candidate and career professional. Lombardi Time means to show up for any important meeting 15 minutes ahead of the scheduled time. During those 15 minutes, you can catch your breath, collect your thoughts, and get focused on what you want to accomplish. During this time, you can also visit the restroom and check your appearance, making sure that ties (or lipstick!) are on straight. While you're there, hop up and down on one foot and recall your value by stating some of the buying motivators developed in chapter 4. This will purge any nervous energy, get blood flowing to your brain, and fill your heart and mind with positive thoughts.

1. **Clear the 30-second hurdle with a positive halo effect:** Psychologists divide job interviews into two parts. Dr. Joyce Brothers refers to the first part as the "30-second hurdle"—a crucial half-minute where most employers make up their minds about a candidate based on the halo effect. This phenomenon refers to an interviewer's first impression of you, which can be negative or positive. A positive halo effect can help people think you are even better than you are. A negative halo effect will make it virtually impossible to ace the second part of the interview, which is everything after the first 30 seconds! You can predispose people to like you by wearing an engaging smile, shaking hands firmly, dressing appropriately, and making the person feel that you are absolutely delighted to meet them. You can also put on a halo by associating yourself with a trusted colleague or friend of the interviewer—this is where networking can really work for you!

Religious Reasons for Not Shaking Hands

If your religion prevents you from shaking hands with women, be consistent in your action. Avoid shaking hands with both women and men to avoid the appearance of favoritism. If asked, "Is there a religious reason why you chose not to shake hands?," state briefly, "Yes, that's the only reason. I intended no ill will because of it."

2. **Share something in common:** When entering an interviewer's office, notice your surroundings. It may be that you can make small talk

about the interviewer's awards on the wall, interesting artwork, pictures of kids, plants, tidy desk, out-of-the-ordinary furniture, and so on. A terrific way to share something in common is to comment on the interviewer's background based on the company research you've done. (Note the openers in the upcoming sidebar.) Another bonding agent is laughter—share it whenever possible.

Be Ready with Openers to Connect with Interviewers

If meeting new people makes you nervous, practice an opener to help you feel more in control. One of these may suit you well:

- "It's so nice to meet you. Congratulations on your latest article. I loved your point about _____ [fill in the blank…using recycled materials, going to a flex-time model, mastering the art of spiel, etc.]"

- "Nice to meet you." Then, if the interviewer's desk is cluttered with family photos, consider saying, "It looks like you've got a budding baseball star there!"

- "I've so looked forward to meeting you. I really enjoyed the presentation you gave at the Widget-Makers Conference last fall."

- "I'm pleased to meet you. I have to tell you that everyone I've met to this point has been nothing but first-class. Your assistant has been especially helpful."

- "Great to meet you. I noticed your company's recent mention in the paper. I hope we'll have time to talk a bit about that."

- "Great to meet you. Jane [your insider contact] has spoken so highly of you. She tells me you've really made some significant strides with your recent program. I'll look forward to hearing more about that."

- "Lovely to meet you. I hear you're an admirer of Egyptian art. I've dabbled in collecting myself."

- "Good to see you again. The last time we spoke was at the regional industry meeting. Did you get to all the breakout sessions you'd hoped to? Which session did you get the most from?"

- "Good to see you again. I'll be interested to catch up on what you've been doing since we last spoke."

- [And, if you have no clue about who the person is] "So glad to meet you. I've been looking forward to better understanding your organization and where I can be of value."

3. **Respect them:** Acknowledge that interviewers likely have demanding schedules and difficult work. Respect them for the position of authority they have earned. You do not have to agree with them on everything. You do, however, need to recognize that they may see, hear, feel, and interpret the world differently and therefore behave differently than you. Seek to respect others first…it's the fastest way to earn it in return.

4. **Support them:** Make the interviewer's job easier by helping them find the right person for the position. You'd probably like it if *you* were that person, and you should do everything in your power to show that you are! If, however, you're not, consider doing what one new grad did when he recognized he wasn't going to fit the needs of a particular department manager. He gave the manager the names of two classmates who he thought would be ideal candidates. Talk about making a lasting impression!

5. **Listen with laser accuracy:** It is impossible to connect with others if you don't listen well. Good listening is fueled by curiosity and compassion.

6. **Communicate exceptionally:** Respond with relevance and an attitude of respect. Recognize that your interviewer's learning style, values, and personality will impact your communication.

Take the 25-Point Communication Check

To better gauge your listening and communication skills, take the 25-Point Communication Check in table 10.1. Take this inventory yourself and then get a third-party perspective by asking a trusted friend or colleague to also rate you.

Table 10.1: 25-Point Communication Check

In business settings, I...				
1. Am complimented for being a good listener.	Seldom	Occasionally	Often	Habitually
2. Allow others to finish their statements before responding.	Seldom	Occasionally	Often	Habitually
3. Allow give-and-take to conversations, where I listen as much as and usually more than I speak.	Seldom	Occasionally	Often	Habitually
4. Remain open to the listener's message rather than assume what I want to hear.	Seldom	Occasionally	Often	Habitually
5. Read between the lines, considering the speaker's values, priorities, and needs.	Seldom	Occasionally	Often	Habitually
6. Avoid thoughts of "right-ness"...that my way of thinking is right or better than the speaker's.	Seldom	Occasionally	Often	Habitually
7. Am respectful of and open to new ideas, not allowing differences in political, social or religious beliefs to distract me from what the speaker is saying.	Seldom	Occasionally	Often	Habitually
8. Look past the irritation to the need when a speaker expresses emotions such as anger or frustration.	Seldom	Occasionally	Often	Habitually
9. Ignore verbal distractions (such as incorrect grammar, generational differences in language, regional accents, or profanity).	Seldom	Occasionally	Often	Habitually
10. Pay attention to body language and tonality to help me get the gist of the speaker's feelings.	Seldom	Occasionally	Often	Habitually
11. Remain fully "present" for the speaker—attentive, interested, curious, and interactive.	Seldom	Occasionally	Often	Habitually

12. Avoid multitasking, such as watching some other activity in the room, reviewing e-mail, clearing my desk, and so on.	Seldom	Occasionally	Often	Habitually
13. Listen for clues on how a speaker prefers to take in information (sequentially/tangibly vs. intuitively/conceptually).	Seldom	Occasionally	Often	Habitually
14. Listen for clues on how a speaker prefers to make decisions (from a thinking/rational perspective vs. a feeling/human-effect perspective).	Seldom	Occasionally	Often	Habitually
15. Keep emotions in check when listening and do not allow emotions to drive my responses.	Seldom	Occasionally	Often	Habitually
16. Use appropriate eye contact and body language when listening.	Seldom	Occasionally	Often	Habitually
17. Use appropriate eye contact, facial animation, and body language when speaking.	Seldom	Occasionally	Often	Habitually
18. Do not steer the conversation toward my agenda or make it about me.	Seldom	Occasionally	Often	Habitually
19. Ask the speaker to clarify if I am not clear on what was said.	Seldom	Occasionally	Often	Habitually
20. Outline the speaker's key points to be certain I understand the message.	Seldom	Occasionally	Often	Habitually
21. Consider whether my response will be relevant to the speaker (in other words, avoid too many extraneous details or too many stories about myself).	Seldom	Occasionally	Often	Habitually
22. Consider the best approach to sharing, so that the speaker finds personal benefit in my response.	Seldom	Occasionally	Often	Habitually
23. Am accurate and concise in my responses.	Seldom	Occasionally	Often	Habitually
24. Keep the conversation focused so that important issues are prioritized.	Seldom	Occasionally	Often	Habitually
25. Respect and appreciate others prior to expecting the same for myself.	Seldom	Occasionally	Often	Habitually

Something magical happens to a relationship when you listen fully—speakers sense that they are important to you, interesting, valued, and respected. They'll then want to extend to you the same respect. This process is foundational to connecting.

L.I.S.T.E.N. Like a Laser

To connect with interviewers as you listen, remember these LISTENing tips:

* **L—Laser your focus.** Lock out distractions and lock on to the whole question, not just a small piece of it. Remain fully present: Look into the speaker's eyes (alternately shift your focus from one eye to the other to avoid staring). Don't multitask (eat, take a phone call, answer e-mail) or drift mentally to your next pressing appointment or any other concern that's on your mind.

* **I—Investigate.** Be curious. Probe beyond the surface…move beyond listening "to" the speaker to listening "for" (empathetically) the speaker's meaning, motives, feelings, priorities, values, perspective, and needs. Further, ask yourself, "How might this person think? Do they take in information in a sequential/sensing mode or in a conceptual/intuitive mode? Do they make decisions from a logical/thinking perspective or a human relations/feeling perspective?" It's impossible to be a good listener without being genuinely interested in the other person.

* **S—Silence your tongue!** Hold judgment and listen with an open mind. Don't take things personally. If what the speaker is saying makes you defensive, irritated, or nervous, there's a greater chance you'll miss the main point. Let the other person finish their sentences. Be comfortable with a little silence in the conversation.

* **T—Take brief notes.** If clarification is needed, repeat the interviewer's question or statement. Take time to formulate your response.

* **E—Elevate the other person.** Good listeners make the other person feel significant, valued, and respected. Act professionally, but resist the urge to be right, show off, or act brilliant with all the right answers. As a candidate, you're there to be a professional solution. Remember the mantra, *"It's about them, not me."*

* **N—Note the nonverbals.** Mirror the body language of your speaker. Does the speaker's body language indicate stress, confusion, frustration, or boredom? If so, how can you respond to improve the situation? Lean forward slightly to show interest.

The Hawthorne Experiments—How Listening Improves Productivity

In the 1920s, General Electric had preliminary evidence that better lighting of the work place improved worker productivity. Wanting to validate these findings to sell more lightbulbs, GE funded the National Research Council (NRC) to conduct an impartial study. AT&T's Western Electric Hawthorne plant in Illinois was chosen as the laboratory. Beginning with this early test, the "Hawthorne Experiments" were a series of studies into worker productivity. The initial study explored the relationship between lighting intensity and worker productivity. The study failed to find any simple relationship, as both poor lighting and improved lighting resulted in increased productivity.

Western Electric's superintendent of inspection suggested that the reason for increased worker productivity was simply that the researchers had shown an interest in—listened to—the workers. This premise ushered in a new era of management theory, breaking from the school of thought that worker productivity was purely a "mechanical" or engineering issue and introducing the concept of "human relations" or social dynamics to impact worker performance.

R.E.S.P.O.N.D. with Relevance and Respect

You can also connect with interviewers by RESPONDing well:

- **R—Remember your objective.** It is to gain employment by educating the interviewer of *your value*. Everything that comes out of your mouth should be *relevant* to this objective. Single-mindedly stay on course with your responses. Be selective about how much you say. Resist the urge to tell all, over-explain, or apologize for any shortcomings.

- **E—Engage the interviewer.** Eye contact, open body language, facial animation, and appropriate gestures are important. Reflect back and confirm your understanding of what is being said. Ask open and closed questions (see "Clarify" in chapter 11). You can also engage interviewers by addressing their different learning styles—such as auditory, visual, and kinesthetic.

- **S—Share succinctly.** Know what your point is, and get to it quickly.

- **P—Point to benefits.** Benefits are the single greatest influencer in communicating your value—the ability to be of benefit to the employer's bottom line, productivity, problems, and so on. Frame your comments in light of how you will benefit the employer. Occasionally, offer what broadcasters refer to as a tease: "I'd love to tell you about how our team went from 82 percent to 99.9 percent accuracy in 30 days. Let me set the stage for you. We had a challenging situation where…".

★ **O—Offer proof.** Whenever you're making a claim about certain skills, make it stand up in court. For instance, instead of saying "I can help your company be more efficient based on my experience and commitment," substantiate your statement: *"I served on a process improvement task force that delivered a 30 percent productivity increase for my last employer, and I'm completely confident that similar productivity gains can be achieved here, as well."*

★ **N—Never drone on.** Two to three minutes seems to be the extent of many people's attention span. After this point, your response has the potential to morph from terrific to tedious. If delivering a SMART Story™, consider a pulse check in the middle of your story to keep interviewers awake and interested. For instance, after describing the situation and action in the SMART Story™, ask "Would more detail be helpful?" Or, "I understand you're experiencing something similar in your department." Or, "Would you like to hear about scenario A or scenario B?"

★ **D—Dedicate yourself to a win-win relationship.** Never manipulate a conversation toward a selfish agenda. Let mutual benefit be your goal.

Quell the Urge to Over-Tell

Have you ever been around someone who regularly tells you more than you need to know? Or, someone who insists on proving they're right? These people suffer from the social ill of over-telling. You don't want to be one of these people on an interview. Situations that prompt the urge to tell include nervousness, passion about your subject, and uncomfortable silence. It's natural to talk more when you're nervous or passionate about your subject, so be aware and pull back on the reins. Learn to be comfortable with silence—stop talking after you've delivered your SMART Story™ or short response—and wait patiently for the interviewer to ask another question.

Telltale signs of over-telling include seeing a glazed look in the interviewer's eye, a yawn, finger or pencil tapping, boredom, or distraction. Re-engage the interviewer by asking a question. Listen. Then refocus on what's more important to the interviewer. *Make it about them, not you!*

Preparing Interviewers for Special Circumstances

Special circumstances are conditions that might cause you to get labeled with a negative halo effect.

Physical Appearance

What should you do if you have a physical situation that might take the interviewer aback? Noted careers author and speaker Denise Bissonette tells the story of working as a job placement specialist and helping a gentleman with special circumstances prepare for interviews. The individual had nearly half his face obliterated by a land mine in Viet Nam and, at first glance, his face was quite disturbing to see. After Bissonette arranged the interview date and time, she said this to the interviewer: "By the way, there's something I want to tell you about Mr. Jones. You see, he nearly died after stepping on a land mine in Viet Nam. His face is quite disfigured, and it will take you some time to get used to. In fact, it took me about a week before I got over it. But after that time passed, I was able to focus on who he was and the talent he possesses. I know you and your staff will come to find the same thing to be true after a week or so."

If your situation is something that may cause interviewers to be surprised or uncomfortable, consider a similar strategy.

Age Discrepancy Between Candidate and Interviewer

If the interviewers are significantly younger than you are and you sense they are uncomfortable about it, make a comment that will put them at ease. For instance, weave into the conversation something along these lines: "It's great to have young, sharp people on staff to blend with older people with more experience. It's been my experience that this brings balance and advantages to a company."

A Surprise Interview Requirement: Is Your Car Clean?

Some interviewers incorporate into their interviews a request that the candidate drive them somewhere. This gives interviewers insights into several areas:

1. How you manage behind the wheel (are you a courteous, alert driver?)

2. How you care for your major property (is the vehicle clean and well maintained?)

3. What your values are (what kind of car do you drive or have you chosen as an extension of your self image?)

An Inexperienced Interviewer

Occasionally you'll encounter an interviewer who doesn't know what to ask beyond, "So, tell me about yourself." This often happens in very small companies where interviewers may not have been trained in interviewing. Take charge of the interview and make the interviewer look good anyway, without acting superior or condescending. Comments such as the following are good starters:

    ★ "I'm sure you are interested in knowing how I can add value to the company" (or save the company money, increase revenues, build market share, and so on).

    ★ "You are probably wondering what attracted me to this position."

Check Your Motive and Attitude

Speech coach Brenda Besdansky of SpeakersWorld.com is fond of quoting Louis Armstrong: "It's not the watcha say but the howcha say it." You've likely experienced a horrible *howcha:* a boss delivers bad news in a callous, matter-of-fact way or a friend corrects you with a judgmental, condescending tone, and it just doesn't hit you right. It wasn't *what* was said; it was *how* it was said. Voice tone, inflection, and motive make all the difference in increasing the receptivity of your interviewer. Check yourself with the following before-and-after examples to make sure you're in the "after" camp:

Before

■ Tone and inflection that doesn't work: whining, begging, manipulating, sarcasm, arrogance, condescension, self-centeredness

After

■ Tone and inflection that does work: respect, confidence, deference, concerned curiosity, attentiveness, thoughtfulness

Before

■ Motive that doesn't work: "I'll tell them anything they need to hear just to get the job." Interviewers see through this! Or, "I've been screwed in the past, and it's my turn now—you owe me this job." Now honestly, would you invite someone with this attitude to join your team?

After

■ Motive that does work: "I'll explore what they need and promote myself 100 percent if it's a good fit both for me and for them." (If it's not a good fit, you should explore whether the position could be tweaked so that you can still be of value.)

Use the Mirroring Technique

Mirroring is a neurolinguistic programming (NLP) technique designed to enhance communication. The principle is to match aspects of your interviewer's voice, mannerisms, and body language. For instance:

- If the interviewer greets you with perfect posture in a brisk, businesslike tone and says, "Jane Doe, good to meet you," then stand up straighter and respond briskly with "John Dokes, good to meet you!"

- If the interviewer uses hand gestures to explain something, feel free to use hand gestures when speaking.

- If the interviewer leans forward to emphasize a point, subtly lean forward to listen.

- If the interviewer asks questions slowly and softly, respond in a similar volume and pace (but be cautious to not speak too slowly or too softly—you want to convey energy and be audible).

- If the interviewer is cold and businesslike and refers to a lot of technical jargon, data, and source material, cite data and source material in your answers and don't attempt to win him or her over by being warm and fuzzy.

The point is not to mimic the speaker, but to match his or her style without losing your personality in the process. Of course, there are some situations where mirroring would not be called for—for instance, when a speaker is angry or emotional. Also, resist the urge to mirror any behaviors that wouldn't win an etiquette award, such as slouching or scratching!

The 7-38-55 Myth about Communication

A number of communications trainers spout statistics that the actual words we use account for only 7 percent of our communication, whereas 38 percent of the message is conveyed by tonality and 55 percent by body language. If that were so, why do candidates have to do so much explaining in interviews?

Curiosity got the better of me, so I went looking for the original source of those numbers. Albert Mehrabian, Ph.D., of UCLA conducted the research with Susan Ferris, the results of which were published in the

Journal of Consulting Psychology (Vol. 31, 1967) and then later in his book, *Silent Message* (Wadsworth Publishing Company, 1971). In both works, Mehrabian explains that the percentages apply only to what he calls the resolution of inconsistent messages, and not normal communications. In fact, his research centered on just one word: maybe. Mehrabian instructed third-party observers to interpret tape-recorded voices paired with photographs to determine whether the speaker's attitude in using the word maybe was one of like, neutrality, or dislike. Observers pointed to body language 55 percent of the time as most helpful in determining attitude, tonality 38 percent of the time, and the actual word only 7 percent of the time.

When it comes to telephone conversations, Jeannie Davis in her book *Beyond Hello* (Now Hear This Inc., 2000) claims that tonality accounts for approximately 70 percent of communication, with the actual words representing 14 to 20 percent of the message. Body language, though it can't be seen, still accounts for between 10 and 16 percent of the message.

Connect with Different Interviewers

A number of factors impact communication, such as one's learning style, personality, values, and priorities. The remainder of this chapter is devoted to better understanding these issues.

Connect with Different Learning Styles

Interviewing involves *educating* your interviewer about the value you bring to the table. Educators are aware that people have different learning styles. Some books on the subject identify as many as a dozen learning styles. For the sake of simplicity, we'll boil them down to three primary categories:

- Auditory
- Visual
- Kinesthetic/tactile

How do you figure out how your interviewer learns best? Table 10.2, adapted from Colin Rose's *Accelerated Learning* (Dell Publishing Company, 1987), will help clue you in to the various learning styles. You can start by identifying your preferred style. Although you may identify with multiple styles, you will usually have one predominant style.

Table 10.2: How to Connect with the Three Learning Styles

Activity	Auditory Learning Style	Visual Learning Style	Kinesthetic/ Tactile Learning Style
Words and phrases used	Uses words such as *hear*, *tune*, and *think* or phrases such as *sounds good*, *I hear what you're saying*, or *let me hear your explanation of that*.	Uses words such as *see*, *picture*, and *imagine*, or phrases such as *it looks to me as though*, or *let me get a clearer picture on that*, or *can you shed some more light on that subject for me?*	Uses words such as *feel*, *gut feeling*, and *comfortable*, and phrases such as *something doesn't feel right*, *feels good*, or *there is/isn't a good connection there*.
Language	Likes to hear factual, sequential thought processes, with steps outlined in a logical, linear fashion	Likes to hear descriptive language to help create a picture in their mind	Likes language that is conceptual or abstract; likes hearing metaphors; may describe knowing something to be true in their "bones" without being able to explain it logically to others
When learning new things at work	Prefers verbal instructions or talking about it with a colleague… needs to hear it to know it	Prefers seeing demonstrations, diagrams, or pictures; likes things in view, with items color-coded… needs to see it to know it	Prefers a hands-on, learn-as-you-do process…needs to do it to know it
When meeting someone again	May forget the face but remember the name or what was talked about at the last meeting	May forget the name but remember the face	May remember what was done together or the feeling associated with the last meeting

(continued)

(continued)

Activity	Auditory Learning Style	Visual Learning Style	Kinesthetic/ Tactile Learning Style
When learning a new term	Likes to repeat the word	Likes to see the word	Likes to write or spell it out
Translation of thoughts	Will pick up a thought and hear it as a word	Will pick up a thought and see it as a picture	Will pick up a thought and feel it as a sensation or associate it with some other memory
Preference for business meetings	Can get just as much out of a telephone meeting as a face-to-face meeting	Prefers face-to-face meetings	Prefers meetings that involve an activity
Distractions	Stays focused on conversation and is not easily distracted by other activity in the room	Notices other activity in the room	Is easily distracted by activity around the room
Note-taking behavior	May take minimal or no notes	Takes notes; often doodles on the page	Takes copious notes

Did you see yourself in one column more than another? Most interviewing emphasizes the auditory learning style (discussing) and to a lesser degree, the kinesthetic style (taking notes). If your interviewer is an auditory learner, it's to your benefit. However, your interviewer may be a visual or kinesthetic learner. To cover all the bases, address the preferences of visual and kinesthetic learners by doing the following:

- Showing work samples

- Drawing an illustration of what you mean on a sheet of paper or white board

- Doing a demonstration that involves the interviewer

- Alternating your language to appeal to each learning style, such as
  - **Auditory:** "How does that sound?" or "Do those steps I just described sound on track? What additional data would you like to hear?"

- **Visual:** "How does that look?" or "With the ideal person in the position, what would this department look like?"

- **Kinesthetic/Tactile:** "Have I been able to give you a feel for how I would perform in the position?" or "Would you like me to touch on a few more ideas?"

What Is Your Body Language Saying?

How you walk, stand, sit, and use body language all add to the overall impression you make! Pay attention to these items:

- **Walk:** Walk into a room as you if belong there—confident and alert. (Women, heed the advice of film stars for making an entrance—enter a room with your hips first. Doing so improves your posture and carriage.) Avoid exiting a room with your back to people. If possible, walk to the door with your interviewer; or, turn toward the interviewer as you head for the door and say something like, "It was nice meeting you" or "I'll be sure to get you that follow-up information by Friday."

- **Stand:** Shoulders square, chest out, stomach held in, head held high. My old marching band instructor used to holler during practice: "skyhooks in your ears…skyhooks in your ears"—a somewhat uncomfortable reminder to stand tall, with heads held high!

- **Sit:** Men, no crossed legs or slouching in the chair. Women, sit like royalty—spine straight and legs crossed at the ankle, not the knee. Shoulders back—when they're hunched forward, it indicates a lack of interest or feelings of inferiority.

- **Lean:** Lean forward slightly (without hunching your shoulders, of course!) as a sign of interest.

- **Eye contact:** Make appropriate eye contact. Avoid staring by looking from one eye to the other, and "smile" with your eyes. If asked a difficult question (for instance, "Who was your worst boss and why?"), keep your eye contact steady. Glancing away or not looking into the interviewer's eyes as you answer is a sign of untruthfulness. If speaking with an interviewer outdoors, avoid wearing sunglasses as this can give the image of being evasive or shifty.

- **Eyebrows:** Relax your eyebrows—tension in eyebrows indicates confusion, stress, or fear.

(continued)

(continued)

- **Mouth:** Mind your mouth! Downward turns or flat lines in the mouth can put people off, while a smile or upward turns in the mouth indicate that you welcome interaction.

- **Head:** Keep head movements to a minimum. Nod occasionally to indicate that you're listening.

- **Arms and hands:** Arms crossed indicates that you are protecting your body. Fidgeting with fingers or a pen indicates that you are agitated or bored, or possibly that you are anxious to say something. When interviewing, remember to keep your hands below your shoulders—no touching the face, nose, or ears; no rubbing your chin; no scratching your head; and so on.

- **Gestures:** To emphasize your key points, consider small hand gestures. When the interviewer is speaking, keep your body still as a sign that you are listening intently.

- **Personal distance:** Be attuned to individuals' personal space—the distance is different for everyone. Try this test: Walk toward a business colleague and maintain eye contact as you move closer. The second you cross into the person's boundary of personal space, their eyes will dart away, telling you you've gotten too close.

- **Nervous activity:** Physical tension in the body may present itself in the form of nail-biting, playing with hair, chewing gum, grinding teeth, or jiggling a leg or foot. One trick for channeling nervous energy that won't be noticed by interviewers is to drive the fingernail from your index finger into the flesh of your thumb on the same hand. Press to the point of creating pain. You'll find it difficult to carry on other, more noticeable nervous movements at the same time.

Connect with Different Temperaments

For centuries, philosophers and observers of human behavior have identified four distinct personality types, or temperaments. Hippocrates spoke of the *choleric, melancholic, phlegmatic,* and *sanguine* temperaments, whereas Plato used the terms *philosopher, guardian, scientist,* and *artisan.* Present-day terms are *idealist, guardian, rational,* and *artisan.* Though different names have been used over the years, there is agreement about the strengths, needs, and values of each group. Understanding the basics around each group will help you appreciate what's most important to them and craft your message so that there is maximum receptivity.

Information from table 10.3 is gleaned from the Myers-Briggs Type Indicator®, David Keirsey's *Please Understand Me II* (Prometheus Nemesis Book Company, 1998), and Dr. Linda Berens' work on temperament. Note that the two-letter heading beneath each temperament corresponds to the letters outlined in chapter 2. Based on the type you identified in chapter 2, you will be able to identify your own temperament here.

Connect with Different Types of Interviewers

Beyond different learning styles, people also have different interviewing styles. In his book, *Hire with Your Head* (John Wiley & Sons, Inc., 2002), Lou Adler teaches interviewers to recognize their default interviewing style, whether emotional, intuitive, or technical. "Interviewers have a tendency to hire in their own image," says Adler. For instance, logic-driven, all-business executives have a tendency to hire logic-driven, all-business candidates. Creative, spontaneous managers have a tendency to hire creative, spontaneous candidates. Instead, advises Adler, it is wiser to hire people who complement the team.

Table 10.4 describes Adler's three interviewer styles. In the right column, I've offered suggestions for what you can do to connect with each type.

Adler proposes that most interviewers are a combination of emotional plus either intuitive or technical. The best combination is intuitive and technical, with an emphasis on gathering performance-based answers from the candidate. Your SMART Stories™ will be critical in this process.

Connect with Different Levels of Interviewers

Companies that do a good job of interviewing make it standard practice for you to meet with a number of people in the organization. Each of these people has a different agenda, as table 10.5 reveals.

How to Tell Whether Someone Is Lying

Although interviewers may be watching you for signs of stretching the truth, you can also observe them to gauge their honesty. Intelligence analysts claim that when people are lying, their eyes will look up and to the left. Other signs to watch for include a sudden change in body posture; an increase in the number of verbal delays (such as, "umm," "errr," or "and-ah"); a change in pitch or rate of speech; sudden jiggling of a foot or leg; or facial expressions that are incongruous with the person's words. So, when you ask an important question, such as, "Do you anticipate any reductions-in-force or reorganizations in the next 6 to 12 months?," observe the interviewer closely!

Table 10.3: Values of the Four Personality Temperaments

	Idealist (NFs, or iNtuiting-Feeling)	Guardian or Traditionalist (SJs, or Sensing-Judging)	Rational or Conceptualizer (NTs, or iNtuiting-Thinking)	Artisan or Experiencer (SPs, or Sensing-Perceiving)
How to identify	Values personal growth and interested in bringing meaning, wholeness, and harmony to people's lives. Creative, intuitive, ethical, sympathetic, insightful. Often drawn to counseling, social work, professional coaching, and facilitator roles.	Typically takes pleasure in playing by the rules, bringing order and structure to organizations, following chain of command, and doing the right thing. Often drawn to management, engineering, programming, and technical roles.	Persistently and consistently rational in their actions. Analytical, systematic, competent, efficient, exacting, and independent. Understands abstract or complex, theoretical ideas. Often drawn to management or executive roles.	Lives for action, adventure, and the present moment. Risk taker. Likes autonomy, action, variety, and freedom for spontaneity. Stays open to possibilities. Stores up useful facts. Often drawn to performer, crisis management, sales, or negotiator roles.
How to connect with	Acknowledge the importance of harmony in work relationships and an ideal, meaningful work environment. Use metaphors to drive home points. Be thoughtful around an Idealist!	Deliver factual, reality-based responses in a sequential, logical, detailed fashion. Value stability, rules, regulations, and conformity. Be respectful around a Guardian or Traditionalist!	Emphasize impressive training or credentials. Stress visioning, logic, innovation, mastery, progress, and excellence. Be confident around a Rational or Conceptualizer!	Deliver solutions that are practical and effective to help them get what they want. Value action, excitement, and variety. Avoid giving too many details. Be practical around an Artisan or Experiencer!
Example wording	"When working with team members, I think it's important to help each one develop and grow, both professionally and personally."	"When working with team members, I like to provide enough structure so that people know what's expected of them."	"When working with team members, I set big-vision goals, assign the most qualified person to individual tasks, and settle for nothing less than excellence."	"When working with team members, I give people the freedom to act autonomously. What's most important is what we accomplish."

Table 10.4: Traits of Three Interviewer Styles

Interviewer Style	Interviewer Traits	How You Can Connect
Emotional interviewer	The emotional interviewer makes decisions based largely on first impressions, personality, appearance, emotional reactions, and feelings about the candidate. Other factors might include academics, personal biases, stereotypes, and racial or gender issues.	Emotional interviewers can be tough to persuade if you miss making a good first impression. If you sense there's been a big disconnect with this type of interviewer, try this line: "I may not be what you initially envisioned as the ideal candidate. I hope you'll keep an open mind. May I share some work examples that point to my ability to deliver the results you need?"
Intuitive interviewer	This interviewer makes decisions based on gut feelings and the candidate having a few critical traits. The decision is then globalized, meaning that in the eyes of the interviewer, because the candidate has those traits he or she can do everything and, without those critical traits, nothing. More general factors include character, religion, values, appropriate style, and location where raised. (Note that many people vote in this manner, thinking the candidate belongs to my party, so that makes him or her the best.) This is where interviewers have the greatest tendency to hire in their own image.	You may sense that things are going swimmingly. Be cautious, though, as the interviewer may have to "sell you" to colleagues or home-office people whom you won't have a chance to meet. If so, consider this language: "It seems we've really hit it off. I know I can do the job and deliver the results you're after. I want to make sure, though, that you've got the solid documentation you need to support my candidacy with your colleagues. May I share some specific successes that relate to the position?"
Technical interviewer	The technical interviewer makes decisions based on the possession of strong skills, experiences, and methodologies. This interviewer does a good job of data collection in the interview, but tends to over-value years of specific experience, degrees held, specific areas of technical competence, and thinking skills. This interviewer has the potential to overlook high-potential candidates who don't yet have the "required" experience.	When lacking a certain skill that the technical interviewer is looking for, say, "How do you want to see those skills implemented?" Then follow with a SMART Story™ that describes how you did something similar using a related skill set. Emphasize what you accomplished without much experience to demonstrate motivation and ability to learn. Consider saying in a respectful, inquisitive tone, "I've been told by managers that motivation and ability to learn is a better predictor of success than identical experience. I'm sure there are people in the company for which this is true. What have you found to be the case?""

Table 10.5: Concerns of Various Company Contacts

Level	Interviewer's Concerns	How You Can Connect
Hiring manager	Will you make *me* look good without being a threat to my job security? Can you do the job? Can you get up to speed quickly? Will you work well with the team? Will you fit in with my management philosophy?	Speak to your overall competency for the position and ability to work under his or her management philosophy. Acknowledge to the interviewer: "You're probably looking for someone who can do the job, get up to speed quickly, and fit in with the team." Then add something like this: "I've done just that in all my new assignments and in a manner that allowed both the team and my boss to receive special recognition." Recognize that the hiring manager is an important vote but often just one of many votes.
Boss's boss	Do you understand the strategic company-wide impacts of the position? Do you fit into the "big picture"? Are you promotable?	Emphasize your bottom-line results, work ethic, ability to work with other departments, and enthusiasm for the future. Share results that are hard, cold facts. Ask questions such as, "How does this position fit in with your vision for the company in the next few years?"
Human resources	Do you have the competencies for the job? Will you be a good cultural fit? Will there be any compliance issues?	At the face-to-face interview stage, you likely already have most of the items on the minimum qualifications "wish-list" for the position. Ask questions that probe for competencies sought in this position. Describe your team skills in a manner that shows a good cultural fit.
Technical people	Do you have the certificates, degrees, and experience to do the job?	Focus on "exact match" technical evidence that verifies your ability.
Sales and marketing	Can you help make this organization more competitive?	Emphasize the competitive advantage accruing to the sales organization as a result of your work.
Managing directors or finance directors	Can you help make this company more profitable?	Display clear, concise benefits to costs, profits, and operating efficiency.

Level	Interviewer's Concerns	How You Can Connect
Peers	Will you be easy to work with? Will you be a grand-stander, seeking all the glory, or will you contribute collaboratively and uphold the acronym for TEAM: **T**ogether **E**veryone **A**chieves **M**ore.	Describe your history of helping peers succeed. Ask questions such as, "What do you need to make this team more successful?"
Subordinates	Will you be easy to work for? Can you give us what we want (rewards, recognition, responsibility, and so on)?	Ask personal questions, such as, "Have you had good managers before? What were their traits? What do you want more of in your job? Less of? What ideas do you have to make things better?" Subordinates may have a hidden agenda, so be alert to this.

Chapter Wrap-Up

Connecting is all about communicating—not just giving out information, but getting through to people. Anthony Robbins said, "To effectively communicate, we must realize that we are all different in the way we perceive the world and use this understanding as a guide to our communication with others." At first, it might feel daunting to figure out how people perceive the world, but it *will* come more easily as you carefully observe and listen to people.

If you're in an interview and can't recall specific information from these pages, don't fret. The simple act of *being aware* that people have different values and temperaments will put you far ahead of most of your competitors.

10 Quick Tips to Create Chemistry and Connect with Interviewers

1. **Share commonalities**—a passion for your field or enthusiasm for a new product/service, as well as personal commonalities such as family (children of the same age), recreational activities, hobbies, or interests. Find common ground—this is relatively easy to do, given the ease of Internet research.

2. **Respect your interviewers.** You do not have to agree with them on everything. Do acknowledge that they may see, hear, feel, and interpret the world differently and therefore behave differently than you. Seek to respect others first…it's the fastest way to earn it in return.

3. **Support your interviewers.** Interviewing isn't a sport, a battle, or a magic show designed to trick someone into hiring you. It's about offering your best case for why you're the right person for the job and able to support the company.

4. **Use the LISTEN acronym,** which stands for **L**aser your focus; **I**nvestigate and be curious; **Si**lence your tongue—hold your judgment and open your mind; **T**ake brief notes and take time to formulate your response; **E**levate the other person; and **N**ote the nonverbals, including your body language and that of your interviewer. It is *impossible* to connect with others if you don't listen well.

5. **RESPOND well,** meaning **R**emember your objective; **E**ngage the interviewer; **S**hare succinctly; **P**oint to benefits; **O**ffer proof; **N**ever drone on; and **D**edicate yourself to a win-win relationship.

6. **Avoid talking too much.** Take turns talking, so that there's a give and take. Keep your responses around the two-minute mark. Walk the fine line between answering the question honestly and giving a version that will put you in the best possible light. Master the art of communicating lots but saying little. Talking too much makes the conversation about you, which causes you to look self-centered, off-target, or arrogant. Remember your interview mantra: "It's about them, not me!"

7. **Pay attention to the *howcha's*.** The howcha's are *how you say it* (as opposed to *what you say*). Tone, inflection, body language, attitude, and motive combine to make how you say it just as important as what you say. To improve your *howcha's*, remain deferential, respectfully curious, and concerned about the interviewer/company's welfare. Use verbal and body-language mirroring to enhance communication, matching aspects of your interviewer's voice, language, mannerisms, and body language.

8. **Connect with interviewers by recognizing their learning style, whether auditory, visual, or kinesthetic/tactile.** Offer variety in your interview so that each style is addressed, such as answering questions for the auditory learners, writing an outline on a whiteboard or showing a PowerPoint demonstration for the visual learners, and engaging the kinesthetic/tactile learners by engaging them in activities or encouraging them to take more thorough notes.

9. **Connect with interviewers by understanding their temperament.** Rational/Conceptualizers (often seen in executives) value impressive training or credentials, and stress visioning, logic, innovation, mastery, progress, and excellence. Idealists (often seen in human service

roles) value harmony in work relationships and ideal, meaningful work environments. Guardians/Traditionalists (often seen in finance and management roles) value factual, reality-based responses in a sequential, detailed fashion. Artisans/Experiencers (often seen in sales/marketing roles) value action, excitement, and variety, and prefer solutions that are practical and effective to help them get what they want.

10. **Connect with each of the various company contacts.** You may meet with the hiring manager, your boss's boss, a human resource representative, technical people, sales and marketing people, finance people, peers, subordinates, and key customers. Each of these individuals has a different agenda that you'll want to be aware of when formulating your responses.

Magical Coaching Questions

How did you score on the 25-Point Communication Check near the beginning of the chapter? Identify a few items from the list that you'd like to improve on.

1. _____
2. _____
3. _____
4. _____

What can you do to put these into practice today?

_____

_____

_____

How will you measure whether you've improved a week from now?

_____

_____

_____

(continued)

(continued)

What is your learning style? _____

In an interview, how can you communicate with the two learning styles that are different from yours?

_____

_____

_____

What is your temperament? _____

Who do you know in your current or most recent work situation that fits the descriptions of the four different temperaments?

Idealist: _____

Guardian/Traditionalist: _____

Rational/Conceptualizer: _____

Artisan/Experiencer: _____

What steps can you take to enhance your communications with people who have each of the four temperaments?

Idealist: _____

Guardian/Traditionalist: _____

Rational/Conceptualizer: _____

Artisan/Experiencer: _____

Chapter

11

Clarify and Collaborate—How to Explore What Needs to Be Done and How It Needs to Be Done

We listened to what our customers wanted and acted on what they said. Good things happen when you pay attention.

—John F. Smith, Chairman, General Motors Corporation

Now that you've learned the essentials of connecting with your interviewer, you're ready for the next two phases in the 4-C process: *Clarify what* needs to be done and *Collaborate* on *how* to do it. Recall that the 4-Cs model involves these phases:

- Phase 1: Connect
- Phase 2: Clarify
- Phase 3: Collaborate
- Phase 4: Close

Let's delve into how to discover and discuss the essentials of what you'll be doing in the target position.

Phase 2: Clarify What Needs to Be Done

As you move into Clarifying *what* needs to be done, let me make one point crystal clear. Out of respect for the interviewer, let him or her take the lead on clarifying whether you can do the job. You don't want to bulldoze your way in and start asking questions out of turn. However, you should be diligent about doing your share of clarifying! As you do, focus on *what the employer needs*—these are the deliverables.

The difference between clarifying and not clarifying the deliverables is like night and day—one keeps you in the dark, the other sheds light on the subject, as table 11.1 illustrates.

Table 11.1: Differences Between Clarifying and Not Clarifying the Deliverables

When You Do Not Clarify the Needs of the Employer	When You Do Clarify the Needs of the Employer
You have nothing to aim at!	You can target your responses to show how you can solve or serve (SOS) the employer's needs.
When no need is established, there is little incentive or urgency on the part of the employer to hire.	You can help keep momentum going to see the need satisfied.
You have no way of knowing whether you are right for the position.	When you are right for the position, you gain more confidence and authority.

Good consultants, sales professionals, or service people *always* find out what the customer needs. Case in point: My husband and I were in a nice Italian restaurant that was famous for its Northern Italian cream sauces. The menu was limited and my husband, not fond of dining out in the first place but accommodating his wife's wishes, was mildly irritated about his lack of choices. The restaurateur, a gracious Italian woman with a lyrical accent, took our order. She immediately picked up on my husband's mood and began asking questions to get clear about his likes and dislikes. I enjoyed watching the process as she nimbly narrowed down what he did and did not like. No more than a half-dozen questions later, she had zeroed in on his tastes. He ended up with an off-the-menu hearty rib-eye and garlic mashed potatoes that suited him to a T. Moral of the story: Don't sell fancy sauces to a fellow who is a meat-and-potatoes man. Your interviewer has certain tastes as well. It's up to you to find out what they are!

Ask for a Job Description

Recall from chapter 8 on telephone interviews that you'll want to request a position description once you pass the telephone screening. This position description may or may not materialize. If it doesn't, be wary. It may mean that the employer doesn't know what they want in the position. When the position description does show up, study it carefully. Some descriptions are well written. Some are outdated. Some aren't even close to the real position. It's your job to clarify what are the real deliverables that the employer needs.

Ask Big-Picture Questions in the First Interview

Use open questions to gather information. Open questions start with what, how, and why. Some of your questions can also start with who, where, and when. In the first face-to-face interview, ask aerial-mode, big-picture questions to clarify what really needs to be done. Here are a dozen to get you started (do *not* ask all of these questions—choose just a few, or the interviewer will feel like they are at the Inquisition):

- What do you want to see accomplished in your team/department/ company in the next three to six months? What would be the ideal outcome?

- How will you measure success?

- How will this position specifically support that goal?

- How does this position impact the organization overall?

- What do you see as the two or three most important tasks for this position in the immediate future?

- With the ideal person in the position, what can be accomplished?

- Who would you point to as a top performer in this position? What traits make them stand out? What specific actions make them so successful? (Interviewers may be hesitant to let the cat out of the bag and tell you specifically what qualities they are looking for; however, these questions can uncover them for you.)

- What percentage of time would you like devoted to each of the key tasks we've spoken of?

- Who will this position work with internally? Externally?

⚝ To whom would I report?

⚝ Are you saying that the most important issues are _____ and _____ ?

⚝ How soon do you want to make a decision?

⚝ Do I understand correctly that when this position is filled, you'll be able to _____ ?(Fill in the blank: get started on the new launch, clean up the backlog, be freed up to do the work you need to do, catch up on your outstanding receivables, and so on.)

Do your best to get a head start on answers to these questions prior to walking into the interview. (See appendix A for tips on researching companies and jobs.) Note that the questions on the prior list center on *the position*. This next list will give you insights into *the company*. Again, learn as much as you can *before* your face-to-face meeting. Assuming answers to the following questions aren't a matter of public record, you may want to ask

⚝ How long has the company been in business? Is it publicly or privately held? If privately held, by whom?

⚝ What are the company's major milestones, key products/services, and strengths?

⚝ How many employees are there? Where? Have there been recent layoffs? Are any planned?

⚝ What does the organizational chart look like? Where does this position fit in?

Bring a notepad to the interview containing questions you want to ask and use it to take notes. Beyond this purpose, a notepad can give you something to hold on to during the interview to ease any nervous tension. Also, remember the fingernail-in-the-thumb trick from chapter 10 to quell nervousness.

The Right Timing Is Important When Asking Questions

A good interviewer will clarify whether you have what it takes to do the job. Before you can start asking deeper clarifying questions of your own, first answer the interviewer's questions with SMART Stories™ that confirm your competencies. "Dance" with the interviewer—if financial subjects are being discussed, don't switch the subject to team development.

Once the interviewer gets a better sense of your qualifications, he or she will be more open to answering your questions. Look for opportunities at the end of your stories to ask tie-in questions that clarify what needs to be done.

This example illustrates how to ask a tie-in question at the end of a SMART Story™:

...Bottom line, we saved more than an hour a day in processing receipts. Is this an area of concern for you, or would you say there are other key challenges your bookkeeping department is facing?

After the interviewer responds, continue with

I'd be curious to hear what you have found that works best.

Ask Deeper-Detail Questions in Second and Third Interviews

As you get further into the interview process, you'll have established the rapport, trust, and mutual interest to ask deeper, more probing questions. The more senior the position, the more questions you can and should ask. Whereas general questions are appropriate for the HR department, detail questions are more appropriate for managers.

Be cautious! If you ask deeper-detail questions too early in the process, you could come across as pushy or presumptuous. Save these types of questions for the second or third interviews.

Questions About the Position

- "What would the ideal person in this job accomplish on a weekly basis?"

- "I'd like to know what it takes to be successful in this company. What kind of effort and hours do top performers put in?" This is a great question to ask to determine whether the company expects 70-hour workweeks without sounding like you're lazy!

- "You mentioned that client retention will be the focus of the position, with about 60 percent of the time spent on this. Is this similar to what the last person in the position did? What other priorities make up the remaining 40 percent?"

- "Is this a newly created position?" Or, "how is it that this position became open? May I ask, did the person leave or get promoted? What results were you most pleased with? What do you need done next? How many people have had this position over the past few years?"

- ✴ "What do you look for when considering someone for promotion?"

- ✴ "How has the position changed over the past few years?"

- ✴ If you don't already have one: "May I see a formal job description?"

- ✴ "May I see an employee handbook?"

- ✴ "Was this position posted internally?"

- ✴ "May I ask how many applied for this position?"

- ✴ "How firm are the company's requirements for the position? What other ways of meeting those requirements are acceptable?"

Questions About Current and Future Challenges

- ✴ "I have appreciated hearing about the goals for this position. What stands between where the project/situation is today and where you want to be?"

- ✴ "What have you already done or put in place to achieve those goals?"

- ✴ "What's gotten in the way in the past?"

- ✴ "What if that weren't an issue?"

- ✴ "Are you concerned about _____ ?" (Fill in the blank with some problem, such as the project not getting done on time, your competitors gaining an advantage if this isn't handled expertly, productivity taking a dip, losing customers because of poor service, and so on.)

- ✴ "Looking down the road to the next several years, what do you see as the key challenges the person in this position will face?"

- ✴ "What is the company's vision for the next 5 to 10 years?"

Questions About People

- ✴ "To whom would I report? When might I meet that person?"

- ✴ "Who will make the final hiring decision?"

- ✴ "Who would be my direct reports? What do you anticipate they need most from a supervisor/leader?"

- ✴ "Who are the key people I'd be servicing/supporting/helping/ leading?"

- ✴ "Who is in charge of _____ ?" (Fill in the blank with resources, outsourcing, or some other aspect of a program or department.)

⭐ "You mentioned I'd be working with _____ internally and _____ externally. How would you describe those relationships currently? Do any of those relationships need to be enhanced? When will I have an opportunity to meet these people?"

⭐ "Could you tell me who makes up the team/department? What are their roles? What do they need most from me? Who is being under-utilized?"

⭐ "What kind of ongoing development or training do you like to see in team members? How does that happen?"

⭐ "What kind of feedback or evaluation system is in place?"

⭐ "Has there been a change in the number of people employed by the company over the past few years [increase, decrease, same]? Do you anticipate changes in the next 6 to 18 months?"

⭐ "When did you join the company? What do you like most about the company?"

Questions About Resources

⭐ "What resources are in place to support this?" Depending on your position, these resources may be financial, human, programmatic, technical, training, and so on. Ask about all that are relevant.

For positions that would normally have access to financial information, ask:

⭐ "What information are you able to share about financial trends?"

⭐ "What kind of revenue and profit trends has the company experienced over the past three years?"

⭐ "What is the budget for this project/program?"

⭐ "What about funding beyond this fiscal year?"

⭐ "When will you know it's time to increase the budget or resources for this?"

⭐ "What has the company done to manage budget cutbacks?"

⭐ "Do you foresee more cutbacks?"

Questions About Strategy

⭐ "What's your short-term and long-term strategy for this initiative/program?" Or, if you're being hired to help develop strategy: "What opportunities are available to us? How has strategy been developed in the past? How can that process be improved upon?"

- "Can you tell me more about how you plan to make this initiative happen?"

- "How will this product/service be positioned in comparison to the competition?"

- "What advantages does the company have over its chief competitors? What are its areas for growth?"

- "What do you see as the single greatest benefit this product/service has?"

- "What do you see as the single greatest asset this company has?"

Questions About Systems and Timeline

- "What systems are in place to measure success?"

- "Tell me about the infrastructure for this project. What's working well? What could be improved upon?"

- "What technology is in place? Does it need to be upgraded?"

- "Where will the majority of the work be done? How much travel is involved?"

- "When do you hope to see this project start?"

- "Do I understand correctly that you need to fill this position in the next 30 days?"

Listen for important issues and problems that need to be resolved—this is where the ultimate motivation to hire comes. Avoid trying to note every single need mentioned by the employer. You'll be better off addressing several key issues than using a diluted, shotgun approach.

Move forward methodically with your questions. Don't jump into explaining how you can solve problems until you have asked enough questions and gathered the key information you need. Solving problems and documenting skills should be reserved for Phase 3, Collaborating.

A Bad Hire Costs a Company Double the Employee's Salary

Bad hiring decisions are not uncommon. Nearly 80 percent of turnover is due to hiring mistakes, according to a study by Harvard University. A professional position that pays $48,000 annually and turns over too quickly can cost a company more than $100,000 in advertising, travel, interview time, training, and other costs, according to the selection systems consulting firm of Development Dimensions International.

Use these statistics to your advantage. For instance, look for an opportune moment in the interview to share these comments: "Mr. Employer, I recognize that your hiring decision is an important one. In fact, I read that nearly 80% of turnover is due to hiring mistakes and that a $48,000 position can cost a company $100,000 in recruiting and training costs if the position turns over too quickly. My desire is to understand what you need accomplished, and then demonstrate my experience and motivation to do that, so you can carefully judge what kind of an asset I would be to this organization."

Ask Questions Based on Intuition, Tempered by Good Judgment

We've all sensed those red flags that tell us to proceed with caution. Some people see them in their head. Others hear a still, small voice that says, "I don't like the way this sounds!" Others get a tight feeling in their stomach that warns them that something is not right.

Sally was interviewing for an executive director position with a professional association. She would report directly to the board of directors, who told her that she would be replacing an incumbent who wasn't performing up to standards. A few things were said that caused Sally to wonder about the board's communication style—was it that they truly gave clear direction that the incumbent willfully ignored, or were they part of the problem, expecting the incumbent to read their minds? Sally developed this list of questions to help her clarify what the real issues were:

- "I believe communication is key to ensuring that your needs and the needs of your members are met." (Note how her approach first addresses concern for the board members.) "Since all of us live in a different city, how will we be communicating?"

- "Will there be a primary point of contact, or several contacts?"

- "Ideally, how often would you like me to be meeting with you?"

- "Would that be by a telephone bridge or videoconference?"

- "Can you tell me about a time when there was a miscommunication between you and the executive director, and what was done to ensure that a similar miscommunication didn't happen in the future?" (Note that this is a behavioral interviewing question asked by the candidate.)

> ★ "What sorts of reporting systems do you currently have in place? Would you say that those are adequate, or would you like me to expand those for you?" (Notice how her language implies that she would be the one doing the expanding, assuming the duties of the position so that they can envision her already on board. The second question leans toward Phase 3 of the interview process, Collaborating on how to do the job.) "I have a sample weekly update form I'd like to show you that might be adapted for our needs."

What does your intuition tell you? Follow it. Trust it. What questions can you ask to probe more deeply?

Phase 3: Collaborate on How to Do the Job

In the Collaborate phase, your objectives are to

> ★ Focus on *how* the deliverables established in Phase 2 will be met.

> ★ Offer evidence of meeting prior deliverables using SMART Stories™ and other documentary aids.

> ★ Demonstrate tangibly how you'd do the job.

> ★ Give the employer a glimpse of you doing the job.

To establish how the deliverables will be met, ask questions such as these:

> ★ "What is currently working well?"

> ★ "What didn't work well?"

> ★ "What did the prior incumbent do well?"

> ★ "What would you like to see more of?"

> ★ "How would you prefer to see this handled?"

> ★ "This is how I might approach that, based on my last position and training I recently attended...what have you found works best inside your company?"

> ★ "I read recently in our trade journal how some companies in California had tried a new strategy for that issue...what are your thoughts on that?"

> ★ "I noted that competitors are trying this approach...what do you think about this?"

> ★ "I really admired the way your team approached that situation. Will you be using the same strategy on the next project?"

Use SMART Stories™ to answer behavioral interviewing questions. As you do, occasionally make the "T" in the SMART Story™ a tie-in with a Clarifying or Collaborating question (see chapter 3 for a review of developing SMART Stories™). This next example shows how you can combine the SMART Story™ format with Collaborating. The description that follows picks up near the end of the SMART Story™ as the candidate described her results:

> …The vendor research I did enabled me to source the part for this special order in less than 24 hours, when it normally took a week to satisfy this kind of request.

Here comes the tie-in, which is actually a collaborating question.

> May I ask, how would you prefer to see something like this handled?

The Secret to Being Able to Ask Any Question

Mary Jansen Scroggins, former sales manager with giftware leader Applause and principal of Jansen & Associates, LLC, offers some sage advice for asking questions: "You can ask anything if you ask permission." For instance, preface your clarifying or collaborating questions with one of these permission-based questions:

- "May I ask more about that?"

- "Could I learn more about that?"

- "When would be a good time to ask a question about your newest product?"

- "Would it be alright if I took a few minutes to explore that?"

Collaborate Using a Demonstration

To demonstrate tangibly how you'd do the job, consider using one of these methods:

- MS PowerPoint presentation addressing a typical challenge if this is something that would be applicable to the position

- Recent sample of work at your past employer (being careful to protect confidential information)

- Fictionalized case study (see more on case studies and simulations in chapter 7)

- Impromptu whiteboard brainstorm of steps you'd take to tackle a challenge

- Interaction with team members in an actual meeting

Case Study
XYZ Company

Marketing Manager

John Jacob Smith

1

Requirements

- Development of long-term strategy for distributor
- Build-out of overall strategic plan
- Analysis and identification of distribution needs
- Analysis of P&L and recommendations
- Category management
- New product development
- Sales meeting and support
- Customer marketing plans and growth strategies

2

A 4-Step Strategy

- **Step 1: Analysis**
  - Background (industry, competitive, consumer landscape)
  - S.W.O.T. (strengths, weaknesses, opportunities, threats)
- **Step 2: Develop Strategic Brand Plan**
  - Brand presence and profitable sales expansion
  - New product development innovations
- **Step 3: Develop Account Strategic Plan**
  - Customer marketing plans and growth strategies
  - Category management
- **Step 4: Execute**
  - Product development
  - Sales force
  - Distributors

3

Step 1: Analysis

- **Industry**
  - Top 15 customers account for 89% of sales of the top 50 customers
  - Group affiliations, private label
  - Value-added products
  - Business partner vs. supplier
- **Competitive**
  - Strong positioned competitors
  - Competition strategy (profitable growth vs. market share)
- **Consumer landscape**
  - Convenience, value-added products — key driver in product selection
  - 48% of meals are consumed away from home
  - Major restaurant chains account for 52% of segment, up 1%

4

Step 2: Strategic Brand Plan

- **Expand brand presence**
  - Maximize branded concepts
  - Leverage e-commerce applications (made to order)
  - National and account specific campaigns and promotions
- **Emerging fast-growth segment**
  - Value-added new product offerings
  - Expand low-carb offerings (individual wrap, ready to serve)
- **New channel of business**
  - Premium, specialty, high-end offerings
  - Private label
- **Financial**
  - Marketing mix enhanced—more value-added products at above-average margins
  - Category management

5

Step 3: Strategic Account Plan

- **Account Strategy**
  - Outside–in approach, solution selling, define the mix of products and services creating a unique value proposition
  - Extract information about customer needs and buying requirements
- **Business Plan**
  - Upstream marketing, sell new low-carb menu offerings to national restaurant chains
  - Emerging fast-growth segments, new item introductions, value-added, low-carb
- **Category**
  - Enhanced customer selection, value and profitability

6

Step 4: Execute – Transition Plan

- **Product Development**
  - Survey and testing
  - Monitor, communicate progress, forecast
- **Sales Force**
  - Sales meeting and support
  - Customer marketing plans and growth strategies
  - National promotions and campaigns
- **Foodservice Distributors**
  - Account specific promotions
  - Upstream marketing
- **Contingency Plan**
  - Monitor progress – results vs. target – make adjustments

7

Beyond Win-Win

- **Strengthened Business Partnership**
  - Solve key account concerns
- **Consumer Demand**
  - Offer size preference
- **Category Development**
  - Enhance sales, market share, and profit
- **Share Best Practices**
  - Share with other account managers
- **Applications for Other Trade Channels**
  - Maximize account opportunities

8

Figure 11.1: A PowerPoint presentation used in an interview to demonstrate skills for the job.

The screen shots in figure 11.1 capture some of the highlights of a MS PowerPoint presentation that helped win one of my clients a job offer in marketing management. For tips on preparing demonstrations, see "Demonstrations" in chapter 6.

Avoid the Word *But*

When collaborating with an employer, avoid using the word *but*. It's inherently negative or confrontational. Substitute the word *and* whenever possible. For instance

- **Before:** "I have heard about that procurement process, *but* I haven't actually used it yet."

- **After:** "I learned about that process through some recent self-study *and* am anxious to see it applied."

- **Before:** "I am familiar with MS Word, *but* I haven't used the Mail Merge feature like you want."

- **After:** "I have used a number of MS Word features, *and* I'm familiar with teaching myself new features." Then, offer a short SMART Story™. For instance, "in my last position, none of the five secretaries knew how to create templates, including me. I noticed how we were either wasting time reinventing the wheel each time we went to create a document, or existing documents were being used as a template, which was dangerous because some text from the original document was often overlooked and found its way into the new document. (Situation and More) I took it upon myself to find an online newsgroup that helped me understand beyond what the standard Help function could tell me. (Action) Bottom line, I set up half a dozen templates for our client newsletter, monthly sales report, and other documents. The templates have saved me several hours each week in creating documents and are now being used by other secretaries so there is more uniformity in our communication materials. (Result) I'm great with learning new programs and features and confident I could learn the Mail Merge function in a similar manner. How often and for what kinds of situations will I be using the Mail Merge function?" (Theme and Tie-in. Note that the theme is being able to learn new programs, and how she uses the last question to Clarify and Collaborate on how to do the job.)

Collaborate by Walking Around

A great way to shift the interview from interrogative question-and-answer to collaborative discussion is to ask the interviewer for a tour. One or more of these areas may be appropriate:

- The office space
- The building
- The grounds
- The production floor
- The warehouse
- The sales office
- A key customer's site
- A vendor's operation
- A retail space where the company's products/services are sold

When walking around or touring, ask lots of questions, take notes, and meet as many insiders as you can (don't forget to note their names and, if it seems appropriate, ask for business cards). This will give you great material for writing follow-up letters or developing leave-behinds (see "Forward Momentum and Communication" in chapter 12).

Chapter Wrap-Up

Getting at the *what* and *how* of the "deliverables" is absolutely key to a successful interview. When you Clarify specifically *what* needs to be done and Collaborate on *how* it will be done, you will

- Know what to aim at and how to target your responses.
- Shift the employer's focus away from a magical "wish list" of certain credentials, years of experience, and so on that would theoretically make a good candidate.
- Keep the employer's focus on the most important factor: your ability to do the job.
- Help the employer to start picturing you in the position.

Bottom line: You look and act like an "A" candidate when you Clarify and Collaborate!

10 Quick Tips to Clarify and Collaborate in an Interview

1. **Once rapport has been established (the Connect phase of the interview), begin to Clarify what the employer needs to have done.** These are called "deliverables." Aim for learning the employer's top two or three deliverables. Once you know what needs to be done, you'll be better able to frame your responses.

2. **Timing is important when asking questions.** Before you start asking clarifying questions of your own, answer the interviewer's questions. Use SMART Stories™ to confirm your competencies. Once interviewers get a better sense of your qualifications, they'll be more open to answering your questions.

3. **In your first face-to-face interview, ask big-picture questions.** "What do you want to see accomplished in your team/department/company in the next three to six months?" "How will you measure success?" "What would the ideal outcome be?" "How will this position specifically support that goal?" "What are the two or three most important tasks for this position in the immediate future?" "With the ideal person in the position, what can be accomplished?" Ideally, you should ask these types of questions to your networking contacts prior to the interview so that you can arrive prepared and ready to position yourself as a solution.

4. **As the interview progresses (either well into the first interview or in a second or subsequent interview), ask deeper-detail questions.** "What would you say are the gaps that need to be overcome to meet those goals?" "What have you already tried?" "What worked best?" "What's your greatest frustration with respect to how things are currently being done?" Use a notepad to take notes during the interview.

5. **Look for opportunities at the end of your SMART Stories™ to tie-in to what needs to be done.** For instance, "I'd be interested to learn how frequently that issue comes up for your team members."

6. **Move forward methodically with your clarifying questions.** Don't jump into explaining how you can solve problems until you have asked sufficient questions to gather the information you need. And, "dance" with the interviewer—if details such as systems and software are being discussed, don't switch the subject to long-term visioning.

7. **The secret to being able to ask potentially difficult questions is to ask permission.** If you're heading into confidential or touchy territory with your questions, preface them with this go-ahead question: "May I ask more about that?"

8. **Once you're entirely clear on what needs to be done, begin the Collaborate phase.** Here, you'll focus on *how* the deliverables will be

met. You can ask questions in this phase also, such as: "What is currently working well?" "What didn't work well?" "What did the prior incumbent do well?" "What would you like to see more of?" "How would you prefer to see this handled?"

9. **In the Collaborate phase, your mission is to discuss and demonstrate how you would do the job.** Discussion might include comments like these: "We had a similar situation at my last employer. The strategy we took involved...which worked out well. How would something like this work within your organizational structure?" Or, "I saw a presentation at the last CMIN conference that addressed that very issue. I'm wondering if we could explore how this might be tailored for your needs."

10. **To demonstrate how you would do the job, TAKE ACTION.** Consider giving an MS PowerPoint presentation to demonstrate your presentation skills, addressing a fictionalized case study to highlight your analytical skills, brainstorming marketing strategies to demonstrate your marketing skills, making a sales presentation to showcase your closing skills, sitting down at the computer to demonstrate your technical skills, sitting in on an actual meeting with potential coworkers to demonstrate your collaborative skills, transcribing a tape to demonstrate your transcription skills, and so on. Whatever you'll be doing on the job, *show the employer how you can do it.* The more the employer can visibly see you doing the work, the better.

⭐ Magical Coaching Questions

What big-picture clarifying questions will you ask your interviewers? Prioritize the list. Review the list just prior to the interview to keep it fresh in your mind. How will you remind yourself to ask these during the interview?

_____

_____

_____

_____

_____

_____

What deeper-detail clarifying questions will you ask?

_____

_____

_____

_____

_____

What clues will you watch for that the interviewer is willing to discuss deeper-detail questions?

_____

_____

_____

Are there any red flags you have about a position you're interviewing for?

_____

_____

_____

What questions can you ask to help sort through these?

_____

_____

_____

_____

(continued)

(continued)

What collaborating questions will you ask?

_____

_____

_____

_____

_____

How will you practice asking tie-in questions at the close of your SMART Stories™ to clarify and collaborate? Who can support you in this?

_____

_____

_____

What specific action can you take to demonstrate to an interviewer your ability to do the job?

_____

_____

_____

Chapter

12

Close with Professionalism— How to Wrap Up and Win

To finish first you must first finish.

—Rick Mears, American race-car driver

Y̲ou've mastered the art of connecting, and learned the importance of clarifying and collaborating from the previous two chapters. Now it's time to understand and apply the art and science of closing.

Phase 4: Close with Professionalism

In a sales transaction, sales professionals are taught to "close" the sale—this is the point near the end of the sales process where the seller asks the prospect to say "Yes!" In an interview, the "Close" is designed to make it logical and easy for the employer to say yes to you.

Closing should never be a manipulative, pressure-packed culmination of the interview. Because the employer holds the decision-making power, it would be inappropriate for you to be pushy or badger them into offering a position. More harm than good would come from such a strategy. It is, however, appropriate to do the following:

261

★ Respectfully gain agreement from the employer that you have what they need.

★ Close any gaps between what the employer wants and what you can deliver.

★ Understand the company's interview process.

★ Express your desire for the position—ask for the job!

★ Keep up the momentum and communication with the employer.

Let's look at how to do these things.

Gain Agreement

Using a collaborative tone of voice, gain agreement by presenting the facts, as these examples show:

★ "As I understand it, you need *xyz* accomplished in this position. I've outlined my experience and results at my last employer that relate to this goal, and I'm confident I could make a solid contribution here. What's more important, though, is how you view my qualifications. *From your perspective, what do you see as my greatest value to the organization?*"

★ "Thanks for providing more details on the company and the position. I'm confident my background will be critical to the success of the priority projects you mentioned. *I'm curious, though, what you sense as my greatest strengths for the position?*"

★ "I've enjoyed our conversation. May I recap my understanding of what you need? We discussed customer retention as the key focus of the position, specifically improving the regularity of weekly e-mail updates and monthly follow-up, as well as creating and implementing a customer survey mechanism in the next three months. *Are you satisfied that my demonstration of how I'd approach the survey will meet your needs?*"

★ "We've covered a lot of territory this morning. To highlight, it sounds as though you want someone who can work independently to research and generate potential contacts for the planned giving department. *May I ask which of my experiences you see as most relevant to the position?*"

Notice the key agreement questions at the end of each of the preceding examples. These questions are designed to help the interviewer favorably summarize your candidacy and conclude that you are the right person for the job.

Close Any Gaps

The interviewer may answer affirmatively to your "gain agreement" questions in an effort to not show their hand. These next questions will help you uncover hidden concerns and gauge where you stand:

* "What would it take to assure you that I would be the best person for this position?"

* "How could I improve my value even more?"

If the interviewer gives you an honest answer to these questions, do not take it personally. Listen objectively and analytically. Do *not* get defensive or irritated. Instead, problem-solve and close the gaps. You might accomplish this by providing the interviewer a sample of your work product. It may be revisiting a particular subject and offering more details and results in a SMART Story™. It may be that you need more training. If it's something like the latter, ask:

* "What would you like me to accomplish in the job as a result of that training?"

This focuses the interviewer back on "doing" the job, as opposed to having the right pedigree. If you're able to deliver the result they want, reiterate this ability. Then, commit to immediately starting on the training program (or whatever they want) while in the job.

Employer Signs of Interest

To gauge whether the employer is interested in you, watch for these signals:

* You are invited to a subsequent interview (second, third, fourth, and so on).

* The interview lasts longer than expected.

* You are offered a tour of the facilities.

* You are invited to interview with additional people in the company.

* You are asked to take assessments—psychometric, cognitive, and so on (see chapter 7).

* You are asked about your availability.

* Salary is discussed beyond an initial early-stage statement of "this is the salary range for the position" or the age-old query "what are your salary requirements?"

* The employer begins to sell you on the company.

* Reference-checking process is started.

Understand the Company's Interview Process

Every company handles its interview process differently. These questions will help you know what to expect next:

- Can you tell me about your interview process?
- How many steps are in the interview process?
- What is the next step? Can we set that up?

Express Desire for the Position

Express your desire for the position and ask for the job. Too many times I have heard interviewers say, "They just didn't seem interested in the position. I really want someone who is motivated and excited about working here." If you're blasé in the interview, interviewers will assume you'll be disengaged in the workplace.

Crank up the energy in your voice and try on one of these closing statements:

- "I'm extremely interested. Although I'm looking at a couple of opportunities right now, this appears to be the one where I could make the biggest contribution." (*Note:* Find any other opportunity so that you can say this truthfully—even if your "other opportunity" is temporary or part time, such as hosting a fireworks stand around the Fourth of July or selling Amway part time. You won't, of course, disclose those opportunities to the interviewer!)

- "I can assure you that if you extended a reasonable offer today, I would be on board tomorrow."

- "I know beyond a shadow of a doubt that this is the perfect position for me. There may be candidates who have heftier resumes than I do, but no one will give you more enthusiasm, commitment, and can-do attitude."

A Great Close Wins a Job with *O* Magazine

Michelle Burford helps shape the voice of one of the most influential women in America, that of Oprah Winfrey. In the April 2004 issue of *Christianity Today*, Burford relays her story of applying for a job with *O* magazine. She was not what you'd call a front-runner candidate. Burford put it bluntly to her interviewer: "There are 100 people out there who have a better resume. But what you'll get with me is a real passion and a real understanding of what she [Oprah] would want to put out there. You won't find anyone who cares more." She was hired two days later, and played a significant role in one of the most successful magazine launches in history.

It might be difficult for you to sound enthusiastic about a position if you're not sure that it's the right one for you. The checklist in table 12.1 outlines 10 areas that will help you determine whether the position is, indeed, a good match. In the column to the right, enter a number between 1 and 10 to indicate your satisfaction level.

Table 13.1: How to Determine Whether This Is the Right Position

Factor	Rate Each Item on a Scale of 1–10 (1 = Intolerable; 5 = I Can Live with This; 10 = Dream Job)
FUNCTIONAL FIT: Is the position in synch with your favorite strengths? Will it allow you to use your honed skills, acquired knowledge, and wired-from-birth talents? Do you get to use these talents/skills the majority of the time? For instance, if analytical tasks invigorate you, will you spend the majority of your time doing this? Or does the position also require that 50 percent of your time be spent doing tasks that aren't your favorite strengths or talents, such as making verbal presentations regarding the results of your analysis? Remember, work is less taxing physically and emotionally when you're doing something that comes easily.	☐
INDUSTRY: Do you have an affinity for this industry? Is it aligned with a cause or higher purpose for you? Will you enjoy working with the products or services that the industry represents? Is this important to you?	☐
INCOME: Is compensation within industry standards? Will you make what you need to meet your financial obligations and goals? If the offer is lower than you had hoped, will you be able to go to work every day without feeling angry, cheated, or undervalued? Your financial situation may influence your decision—in other words, if youare presently unemployed, how long can you afford to wait?	☐

(continued)

(continued)

Factor	Rate Each Item on a Scale of 1–10 (1 = Intolerable; 5 = I Can Live with This; 10 = Dream Job)
COMPANY AND CULTURE: Are employees treated fairly? Are team spirit and fair play evident? Does the company do what it says it will do in its policies and other communications? Are staff members viewed as the company's greatest asset? What about company stability in terms of finances and future…has there been a history of downsizing, mergers, or acquisitions? Do trade-journal articles or conversations with competitors or insiders reveal that the company may be in financial trouble? Is the ambiance and social structure in your comfort zone? Is the company's mission statement aligned with your values? If the company expects everyone to work 60-hour work weeks, is this okay with you? Do you like the company's dress code, stated or unstated?	☐
ADVANCEMENT, GROWTH, AND GOALS: Will this position be a logical fit for your long-term plans? If this is more of a bridge job than a dream job, will it allow you to still have the time and energy you need to work on action steps toward your dream job? If this is a position toward the end of your career, will it allow you to create the legacy you want? If you're in your early or mid-career, is this the right stepping stone? Does the company have a policy for promoting from within? Are professional development and training programs offered? Will the company reimburse you for training completed outside the company?	☐
LEVEL OF RESPONSIBILITY: Does the opportunity offer the responsibility you'd like? Will the position give you what's important to you, for instance, an intellectual challenge, leadership opportunities, an impressive title, clout, freedom, independence, the ability to influence change, and so on?	☐

Factor	Rate Each Item on a Scale of 1–10 (1 = Intolerable; 5 = I Can Live with This; 10 = Dream Job)
CAMARADERIE: Do you like the people you'll work for and with? If you prefer to be with like-minded people, will this be the case? Or, if you prefer to be surrounded by diversity and divergent opinions, will this be the case? Is the social atmosphere of the department or company in synch with what you want, such as honest communications, a sense of connectedness, trust, teamwork, interaction, autonomy, service, and so on?	☐
DIRECT SUPERVISOR: Does your immediate supervisor have a good reputation? Are employee turnover rates low? Does your supervisor-to-be appear to be committed to professional growth and development, as opposed to stuck in a rut and stagnant? What, if any, red flags or concerns might you have about personality conflicts or your boss' management style?	☐
LOCATION AND FACILITIES: Is the company's distance from your home acceptable? If the opportunity requires an excessive commute, is telecommuting or relocation a possibility? If no, are there measures you can put in place that will help salvage the commute time, such as taking a course that involves audiotapes? Beyond commute considerations, is the location safe? Will your work space be conducive to productivity and creativity? Does the company provide the equipment and support you need to do your job effectively?	☐
PERSONAL/FAMILY: Will the position enhance or complement your personal/family commitments? Will the schedule or stress level prevent you from giving what you want to your spouse/partner, children, or other important people in your life?	☐
Total Score:	_____

Sometimes the question of "Am I compromising or settling for less?" comes into play. A preponderance of low scores to the questions in table 12.1 will help you sort that out. You can also use this system to compare multiple employment offers. And, remember that in the 21st century, saying "yes" to a job offer is not a lifetime commitment. The more important question is, is it right for now?

Keep Up the Momentum and Communication

One of the best things you can do at the close of an interview is to keep the door open for future communications. Here are some secrets to make that happen:

⭐ **Give the employer a "leave-behind."** A leave-behind is an item that you leave with the interviewers at the end of the interview, such as a fact sheet (see the examples at the end of this chapter), a case study, before-and-after photos, a collection of testimonials, a bookmark with an apropos quote, or a meaningful but inexpensive gift, such as one of your favorite motivational books. It's a great closing move and makes a lasting impression when you're no longer in front of the employer. If multiple interviews are part of the process, think about what you can offer at the end of the first and second or subsequent interviews.

⭐ **Ask, "What's the next step?"** Try to arrange the next interview before leaving. Then, in your most deferential tone of voice, offer: "I'd like to be able to follow up with you as additional ideas from our discussion come to mind. Is e-mail or phone contact best for you?"

⭐ **When the interviewer says she will get back to you, ask: "When might I expect your call?** May I ask you to use my mobile number, as that's the best way to reach me."

⭐ **Send a performance-based thank you/follow-up note like those at the end of this chapter.**

If communication has come to a standstill, consider these strategies:

⭐ **Enlist the help of insiders.** In your most respectful tone, say: "Joe, this is Susan. I was told I might hear something from your boss at the end of last week. He hasn't called back. What do you think I should do?"

⭐ **Leave the most professional-sounding, upbeat voice mail possible.** Never let fear, frustration, or uncertainty creep into your voice—it serves you absolutely no purpose. For instance, "Hi Mr. Smith. Susan Whitcomb here. Just touching base with you as promised after our meeting last week. I recognize you're busy. If I don't hear back from you, I'll touch base again early next week. I had some additional thoughts on our topic of discussion and will be e-mailing those to you along with a recent article I think you'll find interesting. I'll look forward to keeping our discussions moving forward."

* **Send an upbeat e-mail.** For instance, "Dear Juan. It's been a few weeks since we spoke, and I wanted to touch base to see how you were coming along in your decision process for the position we discussed. Recognizing you're busy, I wonder if you have 5–10 minutes in your schedule where we could talk briefly. I'll call your assistant just before noon today to see if this is possible. By the way, I did a little research and found a solution to that programming script we spoke about. Thanks. ~Jayne Seamour"

* **Send an upbeat letter** (see the example follow-up letters at the end of this chapter).

* **Or this last-ditch effort:** "I sense that I've not fully addressed your needs for the position. I'm committed to building my skills and value so that you'll think of me for future opportunities. From your perspective, what do you consider my greatest strengths to be and what area should I concentrate on building up next?" And, "How would you recommend I stay in touch over the next 6 to 12 months so that I'd be considered for future opportunities?"

The Action Close and the Reaction Close

Milo Frank, in his best-selling *How to Get Your Point Across in 30 Seconds or Less* (Pocket Books), suggests two types of closes. The first, an action close, calls for a specific action on the part of the buyer within a specific time frame. I recommend this only for professions such as sales where decisive action and closing skills are important. For instance, a sales executive might use this action close:

I'm sensing that it's important we keep the momentum going so that your new product launch date is met. Shall we firm up the date and focus for our next meeting?

The second type of close is the reaction close—an indirect approach that is most appropriate for interviewing:

Are you satisfied that we've covered everything we needed to today? What should the next step be?

The reaction close keeps the interviewer in control but allows you to be a collaborative part of the process.

Measure Your Performance in a Post-Interview Analysis

The media and its political pundits love to dissect important speeches of the President and other political leaders. Sometimes the commentary goes on ad nauseam, especially during the campaigning time leading up to a presidential election. Nonetheless, the post-analysis can serve a purpose: helping to clarify pros and cons and give perspective on each candidate.

After you finish an interview, you can do some post-analysis on your performance to help you learn and continue to get better with each interview.

Post-Interview Coaching Questions	Your Answers
What went right?	
What would I change or do differently next time?	
What did I learn from the experience?	

Further, consider rating yourself on a scale of 1 to 10 to measure how effective you were.

Item	Rating Scale
I connected with the interviewer (dressed appropriately, arrived early, exuded professionalism, shared commonalities, used laser listening, and so on).	1 2 3 4 5 6 7 8 9 10
I made the interview about them (the company's needs and how I could satisfy them), not me (what I want, need, or deserve).	1 2 3 4 5 6 7 8 9 10
I clarified both the deliverables of the job and how critical this position is to the interviewer/company.	1 2 3 4 5 6 7 8 9 10
I collaborated with the interviewer on how he or she would like the job done.	1 2 3 4 5 6 7 8 9 10

Item	Rating Scale
I offered a demonstration of how I would do the job; I gave the interviewer a sense of how I would perform in the position.	1 2 3 4 5 6 7 8 9 10
I offered complete SMART Stories™ for behavioral interview questions.	1 2 3 4 5 6 7 8 9 10
Every word out of my mouth was positive, pertinent, and precise.	1 2 3 4 5 6 7 8 9 10
I am a known commodity to the interviewer—people within the company or individuals who have strategic alliances with the company know me and recommended me to the interviewer.	1 2 3 4 5 6 7 8 9 10
I closed the interview by gaining agreement, closing gaps, understanding the company's interviewer process, and expressing desire for the position.	1 2 3 4 5 6 7 8 9 10
I sent a performance-based thank you/follow-up letter within 24 hours.	1 2 3 4 5 6 7 8 9 10
Total Score:	_____ out of 100

The 4 C's in Second and Subsequent Interviews

Remember to cover each of the 4 C's on second and subsequent interviews. Table 12.2 outlines some subtle differences of the 4 C's in first versus subsequent interviews.

 Note When meeting a new individual at second or subsequent interviews, treat the encounter as though it was a first interview and give sufficient time to each of the Connect, Clarify, Collaborate, and Close phases.

Table 12.2: The 4 C's in First and Subsequent Interviews

	First Interview	Second and Subsequent Interviews
Connect	By initial research, commonalities, respect	By continued research, follow through, respect
Clarify	Big-picture details	Fine-tuning details
Collaborate	Depending on length of interview, surface-level to high-level issues	High-level, confidential issues
Close	Establish agreement about mutual interest; close gaps; convey enthusiasm; ask for the job if there is to be only one interview	Confirm mutual commitment; close gaps; convey enthusiasm; ask for the job

Sample Follow-Up Letters and "Leave-Behinds"

CHARLES CANDIDATE

555 N. 14th Street
San Francisco, CA 94111   charlescandidate@msn.com   Work: (415) 555-5555
Mobile: (415) 555-5556

[date]

Javier Gomez, V.P. Marketing
HI-TECH PARTNERS
55 Market Street
San Francisco, CA 94111

Subject: Promotional Market Manager

Dear Javier:

Thank you for the opportunity to interview for the Market Manager position. I appreciated your time and enjoyed talking with you about the position. The interview confirmed my initial positive thoughts of Hi-Tech Partners and the strategic course you have charted for the company.

As I understand it, your goal is to match the position with someone who can deliver these three key priorities:

- **Offer a strong track record**—With 10 years of experience at two respected Fortune companies, I have demonstrated a solid trajectory of advancement. Highlights with Sony include a #1 ranking among 150 sales managers nationwide, with 45% sales growth; for HP, again a #1 ranking among 24 market managers, based on nearly doubling sales volume over the prior year.

- **Be a visionary leader and change agent**—I am currently sharing a new and aggressive vision with my national account to triple sales. This is being accomplished by tapping the right people for the right position, leveraging team members' strengths, and restructuring elements of the sales team to focus on key deliverables.

- **Deliver results**—Generating record-setting results has been the hallmark of my career. My commitment to you in the first few months would be to understand fully the needs of the business, identify underdeveloped and untapped opportunities, and then create a strategic plan that addresses growth in both core business and new business development. This would be the blueprint for executing initiatives to align the sales team with their inherent strengths, implement sales training, develop licensed and branded promotional premiums, and emphasize conceptual selling to generate more business for your accounts.

Given these experiences and competencies, I'm confident the 50% growth you are targeting for the division is attainable. As my track record shows, I have always exceeded growth expectations and am certain I would do the same for Hi-Tech Partners.

I look forward to speaking with you again soon.

Sincerely,

Charles Candidate

Figure 12.1: Performance-based thank-you/follow-up letter.

CRAIG E. COTTERDAM

Five Nonesuch Place   (214) 543-5432
Dallas, TX 75555   cec555@att.net   mobile (214) 432-4321

[date]

Mr. Michael Meeker, Director of Operations
San Juan Surveyors
55 Center Park Place
Dallas, TX 75432

Dear Mr. Meeker:

It's been several weeks since I had the pleasure of meeting you and your team at San Juan Surveyors. I wanted to touch base and get an idea of how the search is coming and what I might do to further my candidacy.

As you know, there are several opportunities I have looked at recently. I must admit, however, that the products, people, and culture of San Juan Surveyors appear to be the best fit. As you commented in our first meeting, this as an opportunity where my industry contacts could provide added value to the company and its clients.

I'll look forward to speaking with you soon. By the way, I had some additional thoughts on how you might expedite the large public works project we spoke of.

Best,

Craig Cotterdam

Figure 12.2: Performance-based follow-up letter.

JOAN E. FONTANELLA

One Wooded Lane   (206) 543-5432
Seattle, WA 98765   joyjoy@inspring.net   mobile (206) 432-4321

[date]

Ms. Jessica Dupree
Regional Manager
Pharma Pharmaceuticals
555 Research Lane
Paramus, NJ 01234

Dear Ms. Dupree:

I understand you will likely be coming to a decision soon about the new District Sales Manager for the Western U.S. In addition to technical competencies for the position, you'll likely want someone with whom you'll be able to work easily…someone who supports you in your initiatives and values teamwork.

I have earned a strong reputation for supporting my regional managers and working well with other managers. Illustrating this is the attached letter of recommendation from Allen Anguiano, Pharmacia Director of Specialty Sales. In it, he writes:

> *"I value sales managers who are proactive drivers, who understand the importance of strategic planning, and who are positive, people-oriented leaders…professionals who consistently deliver. Joan embodies all of these qualities…and more…. Of my eight current direct reports, I would rank her at the top."*

In addition, quotes from other district sales managers include the following:

"[Joan] has always been extremely professional, organized, and willing to do more than her share." ~ Craig Maleski, DSM

"As a new DSM, Joan was my mentor…. Collaboration is one of her strong suits."
~ Judi Zantilla, DSM

"Joan is an open, supportive co-worker … her teamwork is appreciated by myself, our other DM counterparts, and RSD." ~ Hillary Jones, DSM

Jennifer indicated you were tied up in meetings on Friday when I left a voice message. I would like the opportunity to meet again to review your needs and how I can help achieve Pharma's goals.

Best,

Joan Fontanella

Figure 12.3: Follow-up letter after second interview.

MEGAN FENNELSOM

99 Bayshore Way   (213) 543-5432
Los Angeles, CA 92021   meganf2@email.net

[date]

Jeremy Jones
Regional Sales Manager
Mytronics
12345 Century Boulevard
Los Angeles, CA 90210

Dear Jeremy:

Once again, thank you for the opportunity to meet. I was pleased that David Manners and Ruth Meeker could make it down from the Bay Area for our meeting (I will be sending them a follow-up note separately).

As you know by now, I respect your products and know I would enjoy promoting them to your clients. To summarize:

> I *want* to do the job, I *know* I can do the job, and I will work *harder, longer, and smarter* than other candidates to exceed your expectations for the territory.

I look forward to speaking with you regarding the next step.

Sincerely,

Megan Fennelsom

Figure 12.4: Sample follow-up after third interview.

JENNA JONES

32123 W. Belmont
Sacramento, CA 95454

(916) 543-5432
jj2000@email.net

[date]

Francine Pinelle
Wholesome Life Products
123 Westmont Street
Sacramento, CA 95454

Dear Francine:

Despite my disappointment in the Sacramento position being put on hold, I am grateful for the opportunity because it introduced me to you!

I deeply appreciate your enthusiasm, time, and commitment toward my application with Wholesome Life Products. Please keep me in mind should other opportunities arise.

I'll look forward to helping you with the school asthma screening project.

Best regards,

Jenna Jones

Figure 12.5: Sample follow-up letter after not getting the job.

	Program Manager
	Division of Continuing Education
	Prepared by
	Carrie Candidate, M.S.

Goal #1:

**Identify, develop, and promote instructional programs
that effectively meet the continuing-education
needs of individuals and organizations.**

Strategies:

1. Formulate a task force for planning and implementing the preceding objective.

2. Conduct an employer needs assessment, including design of a survey instrument. Analyze results, draw conclusions, and make recommendations to the task force or management team.

3. Establish employer advisory committees by industries and fields.

4. Identify employee skills, knowledge, and competencies in demand by South Texas employers.

5. Incorporate innovative delivery systems to meet the adult learner needs.

6. Develop a comprehensive marketing and promotion plan to target audiences (for example, direct-mail marketing, advertising, and employer visits to targeted organizations).

7. Based on employer feedback, create and develop flyers and brochures and market to target audiences, including

    -   Special-education teachers in the K–12 systems
    -   Human resource managers in education and business
    -   First-line supervisors in management positions
    -   Healthcare professionals
    -   Accountants
    -   Therapists and social workers

8. Be visible at key community events to promote the Division of Continuing Education.

9. Evaluate return-on-investment in all activities to ensure fiscal goals are met.

Figure 12.6: Sample leave-behind document describing strategies the candidate would suggest to meet a specific program goal.

AIDEN B. CARLISLE

(312) 555-5555   abc-win@yahoo.com   (312) 555-5556

FINANCE / OPERATIONS HIGHLIGHTS

Delivered record cash flow, profit & shareholder value in *every* assignment.
Leveraged national/international sales & manufacturing opportunities.
Orchestrated complex turnarounds in record time.
Funded companies in difficult capital markets.
Created/redesigned systems and infrastructure for startups and existing companies.
Well-versed in diverse industries (high-tech manufacturing, software, consumer products, retail).

Strengths:

- Managing P&L, boosting shareholder value (equity, dividends), quickly capturing cost controls & cash-flow gains, building companies into international market leaders, designing process improvements & best practices, optimizing production & logistics, evaluating/implementing domestic & international outsourcing opportunities (China, Hong Kong, Singapore, Taiwan, Mexico).

Turnaround Strategy:

- Led restructuring of widget manufacturing company in 5 months…drove $18 million to bottom line in 1 year…reduced monthly burn from $2 million to $500K (Capital Machine, Inc.).

- Led international business preservation strategy, completing 5-year business plan in 1 month…salvaged $5 million credit facility…crafted operations strategies to capture first-year tangible savings of $1 million in manufacturing and production (Kay Emporium, Inc.).

Corporate Growth:

- Launched unique patented business platform that transformed startup into an international category leader and drove sales from $4 million to $50 million in 3 years (Cartell, Inc.).

- Executed M&A growth strategy that propelled company revenue from $95 million to $700 million in 2 years (Trim-Co, Inc.).

Manufacturing & Distribution Operations:

- Increased manufacturing capacity 900% through consolidation of production and distribution processes—from 500 to 5,000 units per week in 30 days (Cartell, Inc.).

- Conceived operational strategies that accelerated growth of wholly owned centers from 1 to 12 and associated centers from 0 to 1,300 in 12–15 months (Cartell, Inc.).

Finance/ Funding:

- Spearheaded $122 million in public and private debt/equity financings throughout career.

- Key in placing $195 million in debt securities (Trim-Co, Inc.).

- Steered company through successful IPO, netting $26 million…led leveraged management buyout 4 years later (TTC Systems).

Leadership & Team Building:

- Recruited by Boards for ability to set/execute fast-traction strategies, create a sense of urgency, and build momentum.

- Polished corporate/media interface … at ease working with Boards, staff, key partners.

Figure 12.7: Sample leave-behind one-page document highlighting accomplishments in key competency areas.

Chapter Wrap-Up

Closing an interview is both art and science. The latter involves a four-step process wherein you'll gain agreement that you have what the employer needs, close any gaps, express your desire for the position or ask for the job, and keep momentum rolling and communication going. The art of closing requires following your intuition—when to push for an answer and when to pull back and wait. It also requires watching for buying signals from the interviewer. Those signals might be introducing you to additional employees beyond the original interview team, sharing information of a proprietary nature, or questioning you about your availability for a starting date or your salary expectations (see chapter 16 for handling salary negotiations). When buying signals come, emphasize your interest and ask for the job.

Throughout all phases of the 4 C's—Connect, Clarify, Collaborate, and Close—let your personality and natural enthusiasm shine through. *Employers love to hire people who love what they do.* Recognize that the more connection or rapport you gain with the interviewer, the more you'll be able to clarify and collaborate. The more you clarify and collaborate, the more natural it will be to close.

10 Quick Tips to Close with Professionalism

1. **The goal of the close is to make it easy for the employer to say "Yes!, we want you."**

2. **Closing should never be a manipulative, high-pressure process of asking the interviewer to make you an offer.** Eventually, the tables will be turned and the interviewer will close *you*, hoping you will say "Yes!, I want the job."

3. **To close, start by gaining agreement that you have what it takes.** These questions will help: "May I ask what you see as my greatest strengths for the position?" Or, "Are you satisfied that I'd meet your needs in the position?" Or, "May I ask what experience you see as most relevant to the position?"

4. **Next, close any gaps between what the employer wants and what you can deliver.** Helpful questions to close the gap include these: "Is there anything in my background that would prevent you from offering me this position?" "How have I done in confirming that I can deliver the results you're looking for?" "What additional evidence do you need?" "What concerns do you have about my qualifications?" "What would it take to assure you that I would be the best person for this position?"

5. **Express desire for the position, and ask for the job!** Many an interviewer has passed over a wholly qualified candidate because the candidate did not appear motivated to do the job. Motivation to do the job can be as important as qualification to do the job.

6. **Crank up the energy and enthusiasm in your voice and ask for the job with one of these approaches:** "I'm extremely interested. Although I'm looking at a couple of opportunities right now, this appears to be the one where I could make the biggest contribution." Or, "I can assure you that if you extended a reasonable offer today, I would be on board tomorrow." Or, "I am absolutely certain this is the perfect position for me. There may be others who have more impressive 'resume lineage,' but no one will give you more enthusiasm and commitment."

7. **When closing, find a way to keep up the momentum.** To do so, consider a "leave-behind." This item could be a fact sheet relevant to the interviewers, a case study, before-and-after photos, a collection of testimonials, or a meaningful but inexpensive gift, such as one of your favorite motivational books.

8. **Keep the door open for future communications by asking,** "What's the next step?" Ask permission to follow up: "I'd like to be able to touch base with you as additional ideas from our discussion come to mind. Is e-mail or phone best?" If the interviewer says she'll get back to you, ask, "When might I expect your call?"

9. **Send a performance-based thank-you/follow-up note the same day that you interview.** If the interview went really well, also consider a quick telephone call a few hours later in the day: "Jake, this is Sheri Rosenstein. I'll be following up as we discussed, but in the meantime I just had to pick up the phone and tell you that I'm so energized from our meeting. It was really a pleasure to speak with you, and I'll sure look forward to continuing our discussions."

10. **Watch for buying signals from the interviewer:** an introduction to other team members who aren't part of the interview team, disclosure of confidential or proprietary information, inclusion on discussion about business strategy, or questions about your availability or salary requirements. When these signals come, reiterate your interest and ask for the job!

Magical Coaching Questions

What steps can you take to enhance your closing skills?

_____

_____

_____

Do you anticipate any gaps between what your skills are and what the employer wants done?

_____

_____

_____

If so, what actions would help close those gaps?

_____

_____

_____

Refer back to the factors in table 12.1. Which is most important to you? _____

What minimum score do you need for each of the factors before you'd consider taking the job? _____

What is the lowest total score you would accept? _____

Part 3

Preparing for Interview Questions and Negotiating Salary

Chapter
13

How to Respond to Frequently Asked Questions

The truth isn't the truth until people believe you, and they can't believe you if they don't know what you're saying, and they can't know what you're saying if they don't listen to you, and they won't listen to you if you're not interesting, and you won't be interesting unless you say things imaginatively, originally, freshly.

—William Bernbach, American advertising executive

J ob seekers typically make a checklist of the things they will need for a successful job search. Usually near the top of the list is resume preparation and interview practice. You have learned throughout this book, however, that there is much more to a successful job search than polishing a resume and memorizing interview responses.

"A" Candidates first aim for positions that are a solid FIT. They then do sufficient research to understand the needs of the employer. And, from that position of knowledge and power, they demonstrate their ability to do the job. Their interview responses aren't simply memorized scripts, but interactive responses that lead to collaborative dialogue and problem solving.

In chapter 1, I stated in Truth #5 that you do *not* need to memorize answers to 100+ interview questions. That statement remains true. What you *do* need to remember about delivering your responses are these 5 D's:

- ★ **Discover** what the employer truly needs to have done (the deliverables).

- ★ **Document** your knowledge, skills, and experience to capably do the job (talent/competencies).

- ★ **Demonstrate** your ability to do the job with greater profitability to the company than other candidates (value).

- ★ **Display** your ability to motivate yourself and/or others (energy and enthusiasm).

- ★ **Describe** your ability to fit in with the company culture (chemistry).

In this chapter, we'll first look at how long the interview might be and how many questions you should prepare for. The remainder of the chapter outlines answer strategies for Frequently Asked Questions (FAQs), including a *Before* and *After* example for each question to give you a feel for how, and how not, to respond.

How Long Will the Interview Be?

The length of interviews varies. First interviews frequently last between 30 and 45 minutes for nonexempt positions (*nonexempt* refers to employees who are entitled to receive overtime pay), whereas 60 to 90 minutes is common for exempt positions (professional employees who are exempt from overtime pay). Second and subsequent interviews may last longer, or they may be a succession of shorter meetings with other members of the organization.

How Many Questions Will I Be Asked?

Every candidate wonders how many and what questions will be asked. Crystal balls aside, the answer to that will vary from interview to interview. Some recruiting consultants advise interviewers to conduct an interview based on just this one key question: *What is the most significant accomplishment in your career?*

However, most interviewers will ask well beyond this one question. More realistic is a number between 10 and 20. Let's do some math to calculate how many questions will fit into a standard interview. If an interview is 60 minutes in duration, with five or more minutes on either end for opening and closing, that leaves 45 to 50 minutes for discussion. It takes roughly 30 seconds for the interviewer to ask a question, and approximately one to three minutes for the candidate to answer. A candidate's one- to three-minute answer can easily expand into 5 to 10 minutes when the interviewer asks follow-up questions or the candidate asks clarifying questions (see chapter 11).

For purposes of illustration, let's say that on average each question-answer (Q&A) round lasts between five and seven minutes. Fifty minutes divided by five or seven leaves time for just 7 to 10 interview questions, or 11 to 16 questions if the interview goes beyond an hour.

Basic arithmetic shows that you do not need to concern yourself with every FAQ listed in this chapter. It would be impossible for the interviewer to ask that many questions! On top of that, the interviewer will likely ask industry-specific situational or behavioral questions (chapter 14 covers industry-specific questions for a number of professions). So, rest assured you won't be grilled on 50 questions.

Yet the question remains: Which FAQs will I be asked? The answer is clear: God only knows...but trust heaven to help you through!

Frequently Asked Questions
Now let's get on to the questions!

Question
Tell me about yourself.

Strategy
Focus on what the interviewers need to know to determine that you're the best investment they could make.

Give the interviewer a quick "READ" on this question, which stands for

- **Relevant:** First, sift everything you say through the relevance filter. Ask yourself, "is the information I'm sharing important to the interviewers? Will the information make them think more or less favorably of me?"

- **Experience:** Provide a quick overview of years of experience or most important companies worked for, along with position titles and responsibility highlights.

- **Academics:** Mention impressive institutions, degrees, certifications, or alumni networks associated with your education.

- **Deliverables:** Translate your experience into value by offering one or two results.

"Before" Answer
I graduated from college, went to work in the late 70s for an advertising firm; then went to another firm; then started my own business, which was really great because it met my needs to be flexible and raise my kids, plus be my own boss.

"After"—the "Magic Words" Answer

I'd be happy to. Before I do that, I'm wondering if you'd tell me a little more about two or three key strengths you're looking for in the ideal candidate. After the interviewer responds, say *Great, it sounds like we're definitely on the same page. You asked about my background.*

With virtually 20 years of experience, the last seven as a creative director at Smith & Jones Agency, I offer three key strengths that I believe are closely aligned to your needs for the position.

*First, I'm an excellent **advertising strategist**—my skills in this area have delivered an ROI of 10:1 on marketing funds, which as you know is well above average.*

*Second, I'm an excellent **project manager;** have numerous contacts with artists, copywriters, and printers; and am able to bring projects in on time and on a shoestring budget. It wasn't unusual for me to save $5,000 on printing costs when our total budget was $25,000.*

*Third, I have a strong **creative background**. Many of the campaigns I directed earned national advertising awards. Based on our chats thus far, I'm confident that my skill set would be a close match for what you need.*

And, I'd love to hear more about what you need for this position. For instance, what do you consider the most pressing projects or issues I'd be tackling in the first 90 days on the job?

Question
What are the top duties you perform in your current/most recent position?

Strategy
Limit your answer to three duties. If you list more than three, it may be difficult for the interviewer to keep track and tasks will start running together. List fewer than three, and you may appear limited in your skills. Focus on the three that are most relevant to the position at hand.

"Before" Answer
I do mainly accounts receivable and stuff around that, like sending invoices out and collections.

"After"—the "Magic Words" Answer
I perform a range of accounting functions, with a focus on accounts receivable, accounts payable, and payroll. I understand the position you need filled will perform similar duties. I reduced outstanding receivables in the 90- to 120-day window by approximately 75 percent, and sent the rest to collections. Our payables have improved, as well, as I set up a system to take advantage of 2 percent/net 10-day vendor discounts. In the payroll area, I manage biweekly payroll for 10 exempt and 150 hourly employees, including quarterly reports, which was something that was previously handled by my supervisor. Some of the efficiencies I put in place freed my time to be able to help her with this and other department tasks.

Question

What types of decisions do you frequently make in your current/most recent position? How do you go about making them?

Strategy

This question helps reveal to the interviewer how much responsibility you carry, your analytical skills, how you prioritize your day, what initiative you take, and what you consider to be important decisions. If you are in management, describe your ability to make both big-picture and detail decisions that align with long-term strategy, such as responsibility for $300,000 in buying decisions for a "tween" retailer, as well as details regarding trend, fabric, and color direction. If you are not in a supervisory or management role, avoid the misstep of saying that you don't make decisions, as the *Before* answer illustrates.

"Before" Answer

I don't have any supervisory authority, so I really don't make too many decisions.

Magic

"After"—the "Magic Words" Answer

As a customer support rep, I make decisions throughout my day, from deciding how to prioritize the processing of Internet orders that are in my e-mail bin each morning to determining whether I need to consult my supervisor on a customer complaint or special order to solving a particular problem related to one of the orders. For instance, just last week there was a situation where the client wanted a one-day delivery on his order. [Tell a SMART Story™ here with emphasis on **A**ction so that the interviewer sees how you go about making decisions.]

The most important decision I make each day is to choose the right attitude and remember that work is about meeting the needs of our clients.

Question

What is the most significant project or suggestion you have initiated in your career?

Strategy

Note the last three words: *in your career.* This should be your biggest, most salient initiative. The interviewer is looking for your drive and energy here—what is the most important idea or project you personally set into motion, and what do you deem significant. Depending on your functional position and years of experience, it may be something like a new company or major project launched, or it may be on a smaller scale, such as an idea you suggested that was implemented and adopted by others. This before-and-after answer suggests how a college student applying for a management training program might answer the question.

"Before" Answer

Since I've been in college and am just starting my career, I can't say that there is anything too significant yet. But, I'm looking forward to doing some significant projects.

"After"—the "Magic Words" Answer

A number of projects come to mind, such as initiating a college schedule that allowed me to complete my degree in three and a half instead of four years and proposing a philanthropic fund-raiser for my business fraternity that raised $16,000. I'd have to say, though, that the suggestion I'm most proud of is the one I proposed to classmates to identify "best practices" for study groups, which made a dramatic improvement in some people's grades. Let me explain. We were studying best practices in an upper-division management class. I asked the question in class, "what if we were to apply this to how we study?" It turned out that several people were interested, so we agreed to meet outside of class. From that core group of five people, we formed the "Best Practice, Ace-the-Class Study Group." Under my direction, we located and evaluated study groups both on our campus and on six other campuses in the Northeast. From that research, we identified 10 best practices that we put into place. We met twice a week, and I took turns leading the group every other time with another leader. Our group grew and replicated itself, ultimately to 12 separate groups on campus with a total of more than 100 students participating. Most important, we measured progress by our grades. On average, students improved their class grades by one full mark, and we even had some students who started the study groups with Ds who were now making As. I also took the initiative to create a manual so that other groups could easily form and continue without me being there.

Question

What is the most significant project or suggestion you have initiated in each of your positions?

Strategy

Similar to the prior question, the interviewer is looking for a consistent pattern of initiative, energy, drive, and ambition. Use accomplishments on your resume to guide you in choosing the most significant project or initiative for each position. If you have a work history that involves half a dozen or more positions, spend more time describing the significant project at more recent positions and shorten the overall description of each project so that you don't sound long-winded. Describe positions in reverse-chronological order, from the most recent to the most dated experiences. Stop, take a breather after describing two or three projects, and say, "Am I giving you enough detail? Would you like to hear more?" Make sure that you are detailing projects or suggestions you *initiated*, not just a project you worked on.

"Before" Answer

In my first position out of college as a business analyst, I was assigned to a project that involved.... After that, I was promoted to a senior analyst and worked on larger accounts. Then I moved from Indianapolis to Cincinnati and went to work for XYZ Company. My most significant project there was the analysis of a merger and acquisition project.... [Note how the candidate misses entirely the point of the question, giving an overview of his work history but not pointing to projects or ideas he initiated.]

"After"—the "Magic Words" Answer

I'd be happy to outline projects or ideas that I initiated. My most recent position as a Business Analyst Supervisor for Idico Manufacturing actually came about because I took the initiative. The then-supervisor announced that she was pregnant and would be taking a

three-month maternity leave in six months. Because this was a relatively new company, I knew that a solid list of standard operating procedures for her position had not yet been developed. I offered to help develop this list so that the department could run smoothly during her leave. She asked me to shadow her for several months so that SOPs could be documented, which I did. After her baby came, she decided not to return, and I was the one she recommended to take her place. So the initiative of developing the SOPs led to my current position. I've helped formalize SOPs for every position in the department. We've seen an increase in efficiency because of these, but more importantly, when temp workers come in they can be immediately productive.

Prior to this, I worked for Del-Lap Manufacturing, also in a business analyst capacity. This was a small mom-and-pop company with a high-end, quality product that needed to cut purchasing costs to compete with larger manufacturers. Here, I suggested creating a co-op with other smaller manufacturers to purchase commodities at deeper discounts than previously possible. In most cases, we cut our raw materials costs by three percent, for an annual savings of $250,000.

Is this giving you the detail you need? Would you like me to continue with examples for my first two employers?

Question

How many years' experience do you have with _____ (the type of product or service you'll be providing at the company)?

Strategy

If you have the years of experience the interviewer is looking for (this is usually stated on the job announcement), tell them so. If you don't have the experience requested, describe the experience you have in a closely related field, as in this *Before* and *After.*

"Before" Answer

Well, I don't have the three years of experience in extrusion molding you're looking for, but I'm confident I can do the job.

Magic

"After"—the "Magic Words" Answer

Over the past three years, I've worked for a plastics company that supplies gear for the scuba-diving industry and has a great reputation for its quality products. While in the warehouse, I've been exposed to most of the machinery and had the opportunity to provide backup for the operators. For example, on one occasion, the manager of the extrusion molding department sought me out to help them meet a critical deadline. The manager later thanked me for my help and said my dexterity and "team spirit" was instrumental in their meeting a major account order on time.

Question

How would you describe your ideal work environment?

Strategy

Ideally, you'd want to describe the company that you're interviewing with—just be careful to not go overboard and look like a sycophant. Research the company (of course, you've already done this!) and offer details that appeal to all four temperaments (see chapter 10). For instance, mention the company's vision, mission, and commitment to excellence to appeal to the Rational/Conceptualizer types; mention structure, policies, and sense of camaraderie for the Guardian/Traditionalist types; emphasize positive impacts on people and customers for the Idealists; and focus on action and results for the Artisan/Experiencer.

"Before" Answer

I'm really looking for a company that appreciates and rewards its employees...a place where there's a sense of community and people trust one another.

"After"—the "Magic Words" Answer

I noted the mission statement on your Web site that says, "To build a great company that values people and inspires excellence in healthcare." I'm very closely aligned with that statement. I want to be part of a culture that inspires excellence—I believe it's the catalyst for innovation and market leadership. [The prior statement should appeal to the Rational/Conceptualizer.] *That excellence should be applied throughout the organization so that best practices are identified and people know what is expected of them.* [The prior statement should appeal to the Guardian/Traditionalist.] *At the same time, those practices should allow people the freedom to act as needed to fulfill needs.* [The last statement should appeal to the Experiencer.] *I believe people are a company's most important asset, so ideally managers should be committed to matching people to positions that are a good fit. When there's a good fit, employees are naturally motivated and enthusiastic about their work.* [The last statement should appeal to the Idealist.] *And, of course, there should be bottom-line value to everyone, from shareholders and employees to physicians and patients. When all of these elements are in place, there's a naturally occurring synergy that will cause everyone to benefit.*

Question

Describe your ideal boss.

Strategy

The interviewer wants to know 1) if you are manageable and 2) how to manage you. Be brief with your explanation, or you may end up with a disparity between your ideal boss and who will actually be managing you. At the same time, this is an opportunity to convey how you want others to treat you.

"Before" Answer

My ideal boss would be someone who respects me, sets realistic goals, does not micromanage, and does not keep changing the target every other day. [The "does nots" in this answer make it too negative.]

"After"—the "Magic Words" Answer

That's easy, because I've had the privilege of working under ideal bosses. [Note that this sentence doesn't say that every boss was ideal.] *The relationships were based on mutual respect, shared goals, and open communication.*

Question

Have you worked under bosses who weren't ideal?

Strategy

This question may come after the prior question about your ideal boss. If so, don't be drawn into criticizing a prior boss who wasn't ideal. People will only wonder whether you'll later do the same to someone in their company.

"Before" Answer

Well, yes. My current boss. That's part of the reason I am looking for a new position. His ethical standards are not what you'd call pure.

"After"—the "Magic Words" Answer

Magic

I find it helpful to think in terms of a person's assets and potential. Bosses are human, and each one has certain strengths. I consider it my job to recognize and focus on the positives. Looking in the negative direction often creates dissension. Whatever the case, I like to build my relationships on respect, common goals, and direct communication.

Question

That's a good answer. Can you give me an example of someone who wasn't an ideal boss?

Strategy

Keep your cool and don't allow any unresolved feelings of anger or resentment to seep into the response, no matter how badly you may have been mistreated by a boss in the past. Be brief and upbeat in your answer.

"Before" Answer

That would be my current boss. There have been a number of situations where he's asked me to do things that crossed the line of ethics. For instance, when turning in insurance applications, he's asked me to change dates and medical information so that policies would be accepted by the underwriters.

"After"—the "Magic Words" Answer

Magic

I've been fortunate to work with some really talented people over the years, and learned something from a variety of management styles. If I were pressed, I'd have to say that one person with whom I worked was challenging because the target goal changed frequently and, though I was committed to communicating with that person, I wasn't kept in the loop. I value keeping communication lines open and think it's critical to helping not only my boss know that I'm on track and delivering results, but those who report to me as well. I find that communicating is critical to keeping people motivated.

Question

Why are you leaving your current employer (or Why did you leave your last employer?)?

Strategy

Avoid saying anything negative about former employers, or it will look like you are whining or not taking responsibility for yourself. Some of the best reasons for leaving include a desire to

* Learn more (the job provided no opportunity to learn and apply growth)

* Earn more (you needed more salary)

* Grow more (you wanted to take on more responsibility)

* Work more (the job was temporary or part time, the company cut your hours or had a RIF/layoff, or the company relocated its headquarters/offices)

* Commute/travel less

Other acceptable reasons include family relocation and personal situations (maternity, accident/illness, caring for a terminally ill loved one, and so on). Any other answer may raise red flags with the interviewer. Avoid telling too many details, but be factual.

"Before" Answer

My company has had a series of reductions-in-force recently and my boss told me that I'd better start looking since our department goals haven't been reached lately.

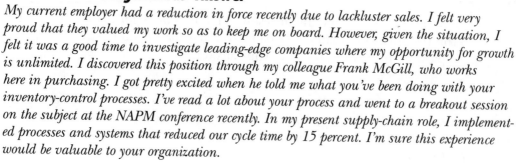

"After"—the "Magic Words" Answer

My current employer had a reduction in force recently due to lackluster sales. I felt very proud that they valued my work so as to keep me on board. However, given the situation, I felt it was a good time to investigate leading-edge companies where my opportunity for growth is unlimited. I discovered this position through my colleague Frank McGill, who works here in purchasing. I got pretty excited when he told me what you've been doing with your inventory-control processes. I've read a lot about your process and went to a breakout session on the subject at the NAPM conference recently. In my present supply-chain role, I implemented processes and systems that reduced our cycle time by 15 percent. I'm sure this experience would be valuable to your organization.

Question

What prompted each of your departures from previous organizations?

Strategy

This is similar to "why are you leaving your current employer?" Here, the interviewer is looking for patterns of why you leave positions. Is it that you get bored after a certain amount of time? Is it that you can't get along with people? Is it that you lose your temper and quit? Is it that you jump ship for any new opportunity that comes along? To answer this question, point to items in the list of acceptable reasons noted in the prior question.

Note that the final sentence in the *After* example allows you to control whom the interviewer calls. If you don't hold favored status with one of your prior bosses, you can steer the interviewer toward someone at the company who will give you a favorable reference.

"Before" Answer

In my last position, I was forced out by a power play. Prior to that, I had a boss whom I didn't see eye to eye with. In the position before that, my manager just wouldn't give me more responsibility and I needed more challenge and variety.

"After"—the "Magic Words" Answer

Magic

In my last position, the company moved its offices farther north, so the commute became more than two hours each way for me. Prior to that, I was recruited to start up a new program similar to the one you have here—I'm confident my knowledge of bringing that program from ground zero to self-sustaining will be of interest to you and I'll look forward to giving you more details on that when you're ready. And finally, before that, I had been with the ABC Company seven years and, being a family-owned company, the organizational structure allowed no room for advancement. I can offer you contact persons and phone numbers for each of those employers if you'd like.

Question
What prompted any internal job changes with your current or previous employers?

Strategy
The interviewer wants to know whether you are promotable. Upward mobility with a prior company will indicate a track record of strong performance, adding to your status as a known and trusted commodity. Conversely, if you were demoted or even had a lateral transfer, this may raise suspicions with the interviewer. If the latter is the case, share the situation in as positive a light as possible, as the *After* example illustrates.

"Before" Answer

While at Adecco, I was on probation due to poor attendance and had to transfer from working with Tier I key accounts to working with Tier II clients.

"After"—the "Magic Words" Answer

Magic

While at Adecco, I transferred from the key accounts work group to the general accounts work group and, while there, honed my multitasking skills in working with a greater number of accounts. On average, the number of projects I worked on each day nearly doubled. It sounds like you've got a similar volume of work in this department, so I'm confident my experience will be of value in servicing your clients. Would you like to hear more about the types of clients and projects I worked with?

Question
What do you know about (or expect from) the position?

Strategy
This is a chance to show off how you've done your homework on the position. State what you understand to be the key competencies needed for the position, the top two or three tasks, the key deliverables expected in the upcoming 6 to 12 months, to whom the position reports, and how it fits in with or supports the overall company.

"Before" Answer

Well, I don't know too much yet—just what the person in the telephone interview mentioned to me. I'd love to hear more.

Magic

"After"—the "Magic Words" Answer

As I understand it, I would support the management and marketing of three product lines. I'd be reporting to the Marketing Supervisor. [Use "I would" and "I'd be" to help interviewers start to visualize you in the position.] You need someone who has excellent organizational skills, is detail-oriented, and communicates well to collaborate with a range of departments like R&D, fabrication, packaging, and distribution. Conversations with people inside and outside the company lead me to believe that the key tasks are coordinating production of marketing materials and keeping communication lines open with internal and external partners, including your graphic designers and printer so that everyone is on the same page about deadlines. From a results standpoint, it sounds as though you'd like to see a system developed to improve internal communications, plus build out the collateral marketing materials for the newest addition to your widget product line.

If now is the best time, I can tell you how I tackled some similar projects in my role as Marketing Manager at XYZ Company.

Question

What do you know about our company?

Strategy

Your response should include both an understanding of the company *and* the industry. Be informed! If it's a public company, research it using Hoovers.com or other resources mentioned in appendix A. If the company has a Web site, read all the significant pages, especially press releases, bios of key decision makers, products and services pages, career opportunities pages, and so on. Talk to external company contacts, such as suppliers, vendors, consultants, and customers. Talk to internal company contacts, including those in the department you will be joining and those in other departments.

"Before" Answer

I know your company has a reputation as a great place to work. Tell me more.

"After"—the "Magic Words" Answer

Magic

I understand from my research that the company is one of the leading regional widget manufacturers, and that your top competitors are Acme Widgets and ABC Widge-co. Vernon Reynolds founded the company 60 years ago and his son has been at the helm since 1990. Under his direction, you've added fiber-optic widgets and expanded your distribution from two states to seven. I've spoken with several people outside the company to learn a bit more, and everything I heard was positive. I'm really interested to learn more about this new device that you'll be launching in the near term. One of the customers I spoke with mentioned that they're anxious to get that item shipped. Is this the most important project that you're working on to date, or is the other initiative involving plastic-coated widgets a higher priority?

Wait for the interviewer to respond. Then, if appropriate, add a SMART Story™ that describes your background as it relates to the company's goals and working priorities.

Question

What contribution do you anticipate being able to make in this position?

Strategy

If this question is asked too early in the interview process, respond with something along these lines: *I'm committed to offering a solid contribution to the department and company and will be better able to indicate what that contribution will be once I know more about the deliverables for the position. May we revisit this question once we've covered some of the results that you're looking for?*

"Before" Answer

I plan to make a solid contribution—I always have in the past and will do so in the future.

Magic

"After"—the "Magic Words" Answer

I anticipate contributing in a way that will make you glad you hired me! Seriously, I'm confident I would do something similar to what I've done in my past positions. For instance, I came in to a situation where _____ [fill in the blank with some numbers-driven fact, such as our accounting department's month-end close was taking 10 days] *and helped to* _____ [fill in the blank, such as reduce the month-end close to just three days].

Question

What contribution could you make to our team?

Strategy

If the interviewer has not yet described the team and its goals to you, ask for more information before responding to this question. If you already have a good understanding of the team and what is expected of you, describe how you function best in a team, whether as creator, doer, facilitator, leader, motivator, scheduler, supporter, and so on. Then, offer a SMART Story™ that describes a success you've had in a similar role.

"Before" Answer

I've been complimented by supervisors and teammates as being very team oriented. I believe that you really can do more together than you can apart. I would make whatever contribution was needed to the team to make it happen.

Magic

"After"—the "Magic Words" Answer

I've worked on a variety of teams and adapted my strengths depending on what was needed at the time. For instance, I have played the role of conceptualizer—the idea person; coordinator—the make sure it happens person; and supporter—the get-it-done person. I'd be happy to offer a tangible example of each of those roles. Is there one that you're interested in more than another? [Wait for the interviewer to answer; then proceed with a SMART Story™ that describes your experience in the specified role.]

Question

How would your boss/coworkers/references describe you?

Strategy

Be positive and offer proof. Consider including in your portfolio/brag book copies of recent performance evaluations (provided they are glowing) or "attaboy" letters from your boss, coworkers, and other references to document your statements. Recall the identity ingredients from table 2.5 that you checked in developing your FIT™. This would be a great time to reinforce those elements. If you don't have letters of reference yet, now (rather than later) would be a good time to ask for them.

"Before" Answer

My boss would describe me as accountable, intelligent, loyal, and willing to go the extra mile.

"After"—the "Magic Words" Answer

I've got a few documents in my binder here that will give you an idea of what my boss thought of me. Some of the terms she uses are "accountable, intelligent, loyal, willing to go the extra mile." I believe she would confirm that I am someone she could depend on to do whatever needed to be done. For instance, when our company was hit by a computer virus and the system was down for 24 hours, we had hundreds of customer orders that couldn't be processed. She made the decision to manually process orders for key retail accounts so that they could receive the merchandise they needed for an upcoming three-day weekend. Although my primary responsibility as an account specialist was to track sales and analyze trends, I offered to help in whatever way I could. My boss and I, along with two sales reps, worked in the warehouse until after midnight to process the priority orders so that they could go out the next morning. The accounts were aware of the computer problems and, although they understood the situation, weren't happy because of potential lost business. Some were threatening to go to our competitor if we hadn't made this extra effort. Our midnight vigil went a long way toward customer goodwill.

Question

Tell me about a time when you worked with a difficult person.

Strategy

Responding to the question affirms that you find some people difficult. Rephrase the question in a way that indicates you don't find people difficult. Avoid the temptation to share horror stories about difficult people you have worked with.

"Before" Answer

Oh my gosh, could I tell you stories. One manager was on an around-the-world ego trip and wouldn't allow anyone to take credit for their own ideas. One time he took one of my ideas and went directly to his director with it. The director loved the idea and implemented it, and I never got a dime for it. That guy was definitely what you'd call difficult.

"After"—the "Magic Words" Answer

I tend to not think of people as difficult. Instead, I view situations as opportunities to problem-solve and learn. For instance, in my last position, there was someone on my team who regularly missed deadlines—I'll call him Ralph, which wasn't his real name. When this happened, it prevented me from generating reports for my supervisor who needed them by the end of each month. Rather than blame Ralph for the report being late, I set up a calendaring system to check in with him five days prior to when I needed the information, and then again one day before I needed the information. Even with this reminder system, he still occasionally missed the deadline. That's when I made an appointment to sit down with him and learn more about what he did.

It turned out that he was trying to do the work of two people and was very hesitant to delegate tasks. Together, we collaborated on how I personally could access the information I needed rather than have him pull the numbers for me. That was eight months ago, and I haven't missed a deadline since then. It takes me about 30 minutes to get the data, which is less time than it was taking to send multiple reminders to Ralph. I figure that I can't control how other people will act; however, I can control my choices and actions. Sometimes it's more important to look at who is willing *to change than who* should *change.*

Question
Is your resume complete and up to date?

Strategy
Ideally, the answer to this would be yes. However, it's possible that the interviewer pulled your resume from the company's resume database, where you submitted it three or more months ago. If you have a more current resume than what the interviewer has, you can deftly pull out your updated resume at this point and offer it to the interviewer.

"Before" Answer
No, I've left my current employer, so the date that reads "2003 to present" isn't correct.

Magic

"After"—the "Magic Words" Answer
It's possible that you have a version that may not be current, since I submitted my resume to your Web site several months ago. Just to make sure we're all on the same page, here is the most recent version. You'll note that the most recent production figures for the last quarter are included on this one, and that our year-to-date numbers are 12 percent higher than goal.

Question
What do you like about your current position?

Tell me about work activities you enjoy so much that you lose track of time.

Strategy
This is a loaded question. If you describe tasks that aren't part of the new position, you may appear to be a poor fit. The *Before* answer that follows would backfire if the position you're interviewing for requires extroverted activity and the ability to deal with ambiguity. If asked this question early in the interview, give a brief response and talk about tasks that are aligned with what you know of the position from the job description or pre-interview research.

"Before" Answer
I really like having structure to my day. I know exactly what's expected of me so that I can shoot for a daily goal and hit it. Each morning, I come in and download the reports that

need to be analyzed and get so engrossed that I don't even realize it when someone walks into my cubicle. I've been known to forget to take a lunch break.

"After"—the "Magic Words" Answer

It's interesting that some of the responsibilities I enjoy the most are similar to what you've described as key to this position. For instance, I really enjoy a day where there's lots of demands and you never quite know what's going to happen next. I work best when there's business action and I can think on my feet. For example….

Question

What do you dislike about your current position?

What interests you least about your current position?

Jobs have pluses and minuses. What do you consider the minuses to your current position?

Strategy

The interviewer will be listening with twofold interest. First, do you point to dislikes about your current position that you'll also have to perform in the target position? If so, this will be a red flag to the interviewer. Second, are you not at a loss to list the things you dislike? If so, you'll be branded as negative. If pressed to list something you dislike, point to some minor housekeeping chore that requires little time, such as "backing up my computer" or "changing my outgoing voice-mail message daily." If you choose the latter, consider saying, "I prefer to just jump in and get started with the day, but I know that it's helpful to customers and my work group to know whether I'm in and when I'll be available to return calls."

"Before" Answer

I guess I'd have to say the deadlines. Sometimes it feels like herding cats to get everyone moving in the same direction and still meet the client's deadlines.

"After"—the "Magic Words" Answer

I don't think that I can point to anything I particularly dislike about managing creative teams. I feel very fortunate that I've found a career that really suits my strengths and talents. Earlier, you mentioned a need for someone who can handle the stress of deadlines. In my last position, I had as many as six significant projects going on at once, all with tight deadlines. I used MS Project to create a tracking system that kept all the projects on a timeline. Prior to two of the six companies contracting with me, they had missed deadlines and gone over budget. I was able to correct that.

Question

What would you want in your next position that you are not getting now?

Strategy

Do not use this question as an opportunity to disparage your current employer, boss, or position. If your list is too long, it begs the question, *Why haven't you taken responsibility to change some of those things sooner?* Review your list of Things That Matter (see chapter 2, "Step 3: Think About the Things That Matter"). From that

list, choose an altruistic value (not a self-serving one) that you are either not getting now or want to see more of.

"Before" Answer

Quite a few things are missing, actually. Right now, I'm not compensated fairly, don't have any upward mobility, work with a micromanaging boss, and don't get credit for innovative ideas or extra effort.

"After"—the "Magic Words" Answer

I think the key thing that I would like to be present in my next position is great communication. It's been my experience that keeping teammates and customers informed really opens the path for understanding, cooperation, and productivity.

Question

What are your strengths?

What is your greatest strength?

What strengths do you bring to the position?

What are your outstanding qualities?

Strategy

This would be a prime time to pull out your Three-Point Marketing Message (see chapter 4) and make sure it is tailored to the interviewer's primary needs. Recall the resume and sound-bite examples of Chris Caballero, who had mastered the 3 R's of sales: **R**esearch, **R**elationships, and **R**evenue Enhancement. Note how she uses this message in the *After* response.

"Before" Answer

Colleagues tell me I have excellent communication skills, am a people person, and am a quick learner. I'm sure all of these skills would be of value.

"After"—the "Magic Words" Answer

I have a number of strengths that would be of value to the position. As it relates to what we've discussed, I'd point to three key factors.

Number one, I'm an excellent researcher—I've developed qualified business leads using traditional and online research methods…. Approximately 40 percent of those leads were converted into new business.

Number two, I'm known for building relationships—I've quickly established loyal and trusting relationships with key accounts, networking contacts, and referral sources.

And number three, I know how to deliver revenue increases—throughout my career I have set new records for group and convention business at boutique hotels, as well as major-brand properties like yours. In my last position, I increased overall sales 45 percent and increased the average sale 17 percent.

May I ask, what kinds of goals are you targeting for the next three to six months?

Question

What is your greatest weakness?

In what areas do you feel you need work?

Strategy

Avoid describing a personality trait as these are harder to "fix." Pointing to a tendency for perfectionism or impatience with lazy people is a worn-out response—interviewers have heard these a million times. Focus on a new skill that can be learned or dazzle them with the insight that your greatest strength can sometimes be your greatest weakness, as the *After* example shows. This strategy moves the interviewer from focusing on the weakness toward hearing a SMART Story™ that describes how you overcame the weakness.

"Before" Answer

I'm a perfectionist and sometimes get impatient with people who don't put in a 110 percent effort.

"After"—the "Magic Words" Answer

I have come to realize that, as a manager, my greatest strength—which is my analytical skill—can sometimes be my greatest weakness if I over-rely on my logical, rational side and don't factor in the human equation. What I've done to counter this is to make sure I ask for input from team members who offer different perspectives. This has worked well to bring a balanced, 360-degree analysis to situations. For instance, there was a situation with XYZ Co. where we needed to make cutbacks. It was clear from a business perspective that at least three people in the department needed to be laid off. I sought input from several of my direct reports before making a final decision, and their thoughts helped me to see some options that would achieve our financial goals without jeopardizing morale and stability. I can offer you more details on how that worked out if you would like. [Then, segue into your SMART Story™.]

Question

What's your greatest fear? What are you most afraid of?

Strategy

Steer clear of answers such as a fear of failure or fear of a difficult relationship, such as not getting along with a boss or coworker. Avoid describing fears that would be outside the realm of the professional environment, such as fear of a terminal illness or terrorist attack.

This would be a great place to weave a quote into the conversation. Here are a few favorites on the subject:

"Nothing in life is to be feared. It is only to be understood."

—Marie Curie

"Courage is not the absence of fear, but rather the judgment that something else is more important than fear."

—Ambrose Redmoon

"Fear is that little darkroom where negatives are developed."

—Michael Pritchard

"It was a high counsel that I once heard given to a young person, 'Always do what you are afraid to do.'"

—Ralph Waldo Emerson

"I don't fear failure. I only fear the slowing up of the engine inside of me which is pounding, saying, 'Keep going, someone must be on top, why not you?'"

—General George S. Patton

"Fortes Fortuna Adiuvat." (Fortune favors the brave.)

—Terence (Latin)

"Fear not that your life will someday end. Fear only that you do nothing with it."

—Anon

"The greatest mistake you can make in life is to be continually fearing that you will make one."

—Elbert Hubbard

"We fear things in proportion to our ignorance of them."

—Livy

FEAR
F = False
E = Evidence
A = Appearing
R = Real

—Veer Sharma

"Before" Answer

I suppose I'm afraid of the things that most people are afraid of: getting a bad medical diagnosis, being the victim of a terrorist attack, or having my child get in a car accident.

"After"—the "Magic Words" Answer

Ralph Waldo Emerson quotes someone he once overhead saying, "Always do what you are afraid to do." If I am continually challenging myself to take on new challenges in order to grow and advance, there will always be a necessity to break through the comfort zones.

For instance, there was a situation several months ago when I was asked by my supervisor to take her place because of a scheduling conflict and make a presentation at a trade show in front of 100 people. The largest group I'd addressed in the past was 20. I felt my comfort zone challenged, but knew that this was an important opportunity. I approached the situation by focusing on the controllables. I worked with a colleague who is an experienced presenter to get ideas on how to engage the audience and structure my information, read books such as What to Say When You're Dying on the Platform, *and practiced before a test audience to work the bugs out. The presentation was well received—of the attendees filling out the speaker feedback forms, 75 percent of the people gave me the highest score possible. My boss, who listened to the tape after the conference, was very pleased and told me that I represented the company well and would plan to give me more platform opportunities in the future.*

Question

What is your greatest failure?

Describe a situation where you failed to reach a goal.

Strategy

The interviewer wants to know if you are human—are you humble enough to admit to failure without blaming someone else for it? And, how do you deal with adversity? If possible, pick a situation that is in the past to distance yourself from a recent disappointment. Avoid a response that veers toward personal issues, such as a failed marriage, bankruptcy, or a child gone astray. Again, referencing a quote may be apropos:

"The difference between average people and achieving people is their perception of and response to failure."

—John Maxwell in *Failing Forward*

"I have not failed. I've just found 10,000 ways that won't work."

—Thomas Edison

"A failure is a man who has blundered but is not capable of cashing in on the experience."

—Elbert Hubbard

"Before" Answer

Last quarter, our team didn't make our quota, although I was over quota. (Although this answer sounds positive, it skirts the heart of the question.)

Magic

"After"—the "Magic Words" Answer

I love the famous quote that says "A failure is a man who has blundered but is not capable of cashing in on the experience." I believe that nothing should be defined as a failure if we learn from it and it gives us more currency of knowledge in the days ahead. For instance, back when I first got out of college, I decided to try my hand as a day trader. I read several books on the subject and opened an online account. To make a long story short, the bottom line was that day trading was not my calling. Although I understood the principles of day trading and made a little money, I didn't meet my financial goals and it wasn't something I thoroughly enjoyed. What I learned from the experience is that I excel at things I am passionate about. That's why my career path over the last four years has been in training and development—it's what I'm passionate about. And obviously, that's benefited the people I serve in the business world. For instance, the last program I wrote and implemented at SDS Corporation helped boost productivity among call-center representatives by nearly 15 percent. I'm anxious to learn more about what you consider the top priorities for your training and development department.

Question
Tell me about a difficult problem you've had to deal with.

Strategy
Don't stress over this question. What you want to convey to the interviewer is how you go about solving problems. Provide a SMART Story™ that details your thought processes, methods, and mindset for managing the problem. Choose a story that doesn't involve a problem with difficult people, as it might appear you are criticizing others.

"Before" Answer
My work is full of difficult problems, including a workload that only the Bionic Man could manage, customers who are demanding, and computer equipment and software so outdated that tech support no longer provides support for it. Once, I had to get a report out and the system kept crashing....

"After"—the "Magic Words" Answer

Magic

I have a formula for challenging situations. First, I take the attitude that "every problem is perfect"—meaning, the problem has surfaced so that I or others can make some change for the better. Second, I step back and get some perspective on the situation. Third, I generate ideas about how to solve it, which often involves collaborating with others, and then prioritize the options. If the solution is something that needs approval from my supervisor, I present the options and recommendation to her. Finally, I implement the solution. Let me give you an example.

When I worked as a service technician for ABC Electronics, my quota required making 15 service calls a day. This was a challenging task in itself, yet I always made my quota, even if it meant working well into the evening. Then, after ABC merged with XYZ, we were given the additional responsibility of selling maintenance contracts. In the past, I had joked that if I had to depend on sales for a living, my family would starve. So, you can well imagine that at first, I wasn't selling any maintenance contracts. My quota was seven contracts a day.

I recognized that I needed to follow my advice about every problem being perfect, so I started thinking about what needed to be done. First, I asked my supervisor if there was sales training support. She said there wasn't a budget for it. I then went to one of my coworkers who was selling contracts left and right, and he gave me some good pointers. I also bought some of Zig Ziglar's books on sales and motivation, and those helped as well.

I realized that the biggest problem wasn't with the quota—it was with my mindset. I changed my thought process from, "I'm taking these people's hard-earned money" to "this will be a valuable service for a number of people." When that attitude was in place, coupled with some tips from my coworker, things started to turn around. The first week, I sold four contracts; the second week, I was up to 10; and, by the end of the quarter, I was hitting quota regularly. This put me in the top 20 percent for sales among a team of 30 technicians.

What I learned from this is that sales had been difficult because I thought it was difficult. Once I changed my thinking, everything else changed. I just had to believe there was an answer, and then find resources to help, and then put it into action.

Question
Tell me about a time when you managed a stressful deadline or situation.

Strategy
The interviewer wants to know whether you can work well under stress. There are several themes you can address when you get a question about stress:

- Setting goals, priorities, and boundaries
- Getting organized and streamlining processes
- Using the right technology and tools

Use a SMART Story™ to respond.

"Before" Answer
Sure. There was a situation where my writing team had to update a 400-page publication for our boiler line. The project got off to a bad start because the engineers kept making changes. Every change meant that we'd either have to rewrite or put the project on the back burner while they figured out what they wanted to do. Meanwhile, one of our writers had a little too much to drink one Saturday night and wrapped his car around a telephone pole. Another writer, who was eight months pregnant, went into labor early. So we were down to just two people. I took charge and told my boss we'd just have to put all our other projects on hold and get permission to skip all the production meetings. I also told her we'd need to work from home to be more productive. We worked like dogs, but we got it all done.

Magic

"After"—the "Magic Words" Answer
I'd be happy to. Our four-person writing team was working on updating a 400-page publication that was to accompany the release of our next-generation industrial boiler line. Normally we schedule two months to do an update, which gives us plenty of breathing room and allows us to work on other projects at the same time. In this particular situation, we had some hurdles to clear. To begin with, the engineers made a necessary change to the product, which delayed our start by two weeks. Then, two weeks into the project, one of the writers was in a bad car accident (thankfully, he's recovered now) and another one who was pregnant went into labor six weeks before her due date. With half a team, we had just six weeks to do what we normally would do in eight weeks.

As the lead writer, I took the initiative in suggesting some strategies to manage the deadline. We reviewed our other concurrent projects and divided those into A and B priorities. I went to my director and asked if the B priorities could be outsourced or put on hold. She offered the help of a freelance writer to write sections that didn't require a lot of technical knowledge. I said it was certainly an option, but I was confident we could make the deadline if we were freed up of some of these other projects and given the okay to work from our home offices where there would be fewer interruptions.

I outlined daily and weekly goals and adjusted the production schedule accordingly. Because the files were quite large with JPEG photographs, I researched and implemented a Web storage system to share files so that we wouldn't have to rely on e-mail, which had been problematic in the past. My writing partner and I put in a few 70-hour work weeks to get it done, but we made the deadline, and we felt such a sense of accomplishment...like we could handle anything that might be thrown at us in the future. The extra effort allowed our sales department to introduce the boilers at the industry's largest trade show and beat the competition, who didn't release their comparable upgrades until the following season. The sales department conservatively estimated a 12 percent gain in market share because of the timing of the product release.

I have a copy of the manual here in my briefcase if you'd like to see some writing samples.

Question

Solve this scenario: Production is down 65 percent due to a 90 percent turnover rate and, in the next six months, we want you to double production from two years when we were at record productivity. How would you solve this problem and meet our goal?

Strategy

This is the "impossible scenario" question. Beware of providing an answer that implies you can solve the issue, or you'll look either inexperienced or unrealistic. It's best to describe the process you would go through and then relate a SMART Story™ that is similar to (but not as Herculean as) what the interviewer wants accomplished.

"Before" Answer

I don't think it can be done.

Magic

"After"—the "Magic Words" Answer

*First, I'd work with the management team to ensure that SMART goals were in place, meaning **S**pecific, **M**easurable, **A**chievable, **R**ealistic, and **T**ime-Sensitive. Then I'd analyze the key components to productivity—people, systems, and equipment. From there, I'd compare what's happening to best practices in the industry. If turnover were one of the main issues, I'd address recruiting, training, and working conditions.*

I'd also invite input from the production floor, as I've achieved double-digit increases in productivity in the past based on great suggestions from my team. Then, I'd write and implement a plan. I can give you an example of how I led a similar turnaround for XYZ Company a few years ago. The results were similar to what you're after, although it took us a bit longer.

Question

What opportunities have you created for yourself in your current position?

Strategy

This is a question designed to gauge your initiative. Offer a SMART Story™. Be cautious that your story doesn't paint you as someone who is self-serving or opportunistic. Employers love self-starters, so make sure you've got a good example for this answer. And, if you don't have an immediate answer, what *can* you do to create opportunity for yourself in your current position?

"Before" Answer

The structure of my current department doesn't really allow for many changes. I suppose I'd have to say that just doing my job well has led to me getting high marks on my most recent performance evaluation.

"After"—the "Magic Words" Answer

I always look for opportunities. When I started work at my current employer, we had monthly staff meetings. I noticed that people often used these as venues for grousing, which impacted the morale and productivity of the meeting. I went to my boss privately and suggested something that was done at my prior employer. The suggestion involved having weekly meetings where each staff member came to the meeting with one opportunity idea. There was to be no criticism of the idea or comments about why something would not work. Then, at the end of the meeting everyone voted secretly on the idea they thought was best. At the end of the month, our boss chose one of the four ideas for the month and implemented it.

This really changed the dynamic of our meetings. People got charged up about what was possible instead of focusing on negatives. My boss liked the idea and put me in charge of leading the portion of the weekly meeting where we discussed the opportunity ideas. Because I took the initiative on this, I was then selected to take the lead on some of the ideas that were chosen for implementation. I can give you an example if you'd like. [Then lead into a SMART Story™ if the interviewer says yes.]

Question

Tell me about a time when you persuaded others to take action.

Strategy

Whether or not you're applying for supervisory/management positions, employers want to know how well you influence others. Pick a situation that will be significant because you may not get another question like this. Use a SMART Story™ that illustrates a benefit to the company/team and not just you, as the following *Before* answer shows.

"Before" Answer

I wanted some time off to travel but had used up all my personal time. I convinced a couple of co-workers to trade several shifts with me so that I could get the time I needed.

"After"—the "Magic Words" Answer

Consider this example for a support-level candidate:

In my role as secretary to the production supervisor for an organic baby-food processor, I noted that we could be doing a better job of communicating with growers about projected harvest dates. Frequently what would happen is the growers would report their picking schedules, with produce available during the second week of July. Production would then schedule a full crew for that Monday; but in reality, the produce wouldn't be ready until Wednesday or Thursday. We had to pay workers for coming in and then send them home. I thought that there had to be a solution to this, but didn't immediately think of anything. A few weeks later, I had jury duty, which required that I call in every night to learn whether I had an assignment. I wondered, why not do something similar for our growers and production crews? I suggested it to my supervisor. At first, he just listened and said he'd think about it. A week later, I approached him about it again and told him that I'd done some research on how a hot line could be set up for growers and then a general information line for employees who would be grouped into Team A, B, and C. When the harvest was heavy, all teams would be called in. I also spoke with the Field Liaison to get his input on how this could work. And, I penciled out a potential savings of 7 percent on labor if we didn't have to call in people and then send them home. My supervisor took this to our operations manager and the system was approved with some modifications. At the end of the season, we achieved a 12 percent reduction in labor, which translated to a five-figure savings. I felt quite proud that I had a part in that.

And consider this example for a management candidate:

We had a situation in my last position as sales manager where quarterly sales were stagnant in comparison to the prior year and my director wanted to see a 15 percent increase in the upcoming two quarters. There were a couple of contributing factors to the sluggish sales, including lack of any new product at a time when our major competitor had just brought out a new line. However, the factor that was most in my control was the attitude and enthusiasm of the sales reps. Rather than issue an edict, I involved all eight reps in the strategy process and explained that, for the health of our company, we needed to see a 15 percent increase over the next six months. It's been my experience that when you give other people input and ownership of a plan, they are more motivated to perform. Together, they proposed several strategies to make this happen. One of the best ideas generated was to offer several combination specials that could be presold at a discount if the client purchased before the end of the month. I also offered them a choice of individual and team rewards if they made their quotas, which helped provide a unique motivator for each rep. I spent about 80 percent of my time in the field with each rep during the next eight weeks. By the end of the first three months, sales had risen 10 percent, and we exceeded our 15 percent goal by 2 percent. I believe that my competency for first motivating myself and then others is absolutely critical to success as a manager.

Question
That is an excellent answer. Could you also give me an example that didn't have such a positive outcome?

Strategy
A skilled interviewer will ask this question to get a balanced perspective, especially if you're acing every question with particularly positive responses. Don't be tempted to don a Superman cape. It is appropriate to share stories that didn't have a neat-and-tidy Hollywood ending. You will be more suspect if you can't admit to things occasionally not going well. Offer a SMART Story™, then wrap up the response with ideas outlined in the *After* example that follows.

"Before" Answer
I really can't think of any.

"After"—the "Magic Words" Answer

Benjamin Franklin said, "The things which hurt, instruct." I can offer an example of how things didn't turn out and what I learned from the event. [Offer a SMART Story™. Then close with something like this:] *When things don't go well, I follow the advice that Dr. John Maxwell presents in his book* Failing Forward.

I first look at the cause. Was it the situation, someone else, or myself?

- ✦ *Was it a failure or just falling short?*
- ✦ *What successes are contained in the failure?*
- ✦ *What can I learn from what happened?*
- ✦ *Am I grateful for the experience?*
- ✦ *How can I turn this into a success?*
- ✦ *Who can help me with this issue?*
- ✦ *Where do I go from here?*

Question

How would you go about solving the following problem: _____?

Strategy

This question probes your decision-making process. The problem presented will be something related to the position, such as reducing the time to do a task, cutting costs, increasing productivity, or improving morale. Describe gathering input from important parties yet without relying totally on others to make the decision. If possible, relate the question to your past experience so that the interviewer sees your experience with this issue.

"Before" Answer

Yes, I've solved that kind of problem before. I analyzed the situation, put a plan into place, and executed the plan. As a result, we went from a product development cycle of 12 months to 7 months.

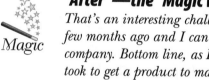

"After"—the "Magic Words" Answer

That's an interesting challenge. I encountered something similar in my current position a few months ago and I can share with you how I approached it and what worked for our company. Bottom line, as Director of Product Development I was able to reduce the time it took to get a product to market from 12 months to 7 months by working more closely with my counterparts in engineering, manufacturing, and marketing. Here's what I did to make that happen. [Offer a complete SMART Story™ with emphasis on the action to reveal your decision-making process.] *Of course, there might be some adjustments necessary to fit this process to your organizational structure, and I'd be happy to hear your thoughts on this.*

Question

Why do you work?

Why do you do what you do?

Why are you a _____?

What are you most passionate about?

Strategy

These questions are all related. The interviewer wants to know both your motives and how to motivate you! Consider linking this answer to the Fulfillment statement you wrote in chapter 2 (see "Step 4: Define Fulfillment"). Remember that Fulfillment is what transforms your position from paycheck to purpose. Purpose produces passion, and passion fuels perseverance, enthusiasm, creativity, productivity, and income to peak levels. You can also point to items from your list of Things That Matter (see chapter 2, "Step 3: Think About the Things That Matter").

"Before" Answer

Well, it's pretty obvious, I guess, since everybody needs to pay the bills!

Or, *I work because I enjoy a sense of accomplishment.*

Magic

"After"—the "Magic Words" Answer

I am a Financial Manager because it's a great venue for my values of order, structure, ethics, and financial integrity. When a company has its financial house in order, it is in a position to thrive and prosper, which means that its shareholders, employees, and customers will also prosper. I take great pleasure and pride in helping make that happen.

Question

What are some of your pet peeves?

What types of things cause you to get angry or lose your temper?

Strategy

The interviewer is measuring your self-control and emotional intelligence here. Do you remain calm, cool, and collected, or are you easily perturbed, impatient, and upset? Assure them you are calm, cool, and collected!

"Before" Answer

My pet peeves are people who don't listen, people who have negative attitudes, people who don't challenge themselves to grow, and people who always have an excuse as to why things aren't done.

Magic

"After"—the "Magic Words" Answer

I'm pretty unflappable when it comes to work. I really can't point to anything that I'd consider as a pet peeve, and truly no one causes me to lose my temper.

If pressed further for an answer, you might say, *You know, I guess I'd say that when I've been short on sleep there might be a tendency toward impatience, but I never lose my temper. And, if I notice that I'm less patient with myself or others, I welcome it as a sign that I need to be super-vigilant about getting enough rest, exercise, and nutrition.*

Question

How do you handle criticism?

Strategy

The underlying question here: "Is this person teachable?" Explain how you've openly received criticism and what you learned from it. Point to an example in the past so that it doesn't appear you made a recent mistake, and choose something that isn't related to character.

"Before" Answer

I take criticism in stride.

"After"—the "Magic Words" Answer

It used to be that I would get annoyed by criticism. It wasn't until I took a different perspective on the subject that I realized it could help me improve and be better at what I do. I especially appreciate it when criticism is constructive, delivered with a respectful attitude, and with the intent to bring benefit to the team. For instance, when I first started at BBB Company, my boss sat in on a meeting that I had with one of our vendors. After the meeting, he first shared with me what went well and what I'd done right. Then, he shared with me what I could do to be even better. Specifically, it was about having better access to the paperwork around the vendor's history so that I could have more leverage in the negotiations. He then helped me visualize how doing that would enhance the negotiations. He was right, and since that time I've been thorough about preparing for meetings and visualizing a positive outcome.

I've used a similar technique in mentoring my staff, where I sandwich the areas for improvement between what they've done well and how the change will enhance their success.

Question

What would you say if I told you that you were giving a poor interview today?

Strategy

Don't assume from the question that you are giving a poor interview, as the bumbled response in the *Before* example shows. This may just be a stress-interview question. Keep a level head and think about the question in this light: What would you say if an important client told you that you were giving a poor presentation? What would you do to meet the needs of the client?

"Before" Answer

Am I? I'm sorry. You know, I just didn't have the time to prepare like I should because I've been sick, and I had a flat tire on the way to the interview…it's just been one of those days. What can I do to turn things around?

"After"—the "Magic Words" Answer

I'd first acknowledge your observation, although I'd hope it would not be true! I'd then ask a few questions to learn what your expectations are for the interview and of me, what you like about my responses thus far, what you'd like to see improved on, and how we might structure things so that could happen easily.

Question

What computer skills do you have?

Strategy

If you are interviewing for a technical position, you will obviously be asked much more sophisticated and in-depth questions about your technology skills. This question is meant for non-techies (admin, sales, operations, and so on) to get a sense of computer literacy. Your response should include common software programs for your profession and, hopefully, knowledge of the system and software the interviewer's company uses. Outline the key programs you use relevant to the position. If your skills are extensive, consider offering a leave-behind (see chapter 12) that details key technology skills and how you used them.

"Before" Answer

I'm computer-proficient and know all the basics in MS Office. I use Word and Outlook the most and also know PowerPoint and basic Excel.

"After"—the "Magic Words" Answer

Magic

As an administrative professional, I have advanced knowledge of MS Word, Outlook, and PowerPoint, and intermediate knowledge of Excel. I have taught myself several other programs, as well, but it doesn't sound like you use them here. I can give you an example of the types of documents I prepared and features used for each of the programs if you like....

In addition, in my last position, I installed new programs and did some basic network maintenance. I also inherited a persnickety printer and got to the point where I didn't have to call the technician out very often because he taught me some of the common things to look for to fix paper jams.

Could you tell me about the key programs you'd want me to use in this position?

Question

Please tell me the meaning of _____ [fill in a list of relevant industry acronyms].

Strategy

Before the interview, you should gather information about the industry, job, and company (see appendix A for ties). Part of the information you'll gather is jargon for your industry. If you've read an industry acronym that you're not certain about, ask a colleague to interpret it or use www.AcronymFinder.com to look up the meaning. Finally, make this response more of a conversation than a test, which is how the *Before* candidate treats the question.

"Before" Answer

Advanced Widget Manufacturing Techniques; Business Development Widgetry; I've never heard of WCCC; ISWC stands for International Standards for Widget Controls; I can't remember WACA; and finally ACWA is Another Crazy Widget Acronym.

"After"—the "Magic Words" Answer

Magic

Let me jot those down to make sure I address them all. AWMT, BDW, WCCC, ISWC, WACA, and ACWA. Okay, from the top, those mean Advanced Widget Manufacturing Techniques; Business Development Widgetry; I'm not familiar with WCCC; then ISWC

stands for International Standards for Widget Controls; I'll come back to WACA; and finally ACWA is Another Crazy Widget Acronym. The individual words for WACA aren't coming to me at the moment since everyone just refers to it as WACA. I know it has something to do with the California Chapter of Widget Associates. Would you be kind enough to refresh my memory? And WCCC? What does that stand for? Oh yes, I have heard of that. We use a little different system at my current employer that I understand is similar.

To keep updated on trends, I read industry publications like _____ and _____, and I attend the National Widget Manufacturers conference each year. What professional associations do most of your staff belong to?

Question
What do you need to do to take yourself to the next level?

Strategy
Some candidates have a tendency to translate this into a question about their weaknesses. Don't! Play it positive, stating that you are, indeed, taking yourself to the next level by applying for this position.

"Before" Answer
Well, I suppose I need to learn how to overcome my fear of public speaking. I've been working on that by going to Toastmasters, and I've made great progress. [Although there's nothing inherently wrong with this response, it is not as positive as it could be because of the phrase "my fear of."]

"After"—the "Magic Words" Answer

Magic

I believe I'm on track to do just that with this position. I have prepared myself through academics, attitude, and action. I can give you an example of each of those if you'd like. Academically, I've added _____ [list whatever designations, certifications, or training you've recently taken]. *From an attitude perspective, I've continually pushed myself to not get comfortable with comfort zones! And from an action standpoint, over the past year I have taken on increasingly challenging projects, some of which I've shared with you already, that have prepared me to make a valuable contribution to this position.*

Question
What's the best book you've read in the last year? What did you like about it?

Strategy
If you're not an avid reader, a trip to your local bookstore will be in order. Check out the sections on management or self-improvement and note the authors who have multiple titles on the shelves, such as Ken Blanchard, Stephen Covey, John Maxwell, Tom Peters, Marshall Goldsmith, and so on. You can reference historical works or classics *if* (and only if) you can show how reading them has improved your work life. This is not the time, however, to describe your favorite book on job search or the latest sci-fi novel you've devoured. Ask your networking contacts or mentors what they recommend for a must-read.

"Before" Answer

I loved Stephen King's last book. His imagination and ability to develop characters is unbe-lievable. [No offense to Stephen King, who is a brilliant writer. Since the interview is about your ability to perform, stick to work-related topics.]

"After"—the "Magic Words" Answer

Magic

It's hard to choose just one because I'm a big fan of just about anything by _____ *and* _____ *(name your favorite business authors). I'd have to say the one I've enjoyed the most is* The 21 Irrefutable Laws of Leadership *by John Maxwell. Although I'm not applying for a senior leadership position, I think that just about anyone can be a leader. In a sense, we all lead, even if we're not supervising someone else. We lead by getting ideas out there, thinking bigger—beyond our self-imposed limitations, surrounding ourselves with sup-port, creating momentum, prioritizing, and so on.*

Two of the laws that I've been applying in my work life are the Law of Momentum and the Law of Priorities. To build momentum, I keep a vision in front of me, focus on what I can do rather than on what I can't, and celebrate victories, no matter how small.

The Law of Priorities encompasses the 80/20 principle and the three Rs of requirement, return, and reward. What is required? What gives the greatest return? And, what brings the greatest reward? I've learned that activity is not necessarily accomplishment.

You'll recall my response to your question, "Tell me about a time when you _____ *"* [Fill in the blank with some question the interviewer has already asked you. If you get this question early in the interview, offer to tell a SMART Story™ that illustrates this law.] *That particular example illustrated how I applied the Law of Priorities.*

Question

Who was your favorite teacher?

Strategy

Your response to this question can reveal both who inspires you and what you learned from him or her. Your options for favorite teacher are the obvious ones—a teacher from elementary school, high school, or college. However, don't over-look the not-so-obvious instructors in your life—your child, a friend who has mod-eled leadership skills, a supervisor who has mentored and coached you, an author you enjoy, and so on. Whomever you choose, offer an example of what the person taught you and how it has made you a better employee/professional.

"Before" Answer

My 10th-grade English teacher. She gave me the tools that I use every day in writing, edit-ing, and communicating with others. [Although this answer is positive, the candidate stops short of how it will be an asset on the job or to the company.]

"After"—the "Magic Words" Answer

Magic

I can think of a number of teachers and business-school instructors who have influenced my life, but I'll point to an unusual teacher for my example, and that would be my friend Marty. You see Marty is an amazing man who has encountered what seems to be more than his fair share of adversity in life. He built a travel-agency business from scratch into a seven-figure business, but the combination of the devastating changes in that industry plus his bookkeeper embezzling funds caused him to go bankrupt. About the same time, his wife and child were killed in a car accident. If anyone had the right to be angry and bitter, it would be him. But he isn't, and he didn't give up. He's started a new business and has gotten back on his feet financially. He also has a CPA firm handling his books. [smile]

I consider Marty my teacher because he taught me that perseverance and attitude go a long way in business and life. We can choose to be either bitter or better. Also, that surrounding yourself with a good team is critical. I've applied these principles in my current position as a team leader for XYZ Corporation.

Question
How do you learn best?

Strategy
This question is a little different from the prior question about your favorite teacher. Now, the interviewer wants to know how you learn best. Review the three primary learning styles outlined in chapter 10 (see table 10.2) so that you understand your own learning style. Then, give an example of how you learned something faster using that style.

"Before" Answer
I think I learn best through trial-and-error. If people just explain something to me, it doesn't seem to stick as well as when they let me have some hands-on practice.

Magic

"After"—the "Magic Words" Answer
I have a friend who is a trainer, so she has helped me understand that there are different learning styles. The three most common are auditory, visual, and kinesthetic. Because I'm committed to learning things as efficiently as possible, I explored and found that my natural style was visual. Let me give you an example of how that helped me learn a new program.

Some time ago, my boss had asked me to learn PowerPoint. I taught myself by carving out some personal time in the evenings to go through the tutorials. Knowing that demonstrations, diagrams, and pictures were helpful to me, this worked out well. Within a week, I was producing PowerPoint presentations that incorporated advanced features like tables, images, and animations. My boss asked me to share some of what I'd learned with other users in our office.

Question
How does this position fit into your long-term career plans? (or Where do you see yourself in 5 to 10 years?)

Strategy
Some people have a clear picture of where they want to be in five years. Some do not. Rather than share a future vision that may not complement what the company needs, consider framing your response in a broad, noncommittal manner. Who can tell the future?

"Before" Answer

I'd like to be in your position in five years. [This may be a good answer if the interviewer is your potential manager and is looking to groom a successor so that he, too, can climb the corporate ladder. However, unless you know it to be the case, this response can be a bit of a risk, not to mention a cliché.]

Magic

"After"—the "Magic Words" Answer

I don't have a crystal ball, but I can tell you what's most important to me for the future. I want to continually add to my skills, take on new challenges, and contribute value to the company. I'm not certain what shape that will take, but I believe it will involve using my strengths in the areas of _____, _____, and _____. [These should be strengths that are required in the position for which you're interviewing.] *I know that this position often branches out into either _____ or _____. At this point, I'd be open to either track, depending on where the company might need me most. In the meantime, I like preparing for "planned happenstance"—meaning that I will develop myself in a manner that attracts opportunities.*

Question

Why are you the best candidate for this position?

Why should we hire you?

Strategy

This question will often be asked at the end of the interview. It's a great time to pull out your Three-Point Marketing Message and link it to important deliverables you've uncovered during the course of the interview.

"Before" Answer

I'm an excellent case manager who is great with people. I have the degree and certifications you're looking for, and this sounds like a great place to work, with people I can really connect with. I'd be more committed than anyone.

Magic

"After"—the "Magic Words" Answer

As a case manager with more than 15 years of experience, I have a unique combination of counseling, teaching, and client advocacy work with high-risk youth—all of which you've indicated as important to the position. I've outlined a number of specific successes in each of those three areas during the course of our conversation.

Beyond those successes, I'd have to say that I have a heart for working with this population. If you don't mind me sharing a personal story…Ten years ago, I had a nephew who committed suicide. Had there been services available to him like your organization is offering now, he might still be alive. That experience has motivated me to become great at what I do. I have letters from parents who've thanked me for making a difference in their child's life, and that is my greatest reward.

Given my experience and commitment, I don't think there's anyone who can bring you more knowledge, resources, or passion for seeing your clients succeed.

Question

How will we know if you were the right person to hire?

Strategy

This is a bit different than the "Why are you the best candidate?" question we just saw. With this "right person" question, address the three key elements shown in the next *After* example. Use language that helps the interviewer see you in the position 6 to 12 months down the road. Notice the bulleted format the candidate uses to help the interviewer follow his points.

"Before" Answer

I am a strong candidate who has delivered the results you are looking for in the past. I can just tell that this is the right job for me.

"After"—the "Magic Words" Answer

There are three ways you'll know you made the right decision. When I…

- *Number one, have added value to the company by going beyond your expectations of me with regard to productivity and teachability;*

- *Number two, have done it with energy, passion, and a positive attitude; and*

- *Number three, fit in well with the company culture, my coworkers, and customers.*

[Wearing a warm smile, finish your response with] *What more could you ask for?*

Question

When would you be available?

Strategy

When asked in a second or third interview, this question may be a trial close to determine your interest in the position. Ask what the interviewer's needs are before responding. Avoid bringing your personal situation into the equation.

"Before" Answer

Well, my babysitter is on vacation, so I'd prefer to start after she gets back but that won't be for another three weeks.

"After"—the "Magic Words" Answer

Could you tell me what your needs are? Then say, *I'm very interested in the position and, given a reasonable offer, would be able to be on board within your time frame.*

Question

The salary range for the position is $__–__,000. Is that acceptable to you? Have you made more than this?

Strategy

This question frequently comes in a telephone interview or first interview. If you answer, "yes," but ask for more when salary negotiations roll around, you will appear insincere or dishonest. To your "yes," add the phrase "provided the actual job is consistent with the job description I was given." This will give you some latitude because positions oftentimes have more responsibility than what's found in the formal job description. See chapter 16 for more on negotiating salary.

"Before" Answer

Yes, that's fine. No, I've not made more than this.

Magic

"After"—the "Magic Words" Answer

[If the salary range is within your range:] Although salary isn't the most important factor in a job, I'm interested in fair compensation for the value I contribute. Your salary range aligns with my research, provided the actual job is consistent with the job description I was given. That range is consistent with my past experience.

Or, That salary range is about 15 percent lower than what my research shows. Actually, I'm wondering whether I could learn more about the position first. It's been my experience that if I'm the right person for the position, we'll be able to come to agreement on the terms. And, yes, I have made more than this in the past. Salary isn't the most important factor in a job for me, although I'm interested in fair compensation for the value I contribute.

Question

What questions do you have?

Strategy

This is a great time to check your notepad that contains the clarifying or collaborating questions you'll want to ask from chapter 11. If there are questions you have that haven't yet been covered, this is the time to ask them.

"Before" Answer

No, I don't. You've been very thorough.

Magic

"After"—the "Magic Words" Answer

Actually, we've really covered a lot of ground already. Most of the questions I have here on my list were already answered. I do have just a couple more that I'd like to discuss. Could you tell me….

Chapter Wrap-Up

Regardless of the interview question, remember the mantra you've heard throughout this book:

It's about them, not you.

Please be clear on why I say this: It is *not* because I want you to be misleading or superficial. It is because every successful professional knows that if you first find the "what's in it for them" in a business relationship, people will open up, cooperate, and support you. Once this is in place, you can then decide on the *what's in it for you.*

Throughout the interview, weave in language you developed from chapter 4, including your

✦ Three-Point Marketing Message—a theme of knowledge, skills, or abilities relevant to the position

✦ Benefits and Buying Motivators—how you can bring more productivity and profitability to the company than your competitors might

10 Quick Tips for Responding to FAQs

Let these 10 tips guide you in responding, remembering that answers should always be

1. **Positive:** Videotape yourself or write out your responses and analyze them for any shades of negativity. Listen for the *howcha's* (see chapter 10, "Check Your Motive and Attitude"). Empty your mind and heart of clutter, cares, and concerns prior to the interview. Then, infuse your voice with energy, optimism, interest, and respect.

   Absolutely no accusing, making veiled inferences, whining, blaming, criticizing, or complaining allowed! For each response you practice, ask yourself:

   • How might this be worded in a more positive light?

   • Is what I'm saying building or busting my case?

   • Is my response making the interviewer more confident and certain I can do the job?

   Never reveal feelings of discouragement in an interview, even if you sense that the interview isn't going well. You have nothing to gain; interviewers won't hire out of pity. They want to hire winners, and winners persevere with positivity!

2. **Pertinent:** Choose the most relevant story or information for your response. Resist the urge to over-tell or share information that does not add to your qualifications.

3. **Precise:** Be brief, succinct, and specific. Avoid rambling, as this *Before* example shows:

   Before: *We had a problem with employees leaving. Actually, they would stay for just a short amount of time because we were hiring a lot of college students. That caused some interesting generational communication issues, actually, but I can tell you about that later if you'd like. So, my boss formed a team and we put in place a number of programs during the time I was there that significantly helped our retention numbers.*

After: I was asked to serve on a four-member team tasked with improving employee retention. We developed and implemented programs that improved our retention from 75 percent to 92 percent over an 18-month period. I can tell you more about my specific role on the team if you'd like.

4. **Profit-Oriented:** Everything you say (and everything you do once you're on the job) should be about contributing value, and therefore profit, to the company.

5. **SMART and Bell-Shaped:** When it comes to behavioral questions, respond with a SMART Story™, one that outlines the **S**ituation and **M**ore, **A**ction taken, **R**esult achieved, and **T**ie-in to the interviewer's question or a competency **T**heme. Remember to make your SMART Story™ bell-shaped (see chapter 9).

6. **Bulleted:** When you're giving a lengthy response (such as a SMART Story™), deliver it in bullet points or with numbers. It will help the interviewer to follow along. And, if ever you sense you're losing or "snoozing" the interviewer, stop and ask a question!

7. **Perceptive:** Don't let your professional guard down when the interviewer seems chatty or informal. Many candidates have lost job offers by misinterpreting interviewer casualness as a signal that the interviewer is befriending them. (One pharmaceutical candidate lost points—and the job offer—when an interviewer used this tactic. The candidate got carried away describing how much time and effort she was putting into planning her wedding. This personal information caused the interviewer to be concerned that the candidate wouldn't be able to give her full attention to an important product launch.)

8. **Timed:** A response lasting one to two minutes, or a little longer if you're answering a behavioral question, is fine. If you need to talk longer, break up the response with a question midway:

   - "Am I giving you the details you need?"

   - "Would you like an example of that?"

   - "What have you seen to be the case in your organization?"

9. **Fresh:** Don't backtrack! You can occasionally reference a story that you've already given, but avoid reusing stories multiple times as it may confuse (or bore) the interviewer. This is why it's important to have plenty of SMART Stories™.

10. **Interactive:** Avoid yes-no answers—they don't encourage conversation. Occasionally use a "menu" approach where you offer the interviewer two or three options and ask which one they'd like to hear more about. For instance, in response to the question, "What are

your greatest strengths?" you might say, "I've been complimented by supervisors for the ability to conceptualize, strategize, and execute. Is one of these more important than another for this position? If so, I'd be happy to start there with an example of how I've used that skill."

Magical Coaching Tips

Do some practice interviewing with a colleague or friend. Practice just 5 to 10 questions at a time. Audiotape or videotape your sessions. Then, review your tape and evaluate your responses using the form on the following page (see "10 Quick Tips for Responding to FAQs" near the end of this chapter for details on each column heading). Give yourself a check mark if your response addresses the column heading. Note that the SMART and Bell-Shape columns (maked by asterisks) apply only when behavioral-based questions are asked.

Question	Positive	Pertinent	Precise	Profit	SMART*	Bell-Shaped	Perceptive	Timed	Fresh	Interactive
Example: Tell me about yourself.		✓	✓		✓		✓	✓	✓	

Chapter

14

Master Your Industry-Specific Questions (ISQs)

The greatest problem in communication is the illusion that it has been accomplished.

—George Bernard Shaw

Bob, determined to do well on his interview for a land surveyor position, had thoroughly prepared himself for Frequently Asked Questions. His responses to "why should we hire you," "tell me about yourself," "where do you see yourself in five years, "and "what are your greatest strengths/weaknesses" were eloquent examples of how to do it right. What's more, he dressed appropriately and exuded confidence.

But Bob didn't get the job.

Why? Because he fell short on answers to Industry-Specific Questions. He faltered on a question about photogrammetry and blew a question about boundary determinations.

Many candidates fall into this trap. To their credit, they are diligent about following the guidance of good interviewing books: Look the part, solve the employer's problems, focus on value, and so on. However, a lot of interview advice overlooks a critical piece of the puzzle: How will you handle questions about specific functions of the job?

Chapter 13 cataloged a number of frequently asked questions that might be asked of any candidate. But that's rarely where the interview ends. Hiring managers want to make sure you have the industry knowledge and depth of experience needed to perform and excel in the job. To determine this, they will ask Industry-Specific Questions (ISQs), many of which will be behavioral interview questions (see chapter 10 for tips on managing behavioral interviews).

In this chapter, you'll find Industry-Specific Questions (ISQs) for numerous professions, along with the strategies and sample answers to equip you for success. To use this chapter to your benefit, follow these steps:

1. Study the sample questions and response strategies for your industry. For purposes of space, only two sample questions and responses are included for each industry. You can find more on my Web site: www.careerandlifecoach.com (click on Interview Magic).

2. If you don't see your industry represented, scan any related categories, as there may be questions that are relevant to your profession.

3. After reviewing your category, jump to the end of this chapter and read the section on "Linking FAQs and ISQs to Your SMART Stories™," as well as the "10 Tips for Answering Industry Specific Questions."

4. Follow the Magical Coaching Tips at the end of this chapter to prepare your own list of Industry Specific Questions.

 Note To review additional Industry Specific Questions, including strategy and sample responses, visit my Web site, www.careerandlife coach.com, and click on Interview Magic.

The ISQs in this chapter were contributed primarily by members of Career Masters Institute (www.cminstitute.com), an international association of career experts, as well as by members of the National Résumé Writers' Association (www.nrwa.com). Each contributor's contact information is listed in the appendix.

Industry-Specific Questions
Here are sample ISQs for 34 different fields.

Accounting (Corporate Finance)

Question
Tell me about a time when cash flow didn't meet projections and what steps you took to cover your credit obligation.

"Magic Words" Strategy
Note that this question requests a specific story, not a theoretical answer. At the same time, be cautious not to reveal confidential information about a prior employer.

I've had experience managing just this type of situation. I'm not at liberty to provide too many details since it was for a privately held company, but I can tell you what steps I took. First, I assessed the timing requirements of key cash outlays and implemented short-term policies to prioritize critical items and release of funds. I then was able to negotiate with certain financial institutions to secure an additional $3 million working line of credit. These steps allowed me the opportunity to streamline operations and reduce SG&A until our sales picked up the following year. We received continued benefit from the SG&A reductions even after the sales improvement, further enhancing our bottom-line growth by nearly x percent.

Question
What experience do you have with inventory management?

"Magic Words" Strategy
Lead off with an overview statement that conveys your turnkey knowledge of inventory management. Then, offer a specific example of how those skills led to an increase in profit or reduction in costs, such as this:

The most recent economic downturn resulted in a buildup of excess inventory before we could react to the reduced demand. While we had to liquidate our overstocked position, I did an analysis of inventory-to-sales ratio to measure how long it would take to sell the existing merchandise. I then instituted methods and procedures such as economic order quantity, reorder points, and safety stock to minimize the costs of inventory we were carrying on our books. As a result, once we were able to normalize our inventory position, we experienced solid double-digit increases in our inventory turnover rates and permanently reduced our carrying costs by 12 percent. I'd like to learn more about your inventory-management system. I understand you're using _____ —how is that working for you?

Accounting (Entry-Level Staff in CPA Firms)

Question
Why have you chosen public accounting over private or governmental accounting?

"Magic Words" Strategy
Answers that will be acceptable include themes such as liking the variety afforded in public accounting, where there is opportunity to work on different clients' projects, as well as a personality that is suited to meeting and interfacing with a diversity of clients.

Question

What area of accounting do you most prefer? Tax or work with audits and financial statements?

"Magic Words" Strategy

The interviewer wants to gauge whether you'll be best assigned to individual work or team work. Those preferring audit and financial statement work must work well in collaborative, interactive settings. These people are often good candidates for supervisory responsibilities down the road.

Administration (Executive Assistant)

Contributed by National Résumé Writers' Association member Melanie Noonan.

Question

What knowledge, skills, and abilities do you consider necessary to be a successful assistant to a high-level executive?

"Magic Words" Strategy

Themes to address here include a solid understanding of business (profit, processes, protocol), superior written and oral communication skills, appropriate technology skills, along with the ability to set priorities and demonstrate initiative, mature judgment, and confidentiality.

Question

Tell me about a situation in which you had to handle conflicting priorities.

"Magic Words" Strategy

The strategy here is to keep executives in the communications loop and take the initiative to offer solutions.

At Prestige Corporation, I supported two vice presidents. Under normal circumstances, I was able to complete month-end reports required by each executive on time and with accuracy. In the fourth month of working there, the office relocated, which caused everyone to lose several days of productivity. I recognized that it would be difficult to do both (move and get the reports completed), so I spoke with the executives and offered some suggestions. One option I proposed was to put another less important project on the back burner for a week, which they both agreed to. This enabled me to move my and my boss' offices, as well as generate reports. Two weeks after we settled in the new offices, I sat down and analyzed how I could cut down the time it took to generate the reports. I came up with a standardized format that was approved by both VPs, which has reduced the time it takes to generate reports by at least 30 percent.

Advertising

Contributed by Career Masters Institute member Evelyn Salvador.

Question

What type of advertising campaigns, marketing programs, or classified advertising have you devised or sold and how well were these campaigns received?

"Magic Words" Strategy

Be prepared to list your range of experience by first identifying those programs that are most applicable to the field of the prospective employer. Highlight various types of campaigns you have developed or effective classified advertising you have sold for your firm or its clients.

After your summary list, you can use a SMART Story™ that is relevant to the employer's needs and offers how well the campaign was received by your firm's customers or the customers of its clients.

Question

What is your involvement with print advertising? Web site design? Radio and television advertising? Retail ads? Multimedia campaigns?

"Magic Words" Strategy

Understanding the "back-office" operations of the business is important in selling advertising. Your familiarity with various media options makes you an asset to a firm considering various means to promote its or its clients' business.

From your research, you should know what media options your prospective employer uses. Lead in by listing all of the media you are familiar with, honing in on the particular options that your prospective employer targets first.

Agribusiness

Question

What have you done to ensure that California's [or any other state's] agriculture is competitive with global competition?

"Magic Words" Strategy

Acknowledge that companies need to be competitive on all key levels, such as materials, energy, and labor. Offer a SMART Story™ about how you've reduced expenses in one of those key areas.

Question

What would you do to curtail Workers' Compensation costs?

"Magic Words" Strategy

Emphasize safety in the field or processing/production facility. Offer a SMART Story™ about how you created a group incentive program that reduced injuries.

Architecture

Contributed by Career Masters Institute member Evelyn Salvador.

Question

What type of structures do you conceptualize and design and what systems and components do your architectural drawings include?

"Magic Words" Strategy

Before answering this question, you need to know whether the prospective employer's firm designs a wide variety of structures, such as a design-and-build or construction-management firm might, or if it specializes in building one type of structure, such as residential homes, commercial buildings, environmental structures, public works projects, manufacturing plants, and so on. This is where your pre-interview research becomes essential.

If the firm's clients are varied, the interviewer wants to know about your experience and flexibility with designing a wide variety of buildings. If the firm specializes in one type of structure, concentrating too much on other projects would be detrimental. This is especially true if your concentration is in residential homes versus commercial buildings versus public works.

Question

What factors do you take into consideration in your designs?

"Magic Words" Strategy

The interviewer is looking for your ability to consider many factors. List aesthetics, functionality, environmental, reliability, climate, safety, effectiveness, location, cost, integration, accessibility, ease of use, availability of transportation, solar power, and so on.

Then provide a SMART Story™ about integrating these components into one project. Lead off with "One project I worked on, for example, which included many of these considerations, was…." Describe how your **A**ctions led to a numbers-oriented **R**esult. Then, **T**ie-in with why these considerations made the project a success.

Banking (Customer Service)

Question

Describe the range of banking functions with which you're experienced.

"Magic Words" Strategy

List your experience, such as transaction processing, check processing, proof procedures, payment processing, vault operations, foreign exchange, as well as new business development, new accounts, cross-selling for consumer lending, insurance sales, or mortgage financing.

Question

Describe the range of your transaction processing experience.

"Magic Words" Strategy

List any of the types of experience you have, such as processing deposits, withdrawals, return items, ATM transactions, cashiers checks, money orders, traveler's checks, loan payments, insurance payments, and so on. Make this response come alive by not simply mentioning a laundry list but adding an accomplishment to it. For instance, "I was asked by my manager to take the lead on handling the more complex transactions." Or, "I learned each of these in about half the time of most new reps." Or, "I was selected by my manager to train new hires on these issues."

Banking (Management)

Question
What have you done to initiate or implement fee-based services?

"Magic Words" Strategy
Acknowledge the trend toward fee-based services and offer a SMART example of how you did so for a current or former employer, with the corresponding increase in revenue. Include information about how marketing was done in a way that was appealing and palatable to customers.

Question
What do you see happening with interest rates?

"Magic Words" Strategy
Crystal balls aside, demonstrate your knowledge of what the financial pundits are saying about long-term interest rates. Offer examples of how you regularly read and research to keep up on this and other critical information.

Collections
Contributed by Career Masters Institute member Evelyn Salvador.

Question
By how much have you reduced outstanding collections/accounts receivable and how did you accomplish this?

"Magic Words" Strategy
The interviewer wants to determine whether you were able to save your previous employers money. State the before and after collections amounts. Describe the **A**ctions, such as utilizing effective skip-tracing methods, correcting large account discrepancies, effectively locating debtors, using successful negotiation tactics, and the like.

Use a SMART Story™ of one of your biggest collection accounts where you received a large-dollar collection, and how you were able to accomplish this. The **T**ie-in can describe how you can help do the same for the prospective employer.

Question
What sources and skip-tracing methods do you use to locate debtors and which methods have you found most successful in collecting delinquent accounts?

"Magic Words" Strategy

Help the interviewer envision your resourcefulness. Describe standard skip-tracing methods you use, as well as any innovative methods you have found successful. This may be informative for the employer, as you may have developed ideas he or she has not previously considered.

This calls for a SMART Story™ where you may have used out-of-the box thinking for a particular client who was having financial difficulties but genuinely wanted to pay their debt. Show how your patience, understanding, and communication skills helped you relate to the debtor and successfully collect what was owed the firm. State the amount saved in the Result.

Customer/Client Service

Question

How have you increased customer satisfaction levels?

"Magic Words" Strategy

A SMART Story™ will be just the vehicle to illustrate how you've taken customer satisfaction levels from point A to point B.

Question

Describe the call-center technology you are familiar with and your skill level with each of these.

"Magic Words" Strategy

Respond with your range of call-center technology experience, such as ACD, IVRU, CTI, predictive dialers, Web-based customer service, or Web-based live interface. If you completed training more quickly than the norm, mention this. If you have taught others, use a SMART Story™ to convey this. If you don't have an official training capacity but are called on by peers to explain advanced functions, mention that you are the unofficial resident expert for certain software.

Education (Administration)

Contributed by National Résumé Writers' Association member Edie Rische.

Question

What money-saving enhancements have you contributed to your school or school system?

"Magic Words" Strategy

This question probes whether you are budget-minded and can be creative in stretching dollars. A SMART Story™ will drive home your point.

Question

Describe how you win support from teachers.

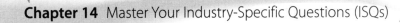

"Magic Words" Strategy

The theme to this answer should be team-building. If you inherited a situation where there was distrust and enmity among the teaching staff, tell a SMART Story™ that describes how you unified the environment (of course, without belittling anyone).

Education (Teachers)

Contributed by Career Masters Institute member Louise Garver.

Question

What is your philosophy of classroom discipline?

"Magic Words" Strategy

The interviewers want to know if you have a classroom-management plan, how you will implement it, why it's important, and whether you know how to control students. Offer a SMART Story™ that uses, for example, a discipline ladder or classroom-management plan.

Question

What are some trends or issues that relate to your specific curriculum area or grade level?

"Magic Words" Strategy

Prepare for this question by being up on your reading of educational journals, talking with peers in your field, attending seminars and association meetings, and visiting schools to observe the latest teaching methods. For example:

One key trend in the area of math and science education is "constructivist learning." I not only read articles on the subject in the American Educator *journal, but also attended a seminar at the recent annual teachers' association convention. This method is based on children constructing their own learning rather than copying what the teacher models. I have incorporated this concept in my math classes with successful results. For example, instead of teaching a standard algorithm, I encourage my students in group settings to find their own methods for solving math problems. Through this method, I have noticed that they are more engaged in learning math. The grades certainly reflect this enhanced learning.*

Engineering (Civil)

Question

Walk me through the projects listed on your resume.

"Magic Words" Strategy

The interviewer will be probing to find out whether you've inflated your resume. Be prepared to state your specific role in those projects. Specifically, were you a project manager or team member? What did you actually design? Which parts? If your resume says you worked on the design for a 2-million-gallon water plant and yet you only designed the drive approach, interviewers will question your credibility. Did you develop the scope of work on your own or was it always given to you? Did you have direct contact with clients? Did you write specifications? Did you file applications? Did you do grant work to obtain funding? These are the details interviewers are looking for.

Question

A contractor is requesting a change order for what he considers as work outside the contract. How would you protect the project from cost overruns while staying on schedule?

"Magic Words" Strategy

Problem-solving skills are being evaluated with this question. If you're dealing with soils or underground work, change orders are inevitable. The theoretical response should include these elements: Evaluate whether the change order is legitimate; if so, is it a fair price (compare the price to similar work on another contract or call another contractor to get a second opinion); then, negotiate to keep costs to a minimum. For instance, pay the contractor time and materials and put an inspector on the job to make sure the contractor stays on track. A SMART Story™ would illustrate this well.

Graphic Design

Contributed by Career Masters Institute member Evelyn Salvador.

Question

What primary graphic design programs do you use to create effective visual communication and how much experience do you have in each?

"Magic Words" Strategy

Lead off with a summary statement about your technology skills that are specific to the industry; then offer the interviewer your level of experience (intermediate or advanced, or number of years) in each, such as QuarkXPress, Adobe Photoshop, Adobe Illustrator, Adobe PageMaker, MultiAd Creator, Microsoft Publisher, and so on. You should know which programs the interviewer's company uses and state your experience with these programs primarily.

Consider offering a "leave-behind" sheet that outlines all of your graphic design program experience (if it is not already in your resume) or some sample projects you have worked on using them. These should be samples of your best work selected from your portfolio, which you might prepare as a media kit (a half dozen examples is sufficient). When showcasing your work, indicate the programs you used and the creative effects you developed using them.

Question

What type of visual communications, corporate identity, marketing campaigns, or other materials do you lay out, design, and/or produce?

"Magic Words" Strategy

Be prepared to list your range of experience by first listing those items that are most applicable to the prospective employer's field.

For example, if you are applying at an ad agency, you could highlight some of these possibilities: corporate identity pieces, advertisements and advertising campaigns, logos, annual reports, brochures, direct-mail pieces, trade publication ads, package design, postcards, and Web site design (if you're experienced in that as well).

If you are applying at a corporate in-house marketing department, include marketing campaigns, presentations, photographs of trade-show exhibits, manuals, news releases, media presentations, and so on. If you are applying for a position with a newspaper, you would include retail display ads, newspaper layouts, newsletters, magazine article layouts, and so on. For a printer, you could include stationery, business cards, catalogs, flyers, forms, and signage as well as more upscale projects if you have them.

After your summary list, consider shifting the conversation toward what the interviewer is most interested in: "I understand you do a lot of Valpac coupons. I can show you some that were particularly successful for our clients." And, "What other advertising and design needs does your firm have right now that I would be working on?"

Healthcare (Clinical)

Contributed by National Résumé Writers' Association member Melanie Noonan.

Question

Describe actions you took in a treatment situation that was out of the ordinary.

"Magic Words" Strategy

Offer a response that underscores your thoroughness and ability to work as a multidisciplinary team member. A good example would be how you worked with a particular patient who was routinely being treated for _____ (fill in your appropriate discipline, such as a respiratory therapy illness or burn treatment) but who you suspected had developed other medical complications. Describe the steps you took, including what other medical team members you alerted, how you followed up, and what the early notice may have prevented.

Question

How have you handled an increase in your patient load?

"Magic Words" Strategy

With the changes in healthcare, it seems that every institution is asking its clinical staff to do more. A SMART Story™ can convey how you accommodated an xx percent increase in patient load while maintaining quality of care. You might also point to how your technology skills have contributed to making this possible. Or, perhaps there is a committee or team you served on that addressed productivity/cost-savings issues.

Healthcare (Management)

Question

How have you engaged physicians to help manage healthcare costs?

Magic

"Magic Words" Strategy

Use a SMART Story™. Provide details, such as how you influenced a dozen orthopedic surgeons to standardize inventory by using the same hip replacement implant, or how you worked with the docs to improve the discharge rate of patients.

Question

What innovations have you recently made to your internal business office operations to address changes in contracting?

Magic

"Magic Words" Strategy

Since the business office is the linchpin in collecting and processing patient data and insurance information, the interviewer likely wants to hear about smooth and timely procedures for reimbursement. Be ready to state before-and-after data that documents how efficient the improvements in your institution's reimbursement have been.

Human Resources (Generalist)

Contributed by Career Masters Institute Member Barbara Safani.

Question

With respect to recruiting, what strategies do you use to ensure a good job-fit?

Magic

"Magic Words" Strategy

Describe your range of recruiting experience and initiatives implemented such as identifying competencies, emphasizing behavioral-based interviewing, requiring skills-based assessments as part of the interview process, and so on.

Question

What are your thoughts on outsourcing or off-shoring human resource functions?

Magic

"Magic Words" Strategy

This can be a politically sensitive issue, so handle it with diplomacy. Consider offering some pros and cons, examples of how it has worked well in the past for your companies, and how you read publications such as SHRM's *HR Executive* to stay abreast of trends.

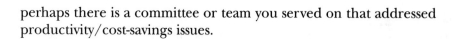

Human Resources (Training and Development)

Contributed by Career Masters Institute member Beverly Harvey.

Question

Tell me about your experience with e-learning systems.

"Magic Words" Strategy

If you have experience with several systems, briefly state the name of the company and the system you used: "At Hughes Supply we managed our e-learning program using Generation21 and at Widget company we used LearnPoint." If you know which e-learning system the company is using, offer a SMART Story™ about your experience with their system. Your tie-in should mention improvements in functionality, content, utilization, and performance that in turn reduced costs and increased revenues.

Question

Describe the range of your experience with respect to content design, development, and delivery?

"Magic Words" Strategy

Convey here your turnkey knowledge of content design, development, and delivery. Describe your ability to create best-in-class training, instructional methodologies, and materials, as well as to execute programs using various delivery methods. Provide an overview of the types of training programs (technical, sales, management) you have designed, developed, and delivered, including the number of people that have received training and their locations (nationwide, worldwide). Communicate the positive outcomes associated with the training. After hearing this, the interviewer will likely ask for a specific example, or you can wrap up your overview response with the phrase, "Would you like a specific example that outlines what was accomplished at XYZ Company?"

Information Technology (CIO, VP, Director, Knowledge Officers)

Question

Describe a situation in which you led a technology initiative that helped add value or profit to the company.

"Magic Words" Strategy

Respond that "any technology initiative should serve and not restrict business. If it does not add value to the company, it may not be in the company's best interest to deploy." Indicate your knowledge of the entire lifecycle of business support systems, speak to the cost versus benefit issues of implementing a new technology or processes, the financial justifications and financial management options (whether to lease or buy outright, how to fund and for how long, and so on), and how to mitigate risks (for example, obsolescence issues, long-term stability of vendors). Then, provide a SMART Story™ that illustrates these points.

Question

What do you think about outsourcing/offshoring?

"Magic Words" Strategy

Magic

Respond diplomatically, assuring the interviewer that as an IT executive, your responsibility is to add value to the organization. In some cases, that means maximizing the capabilities of your existing infrastructure. In others, it means outsourcing so that you don't have to constantly upgrade infrastructure. If you have experience with outsourcing, describe the strategy and processes you used to implement an off-shore solution, along with the results/outcomes associated with the initiative. Provide brief illustrations of acquired knowledge in managing areas such as outsourcing best practices, staff transition, vendor selection, engagements, quality assurance, internal company politics, and performance metrics.

Information Technology (Managers, Assistant Directors)

Question

Tell me about a time when you handled a security intrusion and what steps you took to improve system security.

"Magic Words" Strategy

Magic

The interviewer wants to gauge your ability to strategize the resolution processes; recognize pulse points in a crisis situation; and leverage experience, skills, and wisdom from prior encounters. Impress upon the interviewer your broad span of knowledge at the user level, department level, company level, or enterprise-wide level; however, scope your answer to the size of company with which you are interviewing. For instance, at some companies, security concerns may be not be as extensive, involving only basic perimeter defenses such as firewalls, an antivirus protection suite, and some level of spam control. Larger enterprises are concerned with more comprehensive approaches, including designs to protect against elements such as distributed denial-of-service attacks and strategies for data integrity, security processes, and extensive perimeter defenses. If applicable, convey to the interviewer your experience involving state and federal law enforcement agencies to bring security perpetrators to justice and shore up any financial implications from the security breach.

Question

Tell me about a time when you were directed by senior management to implement a technology initiative that would take you over budget and how you handled it.

"Magic Words" Strategy

Magic

Before responding to the question, first assure the interviewer that you have an excellent record for managing budgets because of your strong forecasting and monitoring skills. Then, convey that you would first analyze whether this initiative

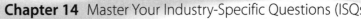

was aligned with the company's strategic plan. The interviewer should appreciate that you're looking at the big picture. If it is not aligned with the company's strategic plan, indicate that you would take into consideration the current internal political landscape. If it is aligned with the long-term strategic direction of the company, explain that you would next proceed to analyzing the financial implications, developing options (will this require a RIF, salary freeze, budget freeze, elimination of commissions; is leadership open to implementing the project in phases over a multi-year time period; what level of support can be provided by the vendor; and so on) and implementing strategies. This process will show that you know the technical aspects, financial implications, and business realities associated with the question.

Information Technology (Technical Staff, Help Desk, Analysts)

Question
What level of responsibility have you held in a help-desk environment?

"Magic Words" Strategy
Typically, the three levels that you might point to are

- Front-line technician: someone with basic skills where issues are resolved in a three- to five-minute timeframe

- Second level: someone with intermediate technical skills where issues affect a wider scope of knowledge

- Third-tier: someone with high-level certifications

If your goal in the interview is to land a position that moves you to a higher level, or if you don't have a desired certification but have equivalent experience, use the strategy of offering a skills inventory to highlight the following:

- Number of years working with certain technology

- Number of people you supported

- How recently you worked with that particular technology

- How frequently you worked with that particular technology (daily, monthly, weekly)

Then, be ready with a SMART Story™ that describes how you resolved, say, a third-tier issue while you were still a second-tier technician.

Question
What do you do when a user cannot log into a network?

"Magic Words" Strategy
The interviewer is looking for your thought process for arriving at the best solution. Offer a SMART Story™ that steps the interviewer through the information you would gather, such as whether the user is local to the site, if this is for a

particular type of user (contractor, full-time employee), whether it is a physical connectivity issue or a software-related issue, or whether the problem is the user's lack of knowledge.

> ## Interviewing Resource for Programmers
>
> If you are a programmer, consider picking up the book *Programming Interviews Exposed: Secrets to Landing Your Next Job* by John Mongan. You'll find dozens of knowledge-based questions and problems on a wide range of topics, from abstract classes to XOR operation.

Insurance Claims and Investigations

Contributed by Career Masters Institute member Evelyn Salvador.

Question

What type of insurance policy claims have you processed or investigated?

"Magic Words" Strategy

Lead off with an overview of the various types of claims you have processed; and then hone in on the type of claims the prospective employer's company handles. For example,

During my career I have processed health insurance claims, Workers' Compensation claims, long- and short-term disability insurance claims, as well as accidental death and dismemberment claims. My particular experience in handling Workers' Compensation claims has involved...

Similarly if you have handled automobile, life, property and casualty, fire, flood, marine, medical malpractice, credit card, or product liability insurance claims, be sure to tie in your experience with the prospective employer's needs.

Question

How do you identify controversial claims and what do you do when you suspect foul play? What investigative techniques have you found most successful?

"Magic Words" Strategy

Explain skills that help you determine whether foul play is a possibility. Depending on the position you hold, you might determine whether an investigation is warranted and refer the suspicious claim to an investigator or conduct the research and field investigations to determine whether, in fact, it is insurance fraud.

Follow with how you identify controversial claims, process investigative requests or orders, conduct legal claims issues research, make claims validity determinations, make suspicious claims referrals, make problem claims closure, and so on.

Provide a SMART Story™ to identify a controversial claim you handled, why you suspected fraud, the investigative techniques used, and the successful outcome attained. Tie this in with how you can do the same for the prospective employer.

Legal

Question
How many trials have you had?

Magic

"Magic Words" Strategy
Offer a straightforward answer, including whether you served as lead attorney, along with a SMART Story™ about a complex, challenging, or relevant case. If you served as second chair, do not immediately volunteer this information. Wait for the interviewer to ask whether you were lead or second chair.

Question
What was your billable rate and production last year? What do you anticipate these to be in the future? Tell me about a time when you had difficulty asking a client for a fee.

Magic

"Magic Words" Strategy
For attorneys interviewing with law firms, the ability to churn out billable hours is critical. If accurate, reference a steady increase in production over the past few years.

Regarding difficulty asking for a fee, clients who are going through bankruptcy or a divorce are often short on cash. The firm wants to know whether you can ask for a fee up front. If appropriate, explain that you do a certain amount of pro bono work yet still generate billable hours that are among the highest of the firm.

Management
Contributed by Career Masters Institute member John O'Connor.

Question
Describe a time when you implemented a change initiative and encountered resistance. What did you do?

Magic

"Magic Words" Strategy
Offer a SMART Story™ that illustrates your leadership influence, as does this example:

Just before the Y2K concerns surfaced in 1999, many of our technology directors at the national level presented a $49 million solution to our division. This so-called solution meant that our division would lose 17 employees. I politely but seriously objected after two weeks of careful competitor analysis. Our industry rivals all put forth the same solution. What did I find out? The solution served the hysteria of Y2K but did not help the company gain revenue or reduce costs. So I wrote a detailed, five-page memo. Several directors *privately e-mailed me to thank me for my research; however, two were not convinced. It took six meetings at our corporate offices in New Jersey, six more detailed papers, and multiple private phone calls to convince all the directors. The result? The multimillion-dollar plan was scratched, Y2K happened and the company saw no burden to the software, and we saved 17 jobs in our division alone. In most of my writing and speaking I acknowledged each director's concern but made sure that each person's point of view and concerns were considered. That helped me build consensus and not alienate anyone. If I had rammed through the change initiative, I would have been right but I would have made a lot of people mad. Instead, we all achieved our main goal: what was best for each division and the company. The big-picture result, of course, was that for the next few years we had a clear edge over, and a lot more cash than, our competition!*

Question

How have you gone about conceiving and implementing a new vision for companies/departments in the past?

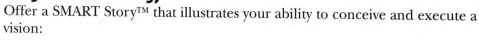

"Magic Words" Strategy

Magic

Offer a SMART Story™ that illustrates your ability to conceive and execute a vision:

I can readily think of several examples over the past five years. Let me focus on one. As Division Manager for ABC Company, our chief competitor had taken 23 percent of our market share in the six months prior to my coming on board. This presented great anxiety for our Southeast division, my division. Tasked with turning around this problem, I turned to what I call my "master mind" team. My master mind team consists of people I work with and also a few trusted colleagues from my past leadership assignments. With their help, I clarified my vision for the division, which was to not only turn it around but make it, over the next five years, the leading provider of widget products in the manufacturing market. I wrote, and with the team, edited the business plan. The buy-in nationally was 100 percent, partly out of necessity and partly out of desperation. Nine months after components of the business plan were implemented, we regained market share. Each month succeeding we added market share until we once again dominated market share. New products were introduced and cycle times were reduced by 56 percent. These successes continue to today.

Manufacturing

Contributed by National Résumé Writers' Association member Melanie Noonan.

Question

Tell me about a situation in which you had to make a difficult decision on whether or not to ship possibly defective product that was urgently needed by a key customer.

"Magic Words" Strategy

Magic

The phrase "Tell me about..." cues you that this is a behavioral interviewing question that demands a SMART Story™, such as this:

To fulfill an urgent customer requirement for certain component parts, we did a rush production run, but time did not allow for the full QC inspection process. Since no defects were immediately noticeable, the product was loaded onto the trailer. Just before the truck was to leave, my shop supervisor informed me that there was a 1 percent failure rate in a test sampling of the parts. Knowing that a complaint from this customer could cost us the loss of their business, I stopped the shipment immediately, called the customer's purchasing manager, and explained the situation. He thanked me for alerting him and gave me the go-ahead to ship anyway. He said he would make sure the product would undergo a thorough inspection before it was used. Meanwhile, I reviewed our production process to find the cause of the defect to prevent further such recurrences.

Consider closing with a tie-in question, such as "What challenges are you having with quality?"

Question
What systems have you put in place to address any deficiencies in quality and on-time shipments?

"Magic Words" Strategy
A SMART Story™ is in order. Convey your ability to quickly note and analyze the situation (if not, questions may arise about why the situation went on as long as it did). Also, indicate how you communicated with key internal contacts, offered solutions with return-on-investment calculations, and implemented those solutions. Remember to provide before-and-after numbers to underscore positive results.

Marketing

Question
Describe a time when you analyzed market research to influence a marketing initiative.

"Magic Words" Strategy
The interviewer wants to know about your research and analytical skills. Use a SMART Story™ that illustrates how you accessed and analyzed market data and then made appropriate recommendations. Finish with the bottom-line outcome.

Question
Describe some of the marketing materials you have written.

"Magic Words" Strategy
Provide an overview statement, such as, "I wrote, developed, and produced annual reports, interim financial disclosures, letters to shareholders, press releases, and all promotional materials for the parent company and its subsidiaries…." Offer the interviewer a glimpse of your portfolio to make these items come to life.

Pharmaceutical Sales

Question

What classes of pharmaceuticals have you sold?

"Magic Words" Strategy

If your product experience isn't perfectly aligned with the company's product, consider a response like this:

I have a range of experience with multiple classes, including anti-obesity, antibiotic, antiviral, loop diuretic, and beta-blockers, where I've called on family practitioners, pediatricians, OB/GYNs, cardiologists, gastroenterologists, allergists, and internal medicine physicians. In researching your company, I've familiarized myself with your and your competitors' HRT products and talked to several physicians in the area. I understand there are both challenges and opportunities to move market share for your newest product. I'm anxious to hear your thoughts and share some of my own about how to accomplish that.

Question

What is your current district sales ranking for your primary product?

"Magic Words" Strategy

The interviewer will want to hear both the ranking number and how many reps are in the district. If you've moved up since beginning with the company, say so. If your numbers have been high but recently took a dip, reference both numbers:

For the majority of the past two years, I've ranked #2 among 12 reps in our district; the last quarter that ranking was #4. I attribute that to…. To counter this, I have aggressively pursued gaining formulary approval for our newest product.

Procurement/Purchasing

Contributed by Career Masters Institute Member Evelyn Salvador.

Question

What buying/purchasing functions do you manage, oversee, and/or handle?

"Magic Words" Strategy

State your total purchasing responsibility, mention any supervisory responsibilities, and provide a summary of your primary functions, such as procurement, category management, merchandising, capital equipment acquisition, market research and identification, order processing/fulfillment, customer service, new item identification, product development, bid specifications and evaluations, vendor selections, contract/price negotiations, cost analysis, inventory control, and warehouse management. Follow up with additional functions as they pertain to your prospective employer, such as manufacturing coordination, product setups, merchandising plans, new item offerings, value analysis, purchase orders, and/or vendor relations.

Question
What methods do you use to analyze and calculate bids?

"Magic Words" Strategy
Explain the methods you use, such as life-cycle costing, weighted value, value analysis, or other methods. This is a good opportunity for a SMART Story™ if you have, for example, changed the methods used to better meet your current or a past employer's needs. For the Action and Result, you can explain the method your employer previously used, why a different method was more cost effective, what steps you took to make the change, and how much the revised method of analyzing and calculating bids saved your employer. If you have an overall percentage of how much you saved previous employers (and you should!), use it. Tie this in with how a knowledge-based evaluation of bids for the prospective employer would save them money as well.

Retail (Store Management)
Contributed by National Resume Writers' Association member Edie Rische.

Question
Tell me the philosophies that have made you a successful store manager.

"Magic Words" Strategy
The interviewer will gauge your core values with this question, in addition to whether you can express your viewpoint articulately. What values do you espouse? Here's what one store manager offered:

I can list three core philosophies that are key to my success as the #1-ranked store in our 12-store region: 1) The customer is the boss, and should be treated in a manner that I would like to be treated were I shopping in the store. 2) The floor sales team determines whether the customer has a positive shopping experience. To that end, I build respect, camaraderie, and unity among my staff by working side-by-side with employees. And 3), mediocrity will never be accepted. High expectations and first-rate training equate to positive outcomes.

Then launch into a SMART Story™ that provides numbers-driven results to substantiate your philosophies.

Question
A customer is angry over the way he was treated by a salesperson. What steps would you take (or have you taken in the past) to resolve this type of complaint?

"Magic Words" Strategy
This is a two-part question: How do you resolve the customer complaint, and how do you manage the salesperson. Start by resolving the customer complaint, for instance, taking the customer to a quiet place, using laser listening to ensure that the customer feels heard, providing options for resolution, and assuring the customer that the situation won't be repeated. Then, explore with the salesperson what happened and why, initiate appropriate consequences, and seek methods to

make sure the salesperson is motivated to exceed future customer-satisfaction goals.

Sales Management

Question

How do you balance the needs of your salespeople with the needs of the management team?

Magic

"Magic Words" Strategy

A SMART Story™ is appropriate here. For instance:

I recently had a situation where management requested we deliver a 20 percent sales increase for the upcoming quarter. This was challenging because we had no new products to offer. I approached it by assembling my team, explaining that the health of our company required a spike in sales, and asking what suggestions they had.

Go on to describe the action taken and, of course, finish with strong results. Your tie-in/theme can be about your management philosophy, such as

I think too often, sales managers dictate rather than involve. True salespeople need to be feel valued—that their thoughts count—and empowered. They need to think of strategies on their own so they have ownership of the idea. It's been my experience that this is the best way to motivate others.

Question

How do you motivate your salespeople?

Magic

"Magic Words" Strategy

The key to your response should *not* be a one-size-fits-all answer. Explain to the interviewer that, if it's someone that you know is a good salesperson, you first identify the problem. The problem could be that the rep just found out a spouse has a serious illness. The old saying, "People don't care how much you know until they know how much you care" applies in this type of situation. Regardless of the cause, explain that you are not a counselor and don't need nitty-gritty details, but that you can help the rep see new solutions. Then, explain to the interviewer how you would come to an agreement on measurable goals with accountability measures built in. Offer a SMART Story™ that illustrates the procedure you've just outlined.

Sales (Outside)

Contributed by Career Masters Institute members Louise Garver and Jane Roqueplot.

Question

Your prospect's secretary says to you, "Mr. Jones is not interested in new products at this time." How would you react to that statement?

"Magic Words" Strategy

Magic

Preface your response with a statement such as, "This is a part of the sales process, and I don't take it personally." Offer a SMART Story™ that explains how you overcome objections in real life. For instance,

I can give you an example of how I managed this very situation on a recent cold call. I expressed appreciation to the secretary for making me aware of his wishes. I then asked if she knew why he was not looking at any new copier products at this time and learned that he had recently purchased a competitor's product. I indicated I'd like to check back with him later to learn whether the product was fully meeting his expectations, and added that action into my follow-up plan. I then inquired who else in the company investigates new products and proceeded accordingly with a new prospect. In meeting with that individual, I uncovered needs for new service contracts. The sale closed just last week and put me at 107 percent of goal for the year, while we're only in the third quarter.

Question

How do you use data to influence your sales strategy?

"Magic Words" Strategy

Magic

Mention the types of data you are familiar with, such as in-house data or data from sources such as IRI, Nielsen, Polk, or Retail Link. Speak to your analytical skills and ability to apply fact-based selling.

Good sales strategy must be driven by accurate data. I've worked in companies where their IT systems captured rich customer data that enabled me to note trends, identify seasonal opportunities, and leverage key account activity. For instance, in my most recent position I was analyzing the monthly sales activity compared to the prior year for a key account and noted a double-digit drop for a particular line item. I immediately investigated what was happening in the store and discovered that a new assistant store manager was not rotating product properly. I worked with the manager and had the problem resolved in two days.

I've also worked at a company that was lacking in historical data. I was instrumental in proposing new systems that captured baseline data, which helped us grow sales 20 percent the following year.

My business analysis skills have served me well in consultative selling and fact-based selling. Could you tell me what type of data sources you're using now and how they're working out for you?

Social Services (Manager)

Contributed by Career Masters Institute member Freddie Cheek.

Question

Tell me about your supervision of professional staff members, interns, and/or volunteers. Did this supervision include field placements? What human resources functions did you handle?

"Magic Words" Strategy

During my five years at XYZ Facility, I managed recruitment, training, scheduling, professional development, evaluation, and disciplinary activities. I have supervised a 65-member team providing integrated treatment services. I trained and supervised bachelors- and masters-level students participating in field placements. My supervisory and HR efforts have resulted in boosting staff retention by more than 15 percent. My team managed a 20 percent increase in caseload without adding additional staff, and enhanced quality of services. This last metric was measured by a client satisfaction survey conducted by a third-party organization. My department earned the highest customer-satisfaction ratings—all in the 90th percentile—among 12 departments throughout the region.

Question

Have you served on quality management/improvement committees and have you monitored quality?

"Magic Words" Strategy

Describe the range of your experience. For instance,

I have monitored the quality of internal and external services, resulting in service integration and outstanding marks for customer service for a culturally diverse population, as measured by customer surveys. I have evaluated and redesigned programs, on an ongoing basis, to respond to the changing needs of insurance providers, consumers, the community, and funding sources.

I have led or served on numerous committees: Standards Compliance Committee, Utilization Review Committee, Policies and Procedures Committee, Code of Conduct Review and Implementation Committee, Performance Evaluation Committee, and Psychiatric Rehabilitation and Recovery Interdisciplinary Task Force.

After providing this type of a list, offer one specific and impressive quantifiable outcome that resulted from service on one of those committees. Ask whether the interviewer would like to hear more examples.

Social Services (Service Provider)

Contributed by Career Masters Institute member Freddie Cheek.

Question

What types of populations or issues do you have experience with?

"Magic Words" Strategy

Your range of experience may include working in the field of chemical or substance abuse; familiarity with 12-step programs; working with people in inpatient rehab programs, outpatient recovery programs, or methadone treatment; children of alcoholic parents; individuals in denial; co-dependents and enablers, and so on. Offer the broad range of experience in your response, but tie it back to the population most relevant to the interviewer's needs.

Question
What type of services have you provided?

"Magic Words" Strategy
Your response may include any combination of these elements: case management, intake/admissions, psychosocial assessment, treatment/care planning, advocacy, crisis intervention, referral/linkage to community resources, and/or discharge planning. Then, depending on the employer's needs and interests, describe one of these areas in more detail.

Warehousing/Distribution

Question
What size inventory do you manage?

"Magic Words" Strategy
Offer the dollar-value or case-number range of inventory you've managed over your career; then hone in on a situation most relevant to the interviewer's situation. Mention one numbers-driven accomplishment, followed by an offer to explain more.

Similar to your DC operation, my current inventory value is $80 million. I've taken our DC ranking from #7 among 12 in the region to #2 in less than 12 months. If you'd like more details about how I accomplished that, I can offer them now.

Question
What kind of a record do you have for inventory variance? Tell me what you've done to lower that number.

"Magic Words" Strategy
Compare your distribution center's inventory variance to the company average or the industry average, provided that your numbers are lower than these averages. Offer a SMART Story™ about how you accomplished the reduction and the dollars represented by the savings.

Linking FAQs and ISQs to Your SMART Stories™
Near the end of chapter 3, we discussed leaving blank the "Potential Interview Questions" section on the SMART Story™ worksheets. Now is the time to pair up FAQs and ISQs with the SMART Stories™ you wrote in chapter 3. To do so, follow these steps:

1. Review the FAQs from chapter 13, as well as the ISQs in this chapter.

2. Complete the "Magical Coaching Tips" worksheet at the end of this chapter. Here, you will develop up to 10 ISQs for your industry.

3. From the FAQs and ISQs in chapters 13 and 14, match as many questions as possible to one or more of your SMART Stories™. (Not all questions will require a behavioral-based SMART Story™ response.)

4. At the bottom of each SMART Story™ worksheet in chapter 3, write in the frequently asked or industry specific question(s) that can be answered by that particular SMART Story™.

5. Enlist the help of a friend to help you practice by acting as an interviewer. This will help program your memory to recall appropriate stories in response to certain questions. (If friends are not easily accessible, make old-fashioned flash cards on 4 × 6 index cards with an interview question on one side and the SMART Story™ on the other.)

Chapter Wrap-Up

Preparing for Industry-Specific Questions is an important aspect of interviewing. As an "A" candidate, this is a must-do in order to Control the Controllables (see chapter 5 on mindset). The exercises in the "Magical Coaching Tips" at the end of this chapter will positively help you learn about current industry questions, gain the latest insider tips, and boost your confidence because of your proactive steps.

10 Tips for Answering Industry-Specific Questions

1. **Ask!:** Network with people in your industry to learn at least five, and preferably 10, Industry-Specific Questions that might be asked in an interview.

2. **Be SMART:** Whenever possible, offer a SMART Story™ to give the interviewer a behavioral, fact-based response. Vary the length of your responses (see chapter 10 on behavioral interviews).

3. **Occasionally preface responses with a *P*hilosophical comment:** State your philosophy or position on a subject. For instance, "I believe that _____ [mention whatever relevant issue is at hand] is one of the top five factors for successful widgetry."

4. **Occasionally preface responses with a *O*verview statement:** Make an overview or umbrella statement. For instance, "With 10 years of experience at ABC Company, I have solid skills in the full widget-making lifecycle, including R&D, testing, marketing, sales, distribution, and customer service. To answer your question more specifically, I can point to a time when."…

5. **Occasionally preface responses with an *E*nthusiastic remark:** Convey enthusiasm, excitement, and passion. For instance, "Absolutely! That's one of my favorite responsibilities. (Or, "I am well-versed in that!") The situation that readily comes to mind is this.…"

6. **Occasionally preface responses with a *Tease*:** Tell them the result at the beginning of the story to hold their attention. For instance, "I can recap how I led a cross-training initiative at ABC Widget Co. that saved $90,000 in overtime costs and improved productivity 7 percent. Here's what the situation looked like...."

7. **Anticipate:** Prepare to shine, even when you don't have the exact experience an interviewer is looking for. See Tips 8 through 10 (Assistance, Observations, Research) for options.

8. **Describe assistance:** Describe how you have assisted with elements of a successful product launch using a SMART Story™ format. "Recently, my current employer launched a new over-the-counter drug that exceeded its projections by 17 percent. My role in the project was as assistant product manager...." After stating the results, tie in the story to your history of continually taking on larger challenges with success and the confidence you have in managing this new responsibility.

9. **Describe observations:** Use a SMART Story™ format to reference how you observed a successful person handle the situation, along with what worked and what you would do differently to improve the situation. "What comes to mind is how I have observed my current company's product manager handling the launch of a new in-home security device. Although I didn't participate directly in the project, I closely observed her actions because of my passion for product management...."

10. **Describe research:** Describe how you would theoretically handle it using the SMART format. Consider introducing your response with, "I anticipated that would be important to you, so I did some research to enhance my knowledge on that topic. Here's how I would handle it."

⭐ **Magical Coaching Tips**

In the spaces below, identify two or three industry contacts you will approach regarding potential interview questions:

1. _____

2. _____

3. _____

(continued)

(continued)

Ask contacts who have been on recent job interviews the following questions:

- What are five industry-specific or technical questions you were asked in your recent interviews?

- What responses did the interviewers react favorably to?

Ask contacts who are experienced in interviewing and hiring the following questions:

- What five industry-specific or technical questions do you regularly ask when interviewing candidates?

- What competencies or knowledge are you probing for with those questions?

- What were some of the A+ responses to those questions by people you hired?

- What constructive criticism could you give me if I were to answer that question in this manner [then, share your answer]?

Itemize and develop your answer strategy for up to 10 ISQs you might be asked on an interview.

Chapter

15

Deal with Illegal and Awkward Interview Questions

One of the basic causes for all the trouble in the world today is that people talk too much and think too little. They act impulsively without thinking. I always try to think before I talk.

—Margaret Chase Smith, American politician

Ever heard of *The $64,000 Question*? Debuted in the 1950s, this television quiz show was one of the earliest of the now-popular game show genre. The program became so popular that the saying, *That's the $64,000 question,* has come to represent *any* question that is difficult to answer. Interviews are certainly loaded with $64,000 questions!

Do You Have Sticky Wickets in Your Background?

A *sticky wicket* is a cricketing allusion and, never having played this British pastime, I'll make my disclaimers for understanding the game fully. A *wicket* is a gate-like set of sticks with cross-pieces at which a ball is bowled. *Wicket* also refers to the turf between the wickets and, by extension, the condition of that turf. If the turf is waterlogged or muddy (not unusual for England), the ball behaves unpredictably and it is difficult to succeed...otherwise known as a *sticky wicket.*

In interviewing, sticky wickets might be a strained relationship with a former boss, a gap in employment during a prolonged job search, an association with a short-lived dot-com that went dot-bomb, the appearance of being overqualified or too old, lack of the "right" degree, an unfinished degree, a health issue, being fired, a prison record, and so on. Any hint of negativity or suggestion of a deficiency may knock you out of the running, and that's the last thing you want. In this chapter, we'll cover strategies for answering those really tough $64,000 questions—namely, illegal inquiries and awkward, sticky-wicket questions!

How to Spot Illegal Interview Questions

Today's employers are pretty savvy about what they can and cannot legally ask in a job interview. Some have learned this lesson the hard way: If discrimination is found, the candidate may be awarded compensatory damages, as well as a job offer, attorney costs, and other benefits. As an example, a candidate who had lost part of his arm in an automobile accident was asked by an untrained interviewer at Wal-Mart, "What current or past medical problems might limit your ability to do the job?" The candidate, after not getting a job offer, filed a charge of disability discrimination pursuant to the Americans with Disabilities Act (ADA), and a jury awarded him $157,500. The entire debacle could have been avoided had the interviewer showed him the job description and, instead, asked whether he could perform the essential functions of the job.

However, this doesn't mean that you won't be asked an illegal question. More than a decade after the passage of the ADA, there is still confusion about exactly what constitutes an illegal question. Employers offer sensitivity training and refresher courses on interviewing compliant with the Equal Pay Act, the Civil Rights Act, the Age Discrimination in Employment Act, the Family Medical Leave Act, and several more. However, with staff changes and the stress of the interview process, many interviewers still ask illegal and inappropriate questions. Your best defense against this is to be prepared with answers to the $64,000 questions. If the interviewer is professional and knowledgeable—all the better. If the interviewer asks a difficult question, you will be ready for it and positioned to win the prize.

The following table outlines illegal and legal (but potentially difficult) questions for a variety of categories.

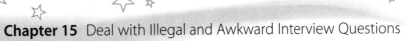

Table 15.1: Illegal and Legal Interview Questions

Category	Illegal Questions	Legal Questions
National Origin/ Citizenship	• Are you a U.S. citizen? • Where were you/your parents born? • What is your native language?	• Are you authorized to work in the United States? • What languages do you read/speak/write fluently? (Legal to ask only when relevant to the performance of the job.)
Marital/ Family Status	• Are you married, single, divorced, separated, engaged, or widowed? • With whom do you live? • Do you plan to have a family? When? • How many children do you have? How old? • What are your child-care arrangements? • Does your husband support your decision to work?	• What's your marital status? • Would you be willing to relocate if necessary? • Is there any reason that you will not be able to come to work every day, on time? (This question is acceptable if it is asked of all candidates.) • Would you be able and willing to travel as needed for the job? (This question is legal if it is asked of all candidates.) • Would you be able and willing to work overtime as necessary? (This question is legal assuming it is asked of all candidates.)
Age	• How old are you? • When did you graduate? • What's your birth date?	• Are you over the age of 18? • Are you old enough to work?
Affiliations	• What clubs or social organizations do you belong to?	• List any memberships in professional groups or other organizations that you consider relevant to your ability to perform this job.
Religion	• What religion do you practice? • Are you a member of a particular church? • The job requires that you work on Fridays, Saturdays, and Sundays. Will your religion cause a problem with this schedule?	• The position requires that you work Fridays, Saturdays, and Sundays. Will you be able to work these days?

(continued)

(continued)

Category	Illegal Questions	Legal Questions
Disabilities	• Do you have any disabilities? • Please complete the following medical history. • Have you had any recent or past illnesses or operations? If yes, list them and give dates when these occurred. • What was the date of your last physical exam? • How's your family's health? • When did you lose your eyesight? How? • Have you ever filed a Workers' Compensation claim?	• Do you need an accommodation to perform the job? (This question can be asked only after a job offer has been made.) • Are you able to perform the essential functions of this job? (This question is fine after the interviewer has thoroughly described the job.) • Can you demonstrate how you would perform the following job-related functions? • As part of the hiring process, after a job offer has been made, you will be required to undergo a medical exam. (This must be a condition of employment for all entering employees in that position. Exam results must be kept strictly confidential, except that medical/safety personnel may be informed if emergency medical treatment is required. Supervisors may also be informed about necessary job accommodations, based on exam results.)
Medical History	• Please complete the following medical history. • What current or past medical problems might limit your ability to do this job? • Do you smoke? • Have you had a history of mental illness?	• Are you able to perform the essential functions of this position? (This can be asked only after the interviewer explains the position.) • Our smoking policy is this… can you adhere to it?
Arrest/Prison Record	• Have you ever been arrested? • Have you ever pled guilty to a crime? • Have you ever been in trouble with the law?	• Have you been convicted of a felony within the past seven years? • Do you have a valid driver's license?

Category	Illegal Questions	Legal Questions
Military	• Were you honorably discharged? • Tell me about your military record. • Have you served in the military of countries other than the United States?	• In what branch of the Armed Forces did you serve? • What type of training or education did you receive in the military?
Credit	• Do you have any credit problems? • Have you recently filed for personal bankruptcy? • Is your salary presently subject to legal attachment or wage garnishment?	• If hired, would you allow us to order a credit report to confirm statements made on your employment application (provided you receive a copy)?

Be aware that it is also illegal for employers to ask:

- For photographs before hiring

- For references from clergy before hiring

- Questions of females that are not asked of males

A Skillful System for Responding to Illegal Questions

Now that you know how to spot illegal questions, how will you respond to them? Basically, you have three options:

- Flat-out tell the interviewer, "That's an illegal question—you're not allowed to ask me that." You may as well tell the interviewer, "You're stupid" or "You're breaking the law"—neither of which will rack up any points for rapport and relationship building. Consider that it's quite possible the interviewer is simply untrained and unaware of the illegality of the question.

- Answer the illegal question, but run the risk of ruining your candidacy.

- Leverage the question as an opportunity to sell your character and strengths.

Obviously, the latter option is the only viable choice. Use this three-step process to leverage questions to your advantage:

1. **Avoid** a direct answer if the illegal question has the slightest chance of hurting your candidacy.

2. **Address** the underlying concern.

3. **Accentuate** a positive character trait or skill in your answer.

Let me illustrate. The interviewer asks: *Are you married?* Although illegal, it seems a fairly innocuous question. No harm in answering, right? Actually, it depends on the interviewer's perspective—something you're not necessarily privy to. A "no" answer might be interpreted as "he is unable to make a commitment or not ready for responsibility." A "yes" answer might be interpreted as "she is too busy with family to put in overtime." Either way, you lose.

Note the following *Before* and *After* responses to the question, "Are you married?"

Before

> Yes, I am married, and happily so for 20 years. We have four kids, with two in college, so you can imagine that my tuition bills are pretty hefty.

The *Before* response focuses wrongly on the candidate's needs. Mentioning college tuition may backfire when it comes time for salary negotiations, as employers want to pay based on your value, not on your economic situation.

After

> I am in a solid relationship and am blessed to have someone who supports me wholly in my career. Some people may wonder whether my personal life will restrict the amount of travel or extended hours necessary for the position. I can assure you there won't be a problem. My last position required 50 percent overnight travel, and I thrive on that sort of schedule. I give the company 18-hour days when I'm traveling, as I find that quiet time in the hotel at night is perfect for getting a jump-start on planning or preparing for presentations.

Note how the *After* response follows the three-point Avoid—Address—Accentuate strategy. The first sentence ("I am in a solid relationship…") avoids a direct answer to the question. The next two sentences ("Some people may wonder…") addresses the underlying concern. And the final two sentences ("My last position required…") accentuates a positive.

Never Commit a "Make-Wrong"

A make-wrong is when you embarrass the interviewer by pointing out an error made. When addressing an underlying concern, choose your words carefully so that you don't make a veiled criticism of the interviewer. This *Before* and *After* illustrates:

> **Before**
>
> You might be concerned that I won't be as productive because of my cane.
>
> **After**
>
> Some people might be concerned that a cane would affect my productivity.

In the coming pages, we'll apply the Avoid—Address—Accentuate strategy to a variety of illegal and challenging questions.

Ethics and Honesty—Don't Say More Than You Should

Let me tell you the story of John (not his real name). John worked with a career consultant to re-enter the job market after his release from prison. His sin? Years before, in a drunken rage, John murdered his father. I cannot offer you statistics on this, but I doubt too many managers are anxious to hire someone with a record of patricide. Let's review a *Before* and *After* response for the difficult, but legal, question: "Have you ever been convicted of a felony?"

Before

> Yes, I was. I was convicted of murdering my father, which I deeply regret. It was during a time when I was drinking. I've been sober since that time. I served my time and got out early for good behavior.

This truthful *Before* answer goes far beyond what is needed. With this answer, the only place he might find work is in organized crime.

After

> I'd love to be able to tell you no, but that's not the case. When I was in my early 20s, I made a severe error in judgment and did some things that I will long regret. Deservedly, the law caught up with me, and I served time. Although it may sound odd, I am grateful for that time. It taught me deep character lessons that I otherwise would not have learned—lessons about humility and self-discipline. I also undertook self-study courses in _____ and _____ and am looking forward to using these skills in this position.

After

If the interviewer comes back again and says, "What things do you regret?," continue the Avoid—Address—Accentuate process.

> Rest assured, they have no bearing on the type of work I'd be doing for you. Again, I'd point to how I've changed and grown since that time and what I can do for you now. For instance, I understand you're expanding your warehousing space. Will my _____ skills be put to use with this project first or is there another priority?

Most people won't have a murder conviction shadowing them. But you may have something much less significant that you're concerned about…something that you feel the employer should know about you to make an informed decision.

Ethics and Honesty—Don't Predict the Future

From an ethical standpoint, many candidates think they should reveal things that *might* (not definitely will) cause a future inconvenience to the employer. For instance:

- "I'm planning on having a baby in the next year or two."

- "I may need to have surgery in the next year."

- "I don't have my full energy because I've been recuperating from an illness."

- "I'll need time off for doctors' appointments."

These things should *not* be shared with interviewers. No one knows what tomorrow holds. Regardless of conscientious intent, stop and think twice when you want to say, "I need to be honest and tell about" this or that. This logic, taken to the extreme, requires that you also mention your family history of, say, coronary disease: "By the way, Mr. Interviewer, I should warn you that I may need time off to recuperate from a potential heart attack, since both my parents had heart attacks around my age!" Of course you wouldn't (and shouldn't) do this.

To avoid situations where you might reveal unnecessary information, use this rule of thumb:

Apply only for positions you can manage.

If any of the following issues are roadblocks for you, don't apply in the first place! It will only cause you to under-perform on the job, which will damage your self-esteem and your work record.

- **Low energy:** If your energy isn't up to working 50-hour weeks, don't apply for a position that requires 50-hour work weeks.

- **Family responsibilities:** If you have family responsibilities that will prevent you from working overtime, don't apply for a position where overtime is the norm.

- **Surgery:** If you know you are scheduled for an upcoming surgery in the near future that will require recuperation time, wait until you are past this before applying for a full-time, permanent position. If you think you *might* need surgery in the long term, don't mention this in an interview. (See the sidebar "Throw Away Your Crystal Ball!")

⚡ **Pregnancy:** If you are pregnant and plan to stay home after the baby comes, apply for a temp job instead of a full-time, permanent position. (If, however, you are pregnant and plan to take only a short time off and then return full-speed-ahead to your career path, go ahead and apply for the position. You are not required to tell the interviewer that you are pregnant; however, if you are applying to a firm that may be adversely affected by your several-week absence, use your best judgment in revealing your circumstances.)

⚡ **Bad back:** If you have a bad back, don't apply for a position that requires tossing boxes around as an essential function of the job. If you have a bad back that goes out occasionally but does not prevent you from doing the essential functions of your position, apply for the position and don't tell the employer that you have a bad back. It has no bearing on your ability to do the job.

⚡ **Serious illness:** If you have a disease that is in remission, go forward with the optimism that it will not come back. Living life with a worrisome "what-if" attitude almost invites that "what-if" to happen. You are not required to tell an employer about past illnesses, and there's no way you can predict the future.

Throw Away Your Crystal Ball!

One candidate wanted to warn an interviewer that he needed knee surgery in the next 6 to 12 months. His career consultant advised him not to tell the employer because it didn't impact his ability to perform the essential functions of the position. Lo and behold, the candidate got the job and ended up not needing the surgery because walking around on the job had the positive effect of physical therapy.

Here's some final food for thought on this topic. Although you wouldn't wish misfortune on anyone, the bottom line is that stuff happens. No one can anticipate a car accident, family illness, natural disaster, and so on. As long as you can do the job and give 100 percent each day, you'll more than earn your pay.

Now, on to communicating how you can give 100 percent each day!

How to Respond to 10 Killer Categories of Questions

In this section, feel free to skip ahead to any category relevant to your situation. Review the potential underlying concerns associated with the category's illegal or difficult questions. Then, after studying the various "magic words," think about how you can customize answers for your needs. Whenever appropriate, tag on a SMART Story™ to verify your statement.

We'll cover these 10 liability-laden areas:

- National origin/citizenship
- Marital/family status
- Age
- Affiliations
- Religion
- Disabilities
- Medical history—physical or mental health/gaps in employment
- Arrest/prison record
- Military service
- Credit history

National Origin/Citizenship Questions

Illegal Questions

- "Are you a U.S. citizen?"
- "Where were you/your parents born?"
- "What is your native language?"

Potential Underlying Concerns

- The valid concern is your eligibility to work in the U.S.
- There may also be prejudicial concerns behind this question borne out of ethnic discrimination. If you sense the latter, think about whether you really want to work for this company.

The "Magic Words" Answers

Magic

- "You may be concerned whether I am eligible to work in the U.S. I am, of course, and can supply verification documents."

- "I read/speak/write English fluently." (Remember the rule of thumb: apply only for positions you can manage!)

- If your English is noticeably halting, say "I am working with a tutor to improve my English. I'm conversant, understand instructions, and can ask questions if I need clarification. My tutor tells me I'm making rapid progress."

- "Is a language other than English a requirement for the position?"

Tactfully Pointing Out Illegal Questions

Some career consultants advise that you tactfully tell the interviewer that his or her question is illegal. For instance, "I recognize that the question has no bearing on my ability to do the job, but I'll answer it anyway," or "From a legal standpoint, you don't really want to ask that, do you?" If the interviewer asks a series of blatantly illegal questions, prying into personal matters that aren't relevant, you can use one of these responses. Otherwise, cut them some slack and diplomatically answer the question—it doesn't hurt to give them the benefit of the doubt, as some hiring managers may not have been trained in the legalities of interviewing.

Marital/Family Status Questions

Illegal Questions

- "Are you married, single, divorced, separated, engaged, or widowed?"

- "With whom do you live?"

- "Do you plan to have a family? When?"

- "How many children do you have? How old?"

- "What are your child-care arrangements?"

- "Does your spouse support your decision to work?"

Potential Underlying Concerns

- If married with children—you will not be completely loyal to the company and its need for overtime or travel; or, children, when ill or in need, may cause you to miss work or generate too many personal phone calls.

- If not married—you might be stereotyped as not stable, or footloose and fancy-free and not inclined to stay for an extended period of time.

- If you have young children—child-care problems may cause numerous absences or tardiness.

- If a spouse relocates or objects to your employment—you might suddenly quit.

The "Magic Words" Answers

- "I assure you that not missing work and being on time are important to me, and I have an excellent attendance record with my prior employer. I can share with you that I have an excellent support system." (You may wish to add to this last sentence something like, "including a mother and two sisters-in-law who live nearby and are able to help with child care").

- "My children are getting to the age where they can be a little more self-sufficient. You may be concerned that they might cause me to miss work." (Then go into your response about child-care arrangements.)

- "I think my single lifestyle gives me an advantage in my career, as it allows me to commit myself wholly to my work. I am very interested in pursuing my career and establishing myself as a valuable member of this company. Fortunately, I have the time and energy to devote to this job."

- "My spouse has no objection to my travel schedule. It actually works well, as it gives him a few nights each week to work late at his position as a research scientist."

- "Our family plans for the future are uncertain, but rest assured, you'll find that I will give this position all the attention it needs, and more. In my last position, I went above and beyond the call of duty by...."

Age Questions

Illegal Questions

- "How old are you?"

- "What year did you graduate?"

- "What's your birth date?"

Potential Underlying Concerns

- Too young—you won't have the work ethic that an older worker will have, or you'll require more training than the employer is willing to invest.

- Too old—you may be too expensive, be overqualified, have poor health or stamina, have outdated skills or be adverse to technology, be set in your ways, be ready to retire, or be slow in performing work.

Magic

The "Magic Words" Answers

Too young (18–30):

⚡ "I'm certainly old enough to work here!" (Smile when you say this.) "Seriously, I know I look young, but I think you'll find I'm very mature. I'm definitely not the type of person who hasn't learned the meaning of work ethic. My former supervisors and colleagues will attest that I take my work quite seriously."

Thirty- to forty-something:

⚡ Smile and say: "Do you think I'm under 18? I feel like I've just been carded...how flattering!"

Fifty-plus-something:

⚡ **General tips:** Make sure your wardrobe and eyeglasses are in style. Consider coloring your hair to cover gray and, men, eliminate beards or mustaches, as these often add years to your appearance. Use language that is up to date and have a basic knowledge of contemporary trends. Check that your attitude doesn't spell stuffy or outdated.

⚡ **Too expensive:** "I recognize the economy has changed and my previous salary reflects an inflated market." Or, "My major objective is an interesting challenge and money is secondary to that." Then discuss how you can add value.

⚡ **Overqualified:** "Some people might have concerns about me having more experience than necessary for this position. I see that as an advantage to both myself and my employer. There was probably something in my resume that interested you to call me in. I'm curious, what was that?" Then, speak to your experiences and how they will bring extra value to the company.

Here's another response that works well: "I personally try to be as overqualified as I can for any job. Every employer wants value from an employee. With my experience, I offer added value. My goal is to be a valuable resource, bringing my years of experience and extensive knowledge to the job and applying them to your goals."

⚡ **Poor health or stamina:** "I can assure you that I have many productive years ahead of me. The benefit of my experience is that I can hit the ground running, and at the same time be a great resource to younger workers." (And, if you have a good fitness routine, this could be a good time to casually mention it.) "Oh, and by the way, I have an excellent attendance record, part of which I attribute to my work with a personal trainer."

⚡ **Outdated skills or adverse to technology:** "I find that over the years, my technology skills have been a consistent strength. I welcome every new software introduction and read *PC World* to learn about the latest gadgets. With each new advancement, I am able to perform my job more efficiently and profitably."

★ **Set in your ways:** "One of the things that keeps me at the top of my game is my openness to change. Without it, you get run over. With it, you have the competition chasing to keep up. I prefer the latter!"

★ **Ready to retire:** Do not bring up the subject of retirement. If the interviewer asks about it, say: "I plan to follow in my father's footsteps, who worked into his 90s! I have no plans to slow down, as I know myself and know that action and results are what I thrive on. I look forward to being a strong contributor for a number of years to come."

★ **Unable to get along with younger coworkers:** "I enjoy working with and learning from my younger coworkers, as well as sharing with them what I know about cost-cutting and labor-saving methods. I've reported to someone in the past who was younger than me, and I know this person would say that we had an excellent working relationship. My most important goal is getting results, not recognition."

★ **Slow worker:** "I know how to work smart, as well as hard. Likewise, I am efficient, accurate, and no-nonsense in getting down to work and getting the job done."

Using Age to Your Advantage

Career Masters Institute member Wendy Gelberg teaches a workshop titled, "Using Age to Your Advantage." In it she clues in job seekers that an interviewer's use of the term "overqualified" is often code for other issues, such as salary or whether you'll stay long enough in the job. If it's the latter, ask what kind of commitment the employer expects (which may be only two or three years, for example). Armed with this knowledge, point to your stable work history at other companies for longer periods of time; offer that, barring unforeseen circumstances, you can commit to the two to three years the employer wants; and end with something like this: "I have the wisdom to know that the grass is not always greener elsewhere. Former employers will point to my loyalty and track record for going above and beyond the call of duty. As an example…." If the employer's concern is salary, refer to the strategies in chapter 16 on salary negotiations.

Affiliations Questions

Illegal Question

★ **"What clubs or social organizations do you belong to?"**

Potential Underlying Concerns

★ You may spend company time and resources (copier, postage, phones, and so on) in support of your organization.

- You may try to "sign up" coworkers and involve them in your activities.

- You may belong to an organization that the interviewer considers silly, frivolous, or weird.

- You may have political beliefs or social views that differ from the interviewer's.

The "Magic Words" Answers

- Relevant is the name of the game here: "I'm active in [or a member of] the major trade organizations for our profession, including ____ and ____ ." Then steer the conversation toward the benefit your membership has for the employer. For instance, "I've found that belonging to these organizations keeps me current on the latest trends and provides me a wealth of networking contacts should I have a question about an industry matter."

- Be careful not to describe a lengthy list of organizations and offices held. You may give the impression that you are overcommitted and won't have time to devote to your job.

- Do not list organizations with religious, political, or activist affiliations.

Religion Questions

Illegal Questions

- **"What religion do you practice?"**

- **"Are you a member of a particular church?"**

- **"The job requires that you work on Fridays, Saturdays, and Sundays. Will your religion cause a problem with this schedule?"**

Potential Underlying Concerns

- You won't be open-minded.

- You will proselytize on the job.

- You may have religious beliefs that differ from the interviewer's.

- You won't be available to work on the weekends.

The "Magic Words" Answers

- "You may be wondering how I will work with people of different faiths. At my last employer, my team members included people of Jewish, Christian, and Muslim faith. We were a tight-knit group and found unity in our commonalities rather than our differences."

- "Like many people, I attend services and have beliefs that bring me a great deal of hope and optimism and guide me in my work ethic…all of which translate into benefits to my employer and my clients."

- "I can manage that weekend schedule with no problem." (Remember the rule of thumb: You are not going to apply for a position that you cannot manage!)

- If you feel comfortable doing so and are absolutely sure it won't affect your candidacy (for instance, you're Catholic and applying to work at Catholic Charities), tell the interviewer your religion.

If You Have Been Discriminated Against

If you believe you have been discriminated against by an employer, labor union, or employment agency when applying for a job because of your race, color, sex, religion, national origin, age, or disability, you may file a charge of discrimination with the U.S. Equal Employment Opportunity Commission (www.EEOC.gov).

Disabilities Questions

Illegal Questions

- **"Do you have any disabilities?"**

- **"Have you had any recent or past illnesses or operations? If yes, list them and give dates when these occurred."**

- **"What was the date of your last physical exam?"**

- **"How's your family's health?"**

- **"When did you lose your eyesight/hearing? How?"**

- **"Do you need an accommodation to perform the job?"** (This question can be asked only *after* a job offer has been made.)

Employment Resources for People with Disabilities

- *Job Search Handbook for People with Disabilities* by Daniel J. Ryan, Ph.D. (JIST Works) will help you assess your strengths and weaknesses, as well as minimize the impact that a disability may have on your job search.

- The Resource Partnership (www.resourcepartnership.org) is a private employer-managed organization committed to the success of both individuals with disabilities and their employers. Since 1978, the Resource Partnership has assisted individuals with varying abilities and disabilities find and experience success at all levels of employment.

Potential Underlying Concerns

* Will your health problems cost this company money in unreasonable accommodations, high medical insurance expenses, or Workers' Compensation claims?

* Will you be able to respond to an emergency?

* Will your disability cause you to be late or absent a lot?

* Will you be able to completely and properly perform the essential functions of the job?

* Will you sue this company for exacerbating your condition (for instance, an allergic reaction to environment, further injury, and so on)?

Magic

The "Magic Words" Answers

* "I've used _____ (a cane, wheelchair, walker, oxygen, and so on) my entire adult life and, rather than be a detriment, it has enabled me to lead a very active and productive life. I have always worked at full-time jobs and pride myself on being completely self-sufficient, including driving and maintaining my own home."

* "Some of my coworkers may wonder whether I can pull my weight. I can assure you it won't be a problem. In my last position, I not only had a better attendance record than most, I was commended for…."

* "This position is exactly what I'm seeking since I have extensive experience in all aspects of the job. In my last place of work, I…."

* "If there is a concern that I will be able to perform the essential functions of the position, I'd like to demonstrate to you how I can."

* "You may be concerned about the fact that I walk with a limp. I can assure you that it has no bearing on my ability to excel at the essential functions of the position you've outlined."

Disabilities: Talking About the Pink Elephant in the Room

The Americans with Disabilities Act (ADA) law offers a measure of protection to persons with disabilities:

* Employers must avoid disability-related questions in interviews or questions about your ability to perform specific job-related tasks or requirements.

* During the interview, employers can *not* inquire what kind of accommodation a candidate needs in order to perform the job properly if hired.

(continued)

(continued)

And yet, if the employer cannot legally ask about your disability but it is clearly obvious you have one, it may feel like the proverbial elephant in the room that no one dares bring up. The consensus of career-transition experts about these pachyderms: Talk about it. If you have a visible disability, bring it up because, legally, the employer cannot.

Freddie Cheek, a Career Masters Institute member, provides career-transition services to people who have disabilities. She notes, "I've had clients lose out on dozens of interviews until they spoke up and addressed their physical disability. Then, they had several offers. Employers will shy away from the unknown—even if the person is well qualified. Once the employer knows there is no problem with the candidate's ability to do the job, the disability is no longer an issue."

"If you have a disability that is noticeable (for instance, you walk with a cane, you wear a prosthesis, or your vision is near legally blind), bring it up almost immediately. Address it in an offhanded way, but do not mention the diagnosis. You can put the interviewer at ease with a comment such as, 'You're likely wondering about my walking stick. It helps improve my balance, and I can assure you that it in no way affects my ability to perform the essential functions of the position. In fact, at an appropriate time in our discussions, I'll look forward to sharing performance evaluations that may be of interest to you....'"

Medical History—Gaps in Employment Questions

Illegal Questions

- "Please complete the following medical history."
- "Have you had any recent or past illnesses or operations?"
- "Do you have any medical conditions that we should know about?"
- "How's your health? We need a high-energy person in this position."
- "Do you smoke?"
- "What current or past medical problems might limit your ability to do this job?"
- "Are you able to lift a 50-pound weight and carry it 100 yards?" (This question is illegal if the task is not part of the essential functions of the job.)

Potential Underlying Concerns

- Do you have the energy to give us 100 percent?
- Will your health problems cost this company money in high medical insurance expenses?

🪄 Will the condition return?

🪄 Will your condition be contagious and infect other workers, bringing on additional liability exposure to the company? Will your child's, spouse's, or parent's medical problems interfere with your ability to concentrate and perform your job? (See answers under "Marital/Family Status Questions.")

Magic

The "Magic Words" Answers

If your medical condition is not visible, do not bring it up:

🪄 "I'm really excited about this position as it allows me to do what I do best."

🪄 "This position is exactly what I'm seeking since I have extensive experience in all aspects of the job. At XYZ Company, I managed similar functions, including…."

🪄 "If there are any questions about how I will be able to perform the essential functions of the position, I'd like to demonstrate how I can."

🪄 If you are a smoker, "I will certainly respect your smoking policy." A note to smokers: Dry-clean your interview suits to remove the smell of cigarette or cigar smoke. A nonsmoker can smell cigarette odor on the clothing, and even the paperwork (resumes included), of a heavy smoker.

🪄 Gap in employment for medical or mental health reasons: "I took some time off for personal reasons and to reevaluate my career goals. After evaluating options that would be a good match for my strengths, I began to focus on _____ , which is aligned well with this position. I'm very much looking forward to adding value to your organization in a role like this."

If your medical condition is visible to the employer, do not mention the illness by name. Be sure you enter the interview upbeat, with enthusiasm and the appearance of health. Then, Avoid—Address—Accentuate:

🪄 **Gap in employment from recent (noticeable) personal illness:** You might say, "That gap in dates was for a medical leave. The doctors are pleased with my full recovery. I'll spare you the details except to say that you won't hire anyone who knows what a gift it is to be healthy and be able to work. I've had a refresher course on what's really important in life, and am committed to being passionately engaged in my work because of it." (Then move on to the deliverables of the job.) You mentioned _____ as an important part of this position. I have some specific accomplishments in that area that you'll likely be interested in.

Other gaps in employment might be addressed in this manner:

🪄 **Gap in employment from past personal illness:** "Yes, there is a break in employment during that time. I took some time off to manage a family obligation (you are not obligated to tell them that you were the family obligation), and that is wrapped up now. During that time, I also took advantage

of brushing up on my computer skills with some classes at _____ , as well as through a self-directed study program. I am excited and chomping at the bit to get back to work."

⚡ **Gap in employment for personal obligation:** "Yes, there is a break in employment during that time. Unfortunately, I had to take some time off to care for a terminally ill family member. He has passed away and I've taken care of the estate matters. It will be a welcome relief to get back to work and use the skills I love using the most."

Arrest/Prison Record Questions

Illegal Questions

⚡ **"Have you ever been arrested?"**

⚡ **"Have you ever pled guilty to a crime?"**

⚡ **"Have you ever been in trouble with the law?"**

⚡ **"Have you ever been convicted of _____?"** (This question is legal is ask if the crime named is reasonably related to the performance of the job in question.)

Potential Underlying Concerns

⚡ Will you have an attitude or be unmanageable?

⚡ Will you be violent in the workplace?

⚡ Will you steal from us?

⚡ Will you be under the influence of illegal substances and cause injury to yourself or others?

⚡ Will you cause our company any liability for future illegal actions?

⚡ Will you attract undesirable people to the business or give customers the wrong impression of the company?

The "Magic Words" Answers

⚡ Never blame someone else for your incarceration. Employers will think you cannot accept responsibility.

⚡ Resist the urge to over-tell. Usually, the less said the better. Be careful of pointing to being under the influence of alcohol or drugs when the crime occurred but now being clean and sober. Employers may wonder what will happen if you fall off the wagon.

⚡ The interviewer may legally ask if you have been convicted of a felony. If your incarceration does not come up in the interview (and you don't offer the information), you run the risk of raising a red flag with employers when they discover it in a background check. Note the *After* response, which incorporates the Avoid—Address—Accentuate strategy:

Before

I have a prison record for embezzlement. Although I admit my part in this, I wasn't entirely at fault because my boss was asking me to do things that I didn't know were entirely legal. Anyway, my boss got more time than me, and I got out early for good behavior.

After

Magic

Several years ago, when I was younger and admittedly lacking in good judgment, I committed a felony. This is something I am certainly *not* proud of. What I *am* proud of, however, is that I'm sitting in front of you today—out in half the time for good behavior. I'm also pleased that I used good judgment during this time—I undertook self-study courses in _____ and _____ and quickly took a leadership role in my work assignment as a _____ [mention "as a ____" only if your work assignment was relevant to your current job target]. The other positive outcome from this experience is that I learned some important character lessons: humility and self-discipline, for example, and that trust is a precious commodity to be earned. The bottom line is this: Like all of us, I'm a different person than I was five years ago and you won't find anyone more committed to staying on the straight-and-narrow. I think you'll agree that I have the skills and motivation to do this job.

No One Is Unemployable!

If there is a particularly challenging sticky wicket in your life, pick up the book *No One Is Unemployable: Creative Solutions for Overcoming Barriers to Employment* by Debra Angel and Elisabeth Harney (WorkNet Publications). The authors will help you overcome even the most overwhelming situations, including addiction, prison records, chronic illnesses, and severe obesity.

Military Questions

Illegal Questions

- "Were you honorably discharged?"
- "Why did you leave the military?"
- "Tell me about your military record."
- "Have you served in the military of countries other than the United States?"

Potential Underlying Concerns

- The interviewer may simply be curious and looking for commonalities if he or she, too, was in the military.

- A dishonorable discharge may raise concerns about your character and conduct.

The "Magic Words" Answers

Magic

* Use a background-checking firm to find out what employers can easily learn about you. It's better to do a preemptive strike, bringing up and explaining an issue instead of letting the interviewer later find out about it and assume you were trying to hide things.

* If you've been dishonorably discharged but the interviewer asks, "Why did you leave the military," one option is to point to a physical problem: for instance, "I wrenched my knee and, as you know, that's not real conducive to combat training and going on 20-mile hikes."

* If you were dishonorably discharged and are specifically asked, "Were you honorably discharged?," consider the ideas listed above for arrest/prison record.

* Never blame someone else, with excuses of following orders, being the scapegoat, being targeted by your commanding officer, and so on.

* Focus on the training or education you received in the military and how it relates to the employer.

Credit History Questions

Illegal Questions

* **"Do you have any credit problems?"**

* **"Have you recently filed for personal bankruptcy?"**

* **"Is your salary presently subject to legal attachment or wage garnishment?"**

Potential Underlying Concerns

* Are you responsible in handling money?

* Will stresses from excessive financial pressures cause you to under-perform on the job?

* If hired, would you allow us to order a credit report to confirm statements made on your employment application (provided you receive a copy)?

The "Magic Words" Answers

Magic

* Don't volunteer information unless asked. For instance, the employer can legally ask you, "Would you allow us to order a credit report to confirm statements made on your employment application, provided you receive a copy?" At this point, you might say something like this: "I've made the mistake that a lot of people make with credit cards...my credit report will show that I'm paying off some debt and making good progress in that area."

* Divorce: One of my clients had gone through a nasty divorce and inherited substantial debt brought on by her husband. Instead of blaming her husband, she said something like this: "One of the fallouts of my divorce,

unfortunately, is that my credit history isn't as positive as I'd like it to be. I've had to share responsibility for some of my ex's small-business debts, which will show up on the report. I'm helping pay this off and making progress."

How to Manage "Sticky Wicket" Questions

We've covered how to respond to dozens of illegal or borderline-illegal questions. Now let's look at just a few more questions that are perfectly legal for the interviewer to ask, but could prove to be sticky wickets for you.

Difficult Question

"Why have you been unemployed so long?"

Magic

The "Magic Words" Answer

Avoid blaming the economy or the state of your industry. Be upbeat and optimistic as you say something like this: "I've taken the time to find something that would be the right fit and, in the meantime, kept busy by sharpening some of my industry knowledge through Web-based courses. I had offers for a couple of opportunities, but they weren't a good fit. With respect to the right fit, I've specifically targeted situations where I can leverage my strengths in a _____ (fill in the blank with the type of company) where I could play a role in setting policy and driving results. I also wanted an environment that would be a good fit. I'm confident that will be the case here. You mentioned, for instance, that you need someone who can…."

Difficult Question

"You have a gap on your resume between your last two employers. What did you do during that time?"

Magic

The "Magic Words" Answers

Honesty is usually the best policy, provided you don't give more details than absolutely necessary. For instance, if the gap was several months to one year, it's acceptable to mention that you were, for instance,

- Taking maternity leave
- Caring for children
- Caring for a terminally ill family member
- Taking time off for travel abroad
- Planning or getting settled after a move
- Taking time to pursue studies

If the time was spent entirely in a longer-than-hoped-for job search, be ready to point to some other concurrent activity, such as

- Taking some industry-relevant classes
- Volunteering in an activity related to your profession
- Taking care of family responsibilities

Consider using this "lottery" analogy to describe your excitement to get back to work. "Many people say that if they won the lottery they'd retire to Tahiti. I can tell you that I'd be climbing the walls if I couldn't work. I love the pace and the energy that I draw from work, and I'm excited that this opportunity looks like such a good match for my skills."

Difficult Question

"Why was your employment period with this company such a short time?"

The "Magic Words" Answers

If the employer was the reason, you might say that the company was undercapitalized and reduced its force. If this wasn't the case, you might say that the position changed significantly after you came on board and didn't offer the level of responsibility that was originally intended. When preparing your answers, recall the options for leaving an employer from chapter 13—to learn more, earn more, grow more, work more, and commute/travel less.

Difficult Question

"Why aren't you making more at this point in your career?"

The "Magic Words" Answers

This may be an opportunity to find out what salary range the employer has in mind. "I recognize that my current salary isn't what it should be, and that's one of the reasons that I'm sitting here with you today! The contributions I've made to my past employer have resulted in tangible cost savings [or profit increases], and I'm confident I can do the same for you. With that in mind, what salary range did you have in mind for someone with my skills?"

Difficult Question

"Have you ever been fired?"

The "Magic Words" Answers

The employer's concern is whether you were dismissed for lack of performance or an inability to get along with people. Use the preemptive strike here—find a way to bring this up early on and on your own terms. For instance, when the interviewer is walking through your resume, you might say, "By the way, I want you to know that the reason I left the position that ended in 1999 was because I was asked to leave. Here's what happened…." (Don't blame or complain about anyone.)

If you messed up, say so without degrading yourself or offering excessive details. Talk about the lessons learned from that experience: "I made the mistake of not following through on an important order—it cost the company some business. I learned an important lesson which is to always…. I wanted to bring this up so that you didn't think I was trying to hide something."

If you were fired because of a change in management, speak to this without belittling the management: "There was a change in management, which led to me and a number of my colleagues being let go."

If it was a personality clash: "I've been fortunate to work with a number of fine supervisors over the years, and I've had excellent relationships with all of them, save one individual. I'm disappointed that there wasn't an opportunity to work further on the relationship. You'd probably like to hear some other people's perspective on this as well, and I'm happy to provide you some references from that employment period." (Then, be sure to let your references know that someone may be calling about this.)

Difficult Question

"Tell me about a situation where you had a strained relationship with a boss or coworker."

The "Magic Words" Answers

The question presumes that you had a strained relationship. Do not admit to strained relationships, and never badmouth or criticize anyone. "I'm happy to report that I can't tell you about a situation where relationships were strained." The word "strained" implies you couldn't or wouldn't take the initiative to resolve a problem. There may have been a situation where another individual was difficult to be around on a regular basis, but that doesn't mean *your* relationship was strained. You can use a similar response strategy to the question, "Have you worked under bosses who weren't ideal?" in chapter 13.

Difficult Question

You don't have the degree we're looking for. Or, why didn't you complete your college degree?

The "Magic Words" Answers

"I can understand your concern about that. Tell me, though, what is it specifically you want to have accomplished as a result of that degree?" After you get some specific deliverables from the interviewer, you can then describe how your experience will allow you to meet those deliverables. Also, if a specific degree is very important to the interviewer, explore whether you could start the training while employed with the company.

Here's another tack you can take with this answer. "I understand that good academic training is important, but I also look at people who didn't complete high school, like the Wright Brothers, Albert Einstein, Steve Jobs of Apple, and Henry

Ford. It was Ford who said, 'Whether you think you can do a thing or not, you're right.' I not only think I can do this, I know I can do it. And, although you may have candidates with more impressive degrees on their resume, I'm confident that no one will give you better hands-on experience, insight into these issues, or passion toward carrying them out than I will."

Difficult Question

What is the biggest work-related mistake you've made?

Magic

The "Magic Words" Answers

Point to something early in your career, rather than a recent mistake. Employers won't buy it if you tell them you haven't made any mistakes. No one walks on water! Here's an example:

I'd have to say that my biggest work-related mistake was not putting contingency plans in place when I planned a presentation to be given by a well-known author. I didn't follow up to confirm 24 hours in advance, and the author had gotten the date mixed up on her calendar so she didn't show up and couldn't be reached. I had a room of 400 people waiting for this person, and she never made it. I had egg on my face, and learned a very critical lesson that day, which is to never assume anything and always double-check everything and always, always, always have a backup plan! To prove I learned my lesson, I can tell you that the last special event I planned, I did have a backup speaker!

Difficult Question

What would you do if your supervisor asked you to do something that went against your ethics?

Magic

The "Magic Words" Answers

Dialogue with the interviewer and do your best to toss this question back into the interviewer's court. Ask questions such as, "Is there a particular situation you can cite that would help me get a better understanding of this?" "Can you tell me what your concern is?" "Has this been an issue in the past?" "How would you prefer I handle the situation?" Your response might include something to this effect: "I would clarify what it was the supervisor needed done. If it appeared to be out of line with company policy, I would bring this up in a nonjudgmental way, as my loyalty would be toward making sure the company remains out of anyone's legal crosshairs." Note that this is a situation where you would *not* want to offer a SMART Story™ because doing so might slander a prior colleague.

What You Should Know About Reference and Background Checks and Pre-Employment Polygraphs

Litigation is driving employers to step up their reference and background checking. A 2003 SHRM survey found 80 percent of companies conducted criminal background checks, up from 51 percent in 1996. Why? Because employers have found themselves embarrassed or engaged in lawsuits by new hires that arrived with unknown baggage. A Florida trucking company was held liable for hiring a driver without a background check when the driver subsequently returned to a delivery site and brutally assaulted a woman. One Pennsylvania university hired an assistant professor who turned out to have a triple murder conviction—luckily, no one was hurt.

Reference and background screening is typically one of the last steps in the hiring process. The employer may check references before (or sometimes after) making an offer. Many companies will make the offer conditional on the results of the background check.

If you have anything in your history that might tarnish your reputation, take the time to do your own investigation so that you're not taken by surprise. One well-established company that provides this service is Allison & Taylor (www.allisontaylor.com), with prices in the $69 to 79 range for basic service.

Reference Checks

Reference checks are used to determine whether the candidate has the skills needed and will fit into corporate culture. What might employers ask when checking references?

- "How do you know the candidate?"
- "What were the candidate's responsibilities during the time you worked together?"
- "How productive was the candidate?"
- "How would you describe the candidate's energy level?"
- "How would you describe the candidate's creativity?"
- "Would you say the candidate is more people or technical oriented?"
- "How has the candidate met deadlines?"
- "How would you compare the candidate's overall performance to that of others you've worked with doing the same job?"
- "How did the candidate interact with others on the job?"
- "How was he or she perceived by others with whom he or she worked?"
- "How would you describe his or her management skills?"
- "In what areas does he or she need to improve?"

- ★ "What could he or she have done to achieve even better results on the job?"

- ★ "What does the candidate need to do to take him or herself to the next level?"

- ★ "Why is he or she looking for other employment?" *or* "Why did he or she leave?"

- ★ "How would you describe the candidate's coachability?"

- ★ "Would you hire him or her again?"

Approach your references and ask them whether they would be comfortable answering most of these questions. If not, find references who will be able to be enthusiastic and supportive of your candidacy.

Background Checks

Background checks verify employment, degrees and licenses, any criminal record, and credit history. Understand your rights with respect to background checks:

- ★ Before background checks can be done, candidates must sign a written disclosure form authorizing the check.

- ★ If an employer bases a decision not to hire on negative information found in a background check, the employer is obligated to provide the results and give the candidate the opportunity to dispute the findings (more details are available through the Federal Trade Commission online at www.ftc.gov).

- ★ The Fair and Accurate Credit Transactions Act (FACT Act) allows you to receive one free copy of your credit report annually. Go to www.experian.com for details.

Never lie to an employer, especially about something that can be learned in a background check. Paul Barada, author of *Reference Checking for Everyone* (McGraw-Hill, 2004), shared stories of candidates who would have been hired, even with "flaws" in their backgrounds, but didn't get hired (or got fired) because of their dishonesty. One involved a candidate for a senior-level position who had 20 years of industry experience. The person lied about completing an undergraduate degree. When the company discovered the lie, they told the person that with 20 years of experience they would not have required the degree, but they could not hire him because of the lie. Another example involved someone who had lied about his previous salary. After being hired, he was asked to bring in a pay stub from his previous job, which didn't match up with what he claimed in the interview.

Pre-Employment Polygraphs

Employers are not permitted to conduct pre-employment polygraphs as a condition of employment except when hiring for armored-car drivers, day-care center workers, or nuclear power plant operators. Law enforcement and other government agencies can also administer pre-employment polygraphs for positions such as police officers, records clerks, dispatchers, and even chaplains. If you fall into these categories, licensed polygraph examiner Melvin King offers these tips to help you prepare:

- Dress as you would for an interview—the polygraph examiner will submit a report to the employer and often includes his or her impressions of you as a candidate.

- Don't worry about personal questions being asked, such as your political, religious, or sexual preferences. You will, however, be asked about convictions, illegal drug use, or drinking (for instance, "Have you ever come to work under the influence of alcohol?").

- All questions will be reviewed with you prior to you being attached to the polygraph, so there are no surprises.

- You have a legal right to obtain a copy of the polygraph and can challenge it if it does not come out in your favor.

Chapter Wrap-Up

Rarely are there candidates with perfect employment backgrounds, notwithstanding spotless reputations or stellar records of contribution. It seems everyone has to "bat across a sticky wicket" at some point in their career. However, with the strategies in this chapter, you'll be able to predict what the interviewer might ask and greatly improve your chances of answering those $64,000 questions!

10 Quick Tips for Responding to Illegal or Awkward Questions

1. **Reconcile yourself to the fact that you will probably have to answer illegal questions.** Give interviewers the benefit of the doubt—perhaps they are stressed or haven't been trained in legally compliant interviewing practices. Correcting them or showing that you know more than they do about legal questions will not win you any points (unless you're applying for a human resources position where you should know these types of laws).

2. **The best option for *answering* illegal or awkward questions is to follow the 3 A's: *Avoid, Address,* and *Accentuate*.** Avoid a direct answer if the question has the slightest chance of hurting your candidacy.

Address the underlying concern. Finally, accentuate a positive character trait or skill in your answer.

3. **Remember to add a SMART Story™ to your Avoid-Address-Accentuate response when appropriate.**

4. **To improve your chances of acing the interview, follow this rule of thumb: Apply only for positions you can manage.** Anything else will cause you to fall short on the job, damaging your self-esteem and work record. For instance, if your energy level isn't up to working 60-hour work weeks, don't apply to a company that expects those hours.

5. **Don't say more than you need to.** Do not tell employers anything they are not legally authorized to ask!

6. **Resist any urge to reveal information that *might* cause a future inconvenience to the employer, such as the possibility of starting a family or requiring surgery in the next year.** No one knows what tomorrow holds! However, if you are pregnant and don't plan to return to work after delivery, don't apply for a full-time, permanent position. If you know you are scheduled for surgery soon, wait until you've recuperated to apply for a full-time, permanent position.

7. **The 10 areas that often lead to illegal or awkward questions include national origin, age, marital/family status, affiliations, religion, disabilities, medical/personal history, arrest/prison record, military service, and credit history.** Which of these might be problematic for you?

8. **Write a personalized list of illegal or awkward questions that you dread being asked.** Practice the Avoid-Address-Accentuate strategy for illegal questions. Practice putting a Positive-Pertinent-Precise spin on awkward questions (see "10 Quick Tips for Responding to FAQs" in chapter 13).

9. **Prepare for reference and background checks by lining up references who will speak about you with enthusiasm and support.**

10. **If you have any concerns about potential skeletons in your closet, pay to have a reference/background check on yourself so that you'll know what employers might learn.** Know your rights about reference/background checks. Employers must obtain prior authorization from you and, if they base a decision not to hire you on negative background information found during the check, are obligated to provide you the results and give you the opportunity to dispute the findings.

Magical Coaching Questions

The 10 areas that often lead to illegal or awkward questions include national origin, age, marital/family status, affiliations, religion, disabilities, medical/personal history, arrest/prison record, military service, and credit history. Which of these areas, if any, might be problematic for you?

_____

_____

List at least five questions in this chapter that might be problematic for you.

_____

_____

_____

_____

What will your Avoid—Address—Accentuate answer be for each of these questions?

_____

_____

_____

_____

_____

_____

_____

_____

_____

(continued)

(continued)

Who will you ask to be references?

_____

_____

_____

_____

_____

What strengths would you like each of them to address when speaking with potential employers? How can you prepare them to focus on these strengths when interviewers call?

_____

_____

_____

_____

_____

Negotiate Your Salary: The Secrets to Knowing and Receiving What You're Worth

In the business world, everyone is paid in two coins: cash and experience. Take the experience first; the cash will come later.

—Harold S. Geneen, Accountant, Industrialist, and CEO

A salary negotiation can resemble a high-wire act, a back-and-forth dance across delicate territory where one false step can spell disaster. Not only that, you're expected to perform this dance during the life-changing period of career transition, when you might already be experiencing new emotional highs and lows and when your entire future depends on your negotiation—or so it seems.

Well, take a deep breath and go back to the core message that you've worked to communicate in every step of your job search: "It's all about value." To effectively negotiate your compensation, you must first understand your value, learn about the value of the position, and base your negotiation on the value you can deliver to the organization. In this chapter we will examine the high-wire dance from first to last steps and give you ideas, strategies, and language you can use to negotiate a compensation package that rewards you fairly for your contributions.

Preparing for the Salary Dance

Be prepared to negotiate salary from day one of your job search! Don't wait to learn how to deal with this issue until you are interviewing or until you are offered a position. Questions about salary often arise in the first telephone screen or even earlier, with a question about your salary requirements included in an ad or online posting. Learn how to deal with these requests so that you don't harm your future negotiating position, box yourself into a lower salary, or eliminate yourself from contention right at the start.

Research Comparable Salaries

Every good high-wire artist spends much more time practicing the act than performing it. Similarly, you will want to put a great deal of time and effort into preparing to negotiate your salary before you actually attempt it "live." First you must lay the groundwork by putting together some hard numbers about average compensation for someone with your skills, qualifications, years of experience, industry focus, and geographic location. Negotiating without this information is like taking to the high wire without carefully checking to be sure your wire is secure: There is no support for your position and your negotiations will soon collapse. With this information, you have a secure base of knowledge that will give you confidence as you negotiate.

How to Research Salary

With abundant resources available on the Web, in the library, and through your network, there's no need to rely on just one source for comparable salary data. It's unlikely that you will be able to identify a precise salary for the exact job you are considering, but the more information you have, the more confident you'll feel about negotiating your salary based on "fair market value."

Salary Tools and Surveys

The Internet abounds with tools and resources that will give you detailed information about salary ranges for specific professions in specific geographic areas. Additional resources are available in print publications, both books and periodicals, that you can find at your local library. Sources exist for jobs at every level, from new college graduates to CEOs! Your reference librarian can help you find the most precise and most comprehensive sources for your particular field and level. Here are a few to get you started:

✦ **JobSmart.org Gateway**—www.jobsmart.org: This Web site is a gateway to hundreds of salary surveys available on the Internet.

✦ **Salary tools:** The following sites are a good place to start; you can easily find many more by entering the word "salary" into your favorite search engine.

workindex.com/salary/
www.careerbuilder.com
www.monster.com
www.salary.com
www.salaryexpert.com
www.salarysource.com
www.wageweb.com

✦ **Professional associations:** If you are a member of one or more professional associations, contact them directly to ask about salary surveys. Or use the *Encyclopedia of Associations* as a reference to find associations relevant to your field, and then call or click to their Web sites for more information.

✦ **U.S. Department of Labor,** *Occupational Outlook Handbook:* This resource is a treasure trove of career information including salary ranges. Explore www.bls.gov/oco/ to find data for your profession.

✦ **Federal government salary tables:** If you are interested in a job with the federal government, you can review salary ranges for every grade and profession at this site: www.opm.gov/oca/04tables/index.asp.

✦ **The Riley Guide to Employment Opportunities and Job Resources on the Internet:** This exceptional site includes a comprehensive resource list for salary information (www.rileyguide.com/salary.html) and a separate section on executive compensation (www.rileyguide.com/execpay.html). You will find links to dozens of helpful sites; there is also a review of one of the fee-based salary reports you can purchase on the Web.

Internet Postings and Want Ads

During your job search, as you review online job postings or print classified ads, you will find that many include salary information that you can add to the data you are collecting. The large job boards such as Monster.com and CareerBuilder.com are also a quick source for some hard salary numbers.

Network Contacts

Include questions about salary as part of your networking interviews. Of course, you would not want to ask your contact how much he or she makes!

But you can inquire about salary ranges and, in general, what you might expect at that company. This phrasing will allow you to ask without stepping into the forbidden territory of someone's personal financial situation:

- "Tell me, what is an average salary for someone with my experience at your company? What would a top performer earn?"

- "How does your company determine its salary ranges?"

- "What does your company pay for Java programmers with five years of experience?"

- "I've been at the same company so long, I'm out of touch with salary ranges. Can you help me out with some general information about your company?"

Be sure to talk to your friends who work at large companies. Most large organizations have fixed salary ranges based on job grade, and these tables are often published in an employee handbook.

Recruiters

Recruiters are an excellent source of salary information. They are usually looking for "tight-fit" candidates within very specific salary ranges. During any contact you have with a recruiter, ask for a "market check" on your salary expectations. You might also ask whether the recruiting firm has conducted any salary surveys for your profession.

Put It All Together

Relying on multiple sources means that you will have a wide range of data that, together, should give you a fairly accurate picture of the "going rate" for your profession. Table 16.1 shows a sample of comparative salary data developed by a Web designer.

Table 16.1: Research on Comparative Salary Data

Source	Low Range	Median	Upper Range
Salary tool: workindex.com/salary/ (national averages)	$46,027	$54,704	$58,315
Salary tool: www.salary.com (national averages)	$45,662	$54,269	$57,853
Salary tool: www.salaryexpert.com (New York/statewide average)	$37,383	$47,798	$56,517

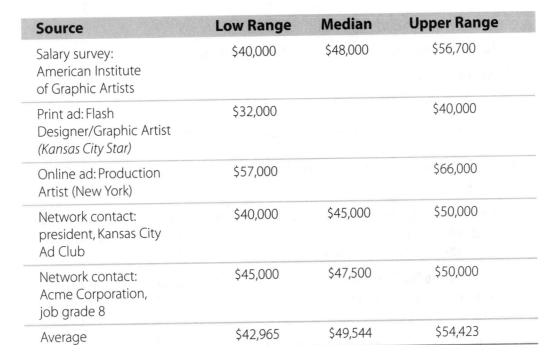

Source	Low Range	Median	Upper Range
Salary survey: American Institute of Graphic Artists	$40,000	$48,000	$56,700
Print ad: Flash Designer/Graphic Artist (*Kansas City Star*)	$32,000		$40,000
Online ad: Production Artist (New York)	$57,000		$66,000
Network contact: president, Kansas City Ad Club	$40,000	$45,000	$50,000
Network contact: Acme Corporation, job grade 8	$45,000	$47,500	$50,000
Average	$42,965	$49,544	$54,423

Keep in mind that these figures do not include benefits, which can vary widely depending on your employer, or performance bonuses, which can drive up your compensation significantly. In most cases, benefits offered by a company are fairly uniform, while bonus payments vary widely and are open to negotiation. Later in this chapter, we discuss negotiating strategies for all of the components of your compensation—salary, benefits, commissions, bonuses, and perks.

Follow the "Magical Coaching Tips" and "10 Quick Tips for Salary Negotiations" at the end of this chapter to research your own comparative salary data.

Develop Your Salary Targets

Now that you know what the "going rate" is for people in your profession, you can begin to develop your target salary ranges for your next position.

Compare your data to your current or most recent salary, taking into consideration the number of years of experience you have, your level of expertise, and the current job market for people in your profession.

As you develop your salary targets, don't forget about projected bonuses or long-term benefits that you might be losing if you leave your current job. Examples include the following:

* Significant year-end bonus
* Sales commissions paid quarterly or annually
* Annual review and projected pay raise
* Stock options that are not yet vested
* Benefit or retirement plans that are not yet vested

After analyzing all of your findings, develop your target compensation in three ranges:

* **Your "Reality" Number:** The lowest salary you will accept; the bottom line you need to pay bills comfortably and work toward your long-term savings and lifestyle goals.
* **Your "Comfort" Number:** An amount you can accept and feel that you are being adequately compensated for your value; a reasonable and realistic goal.
* **Your "Dream" Number:** Your ideal salary and/or the level of compensation commanded by top performers in your target positions.

Supply and Demand

The rules of supply and demand come into play during salary negotiations. If your expertise is in short supply, the demand is stronger and you have more negotiating power. On the other hand, if the market is flooded with people of comparable skill, you will have less room to maneuver in the salary dance. In the fast-growth 1990s, salaries, perks, and bonuses grew astronomically, sometimes to unreasonable heights. With the economy in flux since 2000, some salaries, particularly at the executive level and for technical jobs, have fallen a bit, and perks such as signing bonuses and lucrative buy-out clauses are less common.

The higher your value to the employer, the more likely you will be able to achieve your "Dream" number. What can you do to move yourself up the value chain? Is there a specific skill or expertise that would make you a more desirable candidate? Can you make the case that you are a "star performer" and therefore worthy of higher compensation? Remember, it's not about what you want, need, or deserve (in other words, how long you've been paying your dues); it's all about value.

Use the "Magical Coaching Tips" worksheet at the end of this chapter to identify your own Reality, Comfort, and Dream numbers. Armed with this information, you are prepared to negotiate your salary based on fair market value.

How to Deflect Salary Questions Until the Offer
"Send resume with salary requirements to..."

How often have you seen an ad with this phrase? Or, even more intimidating, "Resumes without salary requirements will not be considered." At what point should you share your requirements and start the salary dance?

In a nutshell, the time to discuss salary is after a firm job offer has been made. Before you receive an offer, you have no negotiating power, and you are more likely to harm than help yourself with a too-early discussion of salary. Think of it this way: Hiring is like shopping. The employer will first peruse a large number of candidates, "try on" a few via interviews, and then make a selection. At that point, the employer has switched from "shopper" to "buyer," and this switch gives a powerful boost to your ability to negotiate.

Don't believe it? Think about your own behavior when you are shopping. Let's say you are looking for a new pair of shoes. You have in mind the style and purpose of the shoes and probably a general idea of how much you want to spend. You try on dozens of pairs of shoes, looking for just the right look, fit, and feel along with the qualities that match your needs. (If you need hiking boots, you probably won't be trying on dress shoes or sandals.) At last, you find them! The perfect pair! They fit like a glove, look great, and have all the features you really need. You look again at the price tag and find that they cost a few dollars more than you had budgeted. When you have made the mental switch from "shopper" to "buyer," you are much more likely to spend just a bit more than you had budgeted, because now the shoes have transformed from an idea into a reality that you can see on your feet and imagine in your life.

Hiring managers are human, too, and when they find an employee they want to join their team, they are more inclined to spend "just a bit more" to get what they want.

To preserve your negotiating power, learn to deflect questions about salary until you have received an offer. Here are some strategies.

In Cover Letters

I recommend that you not provide salary information in your cover letters, even if it is requested. Survey after survey of human resources and hiring managers shows that when they receive applications without the requested salary information, they look at the resume anyway. Thus far, you haven't hurt your chances, so why give them some information that might screen you out of the interviewing process or set your value below what they are willing to pay?

But that is not your only option. There are several ways you can handle the salary question in your cover letters:

- **Ignore.** Make no mention of salary. As mentioned, this is my recommended strategy because, in all likelihood, it will not harm your chances of being selected for an interview.

- **Defer.** "I will be happy to discuss salary considerations during an interview." Remember that it's in your best interest not to discuss salary until a job offer has been made, so you might not want to make this offer.

- **Address without revealing anything.** "My salary requirements are open; I am more interested in the challenges and opportunities of this position and expect that your company pays a competitive salary." This response might be seen as evasive, but it does indicate that you read the ad and are at least responding to the company's request.

- **Share a range.** "Based on my understanding of the fair market value of this position, I anticipate a salary in the $85,000 to $95,000 range." Or, "My current compensation is in the high forties, and I anticipate this would increase 10 to 15 percent in a new position." The only problem with this response is that the employer now knows what you expect and can initiate negotiations at that level…or below.

During a Telephone Screen Interview

In many cases the first stage in the interview process is a telephone screen to determine whether you have the right mix of skills, experience, and achievements to warrant an interview. This interview might be with a recruiter or hiring manager, but often it is administered by a human resources screener armed with a predetermined list of questions. As discussed in chapter 7, your objective is to pass the screen and earn an invitation for an in-person meeting. Try not to screen yourself out by revealing salary information at this point; refer to the next section for specific language you can use to bring the conversation back to your qualifications and your fit for the position.

Recruiters: The Exception to the Rule

With recruiters, it's okay to reveal salary information. Because recruiters are seeking candidates who fit their client company's specifications to a "T," they need to know whether your salary expectations are in line with what the company is offering. Most recruiters will not continue the conversation if you are not forthcoming about your current salary and your expectations. Feel free to share this with them, along with any factors that might influence your request, such as a forthcoming bonus or a two-year salary freeze at your company.

During In-Person Interviews

The purpose of an interview is for both you and the employer to explore your fit with the company and the position. In the early stages of these explorations, you don't have a complete view of the opportunity and its challenges, and the company has not had a chance to learn enough about you to switch from "shopper" to "buyer." As a result, salary discussions at this point are premature.

As a savvy job seeker, you should learn to deflect the question and redirect the discussion toward your qualifications. Here are a few suggestions for turning the question around without appearing difficult, stubborn, uncooperative, or manipulative. Remember the *howcha's:* How you say this will be as important as what you say. Strive for politeness and objective curiosity.

- "Salary is important, but it's not my first consideration. I am more interested in finding the right position, where I can make a real contribution. I'm very interested in what you've told me so far; can we continue that discussion?"

- "I want to be fairly compensated for the value I bring to the company. I'd like to learn more about the challenges you're facing and how I can help."

- "I've always been compensated fairly based on my contributions; I anticipate this would be the case at Widget Products, too. Can you tell me more about your current challenges? So far I'm excited about the position, and I'd like to learn more."

- "Are you offering me the position?" Assuming the answer is no… "Well, I think we should defer discussion of salary until we both determine I'm the right person for the job."

- "I can assure you that if we both feel I am the right person for the job, salary will not be an issue. My research tells me that your company pays competitive salaries, and all I expect is to be treated fairly and rewarded for my contributions."

- "I am sure your company pays competitive salaries. Can you tell me what the range is for this position?"

- "What I'm seeking is simple: a performance-based salary package that will keep me motivated and delivering great results for the company."

★ "To tell you the truth, I don't have enough information about this position yet to be able to determine a meaningful salary. Can you tell me more about the scope of the position and your performance expectations?"

You get the idea. Address the question but stay focused on what's really important—whether you are a good fit for the position and the company.

Because interviewing can be stressful, candidates sometimes lose their composure and blurt out a response when asked a direct question such as "What are your salary requirements?" or "What's your current salary?" If this happens to you, don't be too hard on yourself! The interviewer has probably asked this question dozens if not hundreds of times and knows how to keep pressing to get the information from you. You, on the other hand, are probably much less experienced at interviewing and are concerned with making a great impression. You don't want to get into a stand-off with the interviewer or refuse to answer the question. So, just in case you feel compelled to provide an answer, prepare and practice a statement that includes salary ranges, rather than hard numbers, and is based on your research:

★ "I understand that fair market value for this position is in the $80,000 to $95,000 range. Is that what you expect?"

★ "I've always been paid competitively based on my contributions to the company. Most recently I've earned in the low seventies, and I would expect a 15 to 20 percent increase for this challenging role."

★ "Based on the value I can offer, meeting the challenges we've discussed, compensation in the $150,000 to $180,000 range seems appropriate."

★ "My research tells me that your company pays $22,000 to $25,000 for this level. I am comfortable with this range."

Never State a Range Below Your Reality Number

When stating ranges, never mention a figure that is below your Reality Number. Keep in mind that while you are focusing on the upper end of your range, the employer hears and hones in on the lower number you recite. It's likely you'll receive an offer that is closer to the lower end of your range than the higher.

When an Offer Is Made

Congratulations! You've accomplished your goal in the interview process and earned a job offer. The employer has switched from "shopper" to "buyer," and the salary dance has fully begun. If you prepare diligently for all possibilities, you'll be able to negotiate the high-wire maneuvers with confidence and ease.

The Employer's First Move

The first move might come as a question from the employer: "So, what will it take to bring you on board?" or "We'd like to make you an offer. What salary range were you thinking of?"

Your First Move

Be careful! In your relief at getting the offer, it's tempting to jump right in and share your research and your target ranges. But it's better to keep your cool and remember the strategies for deflecting salary discussions that you practiced earlier in the process. For the most beneficial outcome, you must "deflect" one more time so that the employer, and not you, is the first to associate a salary number with your job offer.

Here's why. As we discussed earlier, the employer has now moved from "shopper" to "buyer" and, because you've clearly demonstrated your value, might be willing to pay a bit more than originally budgeted to bring you on board. But employers have a responsibility to deliver results at the lowest cost to the company. If you chime in with a figure that is in the low end of the company's pay range, they will happily negotiate based on that figure. On the other hand, if your carefully researched, confidently stated figure is significantly above their pay scales, the employer will either be affronted or will think that the two of you are not on the same page with regard to the position scope, responsibilities, challenges, and performance expectations. This could mean a setback in your relationship and could jeopardize the job offer.

Instead, use those well-practiced deflecting techniques to prompt the employer to share a salary offer with you.

- "Thank you! I'm excited about the opportunity! Based on the value I can bring to meet the challenges we discussed, what do you think is fair compensation for this position?"

- "I'm glad we agree that I have the right mix of skills and experience to really make an impact in this position. In what salary range do you see me?"

⭐ "What have you budgeted for this position? I'm sure we can come to an agreement on some combination of salary and performance-based bonuses that will be fair and will motivate me to do my best."

⭐ "Thank you. I appreciate your confidence in me. We've discussed some significant challenges, and I'm looking forward to tackling them. What figure did you have in mind?"

Next comes your first real move in the salary dance. When the employer comes back with a number or a range, your initial response is critically important.

The Moment of Silence

In every case, whatever the number, whether high or low, your first response should be to repeat the number, thoughtfully and non-judgmentally. Then stop talking. This is called the Moment of Silence. Bite your tongue, and let the employer make the next move.

Repeat the Top End of the Range

When the employer states a range, your repetition of the number should be the top end of the range. Let's say the employer answers, "Well, our range for this position is $47,000 to $52,000." Your thoughtful response: "Fifty-two thousand dollars…." Your goal is to plant the top end of the range in your listener's mind, rather than the minimum amount offered.

During the silence, you'll be calculating like mad to compare the number to your Reality, Comfort, and Dream numbers. This can be particularly difficult if the numbers are presented in a different format—hourly, weekly, or monthly, for example, when you've calculated annually. During this Moment of Silence, you will need to determine whether this is a Reality, Comfort, or Dream Number so that you can make your next move with confidence.

How else can the Moment of Silence help you? The employer, now in "buyer" mentality, does not want to lose you. If you don't jump at the offer immediately, it's possible the hiring authority will come right back with a higher figure: "Well, I guess we could go to $55,000." Without saying a word, you've just earned a five percent raise!

If the employer does not respond with a new number, it's your turn to make a move. What you say next will depend on how closely the offer matches your expectations.

Be Sure You Are Clear About the Parameters of the Job

At this point in your discussions you should have an excellent understanding of the position scope, challenges, and performance expectations. But before you start to negotiate your compensation, it is essential to clear up any questions that remain about the following:

- Job description
- Job functions
- Reporting relationships (who you'll report to and who will report to you)
- Start date
- Employment status
- Full-time employee eligible for full benefits
- Part-time employee with perhaps partial benefits

  - Exempt status, where you will be exempt from certain hour and pay laws and thus not be eligible for overtime pay (usually applies to professional and administrative positions)

  - Non-exempt employee, where you will usually be paid an hourly wage and will be eligible for overtime pay for hours beyond those stipulated in your job description (usually applies to assembly, production, customer service, and other nonprofessional positions)

  - Independent contractor, where you will not be considered an employee and therefore will not receive company benefits; with this status, you will be responsible for paying self-employment taxes

Independent Contractor or Employee?

Many employers are hiring workers as independent contractors instead of employees. The distinction has important tax and employment benefits consequences. Those who should be classified as employees but aren't may lose out on Workers' Compensation, unemployment benefits, and, in many cases, group insurance (including life and health) and retirement benefits. In general, a worker is an employee when the business has the right to direct and control the worker. For instance, if the business provides training in required procedures and you receive extensive instructions on how work is to be done, this suggests that you may be an employee. For more information, visit the IRS Web site: www.irs.gov/faqs/faq-kw68.html.

All of these factors can have a significant impact on your compensation and working conditions and therefore will affect the way you react to the salary that has been offered.

Agree on Base Salary Before Benefits or Bonuses

You might also be wondering about benefits, performance bonuses, and perks that you will be entitled to or that you can negotiate. Although these must be factored into your decision, I recommend that at this point you first come to an agreement on base compensation (salary) for a clearly defined position. Then you can tackle the additional issues one by one as you work your way through the negotiation.

Many companies are proud of their benefits packages and might try to use them as a lever to persuade you to accept a lower salary. Only you can determine the compensation level that makes sense for you, your family, your career, and your current circumstances. Keep in mind that if you accept a lower salary now, it will affect your compensation going forward with the company, because most salary increases are given as a percentage of current salary.

The Etiquette of Negotiating Salary

- **Most employers expect you to negotiate.** You will not offend the interviewer by asking for more, provided you do so in a polite, professional manner and base your request on your value, not on what you want, what you deserve, or what you've made in the past.

- **Your research will tell you whether the offer is too low, too high, or just right.** Your response will vary based on the situation. Detailed scenarios for each case are presented in the following sections.

- **Women, be assertive about negotiations!** A recent study at Carnegie Mellon University, investigating pay disparity between men and women, identified an underlying cause: While 57 percent of the men in the survey negotiated for a higher salary, only 7 percent of the women attempted to bargain for more than was offered. Because subsequent pay raises are typically a percentage of salary, a lower starting salary means slower growth during your entire tenure with a company. Thus, the disparity between men and women only widens.

What to Say When the Offer Is Just Right

You've done your research into fair market rates for this kind of position, and you have a full understanding of the job scope and expectations. The interviewer offers you a salary that is in the Comfort or Dream range and is eminently fair given the parameters of the position. It's a great company to work for, and the job will advance your long-term career goals. There's absolutely no reason you can't accept on the spot.

> That sounds terrific, Ms. Williams. My research tells me that that is a very fair market value for this position. I appreciate your confidence in me and am excited about delivering the results we've discussed.

Next, you'll move on to discussion of your complete compensation package, including bonuses, benefits, and perks...and here you can certainly negotiate, even if you haven't negotiated the salary figure.

To Counter-Offer, or Not to Counter-Offer?

News flash! Counter-offers are *not* compulsory. Some companies lay their "best and final" offer on the table when they offer you the job. Because you've done your homework, you will know when an offer is good. In some circumstances, when the job market is very tight—the demand for your expertise is low and the supply of candidates is high—you will have little if any negotiating power. Don't be overconfident or greedy; if the offer is attractive and meets your needs and expectations, take it!

How to Initiate a Counter-Offer

In cases where the employer has not laid his best offer on the table (or his best offer isn't matching up to your Reality Number), you'll have some work to do.

What to Say When the Offer Is Too Low

You have paused for a Moment of Silence, and perhaps the employer has upped the original figure that was offered. In any event, the offer is below your Reality Number and/or below what you consider to be fair compensation for the position. Here's how to reply.

Express appreciation for the offer:

> Mr. Martinez, I'm flattered that you think I'm the right person for the job, and I'm excited about meeting these challenges.

Clarify job parameters:

> Let me be sure we both have the same understanding about the position. This would be a full-time, exempt position as Warehouse Manager for your Columbus facility. I would be reporting to the Operations Director and be responsible for a staff of 10 hourly employees. I would be expected to manage the implementation of new barcoding software in the first six months and lead some vigorous cost-cutting programs to achieve at least 10 percent cost savings in the first year.

Be sure you have accurately summarized the position. Wait for the interviewer's assent and clear up any differences before you proceed.

> Do I have that straight?

Make a persuasive case for a higher salary, based on the *value* you can bring to the position. Mention the employer's *most pressing problem,* as uncovered during the interview process, and your ability to solve it.

> As we discussed, I have the right skill set to make an immediate impact in this position, and I am confident of my ability to deliver 10 percent cost savings or even more in the first year, based on my track record with Acme Corp. And, as you know, I've led successful software implementations of this type twice, and I project a smooth process completed in four to six months. Based on my contributions, and what I understand to be fair market value for this type of position, a salary in the X to Y range would be more appropriate. What can you do in that range?

Other Ways You Can Initiate a Counter-Offer

Here are some other options for language to use when responding to an offer that is too low. The goal is to engage in dialogue, so you want to avoid being confrontational, acting insulted, or being scornful. Such an attitude will harm or even sabotage the negotiation; and even if you don't lose the offer, you will damage your relationship with a future coworker.

- "I've talked to peers in the industry and researched salaries on several well-respected Web sites, and to be honest, I'm a little disappointed. I expected an offer in the X to Y range, based on fair market value. What flexibility do you have?"

- "Quite frankly, I'm disappointed. Is there any room to negotiate?"

- "I have a real problem; can you help me?"

Language to Avoid

Keep in mind that employers are not really interested in what you want, need, or deserve; their fundamental concern is "What can you do for me?" Therefore, steer clear of language that communicates your wants or needs or expresses any sense of entitlement.

Before **You-Centered Language**	After **Employer-Centered Language**
I really need more.	I'm extremely interested, but I must confess I'm disappointed in the proposed salary. Fair market value indicates 15 percent more for a position with this level of responsibility and 25 percent more for someone with my ability to contribute. What flexibility do you have?
Are you sure you can't do more?	How might the position be modified or upgraded to warrant more?
I can't make a move for less than X.	While salary is not my only concern, it is important. I'm eager to contribute and confident of my ability to do so. How can we structure the compensation so that I'm rewarded for meeting established goals?

Three Possible Responses from the Employer

Now it's the employer's move. He has three options, and your next step will depend on what he does.

1. Employer stands pat.

> I'm sorry, but that is what we've budgeted, and we consider it to be a very fair salary for the position.

Don't give up yet! Perhaps you can negotiate performance bonuses that will bring the amount up to your Reality or Comfort level. Maybe the benefits are terrific or you can negotiate some additional perks. Unless the number is totally out of the question, I recommend that you table the base salary discussion and continue negotiating other aspects of your compensation.

> OK, I understand your position. I do feel confident of my ability to achieve these goals for the company, so maybe we can build in some performance bonuses that will make us both happy. And what is the benefit package like? It might be I've overlooked something in my calculations.

2. Employer ups the offer a bit but still below your expectations.

> Well, I guess we could go to X.

Follow the pattern of your initial response—be polite and enthusiastic, reiterate key challenges, and express your confidence in achieving results for the company.

> I appreciate your flexibility. You know, we talked about the problems you're having with personnel and team issues in the warehouse. I know that is affecting your productivity. I have a very consistent history of building strong teams in environments just like this, and I have full confidence in my ability to do the same here at Acme Widgeters. I've calculated that a 5 percent productivity boost would improve your bottom line by $100,000 in the first year alone. Based on this kind of contribution, don't you agree that a salary in the X to Y range is fair?

You can continue in this vein as long as the employer is receptive and you are able to document specific areas where you can help the company. It's always helpful to tie specific dollar benefits to your contributions; this will help the employer see that hiring you will deliver more value than cost to the company.

When you are satisfied that you have negotiated base pay that is appropriate for your value and meets your expectations, accept enthusiastically and move on to phase two, where you negotiate details of your total compensation package, including performance bonuses, benefits, and perks.

3. Employer counter-offers an attractive salary that is in line with what you can deliver to the company.

You don't have to negotiate further; you can move on to discussing your total compensation package, including performance bonuses, benefits, and perks.

> That sounds terrific. I appreciate your flexibility and feel confident of my ability to deliver the results we've discussed.

What to Say When the Offer Is Too High

Believe it or not, this does happen! The employer mentions a figure that is above your Dream Number and substantially higher than your research shows to be fair market value.

When this happens, usually one of two things has occurred: Either you have misconstrued the scope, level, and challenges of the position, or there are serious problems at the company. You need to uncover what's really going on, and to do so you can start with the same response outlined under #1 in the preceding section.

First, express appreciation for the offer:

> Mr. Martinez, I'm flattered that you think I'm the right person for the job, and I'm excited about meeting these challenges.

Clarify job parameters:

> Let me be sure we both have the same understanding about the position. This would be a full-time, exempt position as Warehouse Manager for your Columbus facility. I would be reporting to the Operations Director and be responsible for a staff

of 10 hourly employees. I would be expected to manage the implementation of new barcoding software in the first six months and lead some vigorous cost-cutting programs to achieve at least 10 percent cost savings in the first year.

Be sure you have accurately summarized the position. Wait for the interviewer's assent and clear up any differences before you proceed.

Do I have that straight?

If the position has more responsibility than you thought, and the higher salary is justified, you can feel confident about accepting provided you believe you can handle the job and deliver the expected results. If nothing has changed, you will need to ask some questions to find out what's really going on. Don't be tempted to jump for the bait until you know why it is being dangled.

I must tell you that this is a very attractive offer. In fact, it's significantly higher than I expected based on my research into fair market value for this kind of position. Are there obstacles or challenges we haven't discussed? Do you have expectations you haven't shared with me? Are there circumstances that have prevented you from filling this job? I'm not scared off by challenge, Mr. Martinez, and quite frankly I'm excited about the opportunity. But I need full disclosure so that I can evaluate your offer fairly and make sure I can be successful for you.

Negotiate Additional Elements of Your Compensation Package

Once base salary is settled, you can discuss and negotiate additional components of the compensation package. Company benefits might or might not be negotiable, but your package can also include performance bonuses and additional perquisites (commonly known as "perks") that offer much more room for creativity and flexibility.

You want to be absolutely clear about all the parameters of your compensation package. Here are some ideas to consider as you prepare for and then conduct the next phase of the negotiation. Many of the benefit questions can be answered by the human resources representative.

Compensation/Bonuses/Raises/Performance Evaluations

- Are periodic raises given? If so, what criteria are used to decide increases?

- What is the procedure for job advancement? Is a certain time on the job required before an employee can move up? How are internal openings posted, and what percentage of jobs are filled via internal promotions?

Are performance bonuses paid? If so, what are the specific criteria for earning these bonuses?

- Tie your bonus achievement to specific company goals that you've identified during the interview process.

- As much as possible, remove subjectivity from performance compensation by linking performance bonuses to some provable formula, such as sales volume, profitability, or productivity.

- Negotiate the right to receive your bonus if you lose your job due to a business reorganization, layoff, or any other reason other than gross misconduct. Companies have been known to dismiss employees just before annual bonuses come due, and you want to prevent this from happening to you.

What is the commission structure (if any)? Is there a cap on commissions? Do commissions continue for recurring sales?

Does the company have a profit-sharing plan? If so, are employees required to contribute matching sums? If so, how much? Can you increase or decrease this amount at will? Can the money be accessed prior to retirement without a penalty? What happens to the money if you resign or are let go?

Does the company offer stock options? What are the criteria for these awards? What is the vesting period? How has the stock performed over the last 3, 5, and 10 years? How many shares are in a typical option award?

Does the company have a written severance policy? What is included?

Is overtime offered? At what rate?

Are bonuses paid to hourly employees? What are the criteria for earning those bonuses? How realistic are they? How much was paid in bonuses to hourly employees in the most recent calendar year?

What other bonuses, benefits, or incentives are available?

How often are formal performance evaluations conducted? Are raises tied to these evaluations? Are improvement opportunities identified and followed up on? Are employees reviewed by peers or just by their direct supervisors?

Is there a signing bonus?

Is there a noncompete agreement?

Beware of Noncompete Agreements

Carefully review a noncompete agreement before signing. You might want to have an attorney review it as well, particularly if it seems severely restrictive. While noncompete agreements cannot always be successfully defended (your past employer cannot prevent you from earning a living), you do not want to get involved in the expense, time, and hassle of a lawsuit.

Benefits

- What is the vacation policy? Must vacation days be used within the calendar year, or can they be carried over or converted to cash?

- How many sick days are allowed? What happens if you exceed that allowance?

- Are personal days allowed? If so, how many? Who makes the decision on granting personal time off?

- What is the health insurance policy? Is there a probationary period before insurance goes into effect? What is the cost? What is the co-pay? What does it cost to insure family members?

- Is there dental insurance? Vision insurance? Coverage for alternative medicine such as chiropractic, massage therapy, physical therapy, or acupuncture?

- What are the costs and coverage for life insurance and disability insurance?

- Does the company have a 401(k) or other retirement plan? What options are there for investing?

- Is flex-time available? What about telecommuting? Job sharing?

- Is there a child-care benefit?

- Are benefits provided to life partners or only to spouses?

- Does the company offer wellness programs and benefits such as health club memberships, fitness classes, and after-work team sports?

- What is the company's commitment to community service? Are there corporate volunteer programs? Can volunteering be done on company time?

- What is the company's commitment to education and professional development? What is the policy for reimbursing college tuition or training programs? Who authorizes these expenditures? How many

employees participate? Is there a limit on numbers or dollars? Can every employee earn college tuition reimbursement, or does the field of study have to be job related?

* Is there a formal mentoring program? What is the procedure for aligning with a mentor?

* Will the company pay for relocation? What is covered, and what is the total benefit?

Special Circumstances

Employers sometimes make assumptions about what will motivate and challenge employees based on past compensation. Because they know that money motivates many people, they might be suspicious if you are willing to accept a salary that is much lower than you've made recently. And they want to treat employees equally, so they'll be concerned if you are requesting a salary that is much higher than you've made recently or higher than others at the company with similar responsibilities.

If you have a compelling argument, you can attempt to change their opinion. It's important not to get into an argument with the employer; instead, state your case calmly, logically, and confidently. As always, your reasoning must be based on value.

How to Assure Interviewers You Can Handle a Cut in Salary

What's the problem with getting a bargain? Employers will be concerned that you'll lose interest in the job because it's not challenging enough, based on your past positions and salary. Not only that, they're afraid you won't stay long and they'll have to fill your position again when you leave for a more lucrative opportunity. Your rationale must be valid and convincing.

Rationale for Taking on a Lower-Level Position

This phrasing worked for a manager-turned-technician:

> I assure you, salary is not my first consideration. Before I started this job search, I thought long and hard about what really motivates me and gives me the greatest satisfaction, and that is the hands-on technical work rather than the managerial aspects. I would find it tremendously valuable to be on the ground floor of your new technologies. If down the road I can make a greater contribution leading a technical team, then my management experience will certainly provide added value. But for now, and the immediate future, my greatest interest and greatest value is as a hardware designer. I researched salaries for this kind of role, and I know that what you've offered is fair market value. I am very comfortable with your offer and excited about the opportunity.

Rationale for a Change in Career Focus

Try this language if you are accepting a lower salary because you are transitioning, say, from the corporate sector to the nonprofit sector:

> I can see that you might be concerned about offering me a lower salary than I've been making, but I want you to know that it is not an issue for me. I want to make a difference—that's what drives me. This position meets all of my personal criteria, and my skills are an excellent fit for what you need. I think you'll be getting great value for your investment! And I assure you that I am ready to make a commitment to the organization and help you meet your challenges.

The Risk-Free Counter-Offer

If you're willing to start at a lower amount but want to build in a risk-free salary increase, this language should work:

> Yes, this is a lower salary than I've been accustomed to. And of course I would like to earn more! But I understand your budget constraints, and I'm ready to make an immediate contribution in this position. In fact, I'd like to suggest an idea that would be a win-win for both of us. If after six months I'm able to achieve the revenue and cost-cutting goals we've discussed, let's build in a 15 percent salary increase to reward my performance and reflect the improved financial health of the company.

How to Explain Why You Deserve a Significant Increase over Your Prior Salary

Your compensation should be based on the value you bring, not on what you've made previously or a set percentage above that. Try to make your prior compensation a non-issue, and let them know you've done your homework. Your attitude should convey a bland assumption that the company will do what's reasonable and fair.

> I assumed that compensation would be based on my value to the company, and I'm not sure how my recent salary history is related to that. As we discussed, I have the skills and experience to achieve the cost reductions you're looking for. In fact, with my contacts at Standard Supply, I'm confident we can meet the 10 percent goal within six months. For this kind of performance, don't you agree that a salary in the X to Y range is reasonable?

How to Make a Case for a Salary That Is Higher Than Others in the Company

What others make is not your affair; you want to be compensated for what you can deliver. However, some companies are very concerned about pay equity and don't want to set a precedent by boosting you out of the range for the position.

> I assumed that compensation would be based on my performance and value to the company. I think we agree that the revenue and cost improvements I can achieve will more than make up for the salary I've requested! Perhaps these significant challenges warrant a higher job grade. Or maybe we can make part of the compensation performance based. I'd be happy to discuss performance milestones and appropriate rewards for reaching them.

You might think that companies won't rewrite job descriptions or reclassify jobs into a higher grade, but this is a common practice when companies find a candidate who has the skills, experience, and intangible qualities they want to add to their team.

In all of these situations, emphasize value and negotiate in a calm, professional, confident manner. You're not wrangling over a quarter in the parking lot; you're conducting a business discussion about the value of your services and the ways in which you'll be compensated for them.

Get the Offer in Writing and Think It Over

Your job offer and initial negotiation might take place during your final interview. If that's the case, most likely you will discuss and come to tentative agreement about a general salary figure, as described in the preceding sections. During this discussion, you might agree to some performance bonuses or a commission structure, and the employer might reference the company's benefits package and perhaps some other types of compensation and rewards.

You've conducted a professional negotiation and come to tentative agreement on your basic compensation. Now is the time to get the offer in writing and take it home to think it over.

A formal written offer is standard operating procedure at some companies. Within a reasonable period of time, typically two to five days, you will receive a package of materials that includes a description of the job and detailed information on salary, benefits, bonuses, and total compensation.

Carefully review the material to be sure it reflects everything you discussed with the hiring manager. Undoubtedly, there will be items you'll wish to negotiate further. Write down any questions you have and make notes about further requests or changes. Then contact the hiring manager and set up a time to discuss the package in person. Don't ask for a meeting to talk about "compensation"; instead, ask to get together to answer a few final questions to help you in making your decision.

Negotiate Face-to-Face

Do not attempt to negotiate or counter-offer your compensation package by e-mail. An in-person meeting is the most productive and professional setting and will allow you to review and resolve every item and come to complete agreement. Obviously, if you are living in a different city, you might not be able to conduct this meeting in person, and in that case opt for a phone meeting rather than an e-mail dialogue. At the end of every phone conversation, be sure you recap what was discussed; then follow that up in writing (e-mail is fine) to confirm the discussion. You don't want to leave room for error. Misunderstandings can cause hard feelings and jeopardize the job offer or your future working relationships.

What should you do if the company does not make its offer in writing? You should ask for it at the conclusion of your initial negotiation. Recap what you discussed, corroborating the job details and compensation to be sure you and the hiring manager are in agreement. Then ask for a written offer so that you can mull it over or discuss it with your spouse. Hesitancy or refusal might be a red flag signaling uncertainty about hiring you, so be wary!

During the interim period and final negotiations, continue to be positive, poised, and professional. Be responsive to the company's needs, stress your enthusiasm, ask when they need to have your response, and meet every deadline. The impressions you make during the negotiation phase of a job offer will make a lasting impression on the people you'll be working with every day, so be sure it is a positive impression!

Ask for the Employee Handbook

Ask for a copy of the employee handbook to be sent with your written offer. Many of your questions will be answered by reading this handbook, and you will also learn about any unusual or restrictive policies that might impact your decision.

As you prepare your notes for the next phase of negotiations, analyze the total compensation package—salary, bonuses, benefits, and perks—against your needs, goals, and researched information. Overall, how does the package compare to your Reality, Comfort, and Dream Numbers? Use the "Magical Coaching Tips" worksheet to evaluate this or multiple job offers.

Because every company structures compensation differently, you will find some pluses and some minuses when comparing the new offer with your current situation or a second offer you've received. Only you can decide what's most important to you, where you are willing to make a trade-off, and what you want to ask for in the upcoming meeting.

Bring All the Decision Makers to the Table

Be sure all the decision makers are present at the meeting. It is a frustrating experience to try to negotiate with someone who does not have the authority to make a decision. If you sense or know that your contact is not the final authority, push to have the decision maker present at the meeting. You don't want to offend your contact, but you do want to be sure that matters are resolved with a minimum of back-and-forth discussion between your contact and the decision maker. Try phrasing it as a convenience—"Would it be more convenient if I we include the hiring manager in our discussion?" or "This is an important commitment for me, and I will have quite a few questions. To keep it as convenient as possible, should we include Ms. Chow in our discussions?" You can't force the issue, but give it your best shot.

The saying is that "everything is negotiable," but that might not be true. Some companies offer fixed benefit plans that are the same for every employee; others refuse to adjust salaries outside of a range; still others provide a comprehensive pay/benefits package in their first offer and do not wish to negotiate or "haggle" over details. But unless you ask, you will never know if an item is negotiable. Be creative! You know what's important to you and what will keep you motivated.

When asking for more, be careful not to appear greedy or entitled. Compare the phrasing in these examples and see how simply wording your request more politely creates a more positive, professional image.

Before	After
I couldn't consider less than four weeks of vacation.	I realize you don't have any flexibility on the salary, but I wonder if you'd consider an extra week's vacation. That would mean a lot to me and would enable me to visit my family on the other side of the country.
These health benefits are worthless to me. Can I get cash instead?	Because I have full coverage through my spouse, I won't need to take advantage of your health insurance benefit. Is there a chance this could be swapped for a cash benefit?

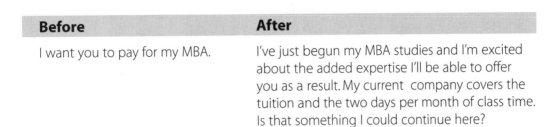

Before	After
I want you to pay for my MBA.	I've just begun my MBA studies and I'm excited about the added expertise I'll be able to offer you as a result. My current company covers the tuition and the two days per month of class time. Is that something I could continue here?

Additional Forms of Compensation

In addition to the questions noted previously in the chapter (see "Negotiate Additional Elements of Your Compensation Package"), review this list of potential benefits to identify those that will make a significant difference to you. When the salary is lower than desired, it is particularly important to negotiate for additional forms of compensation. Although extra time off or a flexible schedule won't make up for cold hard cash, such benefits can increase your job satisfaction and give you a positive feeling about the company.

- Insurance: Life, disability, medical, dental, vision
- Overtime and other supplemental pay programs
- Paid vacation time
- Paid or unpaid leave (leave of absence, maternity/paternity/adoption leave, family leave)
- Flex-time
- Job sharing
- Child-care programs or benefits
- Wellness programs
- Pension and profit-sharing plans (IRAs, 401[k] plans, stock bonus plans, ESOPs)
- Stock options
- Performance-based compensation incentives
- Education and training programs, tuition, books and materials
- Professional association dues and conferences
- Cost-of-living adjustments
- Scheduled raises

- ✳ Relocation expenses
- ✳ Signing bonus
- ✳ Company car or mileage allowance
- ✳ Expense account
- ✳ Technology (laptop, PDA, cell phone)
- ✳ Telecommuting option and support
- ✳ Additional perks (health club membership, parking, first-class travel, company credit card, prepaid legal services, loans at reduced rates of interest, and so on)
- ✳ Termination agreement (severance pay, reason for termination)

Throughout your negotiations, stay upbeat and positive about the job and the company. Be sure all of your questions are answered, and if you have negotiated any changes to the original written offer, ask for a revised offer letter.

Close the meeting by expressing your enthusiasm! Ask the employer when a firm answer is needed. Tell them you want to review everything carefully once more and discuss the opportunity with your spouse. Assure them you'll be back in touch as soon as possible. And be sure to keep your promise!

Evaluate the Offer or Multiple Offers

Analyzing a job offer is a complex process that involves emotion as well logic. The job and company must be a good FIT for your career goals, skills, interests, and personal style. You should be excited about the challenges, satisfied with the compensation package, and confident that you have the ability to achieve the stated goals. A little bit of trepidation is normal!

Use the "Magical Coaching Tips" worksheet at the end of this chapter to ask yourself several questions that will help evaluate the offer or compare this offer to another offer.

If you already have a job offer from another employer (Company X), it's acceptable to let the first employer (Company Y) know and to use this as leverage. For instance, "I'm evaluating a second offer at this time. To be honest, Company Y is my first choice, although the base salary you're proposing is 10 percent less. I'm wondering what room there might be to get closer to, or even match, that 10 percent difference."

Another situation that often arises is that you've received a job offer from Employer A while you're waiting to be called back for a second interview by Employer B, who happens to be your first-choice employer. If this happens, contact Employer B and say, "I wanted to touch base on your timeframe for this position. It happens that I have an offer from another employer that I'll need to make a decision about and yet my preference is to make a commitment to your company. Is it possible we might meet soon?"

Accept and Finalize Your Agreement

When you've made the decision to accept a job offer, confirm it in writing as soon as possible, and always within the time you promised. Your professional, positive, enthusiastic acceptance will set the right tone as you start your new position. Your acceptance letter may look something like figure 16.1.

Chapter Wrap-Up

Hiring costs money, and companies want a return on that investment. They are not looking for seat warmers, cubicle fillers, or office decorations; they want people who will add value to the company and improve its bottom line. Be confident of your value and assured in your negotiations. Such an attitude will enable you to dance across the high wire with ease and arrive safely at your career destination.

10 Quick Tips for Salary Negotiations

1. **Communicate your value during interviews and on through salary negotiations.** Enter negotiations as a confident optimist—if you expect more, you'll be more likely to get more.

2. **Memorize responses to deflect salary discussions until the employer has shifted from "shopper" to "buyer."**

3. **Be prepared**—learn the fair market value for your talents by researching the low, median, and high range for similar positions.

4. **Identify your Reality, Comfort, and Dream Number salary range.**

5. **Base your salary requests on what you bring to the company and what you will achieve**—not on what you need, want, or deserve.

6. **First, agree in principle on base compensation. Then, explore and negotiate bonuses, benefits, and perks.** Know what "throw-aways" you are willing to concede. When you are willing to give something away

Jayne Smythe
123 West 53rd Street
Airtown, NY 12345
(917) 543-2100
jaynesmythe@msn.com

[date]

[Certified Mail; return receipt requested]

Name, Title
Company
Street Address
City, State, ZIP

Dear Ms. _____ :

It's been a pleasure meeting with you and other members of the Widget Manufacturers, Inc. team. This letter confirms that I agree to be employed by _____ [name of company] as a _____ [position title] beginning _____ [start date].

As compensation, I agree to accept an annual salary of $_____ payable in _____ [monthly, weekly] installments in the sum of $_____. Additionally, I understand that I will receive _____ [state benefits agreed to].

Upon termination of our agreement for any reason other than gross negligence on my part, I shall be entitled to receive my bonus and salary for the remaining period of the quarter in which my termination occurs.

If any terms of this letter are unclear or incorrect, please reply in writing within three days of receipt of this letter. I can be reached at (917) 543-2100 should you need anything from me prior to my start date.

I am thoroughly looking forward to joining the team and making a valuable contribution to the organization.

Sincerely,

Jayne Smythe

Figure 16.1: An acceptance letter.

(tuition reimbursement, for example), it makes you look flexible. In other cases, offer a concession in exchange for something that is of importance to you.

7. **Frame any counter-offer requests in employer-centered language instead of you-centered language.** Express your requests without anxiety, anger, or attitude, but in a manner that is positive, poised, and professional.

8. **Get the offer in writing.** If you can't, draft and submit your own letter outlining your understanding of the position. Evaluate offers on multiple planes—salary, job duties, future potential, location, commute, schedule, company culture, and so on.

9. **Be willing to walk away.** Consider what the consequences will be of accepting a salary and benefit package below your Reality Number.

10. **Don't cut off other options until you have actually started work.** Wait to share the good news with your broader circles of contacts until you are actually on board. And, remain courteous and professional… don't forget that you will be working with the people with whom you are now negotiating.

Magical Coaching Tips

When Researching Salary
Using table 16.1 near the beginning of this chapter as a guide, develop your own comparative salary data.

My Research on Comparative Salary Data

Source	Low Range	Median	Upper Range
Salary tool: workindex.com/ salary/ (national averages)	$	$	$
Salary tool: www.salary.com (national averages)	$	$	$
Salary tool: www.salaryexpert.com (New York/statewide average)	$	$	$
Salary survey: professional association or other source	$	$	$

(continued)

(continued)

My Research on Comparative Salary Data

Source	Low Range	Median	Upper Range
Print ad/source	$	$	$
Online ad	$	$	$
Network contact	$	$	$
Network contact	$	$	$
Average	$	$	$

When Developing Your Salary Target

Develop your own salary range of Reality, Comfort, and Dream numbers.

	Current Salary	Reality Number	Comfort Number	Dream Number
Base				
Bonus				
Commissions				
Projected raise				
Stock options not yet vested				
Benefit/retirement plans not yet vested				
Other				
Total				

When Evaluating an Offer or Multiple Job Offers

When evaluating an offer, ask yourself some of these questions as you weigh the pros and cons of each unique opportunity.

The Job	Offer #1 Negative Neutral Positive − o + (Circle one)			Offer #2 Negative Neutral Positive − o + (Circle one)		
Is the job a good fit for my professional strengths?	−	o	+	−	o	+
Will I be doing what I love to do most of the time (or will I be doing a lot of tasks that frustrate me or burn me out)?	−	o	+	−	o	+
Will the work challenge me?	−	o	+	−	o	+
Do I have all the training and education I need to do the job well? If not, will the company provide it?	−	o	+	−	o	+
Will I have the resources necessary to do the job well?	−	o	+	−	o	+
Did I feel good rapport with coworkers?	−	o	+	−	o	+
Do I like my boss? (Also analyze the individual's behavioral style, managerial style, record of promoting staff, ability to mentor, grasp of his or her job, and relationship within company hierarchy.)	−	o	+	−	o	+
Are there opportunities for advancement? Realistically, how long will this take and how straightforward is the process?	−	o	+	−	o	+
Will I be compensated adequately for my efforts?	−	o	+	−	o	+
Can I earn bonus pay for performance?	−	o	+	−	o	+

(continued)

(continued)

	Offer #1 Negative Neutral Positive **– o +** (Circle one)			Offer #2 Negative Neutral Positive **– o +** (Circle one)		
Is there potential to increase my salary in the near future?	–	o	+	–	o	+
Are the benefits adequate for me and my family?	–	o	+	–	o	+
Is there anything that's missing that I consider important?	–	o	+	–	o	+
Are performance expectations achievable? Does the level of challenge frighten or stimulate me?	–	o	+	–	o	+
Will I be excited about going to work most days?	–	o	+	–	o	+
The Culture						
What hours am I expected to work? What are the unwritten "rules" for arrival and departure times? Is evening and weekend work the norm?	–	o	+	–	o	+
What social opportunities exist? Are these congruent with my interests?	–	o	+	–	o	+
What does the atmosphere feel like? Is it friendly, brisk and businesslike, laid back, casual, formal? How does this match with my style?	–	o	+	–	o	+
Is there a lot of deadline pressure? Will I perform my best under these circumstances?	–	o	+	–	o	+
Is the level of intensity about right for me?	–	o	+	–	o	+

Is the balance of individual and teamwork right for me?	–	o	+	–	o	+
What kind of political currents do I sense? Am I comfortable with those?	–	o	+	–	o	+
Is the job highly structured or unstructured? Is this what I prefer?	–	o	+	–	o	+
What has the negotiation been like? Has it been courteous and professional, or do I get a sense that the company begrudges paying me what I'm worth?	–	o	+	–	o	+
What is the average tenure of people in my department?	–	o	+	–	o	+
Is the leadership team in my area new or well established? How do I feel about that?	–	o	+	–	o	+

The Company

Is the company growing or downsizing?	–	o	+	–	o	+
What are its future plans? How do I feel about those?	–	o	+	–	o	+
Does it seem to be seizing market opportunities, or are competitors leaving it in the dust?	–	o	+	–	o	+
How stable is the executive team?	–	o	+	–	o	+
What is the public image of the company? Do my interviews confirm or refute it?	–	o	+	–	o	+
Is the company an industry leader or struggling to keep up with the competition?	–	o	+	–	o	+

(continued)

(continued)

	Offer #1 Negative Neutral Positive – o + (Circle one)			Offer #2 Negative Neutral Positive – o + (Circle one)		
Has the company had financial or legal woes recently? What is the status?	–	o	+	–	o	+
How competitive are its core products? What is on the horizon?	–	o	+	–	o	+
What are the most significant market challenges the company faces?	–	o	+	–	o	+
How has the company handled downsizing in the past?	–	o	+	–	o	+
Are the location and commute acceptable?	–	o	+	–	o	+

When evaluating multiple job offers, look at the number of positives circled in each column. Depending on how you weight each item, it's likely that the column with more positives (+) is the better of the two offers.

Appendix A

Resources for Researching Companies

Research—knowing the insider scoop—is essential. Most job seekers wait to do research until they've got an interview lined up. In a targeted job search, research comes prior to contacting the company–it's what helps you land the interview in the first place! Information you should gather includes the following:

1. Company data, including length of time in business, major milestones, strengths

2. Company's key products/services

3. Company's current TOP issues:

   - **T**rends—the company's five-year financial trends, strategic direction, and industry trends

   - **O**pportunities—new projects on the drawing board and company priorities

   - **P**roblems/Projects—competition or challenges that are keeping the organization from being as productive or profitable as possible

4. How your skills can be integrated with, and bring value to, the company's TOP issues

5. Names and bios of key decision makers at the company

6. Strategic stakeholders—customers, corporate alliances, vendors, suppliers, and consultants

7. Analysis of key competitive companies

Use the following resources to help you access information about your target companies:

People who are closely linked to decision makers at the companies.

- **Business information sites:**

  - Hoovers: www.hoovers.com

  - Bizjournals: www.bizjournals.com/search.html

  - Dunn and Bradstreet: www.dnb.com

  - CEO Express: www.ceoexpress.com

  - Corporate Information: www.corporateinformation.com

  - Bloomberg: www.bloomberg.com (this site caters to institutional investors, with a price tag out of reach for most individuals; as an alternative, explore access to this data via any of your network contacts in the brokerage/financial services business)

- **Company Web site:** Read the careers section, which might give you an idea of the company's culture, affinity groups, succession planning, and advancement opportunities. In addition, review the site's press releases, about us, history, and investor relations pages, as well as its products/services pages.

- **Company marketing material:** Call and ask for marketing or sales literature if none is available at the Web site.

- **News sources:** Google.com searches can turn up interesting support information about the company or its industry. Journals for your industry can also provide leads.

- **Libraries:** Ask the resource librarian to run a periodical search using the company name and your functional area as keywords.

- **Associations:** Review your professional association(s) to search for any references to your target company. It might be that an employee from the target company will be presenting at an upcoming conference, or you might find an article that is of relevance to your target company's TOP issues.

- **Career Web sites:** Several career Web sites offer access to company research, such as vault.com, wetfeet.com, and craigslist.com.

- **Company annual report:** Often available at the company's Web site or through the investor relations department.

- **Publicly traded companies' 10-K (annual report) or 10-Q (quarterly report) filed with the Securities and Exchange Commission:** These reports are available at www.edgar-online.com (EDGAR stands for Electronic Data Gathering, Analysis, and Retrieval system). Similar to an annual report, the 10-K contains more detailed information about the company's business, finances, and management and is loaded with contact names. For an excellent guide on reading an annual report, visit www.investorguide.com/igustockreport.html.

- **Analyst reports intended for the investment community:** Read warily; analysts (who are employed by banks and won't want to offend potential client companies) might be tempted to issue a rosier outlook for the company than what it really deserves. Use Google to find analyst reports on your company, or check sites such as Zacks (www.zacks.com) or Thompson Financial (www.thomson.com/financial/fi_investmgr.jsp).

Appendix
B

Interview Question Contributors

T he following members of Career Masters Institute (www.cminstitute.com) and National Résumé Writers' Association (www.nrwa.com) contributed to the question-and-answer strategies in chapters 13, 14, and 15. Please feel free to contact these members should you need additional help with your career transition, including focusing and creating an orchestrated strategy for your search, developing resumes and other campaign materials, preparing for interviews, and putting a strategy in place for ongoing career management.

Freddie Cheek, M.S.Ed., CCM, CPRW, CWDP
Cheek & Associates
406 Maynard Dr.
Amherst, NY 14226
Phone: (716) 839-3635
Fax: (716) 831-9320
E-mail: fscheek@adelphia.net
www.CheekandCristantello.com

Julianne S. Franke, MS, CPRW, CCM
President
The Right Connections
258 Shire Way
Lawrenceville, GA 30044
Phone: (770) 381-0876
Fax: (770) 381-0877
E-mail: jfranke1@bellsouth.net

Sheila Garofalo, B.A., M.A., CCMC, MBTI Qualified
SFC Consulting, Inc.
P.O. Box 2103
Woburn, MA 01888
E-mail: sfccons@verizon.net

Louise Garver, MA, JCTC, CMP, CPRW, MCDP, CEIP
President
Career Directions, LLC
115 Elm St., Ste. 203
Enfield, CT 06082
Phone: (860) 623-9476
Fax: (860) 623-9473
E-mail: TheCareerPro@aol.com
www.CareerEdgeCoach.com and
www.resumeimpact.com

Wendy Gelberg, M.Ed., CPRW, IJCTC
President
Advantage Resumes
21 Hawthorn Ave.
Needham, MA 02492
Phone: (781) 444-0778
Fax: (781) 444-2778
E-mail: WGelberg@aol.com

Beverly Harvey, CPRW, JCTC, CCM, CCMC, MRW
President
Beverly Harvey Resume & Career Services
P.O. Box 750
Pierson, FL 32180
Phone: (386) 749-3111
Fax: (386) 749-4881
E-mail: beverly@harveycareers.com
www.harveycareers.com

Melanie Noonan, CPS
Peripheral Pro
West Paterson, NJ 07424
Phone: (973) 785-3011
Fax: (973) 785-3071
E-mail: Peripro1@aol.com

John M. O'Connor, MFA, CRW, CPRW, CECC, CCM
President
CareerPro Resumes & Career Advancement
3301 Women's Club Dr. #125
Raleigh, NC 27612-4812
Phone: (919) 787-2400
Fax: (866) 447-9599
E-mail: john@careerproresumes.com
www.careerproresumes.com

Barb Poole, CPRW, CRW, BS, CCMC
President
Hire Imaging
1812 Red Fox Rd.
St. Cloud, MN 56301
Phone: (320) 253-0975
Fax: (320) 253-1790
E-mail: barb@hireimaging.com
www.hireimaging.com

Edie Rische, JCTC, NCRW
Write Away Resume
5908 73rd St.
Lubbock, TX 79424-1920
Phone: (806) 798-0881
E-mail: erische@door.net
www.writeawayresume.com

Jane Roqueplot, CWDP, CBC
President / Owner
JaneCo's Sensible Solutions
194 N. Oakland Ave.
Sharon, PA 16146
Phone: (724) 342-0100
Fax: (724) 346-5263
E-mail: jane@janecos.com
www.janecos.com

Barbara Safani, MA, CPRW
Career Solvers
980 Madison Ave.
New York, NY 10021
Phone: (866) 333-1800
Fax: (212) 580-2388
E-mail: info@careersolvers.com
www.careersolvers.com

Evelyn U. Salvador, NCRW, JCTC*
Creative Image Builders, Inc.
8 Marla Dr.
Coram, NY 11727
Phone: (631) 698-7777
Fax: (631) 698-0984
E-mail: CareerCatapult@aol.com
www.DesignerResumes.com

Julie Thomas
Julie's Typing & Notary Service
West Monroe, LA 71294-0391
Phone: (318) 322-2199
Fax: (318) 322-2199
E-mail: JCThomas@bellsouth.net

Daisy Wright, BA, CDP
The Wright Career Solution
7 Woodcreek Dr.
Brampton, Ontario, L6Z 4V6 Canada
Phone: (905) 840-7039
E-mail: wcs@thewrightcareer.com
www.thewrightcareer.com

Contributions excerpted from Step by Step Resumes *by Evelyn Salvador.*

Index

The Magic Continues!

Now that you're interviewing with confidence, you can apply Susan's magical advice to your résumé as well!